SECURITY IN THE PERSIAN GULF

Origins, Obstacles, and the Search for Consensus

EDITED BY

LAWRENCE G. POTTER
AND GARY G. SICK

palgrave

SECURITY IN THE PERSIAN GULF

© Lawrence G. Potter and Gary G. Sick, 2002

First published in 2002 by PALGRAVE™
175 Fifth Avenue, New York, N.Y.10010 and
Houndmills, Basingstoke, Hampshire RG21 6XS.
Companies and representatives throughout the world

PALGRAVE is the new global publishing imprint of St. Martin's Press LLC Scholarly and Reference Division and Palgrave Publishers Ltd (formerly Macmillan Press Ltd).

ISBN 0-312-23836-3 cloth
ISBN 0-312-23950-5 paperback

Library of Congress Cataloging-in-Publication Data
Security in the Persian Gulf : origins, obstacles, and the search for consensus / edited by Lawrence G. Potter and Gary G. Sick.
    p.   cm.
  ISBN 0-312-23950-5 (pbk.)—ISBN 0-312-23836-3 (cloth)
    1. National security—Persian Gulf Region.   2. Persian Gulf Region—Military policy.
I. Potter, Lawrence G.   II. Sick, Gary, 1935-
UA832.S44   2001
327'.09536—dc21   2001044655

A catalogue record for this book is available from the British Library.

Design by Letra Libre, Inc.

First edition: January 2002
10 9 8 7 6 5 4 3 2 1

Printed in the United States of America.

CONTENTS

INTRODUCTION

LAWRENCE G. POTTER AND GARY G. SICK

Most of the chapters of this volume originated as papers presented at a conference on "Mutual Security in the Gulf: Tradition and Transformation" at Castelgandolfo, Italy, in July 1998.[1] This was the fifth international conference of Gulf/2000, a research and documentation project on the Persian Gulf states based at Columbia University in New York. Gulf/2000 periodically has brought together small groups of Gulf experts in an effort to stimulate greater understanding and promote future cooperation. This book may be regarded as a follow-up to the volume of earlier papers published by the same editors in 1997, *The Persian Gulf at the Millennium: Essays in Politics, Economy, Security, and Religion*. Whereas the majority of the authors of the earlier work were outsiders, most contributors to the present volume are themselves from the Persian Gulf states. Many share here the results of ongoing research on the societies and peoples of the Gulf today.[2]

This volume's theme is regional security—its past, present, and future. Security here is broadly defined, and includes not only "hard" military issues such as the arms race in the Gulf, addressed by Saideh Lotfian, but also "soft" issues such as tensions arising from cultural differences between Arabs and Iranians. Authors in this work assess the crucial human indicators of the region's future, including the issue of mutual perceptions (with an Iranian perspective by analyst Bijan Khajehpour-Khoei and a Kuwaiti one by political scientist Abdullah Alshayji) and the role of the coming generations (by Iranian political scientist Mohammad Hadi Semati and Saudi anthropologist Mai Yamani).

The initial two articles explore the influence of the outside world on the Gulf and the Gulf on the outside world. There is a long tradition of external involvement in the region that persists today, as documented in historian John Peterson's review. As he demonstrates, the Gulf was an area of geopolitical importance long before oil, as imperial powers fought for trade and security advantage. In a provocative and pathbreaking analysis, M. R. Izady makes the case that the Gulf constitutes a distinct society of its own, having more in common with the societies of the Indian Ocean basin than with the Middle East.

Mention of the Persian Gulf immediately brings to mind oil and the riches it brings. Yet while the present-day prosperity is indeed built on oil, this has been true for only the past half-century, merely a moment in the long history of the Gulf. As Kuwaiti historian Muhammad Rumaihi reminds us, "The Gulf is not oil. The Gulf is its people and its land. So it was before the discovery of oil, and so it will remain when the oil disappears. Oil is no more than a historical phase in this part of the Arab world—and a rather short one at that."[3] It is the consequence of this oil wealth—what it has done to society and how it has affected political life and thus the security of the littoral states—that concerns the authors of this volume.

It is an aim of Gulf/2000 to consider long-term trends in the Gulf, not to restrict analysis to any one state but rather to focus on the region as a whole. The modern state system in the region is largely a product of the twentieth century; of the littoral states only Iran and Oman have distinct historical identities. The most serious challenges facing the Gulf states today are the domestic ones they all share, including weak economies, rising unemployment, the threat of political Islam, and demands for greater political participation, even democratization.[4] All these states depend heavily on revenues from petroleum exports, which are highly uncertain: while at record highs in 2000, they were at record lows in 1998.

The long-term regional perspective is important, yet often missing in people's mindset as well as recent analyses. Historically the Gulf was an integrated region characterized by the constant interchange of people, commerce, and religious movements. Before the modern era, peoples of the region shared a maritime culture based on pearling, fishing, and long-distance trade. In cities such as Kuwait, large merchant families arose that established trade networks both within the Gulf and throughout the larger Indian Ocean region. Because of physical impediments such as mountains and deserts, in the past people living on the shores of the Gulf had closer relations with each other than with those living in the interior. All of this led to a certain mutual tolerance and helped to create a common Gulf identity. Over the past century or more, however, this Gulf or *khaliji* identity has been obscured by a sense of separateness that was fostered by a century and a half of British hegemony followed by the rise of new national states.[5]

In the Gulf today there is a widespread feeling of vulnerability and a sense that local actors are not in control of their own destiny. This is reflected in the chapter by Abdullah K. Alshayji, a political scientist from Kuwait. Rather, the three largest players, Iran, Iraq, and Saudi Arabia, have competed for hegemony as the smaller, more vulnerable Arab monarchies have turned to the United States for protection. The American attempt to exclude the two largest regional states, Iran and Iraq, from regional affairs is surely untenable over the long term and has postponed the moment when the Gulf residents will have to face their own future and devise their own security system. Iraq is eager to reclaim what it sees as its rightful role in the Gulf, as noted in the paper by Raad Alkadiri, and its neighbors will have to find a way to accommodate this desire. Starting in the autumn of 2000, Iraq took advantage of the revival of the Palestinian *intifada* to reassert its political role in regional affairs.[6]

One of the main sources of instability in the Gulf region is unsettled borders and boundary disputes, largely arising from the colonial powers' redrawing the map of the Middle East after the collapse of the Ottoman Empire in World War I. Iraq's sense of grievance over its boundaries with Iran and Kuwait led directly to the two most destructive regional conflicts in the twentieth century—the eight-year war between Iran and Iraq (1980–88) and the Allied coalition's campaign to evict the Iraqi army from Kuwait (1990–91). Border disputes in the region, however, are increasingly being settled, partly in order to facilitate oil operations.[7] One of the most dramatic examples came in March 2001, when Bahrain and Qatar accepted the verdict of the World Court that settled their longstanding border dispute, largely in favor of the former.[8]

Nevertheless, at least two potentially dangerous disputes remain. The division of the Shatt al-Arab, the waterway dividing Iran and Iraq, was a major factor in Iraq's 1980 invasion of Iran and remains unresolved. But the key problem blocking regional détente is the century-long dispute between Iran and the United Arab Emirates over the sovereignty of three tiny islands at the mouth of the Gulf: Abu Musa and the two Tunbs. The governments involved have increasingly invoked this issue in emotional terms as a nonnegotiable issue of sovereignty, thus complicating any eventual compromise. The islands issue is tackled here by Jalil Roshandel and Hassan Al-Alkim, an Iranian and an Emirati respectively, with an illuminating commentary by a leading expert on the subject, British geographer Richard Schofield.

The second millennium ushered in a new era in the Gulf. A decade had already passed since Desert Storm and countries moved on, with the exception of Iraq, whose government had been relegated to outlaw status and its people to pauperization. The region's isolation, enforced by the British for so long, was now over; no longer could governments closely control what their people could hear or see. A new generation had emerged whose political consciousness was rising and whose aims seemed destined to challenge or change those of the state. This generation was beginning to take its place as part of the global community thanks to an explosion of information via the Internet and satellite broadcasts.[9] The Al-Jazeera satellite-television channel, for example, which began broadcasting from Qatar in 1996, infuriated practically every Arab government by fearlessly broadcasting opinions on previously taboo topics such as human rights, corruption, and religion. At a different level, the Gulf/2000 project provided current information and informed opinion to its more than 900 members—many of whom reside in the Gulf—through its online discussions and electronic library, in addition to the many other rapidly growing global information resources of the Internet. Policymakers increasingly need to take the effect of the information revolution on public opinion into account. As Ambassador Edward S. Walker, president of the Middle East Institute, declared in June 2001, "There is a new phenomenon in the region called public accountability, which we have seldom had to factor into our projections of Arab behavior in the past.[10]

The new generation in Iran and Saudi Arabia is analyzed by Semati and Yamani. In 1950, the combined population of the eight Gulf states was estimated at a little over 26 million people.[11] In the year 2001, this population was around 120 million and in 2050 it is projected to be 237 million. Not only is the current population huge, but it is also very young: a third of the people in the littoral states are under the age of 15.[12]

The Gulf states, as depicted in this book, are clearly in a period of transition and transformation. In common with the change of leadership taking place throughout the Middle East that saw new monarchs take over in 1999 in Jordan and Morocco, and a new president in 2000 in Syria, a similar transition has already begun in the Gulf with the accession of a new leader in Qatar in 1995 and in Bahrain in 1999. Leadership change is probably not far off in Saudi Arabia and the UAE. Uncertainty over the longevity of Saddam Hussein or the nature of his successor in Iraq, however, continues to unsettle the region. In Iran, unique among the littoral states, regular elections were institutionalized to bring new presidents and parliaments to power; however, that was no guarantee against relentless struggles over access to power and uncertainty over the outcome.

To what extent is a transformation of attitudes, which alone can enable a relaxation of tensions and provide real mutual security, possible in the Gulf? The necessity of correcting a history of misperceptions, as suggested by Khajehpour-Khoei's paper, is a key to the success of the confidence-building process that is now underway in the Gulf. Since the election of Iranian President Khatami in 1997, we have witnessed unprecedented acts of regional cooperation, which gave rise to hopes that a new rethinking and reimagining of relationships was underway. Khatami's reelection in June 2001 increased hopes for regional détente. Iran and Saudi Arabia have led the way in promoting confidence-building measures in the region. Saudi Crown Prince Abdullah's attendance at the Organization of the Islamic Conference (OIC) meeting in Tehran in December 1997 was a major watershed, and President Khatami's triumphant tour of the Gulf in May 1999, with visits to Saudi Arabia, Qatar, and Damascus, set the stage for a new politics of rapprochement.

The signing of an unprecedented security pact between Iran and Saudi Arabia in April 2001 signaled greater Arab trust of Iran and could prove to be a harbinger of improved regional relations.[13] Indeed, this was shortly followed by a historic apology by Kuwait to Iran for backing Iraq during the Iran-Iraq War.[14] Despite internal power struggles, all major factions in Iran appeared to embrace the idea of reconciliation in the Gulf, moving away from the confrontational and interventionist mode of the immediate post-revolutionary period. This was welcomed by nearly all the Arab states of the region, including even Bahrain, which had long feared Iran's export of a radical Islamist vision. By the turn of the century, a more familiar Iranian nationalism once again seemed to emerge as the driving force, a fact even acknowledged by U.S. policymakers.[15] The Iranian revolution, however, had not yet run its course, and Arabs as well as Iranians could not confidently predict the shape of a future government or its policies.

Although outside powers will continue to play an important role in Gulf security as they always have, if only because of their interest in guaranteeing oil exports, it is likely that the regional states will increasingly take charge of their own destiny. This will inevitably mean a smaller role for U.S. forces there, which is probably a good thing for all parties. The return of Russian influence in the Gulf, initially via Iraq, certainly must be expected over the long term. The return of Iran and Iraq to a greater role in littoral affairs is also inevitable, if unsettling to the Gulf monarchies. Increased economic cooperation between regional states to exploit shared resources, such as the North Dome/South Pars gas field between Qatar and Iran, may be the surest way to tamp down political differences.[16] For the Gulf states have a legacy of cooperation as well as conflict. Perhaps the coming generations, who will drive the new regional rapprochement, will help bring the Gulf back to a sense of its own identity and destiny, apart from the West or even the rest of the Middle East. A search for consensus in the Gulf has just begun.

NOTES

1. The meeting was held at Villa Montecucco, the conference center of ENI, the Italian energy company, to which Gulf/2000 extends its appreciation.
2. Two papers that were not given at the conference, those by M. R. Izady and Abdullah K. Alshayji, were commissioned for this volume.
3. Muhammad Rumaihi, *Beyond Oil: Unity and Development in the Gulf,* trans. James Dickins (London: Al Saqi Books, 1986), p. 11.

4. "The Coming Crisis in the Persian Gulf," by Gary G. Sick, in *The Persian Gulf at the Millennium: Essays in Politics, Economy, Security, and Religion,* Gary G. Sick and Lawrence G. Potter, eds., (New York: St. Martin's Press, 1997), pp. 11–30.

5. "The Persian Gulf in Transition" by Lawrence G. Potter, in *Headline Series* No. 315 (New York: Foreign Policy Association, 1998).

6. See *Middle East Policy,* vol. 7 no. 4 (October 2000), with proceedings of Gulf/2000 conference on "The Future of Iraq."

7. "Border Disputes in the Gulf: Past, Present and Future," by Richard Schofield, in *The Persian Gulf at the Millennium,* pp. 127–66.

8. "Court ruling on Gulf border row," by Robin Allen, *Financial Times,* March 17, 2001 (online).

9. See *The Middle East Journal,* Summer 2000, special issue on "The Information Revolution."

10. Edward S. Walker, "The New U.S. Administration's Middle East Policy," speech at the second annual Middle East Oil and Gas Conference, Houston, Texas, June 19, 2001, in *Middle East Economic Survey,* June 25, 2001.

11. 1950 population estimate derived from U.S. Census Bureau, International Data Base.

12. Figures for current and future population, and percentage under the age of 15, from 2001 *World Population Data Sheet* (Washington: Population Reference Bureau, 2001), p. 6.

13. AP (Tehran), April 14, 2001 (online). "Iran hopes that security accords can soon be reached with Bahrain, Oman and Yemen." *Middle East Newsline,* June 9, 2001 (online).

14. Iran Press Service, May 6, 2001 (online)

15. See Martin Indyk, Assistant Secretary for Near East Affairs, Department of State, Hearing of the House International Relations Committee, "Developments in the Middle East," June 8, 1999.

16. It is well to keep in mind that despite all the rhetoric over Abu Musa, Iran and Sharjah quietly split oil revenues from local waters, as specified in the 1971 Memorandum of Understanding, with no problem.

CHAPTER 1

THE HISTORICAL PATTERN
OF GULF SECURITY

J. E. PETERSON

More than a century ago, Bismarck declared, "In international affairs, there are three wasps' nests besides the Balkans: Morocco and the Mediterranean, the Persian Gulf, and the American Monroe Doctrine; God grant that we may never fall into one of them."[1]

Today it is an obvious truism that the primary factor behind concerns for Gulf security is access to oil. It is also self-evident that the key global significance of Gulf oil is a manifestation of only the past few decades. But, as Bismarck's observation demonstrates, the Gulf has been an area of geopolitical importance long before the discovery of oil. Indeed, the Gulf has served as an arena of international concentration and rivalry for centuries and even millennia.

At the same time, it can be observed that the role played by oil today in international concern about Gulf security is not dissimilar to the manner in which other commodities and motives concerned international actors in the past. A closer examination of certain of these themes of continuity in external actors' goals in the Gulf region may well contain worthy lessons for the present and salutary considerations for the future.

It can be postulated that the involvement of external powers in Gulf security has arisen from one or more of three principal motivations: trade, political rivalry, and imperial security. Of these, commerce is perhaps the most obvious factor and itself is divisible into two overlapping subcategories: the protection of (or the desire to penetrate) long trading routes crossing or deriving in the Gulf; and local or regional trading. The earliest well-known example of a trading route traversing the Gulf region was that of the Silk Road, originating in China and terminating in the Mediterranean. Although its heyday was during the period of Roman control of its western terminus and while it declined after the rise of Islam, the Silk Road remained an important route through the time of Marco Polo.

The spice route was in many ways even more central to the Gulf. In addition to transporting cinnamon, cassia, cardamom, ginger, and turmeric from East to West, Arab merchants also exported the southern Arabian products of frankincense and myrrh. Unlike the silk route, which was mainly overland, the spice route proceeded largely by sea. Although first the Egyptians and then the Romans commanded the western terminus in antiquity, control of the spice route through its central course was jealously controlled by Arab merchants and states, despite periodic attempts to break the Muslim monopoly (shared in medieval times with Venice and to a lesser extent Genoa). The desire to deal directly with the sources of spices was a principal motivation in the launching of the European age of exploration.

Properly speaking, the frankincense trade can be considered local trade within the Gulf. And of course trade between the Gulf and the Indian subcontinent and Southeast Asia is an age-old occurrence. Direct European trade with the region, however, awaited the development of the maritime routes around the Cape of Good Hope. In this light, oil can be regarded as both a modern manifestation of local trade and as a network of long trading routes requiring protection as part of the necessity of guaranteeing access to oil.

The second fundamental factor in external concerns, that of political rivalry, stems from the drive of one or more countries to secure control or domination of the Gulf, whether its littoral(s), its hinterland, or its waters. Through the course of history, one of three broad situations can be discerned as existing at any one time: effective domination by a hegemon seeking to protect entrenched interests (such as the Portuguese in the sixteenth century and the British in the nineteenth and early twentieth centuries); a bipolar balance-of-power state of affairs (the Byzantines and the Sasanids; the Ottomans and the Safavids; the United States and the Soviet Union); or a more fluid condition of multilateral sparring and jostling.

As to the third motivation, several dimensions to the rather imprecise category of imperial security can be discerned. The imperial impetus assumes that an actor seeking to or having already incorporated the Gulf, or parts thereof, into its imperial domain or sphere of influence will display unequivocal interests or actions in defense of its imperial position. These may be prompted by such factors as national prestige, advancement of ideology or religion, or perceived threats to the status quo. In part, imperial security is internal in that it requires the security of imperial possessions either through direct control or by the maintenance of secure areas of influence. Inevitably this raises the problem of frontiers: where they logically should lie and, once having been defined, how they must be secured. But paradoxically, imperial frontiers can never be established in a definitive sense since their importance lies only in the security they provide for the territory within the imperial dominions or sphere of influence. As a consequence, there is a constant impetus for forward policies—that is, the frontiers can be secured only by securing the further frontier that lies beyond the secured frontier and so on.

Still, as the Gulf essentially has rested on the periphery of empires through the ages—and as the Middle East constitutes a strategic land bridge between three continents—the most important enduring factor in this category seems to be that of establishing and protecting imperial lines of communication. Furthermore, it can be perceived that the construction and relevance of such lines of communications have evolved throughout history as a result of technological progress. Such advances have embraced inter alia the development of deep-water maritime vessels, subsequent advances in ship construction and navigational capabilities, especially as utilized by European explorers, the advent of the steamship, telegraphic communications, railroads, and aircraft.

The enduring themes in Gulf security outlined above can best be illustrated by a brief retrospective of Gulf security scenarios throughout history. Before the rise of Islam, two equally matched empires vied for supremacy in the greater Gulf region. The Byzantine Empire controlled the western approaches of the Gulf while the Sasanids held the eastern approaches and the Gulf itself. Constantinople had built a monopoly on trade between Asia and Europe, but it was prevented from dealing directly with China by Persian control of the central segments of the commercial routes. Byzantine-Sasanid relations were in constant tension, and frequent warfare along the frontier failed to budge the status quo. In an effort to cut out the intermediaries in the Asia trade, Justinian I (r. 527–565) sought to establish alternative routes circumventing the Sasanids. On the one hand, he explored the northern alternative, by crossing the Black Sea, establishing bases in the Crimea, and opening relations with the peoples of the Steppes. Justinian II (r. 565–578) carried this policy forward by building an alliance with the Turks against the Persians. On the other hand, Justinian I deepened ties with the Ethiopian kingdom of Axum in an effort to develop a maritime route through the Red Sea and across the Indian Ocean. These efforts were not successful, however, and instead the Byzantines' greatest coup was discovery of the secret of silk and its subsequent manufacture in Byzantine territories.[2]

The struggle between Constantinople and Ctesiphon continued unabated until the rise of Islam. The Islamic armies from Arabia first drove a wedge between the two ancient warring states and then succeeded in displacing the Byzantines in their Middle Eastern possessions and in conquering Persia as well. Thus the Islamic empire ended a balance-of-power regime in the Gulf/Middle East by establishing a centuries-long predominant empire controlling the heart of the region.

As Umayyad rule gave way to 'Abbasid, the locus of the Islamic state moved to the northern Gulf. Although the foundation of Basra in the early days of the Islamic state was the consequence of military requirements, its strategic location ensured that it soon prospered as a center of trade, for the same reasons as had previous commercial hubs in the same area. The positioning of the 'Abbasid capital at the new city of Baghdad, founded in 762, and the predominance of a single powerful political authority in the region helped ensure a shift in the relative importance of long-distance trading routes from the Red Sea to the Gulf. Even the decline and fall of the 'Abbasids as a result of the Mongol invasion did not erase the significance of Gulf trade: the emporia of Siraf, Qays, and Hormuz thrived in turn.

Politically, however, the collapse of the 'Abbasid state led to a long period of fragmentation during which Arab, Mongol, Turkish, and other rulers vied for power and territory. It took several centuries before the Gulf returned to a more durable balance-of-power status, this time with the Ottomans standing in for the Byzantines and the Safavids (and later the Qajars) succeeding the Sasanids. This was the prevailing situation on the eve of European penetration of the Indian Ocean.

The Portuguese impetus to explore the seas and lands beyond their immediate shores resulted from a combination of scientific, economic, military, political, and religious motives.[3] A contemporary Portuguese chronicler advanced five motives behind the Portuguese drive to explore. The first of these was to explore the African coast beyond the cape of Bojador in order to know what existed there. The second was to find out whether there were any Christian people in Africa with whom it might be possible to conduct profitable trade. The third was to ascertain correctly the extent of the territories of the

Muslims because every sensible man naturally would like to know the power of his enemy. The fourth was to discover if there was any Christian kingdom which would help in the war against the Muslims. The fifth and final motive was to extend the Christian faith and "to bring to Him all souls that wish to be saved."[4]

Without doubt, the Portuguese court, especially through the influence of Prince Henry the Navigator, was intrigued by the complementary challenges of expanding geographic knowledge (and dispelling myths about the dangers of the Atlantic), setting new standards of navigational principles and cartography, and establishing a fleet of state-of-the-art ships. But, not surprisingly, a commercial motive was also central to Portuguese thinking. In the same way that the Byzantines had monopolized the western terminus of the Oriental trade routes, so the Ottoman conquest of Constantinople enabled them to control Europe's supply of spices, pearls, ivory, silk, and other textiles. Like other European powers, the Portuguese ambition was to discover trade routes independent of the Ottomans.

In addition, five centuries of struggle for independence against the Muslims had produced a keen sense in the Portuguese psyche of the Islamic world as enemy. This manifested itself in both the political and the religious spheres. On the one hand, a successful undermining of the Ottoman control over Oriental trade would seriously weaken Europe's greatest rival. On the other, Christian expansion into Asian waters was regarded as a maritime extension of the Crusades. Hand in hand with conquest went conversion, and Portuguese accounts of their exploits frequently spoke of carrying the sword in one hand and the crucifix in the other. Even the legend of Prester John seemingly had played its part in stoking religious fervor, and his "lost" Christian kingdom was seen as a potential ally against the Muslims and as a possible base of operations.

Beginning early in the fifteenth century, the Portuguese used their caravels to extend the limits of navigation down the coast of Africa until Bartolomeu Dias rounded the Cape of Good Hope in 1488. By 1498, Vasco da Gama had reached India and he returned home the following year with the first wares from the Orient. In subsequent years, Portuguese ships captured ports along the Indian Ocean littoral and established factories, particularly along India's Malabar Coast. The first Portuguese fort in Asia was constructed at Cochin by Afonso de Albuquerque in 1504.

It was quickly realized that the protection of Portuguese trading interests would require a strong presence and a permanent fleet. Accordingly, Francisco de Almeida arrived in India as Portuguese viceroy in 1505. With an Indian base centered first on Cochin, Portugal moved in two directions. Expansion in the direction of the Gulf to the northwest was intended to disrupt Muslim commerce, to place pressure on the Ottomans, and to consolidate control of the spice trade. With this in mind, Albuquerque made his way up the East African coast, established a short-lived fort on Socotra Island in 1507, and then captured Qalhat, Quriyat, Muscat, Suhar, and Khawr Fakkan on his way to the Gulf. Hormuz was reduced (although not permanently captured until 1515), which not only provided the Portuguese with control of the entrance to the Gulf but eliminated any threat from the kings of Hormuz and opened Persia to direct trade with Europe. An unsuccessful attempt to take Aden in order to control the entrance to the Red Sea was also made at the same time.

Meanwhile, the Portuguese were also expanding their presence and trade opportunities eastward, capturing Malacca in 1511 and founding Macau in 1557. Although Malacca, at the epicenter of Asian trade, would have made the better Portuguese capital for economic reasons, it remained at Goa in order to better confront the Ottoman threat.

As early as the Almeida viceroyalty (1505–1509), Portugal had established mastery of the Indian Ocean. Rather than relying on a strategy of defending factories when attacked by local rulers, Almeida placed emphasis on the expansion of the armada backed by coastal forts qua naval bases at key positions. The vigorous application of sea power enabled a monopoly to be established over navigation and long-distance maritime trade.

Albuquerque, Almeida's successor, strengthened Portugal's hegemonic position and even altered the strategy from one of protection of navigation and trading interests through overwhelming sea power to the acquisition of territory in order to better safeguard interests. This marked the emergence of a Portuguese empire in India with Goa (captured in 1510) as its capital. Other forts were built along the Indian coast as well as at Malacca, Ceylon, East Africa, and, in the Gulf, Muscat (1507) and Hormuz (1515).[5]

Thus the Portuguese enjoyed hegemony over the Gulf, as well as the rest of the Indian Ocean, for nearly a century before fading in the face of serious challenges by European rivals and resurgent local rulers. There had always been an aura of fragility to the empire, a consequence of the wide geographic dispersion of its strongholds, as true in the Atlantic as in the Indian Ocean basin, and the constant and severe lack of manpower that more than once left the Portuguese vulnerable to opportunistic Ottoman raiders. Indeed, the Portuguese hegemonic position in the Gulf was threatened throughout this period by Ottoman expansionism into Syria, Egypt, Yemen, and Mesopotamia, which was checked largely by Lisbon's alliance with Persia.

The end to Portuguese predominance in the Gulf came when a joint expedition of Shah 'Abbas and the English East India Company captured the Portuguese stronghold of Hormuz in 1622 and Muscat, to where the Portuguese garrison had fled, fell to the Omanis in 1650. In fact, this marked the emergence of a period of Omani seapower between 1650 and 1730, during which the Arabs expelled the Portuguese from much of the East African littoral and harassed their remaining possessions on the western coast of India.

With the Portuguese decline, the power situation in the Gulf and Indian Ocean expanded from hegemonic to multilateral, with the Dutch making an early bid to supplant Portuguese dominance in the face of vigorous English and French competition.[6] Following the establishment of the Dutch East India Company in 1602, the Dutch gradually usurped Portuguese forts, factories, and settlements around the Indian Ocean, including the capture of Malacca in 1641 and Cochin in 1663.

After the establishment of the company's headquarters on Java in 1607, the Dutch successfully forced England to restrict its interests to India. Besides seeking to monopolize local trade throughout the area, the Dutch concentrated on directing the China trade through their base on Java and protecting the onward route by establishing a station at Cape Town in 1652. The wealth of the company was assured as well by controlling the production, in addition to the exportation, of spices such as nutmeg, cloves, cinnamon, pepper, and coffee.

In the Gulf, Dutch aggressiveness moved into the vacuum left by the declining Portuguese, and they frequently were successful in besting the English both in trade with Persia and Iraq and in naval engagements. But in the first half of the eighteenth century, Dutch power in the western Indian Ocean began to decline, principally as a result of reverses in European wars, including the War of the Spanish Succession (1713–14).

Britain eventually superseded the Portuguese as hegemon in the region. Britain's initial involvement with the Gulf was predicated exclusively upon commercial interests.[7] The English East India Company was incorporated in 1600 and trade with the Gulf quickly supplanted declining Portuguese commerce while competing favorably with the Dutch and the French. A century later, though, the importance of Gulf trade had diminished considerably, and by the end of the eighteenth century it had virtually disappeared.[8] Continued British representation in the Gulf and the occasional patrols there by the Bombay Marine could be reasonably justified only in terms of protection of the minor "country" trade from India. Nevertheless, new factors appeared to prevent complete British withdrawal from the area.

Not the least among these factors was the rivalry with Britain's old enemy France. Under the prodding of Colbert, the French established their own East India Company in 1664 and made Madagascar and Ile de France their base of operations. French advances in India, however, apart from the capture of Pondicherry and several other ports, were slow to come, partly due to the strength of Aurangzeb, the last great Mughal emperor, and partly because of competition from the English East India Company. Nevertheless, by 1677 the French company possessed a factory at Bandar 'Abbas. In conjunction with military successes in Europe in the 1740s, the French governor-general of India, Dupleix, succeeded in capturing Madras, but a subsequent treaty returned to Britain its center of power in India and the French East India Company was never able to recover.

The preceding neatly illustrates the point that changing fortunes in colonial arenas and local contentions often were outgrowths of home rivalries in Europe. While France's presence in the Indian Ocean basin never again seriously challenged British predominance, the mere whisper of French intrigues was taken very seriously indeed. In 1798, Napoleon Bonaparte landed an army in Egypt and easily overpowered that country's Mamluk rulers. In British eyes, however, the real goal was India, and this suspicion was given additional credence with the interception of Napoleon's letters to the rulers of Muscat and Mysore. The destruction of the French fleet at the Battle of Aboukir in 1798 and then Napoleon's ignominious flight to Europe after the unsuccessful siege of Acre in 1799 proved to be only temporary setbacks to French designs. Indeed, it took Napoleon's occupation of Egypt to alert the British belatedly to the country's geopolitical importance.

Instead, France changed tactics and a small fleet was dispatched to the Indian Ocean in 1803, and was followed by the posting of a commercial agent to Muscat in 1807. The treaty of Finkenstein, signed in the same year, would have obliged Napoleon to restrain Russian expansionism in the direction of Persia in return for the Qajar shah's declaration of war upon Britain and his participation with Afghans in an attack on India. This agreement came to naught, however, as France soon reconciled with Russia and Britain subsequently reached a new treaty with Persia in 1809. The final blow to Napoleonic ambitions came with the British capture of Ile de France (thereafter named Mauritius) in 1810, depriving France of its last major base in the Indian Ocean.

British mastery of the Indian Ocean clearly rested on its supremacy at sea. In this respect, its thinking and practice differed little from that of Portugal several centuries earlier, even though its methods of ruling possessions differed markedly. The British

Empire was built on and kept ascendant by sea power. The eminent theorist on the subject, Alfred Thayer Mahan, defined sea power as command of the sea through naval superiority; and that combination of maritime commerce, overseas possessions, and privileged access to foreign markets that produces national "wealth and greatness."[9] For two centuries or more, the technology of sea power—ship design, armaments, and the science of naval warfare—remained virtually unchanged and preserved Britain's advantage, although this began to shift in the latter part of the nineteenth century.[10] Imperial policy depended not only on mastery of the seas but also on control of vital choke points and ports of entry. Thus British possessions came to include Gibraltar, Suez, Aden, South Africa, India, Ceylon, Singapore, and Hong Kong.

By the beginning of the nineteenth century, Britain had vanquished effective threats from European rivals and was in a position to dominate all maritime activity in the Gulf. A first requirement, however, was to defuse regional threats to the British position. Despite the decline in trade, British and British-protected vessels continued to ply Gulf waters and were attacked with increasing frequency in the early years of the nineteenth century. There are various reasons for the emergence of what the British termed "piracy," including depressed economic conditions along Gulf shores and the decline of existing political authority in the region.

The Portuguese had first applied the term "pirates" in the seventeenth century to the Ya'rubi (pl. Ya'aribah) rulers of Oman, who were then engaged in expelling the Portuguese from their strongholds in the Gulf and East Africa. A century and a half later, the British tended to regard the activities of the Qawasim (sing., Qasimi), who were based along the southern shore of the Arabian littoral, in the same light.[11] The strength of Muscat's rulers was quickly fading at the time and local opposition in Oman to their dominance was enflamed by the alliance with the British. In short order, Muscat's possessions on both shores of the Gulf fell to Qasimi control. The anti-Muscat and anti-European inclinations of the Qawasim were further exacerbated by their conversion to Wahhabism, the puritanical strain of Sunni Islam prevailing in central Arabia and being spread by the efforts of the Al Sa'ud.

To the British, these attacks on the shipping of various flags were an annoyance and were lumped together with the activities of the Gulf's freebooters as "piracy"; as a consequence, the territory of the Qasimi lairs was labeled "the Pirate Coast." The principal British response to this "piracy" came in the form of punitive expeditions launched against Qasimi ports. The first of these was prompted by the growing seriousness of the situation in 1808 when many of those aboard an East India Company cruiser were massacred and Qasimi vessels began to appear for the first time in Indian waters. Consequently, an 11–ship armada laid siege in 1809 to the Qasimi capital at Julfar (modern Ras al-Khaimah) and burned it. Another Qasimi stronghold at Lingeh (on the Persian coast) was stormed next, and finally a joint British-Muscati fleet captured Shinas (on Oman's Batinah coast) following a fierce battle. Despite these successes, the power of the Qawasim was broken only temporarily.

By 1812, the Qasimi fleet had been restored and soon their dhows reappeared off the coast of India. British resolve to act forcefully against the renewed threat was stiffened by the success of Egypt's Muhammad 'Ali in defeating the Al Sa'ud, presumed to be backing their fellow Wahhabis. After extensive planning and a suitable respite in internal Indian troubles, a second expedition, again relying on Muscat's help, stormed Ras al-Khaimah in 1819–1820. The town was captured after considerable loss of Arab life while smaller parties were sent out to gain the surrender of neighboring ports and towns. A small garrison left behind when the fleet withdrew subsequently transferred to Qeshm Island.

The idea of a base in the Gulf to protect commercial interests had been broached a century earlier, but the scheme advanced in 1808 derived from political and strategic considerations. A military presence on, say, Kharg Island or Qeshm Island, it was argued, would not only offer protection against pirates but also serve to counter Persian and French designs in the area. While the scheme enjoyed the support of officialdom in India, it was rejected by London, which preferred instead to rely upon diplomacy to advance its strategic interests in the Gulf. Actual occupation of Qeshm Island in 1820 proved short-lived as the garrison quickly fell prey to disease and entanglement in local politics and warfare.[12] It was withdrawn in 1823 and the idea of a military base languished, with a few limited exceptions, for nearly another century. A more fruitful idea arising from the efforts of the Government of Bombay to eradicate piracy eventually culminated in the Trucial system operating under British aegis.

The first step in the erection of a productive and durable Trucial system appeared in the aftermath of the 1820 siege of Ras al-Khaimah.[13] The "General Treaty of Peace with the Arab Tribes," which the area's shaikhs (tribal heads) were forced to sign, prohibited piracy and plunder by sea and required their vessels to fly a recognized flag and be registered. Enforcement was provided at first by the short-lived base on Qeshm Island. Then regular Bombay Marine patrols in the Gulf, introduced shortly thereafter, were able to deal effectively with the occasional attacks perpetrated over the next few decades.

One limitation of the 1820 treaty was its failure to regulate the conduct of warfare at sea among the Arab tribes, which tended to disrupt the fishing and pearling seasons with some regularity. The British were able finally to arrange a maritime truce in 1835 that forbade all hostilities by sea for a period of six months, with the understanding that Britain would not interfere with wars on land. In British eyes, the "Pirate Coast" was thereby transformed into the "Trucial Coast" (or "Trucial Oman"), a sobriquet it was to retain until full independence in 1971. This maritime truce proved so successful that it was renewed regularly until 1843 when a ten-years' truce was signed. Upon its expiry, Britain induced the shaikhs to accept a "Treaty of Perpetual Maritime Peace." By its terms, the British government assumed responsibility for enforcing the treaty. Aggression by any signatory upon another was not to be met with retaliation but instead referred to the British authorities.

The foundation had been laid for Britain's legal and formal predominance in the Gulf itself to be combined with British mastery of its external allies into a truly hegemonic position. But permanent responsibility entailed permanent in situ supervision and so official representatives gradually were stationed around the Gulf. In final form, British administration there formed one part of the Government of India's far-flung residency system, with a Political Resident in the Persian Gulf (PRPG) headquartered at Bushehr (on the Persian coast) until 1947 and thereafter at Manamah, Bahrain. The Resident's subordinates at one time or another included political agents, political officers, and native agents, stationed at Muscat, Bandar 'Abbas, Sharjah, Dubai, Abu Dhabi, Doha, Manamah, Kuwait, and Basra (located in what was an Ottoman wilayat until 1914).[14]

In addition to establishing and maintaining maritime peace, the British pursued other ancillary interests during the mid-nineteenth century. One of these involved the restriction and then the elimination of the slave trade. By 1848, Britain had succeeded in pressuring most of the Gulf's rulers to declare illegal the carriage of African slaves in Gulf vessels and later in the century British legations routinely manumitted slaves upon request.[15]

—=◉=—

The next step in enhancing British control of the Gulf came about partly as the result of European challenges to British supremacy and partly due to the inexorable logic of the defense of India. As Britain solidified its position in India, the natural concern about external threats meant that zones of influence should be extended beyond the Indian frontiers. But as frontiers were secured, they in turn required protection and thus securing the zones of influence became fresh objectives. This seemed to require an ever-expanding circle of engagement and pacification. The seemingly baffling involvement in Afghanistan was at least in part a product of this impulse. By the 1890s, the debate had become fully engaged between the Government of India on one hand, arguing that Britain must seize control of additional buffers of territory in order to safeguard India, and Whitehall on the other, countering that the empire could not support unending expansion and that influence and indirect control were preferable to conquest and direct administration.

In the Gulf, which had by this time become a vital communications route for the British Empire, the impulse to protect the outer perimeters of India and its lifelines took two forms. Britain allowed the Qajar shahs to reign relatively unimpeded in interior Iran but exercised strong influence in, if not outright control of, the Gulf coast through a consul-general who was also the political resident. On the Arab littoral, a new series of formal treaties was engineered with all the chieftains of the coast. In return for cession of responsibility for defense and foreign relations to the British, the local shaikhs were recognized as legitimate rulers (*hakim* in the singular). What had been a fluid system of authority based on tribal leadership and alliances was transformed into the emergence of territorial states complete with hereditary rule through designated individuals and their families.[16]

In this manner, the Al Thani rose to prominence in Qatar despite their having been virtually unknown prior to the nineteenth century. By reason of his protected relationship with Britain, Shaikh Mubarak of Kuwait was able not only to hold off the Ottomans but to strengthen his position vis-à-vis the other leading families of Kuwait. Along the Trucial Coast, the resurgence of the Al Bu Falah under the Al Nahyan led to recognition of the shaikhs of Abu Dhabi while the role of the Al Maktum in creating an *entrepôt* in Dubai assured their recognition. The Qasimi shaikhs at Ras al-Khaimah and Sharjah retained enough significance to be recognized as well (although Ras al-Khaimah did not acquire Trucial status until 1921). Other shaikhs gained and lost recognition as their fortunes waxed and waned. Even Oman, always independent even if only nominally so, was forced to adhere to a similar treaty in 1891. The weak link in this system was Mesopotamia, which remained under Ottoman sovereignty until World War I.

—=◉=—

Insofar as the Gulf had become a "British lake," the paramount position was not, however, without challenges, sparked by technological change. The earliest and most prolonged manifestation of British concern with the Gulf's impact on India's security was to guarantee the security of imperial lines of communications between India and Britain. A quick glance at the map reveals two alternative routes: the Gulf and the Red Sea. The advantage of the Red Sea was its maritime nature, which permitted Britain to rely on its principal strength, mastery of the seas, and suggested that it need not be dependent on the goodwill of other powers along the route. The disadvantage of this route lay in the choke points at Bab al-Mandab, the Gulf of Suez, and Gibraltar. Indeed, Suez was a weak link in the chain as it required an overland transfer. As the geopolitical importance of Egypt had been recognized by the beginning of the nineteenth century, it is not surprising that Britain enthusiastically backed the construction of the Suez Canal, nor that it soon asserted its control over Egypt. At the opposite end of the Red Sea, Britain had taken Aden in 1839 for use as a base to protect the southern approaches to the Red Sea.[17]

On the other hand, the Gulf provided a more direct route, despite the disadvantages of an absence of control over overland segments. The Gulf had served as a principal mail route between London and India until superseded in 1833 by a Red Sea alternative. Direct and reliable postal connections with the Gulf were restored only in 1862 with the introduction of a Bombay-to-Basra steamer mail service, but the connection to Europe was never renewed. However, advances in technology soon allowed quicker and more direct communications using the Gulf route. Indeed, technology was quickly becoming a key ingredient in changing or intensifying conceptions of Gulf security. Important for imperial purposes was the laying of a submarine-and-coastal telegraph cable along the Gulf in 1864. This link enabled the Indo-European Telegraph Department (later Cable and Wireless) to provide an essential and profitable service until undercut by wireless competition in the 1920s.[18]

Another technological advance was responsible for the "steamship" challenge of the 1860s. While it has been suggested that new technology was responsible for altering the pattern of trade, as European steamships replaced coastal craft and European textile mills rendered local weaving uncompetitive, it seems equally likely that competition between European powers drove a quickening of interest in the Gulf. In any case, the decade saw a profusion of Russian, French, and German steamships establishing regular routes up and down the Gulf, in direct competition with the British India Steam Navigation Company. But the interest eventually wore off, most likely because the trade advantages were meager and the costs of maintaining such transparently political maneuvers were too high.[19]

British supervision of Gulf maritime activities and the development of communications lines through the area, in turn, served to strengthen the British stake in what was seen increasingly as a region of some geopolitical importance. Lord Curzon, the viceroy of India at the turn of the century (1898–1905), categorized British interests in the Gulf as being commercial, political, strategical, and telegraphic.[20] As one scholar has put it, the Gulf in fact was not a "British lake" at this time but "an international waterway of steadily increasing importance in an age of imperial rivalries, diplomatic flux, and sizable dangers to international peace of mind in the cycles of decay and revolutionary activity in the Ottoman and Persian states."[21] The growing importance of the Gulf, especially as a backup to the all-water Suez route, was noted by Mahan in his article, "The Persian Gulf and International Relations."[22] Between the middle of the nineteenth century and World War I, Britain consistently worked to consolidate its position in the Gulf and to deny access to other non-regional powers. The principal threats were seen as emanating from France, Russia, Germany, and the Ottoman Empire.

The most spirited threat to the British position, however, came with the French challenge of the 1890s and beyond the turn of the century. Despite the Entente Cordiale,

Anglo-French relations hovered on the verge of crisis in the Gulf during this time, most particularly in Oman. The French offensive caused friction in several ways. First, dhows from the Omani port of Sur were allowed to hoist the French flag, thus providing them with immunity from the British and the Sultan in their smuggling activities, principally arms and slaves. Second, French arms dealers plied their wares openly in the markets of Muscat and adjoining Matrah, with the consequence that many of these weapons made their way to the North-West Frontier where they were used against British forces. Third, France sought to insinuate itself into Oman on an equal status with Britain first by the appointment of a French consul in Muscat, initially the redoubtable Paul Ottavi, and then, more seriously, by the securing of the sultan's permission to establish a coaling station at Bandar Jissah, just outside the capital.

This provoked the British to issue a strong warning to the sultan to revoke the license or face the wrath of the Government of India. The sultan capitulated, the coaling station was never constructed, and Britain offered an olive branch in the form of shared coaling facilities in Muscat harbor. At the same time, the British notion of thwarting the French challenge in Oman by making Muscat a protectorate ironically was stymied by the Anglo-French Declaration of 1862, which stipulated that neither power would seek to alter Oman's sovereign status without reference to the other power. Thus, the addition of another imperial frontier to be defended was narrowly avoided.

In the meantime, India was facing a challenge from another direction with considerable potential impact for the Gulf. The Russian threat to British hegemony in the Gulf took two concrete forms. One was the intrigue of the "Great Game," especially in Afghanistan, which was viewed as a deliberate attempt to extend the Russian sphere of influence and to frustrate Britain's expansion of its zone of influence. Britain feared a Russian push from the North, which was frequently expressed in the premise of a Russian drive for a warm-water port. In short, nineteenth-century suspicions were driven by tsarist expansionism in Asia, competition for influence in Afghanistan, and fears that Russia, in competition with Germany, would seek a port in the Gulf to connect with a railway.

The other perceived threat was an intensification of Russian influence over the Qajar court. Disastrous wars with Russia early in the nineteenth century forced Persia to cede its Caucasus territories and Russian influence in Tehran reached its apex in the early years of the twentieth century, marked in part by the establishment of formal Russian and British zones in the country. The Russian-officered Cossack brigade played a significant role during the Constitutional Revolution and it was an officer from this brigade, Reza Khan, who took control in 1921 and made himself shah in 1925. The Russian role in Iran abated as a result of the Russian Revolution but increased dramatically early in World War II, when the Soviet Union joined Britain in invading Iran. Thereafter, the Russian threat found expression in the Cold War, with the apex occurring in the late 1940s with Soviet sponsorship of the short-lived Azerbaijan and Kurdish republics and close relations with the communist Tudeh party.

By the turn of the twentieth century, the Russian threat was perceived not just as a drive for influence in the murky region of Russo-British frontiers but was given new importance by emerging conceptions of geopolitical theory. The central idea was embodied in Sir Halford Mackinder's thesis of a world "Heartland" stretching from the Volga to the Yangtze and from the Himalayas to the Arctic Ocean.[23] Russia was located at the pivot of world politics. Cradling it was a great inner crescent including Germany, Austria, Turkey, India, and China, while Britain, South Africa, Australia, the United States, Canada, and Japan comprised an outer crescent. At stake was no less than a "World-Island" composed of Europe, Asia, and Africa. As Mackinder put it, "Who rules East Europe commands the Heartland; Who rules the Heartland commands the World-Island; Who rules the World-Island commands the World."[24]

In large part, technology again was seen as being at the root of this shift in strategic power. Whereas once the great land mass of Eurasia was a liability in strategic terms, technological advances reversed the picture. For centuries, sea power had defined world domination since ships could project power across far distances much more quickly and efficiently than land-based armies. But the development of the railroad meant that troops and supplies could be sent great distances more advantageously than by sea.

Not only was Russia ideally placed to take advantage of this new equation but Germany, at least potentially, posed as great a threat. The Gulf figured prominently in this new struggle as British control of India, including its periphery, was necessary in order to thwart domination of the "World-Island." This thinking not only intensified concern about a Russian threat from the North but Germany's influence in Istanbul and the projected Berlin-to-Baghdad railway with its terminus on the Gulf also gave great cause for alarm. Britain's Middle East strategy in World War I was aimed not only at removing the weak Ottoman Empire from the scene but at seizing Mesopotamia to seal off the last unsecured access to the Gulf and thus eliminate a vulnerable shortcut to India as well as a potential threat to imperial lines of communication.

———◦◉◦———

British confidence in the Gulf/overland route could not be assured as long as the Ottoman Empire sat astride it. And in the early years of the twentieth century, the penetration of German influence within the Ottoman Empire was a growing cause for concern, not least because of the projected railway. Indeed, the development of railroads with their superior ability to shunt troops and supplies from one place to another threatened more generally to negate the heretofore effective British strategy of relying upon its maritime supremacy to defend its imperial interests. For this reason, it was not surprising that Britain reacted with alacrity when Germany began actively searching for a Gulf terminus.

Although the spearhead of the German assault lay in the establishment of various commercial interests in the Gulf, the real threat clearly was posed by the proposed location of the eastern terminus of the German-built Ottoman railway at Kuwait, the site favored by Berlin and Istanbul. Britain adamantly opposed the unambiguous incorporation of Kuwait into Ottoman territory as well as the construction of a railhead and port that would threaten British strategic interests. Following years of negotiation, the Anglo-Ottoman treaty of 1913 included an agreement to terminate the line in Basra, but the two powers found themselves at war before ratification was completed.

The railway, however, formed only one aspect of the protracted Anglo-Turkish rivalry. The Ottoman Empire, long sovereign in Mesopotamia, had become increasingly expansionist in the mid-nineteenth century. As early as the 1860s, claim was laid to

Kuwait, Bahrain, central Arabia, Qatar, and even the Trucial Coast. Al-Hasa (now part of Saudi Arabia's Eastern Province) was occupied in 1871 and became a permanent, if unruly, possession until its recapture by the Al Sa'ud in 1913. An attack on Qatar in 1892 ended in disaster, and the effort a decade later to introduce Ottoman officials there was aborted by British representations in Istanbul. Ottoman claims to Qatar and parts of Abu Dhabi were eliminated only by the "Blue Line" Agreement of 1913. The status of Kuwait was considerably more ambiguous and was complicated by the railway question. Tentative agreement on recognition of nominal Turkish sovereignty over the shaikhdom in return for its autonomy was overtaken by the outbreak of World War I and subsequently Kuwait was regarded as an independent state under British protection. Thus, the extension of a British umbrella of protection to Kuwait was done not really for local considerations but for the wider goal of maintaining Gulf security within the imperial context.

In a related manner, British strategy in the Middle East during World War I was predicated on the dismemberment of the Ottoman Empire, as well as its dissolution, in order to remove a chronically weak—and thus unstable—element in the European equation. The extension of British control or influence over Mesopotamia, Palestine, and Hijaz (as well as the allied French paramountcy in Lebanon and Syria) enhanced imperial security along both the Gulf and Red Sea lines of communication.

The war enabled Britain finally to take control of Mesopotamia. This region long had been a center of British interests for such reasons as several centuries of British commerce in Mesopotamia; a tradition of political representation there since 1728; the establishment of postal service in 1862 through the (British) Euphrates and Tigris Steam Navigation Company; the increasing desire to protect the northern reaches of the Gulf from European ambitions and Ottoman expansionism; the perceived need for control over any eventual railhead on the Gulf; and lastly the desire to participate in and control oil exploration. An expeditionary force of the Indian Army landed in Ottoman territory almost immediately upon declaration of war and marched into Basra a few weeks later. But Baghdad was not captured until 1917, after the catastrophic defeat at al-Kut, and Mosul was not entered until after the armistice had been signed. In the end, though, France, Britain's remaining European rival in the Middle East, bowed to Britain's claims in Mesopotamia and existing control was ratified through the granting of the League of Nations mandate for Iraq to Britain.[25]

By the time hostilities were terminated in 1918, the Gulf had very nearly become a "British lake" in truth. Through a series of formal arrangements in the 1890s, prompted by the "forward policy" of Lord Curzon, Kuwait, Bahrain, Qatar, and the Trucial shaikhs had legally accepted British protection and advice.[26] Similar terms had brought the nominally independent sultanate in Muscat within the British sphere of influence. Iraq had become a British mandate. Only Persia and the Al Sa'ud retained any degree of real independence, yet Britain exercised considerable leverage in Tehran and Saudi authority was confined largely to its Najdi base. With British supremacy in the Gulf finally and unquestionably assured, the thrust of British policy increasingly turned toward involvement in local politics to protect its growing list of accrued interests.

The ensuing Gulf security concern involved another advance in technology—the airplane—concomitant with new geopolitical theories regarding the role of air power. While the classical proponents of air power theory, Giulio Douhet and his near-contemporaries Billy Mitchell and Alexander de Seversky,[27] were concerned with total warfare, the application of air power to the Gulf was more narrowly restricted to the establishment and maintenance of aerial lines of communication and colonial policing. As Lord Wavell, viceroy of India (1943–1947), remarked, "There are two main material factors in the revolutionary change that has come over the strategical face of Asia. One is air power, the other is oil."[28] The discovery and exploitation of oil in the Gulf has been the more important and permanent factor catapulting the region to global attention, but the necessities of air communications and air power were first responsible for British concern with the security of the Arabian Peninsula itself. Not long after the technology of air power had been developed, it was applied to Arabia and the Gulf.[29] It was to remain a principal British tool for providing both internal and external security until final withdrawal in 1971.

Prior to the 1920s, British concern with the affairs of the Arab littoral states of the Gulf was prevention of warfare by sea but otherwise generally non-interference in internal affairs, including warfare by land.[30] To repeat, British concern was centered on the security of imperial lines of communication, which were essentially maritime and where they were not, as in the Indo-European Telegraph, the telegraph line had been deliberately laid along the Persian coast in order to avoid the lack of security on the Arab littoral.

This "hands-off" attitude changed in the second decade of this century. A principal factor in the application of air power to the Gulf was the emergence of the Royal Air Force (RAF) as a full-fledged Service and, especially, the success of the chief of the air staff, Air Marshal Sir Hugh Trenchard, known as "the father of the RAF," in carving out a role for the RAF as the primary policing force in the Middle East. The RAF not only carried out security responsibilities in Iraq but assumed administrative control of the mandate in 1922. Meanwhile, the RAF had been active in protecting Aden from the Ottomans during World War I and air sorties were carried out against recalcitrant tribes as early as 1919. Trenchard argued vigorously that the RAF could provide a more cost-effective policing function in the protectorates of southern Yemen. In 1928, the RAF was given overall responsibility for the defense of Aden Colony and Protectorate, replacing a British and Indian garrison. Other RAF duties in the Gulf included protecting Kuwait and Iraq from incursions by the Ikhwan of the Najd and bombarding one of the sultan of Oman's tribes in Sur.

With the assumption of the two noncontiguous areas of responsibility in Iraq and Aden, it was necessary to establish a chain of aerodromes and emergency landing grounds along the coastal route from Basra to Aden. Political arrangements and surveying of the complete route began in earnest in 1929, in conjunction with the civil air route to India. This involved additional negotiations with littoral rulers regarding security and procedures for dealing with unruly tribes. For various reasons, particularly uncertainty surrounding security in remote stretches of the route, especially along Oman's Arabian Sea coast, completion of the route was held up until 1936.

As another aspect of the new technology, developments in aircraft meant that for the first time it was feasible to introduce long-distance civil air routes. Naturally, the route from London to India was a high priority, and the RAF established a mail-carrying air service through the Middle East in 1921. Accordingly, Imperial Airways (the forerunner to British Airways) set to work making arrangements for such a route in the late 1920s, involving both land-based aircraft and flying boats. While initial arrangements were made to route the Gulf segments along the south Persian coast, it soon became clear that for political reasons this was not a permanent solution.[31]

As a consequence, Government of India officials in the Gulf were instructed to enter into negotiations with the various Arab rulers for rights to establish aerodromes and maritime landing areas, and the RAF carried out the surveying. Facilities were quickly arranged in Kuwait and Bahrain but negotiations proved more difficult along the Trucial Coast. Eventually, the ruler of Sharjah was persuaded to permit a landing ground and rest house and the Imperial Airways service was switched from the Persian coast to the Arabian littoral in late 1932, using stops at Kuwait, Bahrain, Sharjah, and Gwadar (the Omani enclave on the Pakistan coast).[32] These air-driven developments prompted a significant change of policy: for the first time, the British required assurance that the rulers with whom they had established treaty recognition would be responsible for the security of their onshore territory. While the determination of borders between the states remained unsettled and the allegiance of Bedouin tribes was not always certain, an important step had been taken in the evolution from tribally-based shaikhs to territorial rulers.

At the same time, it was recognized that circumstances in the Gulf had changed since Curzon's day. As remarks of a Foreign Office official were summarized in 1935, "To-day the Persian Gulf was one of the world's highways, bordered by strongly nationalist States, whose interest in the Gulf was real and active, and the discovery of oil had led other foreign Powers to take an increasing interest in Gulf affairs. In his view, the time had come, or was at least rapidly approaching, when His Majesty's Government would no longer be able to maintain their previous policy of merely keeping others out, and living, as it were, from hand to mouth, but would be faced with the necessity of going either forwards or backwards."[33]

This then introduces the paramount catalyst for Gulf security over the last half century or more: access to Gulf oil. Oil was first discovered in Iran in 1908 and then in Iraq shortly after World War I. The geopolitical importance of Gulf oil manifested itself as early as World War II, when Bahrain served as one of Britain's three major sources of East-of-Suez oil requirements. During the war, fears of Axis threats to the supply of Gulf oil were responsible for an interruption of production in Saudi Arabia and Kuwait. In an amazing, even if less than effective, feat of aerial bravado, Italian bombers made their way from Rhodes to the Gulf, dropping bombs on Bahrain and Dhahran—but missing their intended targets and landing in Eritrea. At the same time, the Gulf assumed another important, if transitory, role as a conduit of Allied war supplies to the Soviet Union. American and British ships deposited their cargoes at Persian ports, which were then ferried overland by truck to the Soviet Union.

There were other reasons for the strategic importance of the Gulf during the war. In the words of the Political Resident just before the war, "The importance of [the air route through the Gulf] is obvious, as if it is 'cut' in time of war, for the period that it remains cut no British civil aircraft, and RAF aircraft only with difficulty (by the Aden Muscat Route) . . . can reach India, Singapore or Australia."[34] Bahrain was a significant asset because of its oil fields and refinery, the naval base at Jufayr, and its selection already as the future home of the Political Residency in the Persian Gulf. The Gulf and Iranian corridor was used as a key Allied supply route to the Soviet Union. The Arabian Peninsula and its surrounding bodies of water—the Gulf, the Red Sea, and the Arabian Sea—provided the air and sea gateways to the Indian Ocean, Asia, and the Pacific. In particular, air routes through the Gulf and along the southern Arabian rim served as important links in the ferrying of men and matériel to the Pacific theater in the latter stages of the war. This was especially important for Britain but it was also valuable for the United States, which not only utilized British facilities but established its own, such as the Dhahran airfield in Saudi Arabia. In addition, bombing raids were conducted from Aden during the Italian East Africa campaign early in the war, and southern Arabia and Gulf bases were used to provide convoy escorts and conduct anti-submarine patrols.

The spirit of East-West cooperation during the war was not to last, of course, and in the decades after the war the Gulf became yet another arena of Cold War competition. To at least some extent, this shift in perceptions of a changed global strategic environment was driven by the emergence of a sort of "rimland" elaboration of Mackinder's "heartland" thesis, with the rimland corresponding to his "Inner Crescent."[35] In the minds of Western policymakers, the heartland was now occupied by a hostile Soviet Union brandishing an expansionist ideology. Consequently, it was imperative to contain this threat by controlling the encircling rimland. NATO secured the western perimeter, although the eastern reaches were threatened by Communist victory in China. In the middle, however, lay the Middle East and the Gulf. Western strategy concentrated on securing the Gulf—both its oil supplies and the survival of friendly regimes—against the perceived Communist threat. Friendly countries in the region were encouraged to form the Baghdad Pact in the 1950s as a kind of protective arc around the vital Gulf oil-producing regions.

Given the existing British paramountcy in the Gulf, defending the region from the renewed threat from the north was regarded in the immediate postwar years primarily as a British responsibility. Nevertheless, the decline of British standing in the Middle East and the perceived seriousness of the Cold War danger served to refocus Washington's attention on the Gulf.

American penetration of this British domain, bitterly resented by the British, had begun in the decade before the war but benefited heavily from the need for cooperation in war efforts and it became more pronounced in subsequent years. The process had started with American minority interests in British oil concessions and it then became pronounced with the establishment of the Arabian-American Oil Company (ARAMCO) concession in Saudi Arabia. American armed forces utilized Gulf air facilities during World War II. Subsequently, the United States built an airfield at Dhahran, established a small naval presence in the Gulf (headquartered in Bahrain), and initiated a long and close relationship with Iran under the rule of Mohammad Reza Shah. Thus, by the early 1950s, the British influence in two of the most important countries of the Gulf had been eroded and replaced by American influence.

The slowly emerging American insinuation into the Peninsula occurred simultaneously with a gradual British retrenchment from the existing position in the Gulf and Middle East. This phenomenon was only the local manifestation of a broader process involving the dismemberment of the British empire and the cumulative relinquishing of long-held East-of-Suez responsibilities. The Peninsula and Gulf constituted the tail end of a retreat punctuated by exits from India in 1947 and Egypt in 1954, the Suez debacle in 1956, the Iraqi revolution in 1958, the surrender of Aden in 1967, and finally withdrawal from the Gulf in 1971.

Withdrawal from Aden—also signifying abandonment of Britain's last major military installation in the Middle East—turned out to be a long, involved, and bloody process. In contrast, withdrawal from the Gulf was far less painful. The military implications were negligible, and at the time the political impact as seen from London and Washington seemed relatively minimal. The impact on the Gulf was more substantial, especially for the smaller emirates. Britain had served as judge, arbiter, administrator, and, of course, protector of this littoral for well over a century. Departure in 1971 was tantamount to removal of the safety net. Obviously, the currents of nationalist and modernist sentiments and ideas had begun to circulate along the shores of the Gulf even before the influx of oil revenues. Apart from Iraq and perhaps Kuwait and Saudi Arabia, few people of the Arab littoral seemed really prepared for the burden of complete political and international responsibilities. Nevertheless, the newly independent states of Bahrain, Qatar, and the United Arab Emirates—along with the not-so-much-older nations of Kuwait and Saudi Arabia—adjusted quickly enough.

The "changing of the guard" in the Gulf from Britain to the United States constituted a lengthy process stretching over several decades. American policy in the Gulf since British withdrawal can be divided into two distinct and contrasting periods: an interval of relatively low commitment during the 1970s followed by two subsequent decades of increasing involvement and concern.[36]

U.S. interests in the Gulf were considerable when Britain withdrew in 1971. Still, even with three years or more advance notice, the United States was not fully prepared to accept direct responsibility for the security of the Gulf and Peninsula, let alone take up Britain's shield. Close working relations existed only with Iran and Saudi Arabia, American diplomats had yet to take up residence in the newly independent states, U.S. military capabilities in the Gulf were miniscule, and apart from the oil companies, there were few politicians, officials, or businessmen who were familiar with the region.

The seeming American inaction concerning the Gulf during the first period cannot be put down solely to indifference, although the Gulf's pivotal role in the looming global oil crisis was not generally appreciated at the outset of the 1970s. Rather, the explanation lay elsewhere. Except for the ties to Iran and, to a lesser extent, Saudi Arabia, the Gulf had always been unfamiliar territory. Even later, Washington's perceptions of events and situations in the region in large part were filtered through Pahlavi Tehran and Riyadh. In addition, the simultaneous American dilemma in Vietnam made direct involvement along the lines of the British experience impossible. The Nixon Doctrine of 1969 was formulated as an attempt to shift the burden of "world policekeeping" away from the application of American force to a reliance on surrogates. Thus, American policy in the Gulf during the period from 1971 to 1979 could well be described as benign inaction, essentially dependent on a "twin pillars" policy whereby the military establishments of the two principal American allies, Iran and Saudi Arabia, were built up with American arms and training assistance.

In addition to a different approach and policy outlook, the United States also faced a radically changed situation from the prewar era of British predominance. While Gulf oil had been important to Britain then, in the 1970s that oil was at the heart of global dependence on an increasingly "vital" resource. The political environment had changed as well: no longer was the Gulf ringed by minor possessions and quasi dependencies of an empire but independent states had appeared and been fully integrated into the international system.

Even though the American strategic interest of denying entry to the Gulf to its superpower rival echoed earlier British attempts at quarantine, there were differences even here. The East-West rivalry and the supremacy of the United States and the Soviet Union in a bipolar system represented a far more direct challenge than those of previous years, as illustrated in the stubborn Soviet presence in northern Iran after World War II and emerging Soviet influence in Iraq after 1958.

Finally, the United States came cold to its role as guardian of the Gulf. Britain had had three and a half centuries of experience in the region and had worked up to its position of predominance and security responsibility gradually over the course of at least a century. In 1971, the United States found itself thrust into a role not of its choosing. For most of the ensuing decade, Washington looked benignly on the Gulf from a distance, blithely assuming that the status quo would remain undisturbed and that the amount of regulation required could be provided by its Iranian and Saudi clients. Neither the oil crisis of 1973–1974 nor the spillover from continued Arab-Israeli strife shook this complacency, but only the events of 1979. The laissez-faire attitude of the 1970s finally gave way to a skittish, hawkish attitude in the 1980s and an increasingly bullying posture in the 1990s.

It took the combination of a number of worrying events around 1979 to give added impetus to a perceived requirement for a more active and direct American security capability in the Gulf. These included the Marxist revolution in Ethiopia, the war between Ethiopia and Somalia in the Ogaden, the short border war between the two Yemens that seemed to favor radical South Yemen, and especially the Soviet invasion of Afghanistan. But the most important of these developments was the revolution in Iran. This epochal event not only removed the key element in the American "twin pillar" strategy but gave birth to a regime hostile to the United States and its friends and one that seemed intent on exporting its revolutionary ideology to the region.

As a result of these developments, the Gulf and the broader region came to be regarded as the "Arc of Crisis," a term coined by U.S. national security adviser Zbigniew Brzezinski. Echoes of Mackinder's "heartland" and Spykman's "rimland" rumbled loudly through the rhetoric around the so-called Arc of Crisis and its close cousin, the Crescent of Crisis.[37] It was felt in Washington that the United States could no longer stand idly by and expect the course of Gulf events to continue along a favorable heading. Intervention was increasingly seen as proper, necessary, and even a duty. Thus, in his State of the Union address of January 23, 1980, U.S. president Jimmy Carter announced that "An attempt by any outside force to gain control of the Persian Gulf region will be regarded as an assault on the vital interests of the United States of America. And such an assault will be repelled by any means necessary, including military force." The Carter Doctrine introduced by this declaration bears a remarkable similarity to the enunciation of British policy in 1903 when Lord Lansdowne, the secretary of state for foreign affairs, stated in Parliament that "we should regard the establishment of a naval base, or of a fortified port, in the Persian Gulf by any other Power as a very grave menace to British interests, and we should certainly resist it with all the means at our disposal."[38]

Much as Egyptian attacks on Saudi territory during the Yemen civil war of the 1960s prompted Washington to dispatch a fighter squadron and to encourage Britain to provide the kingdom with Lightning and Hunter aircraft, the looming Iranian threat in the Gulf caused Washington to accede to Riyadh's request for five AWACS (Airborne Warning and Control System) aircraft to provide long-distance radar coverage. In some ways, this decision can be seen as marking the beginning of a qualitative change in U.S. policy: no longer content with assisting surrogates from afar, the United States found it necessary to insert its own equipment and personnel into the region.

While the outbreak of the Iran-Iraq War in 1980 seemed to benefit U.S. interests by diverting Iran's attention and moderating Iraqi attitudes towards friendly Arab states, the shift in fortunes of war to Tehran's favor eventually forced the United States into deeper involvement, as evidenced most obviously by the commitment to reflag vulnerable Kuwaiti oil tankers under the U.S. standard. Henceforth, a permanent naval presence (the long-present but minuscule U.S. Navy's Mideastfor notwithstanding) was added to an air force presence.

But assistance to allied nations was only part of the sea change in U.S. policy. In response to the perceived threats at the end of the 1970s, the first serious planning for military intervention began to take place. The Rapid Deployment Joint Task Force was established at Tampa, Florida, in 1980. By the beginning of 1983, it had evolved into the U.S. Central Command, one of six U.S. unified, multiservice commands, with a theater of operations centered in Southwest Asia and Northeast Africa.

Still, for much of the decade of the 1980s, the U.S. Central Command was an onlooker to regional strife that it could not control, could not influence, could not ameliorate, and in which it could not intervene. The Iran-Iraq War was perhaps the first concrete indication in Western capitals that the primary threat to security in the Gulf did not come from the Communist bloc but from regional actors. The end of the Iran-Iraq War and the collapse of the Soviet Union served finally to refocus American attention on more immediate, regional threats to Western conceptions of Gulf security. The culmination of this redirection was, of course, the Iraqi invasion of Kuwait and the subsequent Desert Storm war.

It can be debated whether Operation Desert Storm could have taken place in the absence of the collapse of the Soviet Union. For all the rhetoric of the time, not least of which being George Bush's proclamation of a "new world order," it seems abundantly clear in retrospect that the war was a classic illustration of American force projection supported by a diverse and diffuse coalition. Both the scale of the buildup and Washington's success in manipulating the playing field had not been witnessed since the Korean War nearly 40 years before. On the one hand, the massive orchestrated buildup of forces and then their successful and vigorous application utilizing the latest in warfare technology seemed to be a vindication of those who had earlier advocated the adoption of a half-war doctrine in American defense strategy.

On the other hand, however, the Kuwait campaign demonstrated the pitfalls inherent in pursuing limited war. By Western reckoning, Iraq had lost the war most definitively and therefore should have capitulated in full to the demands and requirements of the victors. But in the mind of Saddam Hussein, he had taken on the combined might of the world and he and his regime survived intact. It was not a defeat so much as a temporary setback on the field of combat. It could even be construed as a victory in much the same way that Saddam was able to portray his near-fatal escape from Iranian counterattack during his long war with his larger neighbor as a glorious victory.

The implementation of no-fly zones in Iraq's north and south and the introduction of the sanctions regime demonstrably failed to force Saddam's submission after a decade of enforcement. Indeed, they did not significantly weaken Saddam's regime internally as they were intended to do, at least in part. Rather, their continuation, combined with the periodic mouse traps that Saddam set and into which Washington repeatedly stumbled, aroused widespread sympathy for the plight of the Iraqi people while solidifying Arab, Islamic, and wider indignation and anger against American (and British) "bullying." At the end of the decade of the 1990s, American policy seemed to return to a vague wishfulness that an end to the drama would be forthcoming through Saddam's ouster from within—not, it has been notably emphasized, through an uprising by the people but by action within those inner elites of the regime closest to him (and, paradoxically, in combination with those exiles farthest away from the regime).

The application of American security goals in the Gulf today rests upon variations of earlier external powers' strategies. Douhet's vision of the overwhelming nature of air power found form in the massive aerial bombardment of Iraq in early 1991. There is an echo of the RAF's past role in Western air forces' enforcement of the no-fly zones in Iraq, as well as in the American-backed Saudi emphasis on air mobility as its most effective defensive strategy. But sea power has not disappeared either. American ships seek to protect Western interests to, from, and in the Gulf through naval superiority, and the dispatch of an aircraft carrier or two sends a powerful psychological message. The parallels can even be stretched back a century or more. The British and European powers were prone to regard annoying local powers opposing them as "pirates"; the present-day equivalents are dismissed as "rogue states."

The pendulum of Gulf security has swung once again. British hegemony evolved into a Cold War bipolar situation and then into American hegemony. But clearly, despite the triumphal posturing following the hostilities in 1991, American power in the Gulf was only a shadow of past British supremacy. International sensibilities had changed and direct intervention in Iraq was not a possibility. Washington's pro-Israeli policy alienated public opinion throughout the Arab world and hampered relations with even friendly regimes. Despite the promulgation of a policy of "dual containment," the United States was unable to force Baghdad to bow to its demands and found itself reduced by domestic constraints to await those initiatives by Tehran tentatively permitted by changes in Iranian politics. At one time the Portuguese crown could simply send a flotilla to enforce compliance with its demands as bloodily as it liked. No longer. It's not easy being a hegemon in the twenty-first century, not even a demi-hegemon.

The state of affairs today in the Gulf fundamentally follows the same rules and conditions as it has throughout history, notwithstanding changes in actors and the impact of technological change. The primal factors essentially remain the same. Trade is still the raison d'être of Gulf security: external actors are still concerned about access to and control of the supply of a valued commodity, today defined as oil, and they seek access to regional markets. Lines of communication no longer may be imperial, but they still exist. The flow of oil from Gulf terminus to end consumer is regarded as a key element of international security, and thus protection of lines of communication is as vital as ever.

Political rivalries continue unabated, of course. A decade or more ago, the United States sought to maintain and expand its influence in the region in order to deny any gains to the Soviet Union, with the Gulf comprising one subsystem in the larger bipolar, balance-of-power Cold War struggle. Today, as the dominant external power, the United States replicates the policy of earlier predominant powers in seeking to maintain the status quo and to prevent the rise of hostile regional powers that would threaten friendly regimes. Regional turbulence is seen as potentially destabilizing the region and thus, given the importance of oil, jeopardizing global security.

There are even echoes of earlier stimuli of ideology and religion. While the sense of religious mission does not apply as it did in earlier periods, one can still speak of a motive of conversion. This is not conversion in traditional religious terms, although there are occasionally reverberations of the revival of the conception of an "Islamic threat" and the consequent perceived need for a new "crusade." Nor is Western, and specifically American, concern any longer cast in terms of a struggle between "good and evil," between capitalism and communism. But it is clear that American economic views predominate, and riding on their crest is a triumphant wave of American pop culture. The West, and specifically the United States, is frequently accused of seeking to propagate not only a capitalist, free-market economy but a global culture based on "the American way."

The Gulf essentially has rested on the periphery of empires through the ages, sometimes under the thrall of a dominant power, sometimes as the prize contested by political rivals, and on occasion at the mercy of a wider mix of competing local and external powers. While the concoction of goals and rewards to be found in the Gulf have changed over the centuries, its central location astride the world's major commerce routes and zones of competition ensures a continued presence on the world stage.

NOTES

1. Cited in Mary Evelyn Townsend, *The Rise and Fall of the German Colonial Empire, 1884–1918* (New York: Macmillan, 1930), p. 309.
2. Georges Ostrogorsky, *Histoire de l'Empire Byzantin* (Paris: Payot, 1956), pp. 103–105.
3. Discussion of these motives is drawn from K. M. Mathew, *History of the Portuguese Navigation in India (1497–1600)* (Delhi: Mittal, 1988), pp. 74–81, who relies upon H. V. Livermore, *A New History of Portugal* (Cambridge: Cambridge University Press, 1966), p. 1. Other sources on the Portuguese in the Indian Ocean include C. R. Boxer, *The Portuguese Sea-borne Empire (1415–1825)* (London: Hutchinson; 1969); ibid., *Portuguese Conquest and Commerce in Southern Asia, 1500–1750* (London: Variorum Reprints, 1985); Paulo Craesbeeck, *The Commentaries of Ruy Freyre de Andrada: In which are Related his Exploits from the Year 1619, in which he left this Kingdom of Portugal as General of the Sea of Ormuz, and Coast of Persia, and Arabia, until his Death* (ed. with introduction by C. R. Boxer, London: George Routledge & Sons, 1930); F. C. Danvers, *The Portuguese in India: Being a History of the Rise and Decline of Their Eastern Empire* (2 vols.; London: W. H. Allen, 1894; reprinted New York: Octagon Books, 1966; and reprinted New Delhi: Asian Educational Services, 1992); and R. B. Serjeant, *The Portuguese Off the South Arabian Coast* (Beirut, 1974).
4. Gomes de Azurara, *Chronica de Descobrimento e Conquista de Guinea* (Paris, 1841), p. 28; cited in Mathew, *Portuguese Navigation*, p. 74.
5. One fascinating facet of Albuquerque's imperial policy was the encouragement given to Portuguese ranks, particularly artisans such as shipbuilders, ropemakers, gunners, and other workers in the arsenal and dockyard, to marry native women from Goa in order to form a loyal population who would remain in India for life. Despite opposition from other officers and the clergy, as many as 450 marriages took place before Albuquerque left Goa for Malacca. H. Morse Stephens, *Rulers of India: Albuquerque* (Oxford: Clarendon Press, 1912), pp. 152–55.
6. C. R. Boxer, *The Dutch Seaborne Empire, 1600–1800* (1965, reprinted 1990); Holden Furber, *Rival Empires of Trade in the Orient, 1600–1800* (Minneapolis: University of Minnesota Press, 1976); and Boxer, *The Portuguese Sea-borne Empire*.

7. Principal sources on British involvement in the Gulf include J. G. Lorimer, comp., *Gazetteer of the Persian Gulf, 'Omān, and Central Arabia* (Calcutta: Superintendent Government Printing, 1908–1915; reprinted Farnborough, Hants.: Gregg International Publishers, 1970); J. B. Kelly, *Britain and the Persian Gulf, 1795–1880* (Oxford: Clarendon Press, 1968); Briton Cooper Busch, *Britain and the Persian Gulf, 1894–1914* (Berkeley: University of California Press, 1967); and Malcolm Yapp, "British Policy in the Persian Gulf," in Alvin G. Cottrell, gen. ed., *The Persian Gulf States: A General Survey* (Baltimore: Johns Hopkins University Press, 1980), pp. 70–100. On the maritime role, see R. St. P. Parry, "The Navy in the Persian Gulf," *Journal of the Royal United Service Institution,* Vol. 75 (May 1930), pp. 314–31; and J. F. Standish, "British Maritime Policy in the Persian Gulf," *Middle Eastern Studies,* Vol. 3, No. 4 (1967), pp. 324–54.

8. Furber, *Rival Empires of Trade in the Orient,* p. 330, notes a sea change in the nature of European imperialism in Asia at this time with competing East India companies being replaced by an emerging *Pax Britannica,* and he pins it precisely to "the first appearance of Indian sepoys on the Mediterranean margins of the European world" when a fleet with British and Indian troops was dispatched to Egypt in 1801 to help expel Napoleon.

9. Philip A. Crowl, "Alfred Thayer Mahan: The Naval Historian," in Peter Paret, ed., with the collaboration of Gordon A. Craig and Felix Gilbert, *Makers of Modern Strategy from Machiavelli to the Nuclear Age* (Oxford: Clarendon Press, 1986), pp. 450–51; citing Mahan's two principal works, *The Influence of Sea Power Upon History, 1660–1783* (1890), and *The Influence of Sea Power Upon the French Revolution and Empire, 1793–1812* (1892).

10. Arthur J. Marder, *British Naval Policy, 1880–1905: The Anatomy of British Sea Power* (London: Putnam, 1942), pp. 3–4. "With the introduction of steam power, the screw propeller, the shell gun, and the use of iron and steel as shipbuilding materials, a new era began. The science of naval architecture underwent a greater change in the latter half of the nineteenth century than in the preceding ten centuries combined." Ibid.

11. The Al-Qawasim constituted a maritime force based on a family of the same name who first appeared in Lingeh, a port on the Persian coast. By the early nineteenth century, the family had relocated its center of activities to the Arabian coast, particularly Julfar (subsequently known as Ras al-Khaimah). From there, maritime raids were carried out against both local and European shipping.

12. Ordered to investigate reports of piracy by the Bani Bu 'Ali tribe (residing at the southeastern corner of the Omani coast), a ship from the Qeshm garrison was attacked by the tribe. The attempt of the garrison's commander, Captain T. Perronet Thompson, to punish the Bani Bu 'Ali ended in catastrophe when the tribe counterattacked and nearly massacred Thompson's forces. A new punitive expedition was sent out from India. In early 1821, in combination with Muscati troops, the Bani Bu 'Ali were defeated in a fierce battle, their main settlements razed, and their leaders imprisoned in Muscat. Subsequently, Thompson was court-martialed for unnecessarily involving Britain in a campaign in the interior of Arabia and publicly reprimanded, although his social standing allowed him to escape punishment.

13. The texts of the relevant treaties and discussion of their background are to be found in C. U. Aitchison, comp., *A Collection of Treaties, Engagements and Sanads Relating to India and Neighbouring Countries* (5th ed.; Delhi: Manager of Publications, Government of India, 1933), Vol. 11. The Ruler of Sharjah, Dr. Shaikh Sultan b. Muhammad al-Qasimi, has refuted the idea that his ancestors were pirates in *The Myth of Arab Piracy in the Gulf* (London: Croom Helm, 1986; 2nd ed.; London: Routledge, 1988).

14. J. B. Kelly discusses the evolution of this administrative network in "The Legal and Historical Basis of the British Position in the Persian Gulf," in *St. Antony's Papers,* No. 4 (London: Chatto & Windus; New York: Praeger, 1959; Middle Eastern Affairs, No. 1), pp. 119–40.

15. On the slave trade see Lorimer, *Gazetteer,* Appendix L, "The Slave Trade in the Persian Gulf Region," pp. 2475–2516.

16. This evolution of authority has been outlined in J. E. Peterson, "Tribes and Politics in Eastern Arabia," *Middle East Journal,* Vol. 31, No. 3 (1977), pp. 297–312.

17. The problem of secure frontiers arose here as well. The security of the settlement (later colony) of Aden could be guaranteed only by satisfactory agreement with the adjacent petty states. But the establishment of treaty relations with the surrounding rulers forced Britain to ensure both their internal and external security, and the encircling band of protectorates grew until confronted with a similar Ottoman expansionism from the north.

18. On communications, see Lorimer, *Gazetteer,* Appendix J, "The Telegraphs of the Persian Gulf in Their Relation to the Telegraph Systems of Persia and Turkey," pp. 2400–38, and Appendix K, "Mail Communications and the Indian Post Office in the Persian Gulf," pp. 2439–74; and Christina Phelps Harris, "The Persian Gulf Submarine Telegraph of 1864," *The Geographical Journal,* Vol. 135, Pt. 2 (June 1969), pp. 169–90.

19. The debate over the role of technology in the introduction of steamships to the Gulf can be followed in Robert G. Landen, *Oman Since 1856: Disruptive Modernization in a Traditional Arab Society* (Princeton: Princeton University Press, 1967); Kelly, *Britain and the Persian Gulf;* T. Cuyler Young, ed., *Middle East Focus: The Persian Gulf* (Princeton: Princeton University Conference, 1969; Proceedings of the Twentieth Annual Near East Conference); and Busch, *Britain and the Persian Gulf.*

20. Cited in Standish, "British Maritime Policy," p. 345.

21. Busch, *Britain and the Persian Gulf,* pp. 1–2.

22. *National and English Review,* Vol. 40 (Sept. 1902), pp. 27–45. Mahan is credited with coining the term "Middle East" on p. 39 of this article.

23. H. J. Mackinder, "The Geographical Pivot of History," *The Geographical Journal,* Vol. 23, No. 4 (April 1904), pp. 421–44.

24. Mackinder, *Democratic Ideals and Reality* (New York: Henry Holt, 1919), p. 150.

25. On the establishment of British control over Iraq, see A. J. Barker, *The Neglected War: Mesopotamia, 1914–1918* (London: Faber & Faber, 1967); Edith and E. F. Penrose, *Iraq: International Relations and National Development* (London: Ernest Benn; Boulder, CO: Westview Press, 1978); and V. H. Rothwell, "Mesopotamia in British War Aims, 1914–1918," *The Historical Journal,* Vol. 13, No. 2 (1970), pp. 273–94.

26. "In Southern Persia and the Persian Gulf Lord Curzon restored the waning prestige of Great Britain, and demonstrated the determination of the Government not to permit any violation of the preferential position which Great Britain has acquired in that great land-locked sea after keeping the peace for three hundred years at a heavy cost in blood and treasure." Lovat Fraser, *India Under Curzon and After* (London: William Heinemann, 1911), p. 25.

27. Giulio Douhet, *The Command of the Air,* translated by Dino Ferrari (New York: Coward-McCann, 1942; London: Faber & Faber, 1943; 1st Italian ed. published 1921 and 2nd edition published 1927); Edward Warner, "Douhet, Mitchell, Seversky: Theories of Air Warfare," in Edward Meade Earle, ed., *Makers of Modern Strategy* (Princeton: Princeton University Press, 1943), pp. 485–503; and David MacIsaac, "Voices from the Central Blue: The Air Power Theorists," in Peter Paret, ed., with the collaboration of Gordon A. Craig and Felix Gilbert, *Makers of Modern Strategy from Machiavelli to the Nuclear Age* (Oxford: Clarendon Press, 1986), pp. 624–47.

28. Address to the Royal Central Asian Society, June 1949; cited in Olaf Caroe, *The Wells of Power: The Oil-Fields of South-Western Asia* (London: Macmillan, 1951), p. 184.

29. The British, French, and Germans all used aircraft for reconnaissance in Arabia during World War I. British airplanes bombed Ottoman forces besieging Aden in 1916 and attacked other Ottoman troops outside al-Kut in Mesopotamia during the same

year. Britain utilized air power in colonial policing along the North-West Frontier and in Afghanistan during 1918–1920; the attack by one bomber on Kabul in May 1920 was seen as an important factor in the decision to sue for peace. Aircraft were used to even greater effect in Somaliland in early 1920, when the forces of Muhammad bin 'Abdullah (the "Mad Mullah") were routed by a single bomber squadron in only three weeks. The rulers of Najd (later Saudi Arabia) and Yemen acquired their first aircraft in the mid-1920s, although the effectiveness of these purchases for military use was extremely limited by the unsuitability of the particular airplanes, the lack of skilled pilots (all of whom were Europeans), inadequate supplies, and haphazard maintenance. For more details, see J. E. Peterson, *Defending Arabia* (London: Croom Helm, 1986), pp. 18–20.

30. The optimal outlines of British policy in the Gulf were summarized by the Political Resident, H. V. Biscoe, in 1931: "to maintain the independence of the Arab Shaikhdoms so long as they preserve law and order and maintain a system of administration that will satisfy or at any rate be tolerated by their subjects, to avoid any greater degree of interference in their internal affairs than is forced upon us but at the same time to prevent any other foreign power from dominating them or obtaining any special privileges in the Gulf." India Office Library and Records (London), L/P&S/12/3727, Biscoe to F. V. Wylie, Deputy Secretary (Foreign) to the Government of India, November 24, 1931. It should be noted as well that another British consideration was the protection of British Indian subjects resident in the Gulf. In practice, this required direct involvement only in a few special circumstances.

31. Opposition to the British route was voiced within the Persian Majlis (Parliament), in part because of Soviet influence. Persia insisted on a route through the central part of the country which would have meant additional difficulties from an operational point of view, and a competing German service from Berlin to Tehran via the Soviet Union had begun operations in 1924. Eventually, a South Persian routing operated from 1929 to 1932. Peterson, *Defending Arabia*, pp. 20–22.

32. The intractability of the rulers of Ras al-Khaimah and Dubai meant that the proposed use of flying boats, already employed by the RAF in the region, had to be abandoned as Sharjah could not provide a suitable anchorage.

33. Remarks of G. W. Rendel, Counsellor in the Foreign Office, summarized in Public Record Office (London), Air Ministry Records, AIR/2/1612, Committee of Imperial Defence, Standing Official Sub-Committee for Questions Concerning the Middle East, Minutes of the 42nd Meeting, September 24, 1935.

34. L/P&S/12/3727, T. C. Fowle, Political Resident in the Persian Gulf, to J. C. Walton, India Office, January 18, 1938; copy in Public Record Office, Cabinet Papers, CAB/104/71.

35. The theorist probably most closely identified with the rimland thesis was Nicholas Spykman. In his words, "If there is to be a slogan for the power politics of the Old World, it must be 'Who controls the Rimland rules Eurasia; who rules Eurasia controls the destinies of the world.'" *The Geography of Peace* (New York: Harcourt Brace, 1944), p. 43.

36. It is outside the scope of this essay to discuss or even cite the voluminous literature that has grown up around Gulf security and especially the American role. My *Security in the Arabian Peninsula and Gulf States, 1973–1984* (Washington: National Council on U.S.-Arab Relations, 1985; Occasional Paper No. 7) provides a comprehensive annotated bibliography of this literature, albeit now very dated. An updated and greatly expanded revision is forthcoming.

37. One can postulate that the linear descendant of this shift in perceptions of the region and its importance (i.e., toward regarding it as a zone threatening Western interests because of its internal instability and vulnerability) is the notion of the zone itself constituting an

implacable Islamic "cultural" threat to the West, as expressed by Samuel P. Huntington in *The Clash of Civilizations and Remaking of World Order* (New York: Simon and Schuster, 1996).

38. The Carter Doctrine is quoted in Peterson, *Defending Arabia,* p. 126, while the Lansdowne Declaration is quoted in Busch, *Britain and the Persian Gulf,* p. 256 (citing the Parliamentary Debates), and Lorimer, *Gazetteer,* Vol. I, pp. 367–68 (citing *The Times,* May 6, 1903).

CHAPTER 2

THE GULF'S ETHNIC DIVERSITY
An Evolutionary History

M. R. IZADY

INTRODUCTION

At present, no part of the Middle East is as ethnically diverse as the basin of the Persian Gulf–Gulf of Oman–northwest Arabian Sea (henceforth, the "Gulf"). In the past few decades, an inherent diversity has been augmented by the influx of a vast body of expatriate workers, many having lived there for over two generations. But diversity— old and new—in religion, language, and race has been a hallmark of the Gulf throughout its long history. Much ethnic diversity was imparted to the Gulf population by the introduction of new settlers (primarily artisans, skilled and unskilled laborers, and brides) for millennia via trade and political connections with other oceanic societies around the rim of the Indian Ocean and South China Sea. The genetic imprint of East Africa, Southeast Asia, and the Indian subcontinent was already strongly present in the Gulf population long before the twentieth century. The recent oil boom and the flood of expatriate workers into the region has just increased that diversity, not created it. The most fascinating point is that a vast majority of the newly arrived expatriates into the Gulf area are not from the continental Middle East, but from the same oceanic societies around the Indian Ocean and the South China Sea with which the Gulf shares a common history stretching back into antiquity.

Any ethnographic study necessitates reviewing the history of premodern immigration into the Gulf basin to appreciate the magnitude of diversity that has been otherwise masked by the routine intermarriage occurring in this "melting pot."[1]

Fundamentally a liberal society that has taken commerce as its primary interest for millennia, the Gulf basin has served as a refuge for many exotic or persecuted religious and linguistic groups who have found sanctuary there from a restrictive outside world. The effective geographic isolation of the Gulf basin from the continental Middle East has allowed these "refugee" groups to survive and prosper in the Gulf, while they died out in the rest of the Middle East. The best examples of this sanctuary quality of Gulf society are found in the extensive Ibadi community[2] that dominates Oman; the community of the Sabaeans/Mandians, the last remnant of the

Christians of John the Baptist in the world, now surviving only in the marshlands of southern Iraq and Khuzistan; and the continued practice of African animism, most visible in the prevalent rite of *Zâr*, or "voodoo" by the old African communities on the Iranian coast of the Gulf. The survival of languages as ancient as Aramaic, Kumzari, Bashagirdi, and Qeshmi, or as remote as Malayalam, Somali, Ethiopic, and Bantu among the indigenous Gulf inhabitants, further corroborates the same liberal (or indifferent) attitude toward linguistic, religious or racial distinctions observed in that cultural world. These will be examined below in detail.

A seafaring society in need of widespread contacts and bonds, the Gulf communities for millennia have used migration (into and out of the Gulf) and cultural exchange as foundation blocks for forming commercial and defensive alliances that brought wealth and diversity to the region. The degree of influence the Gulf exercised overseas may seem as disproportionate to its relatively small land and population. One need only compare it with other seafaring mercantile societies such as the Netherlands, Portugal, and England to see what can be and has been achieved with little capital in base population and geographic size when oceans are thrown into the equation.

Despite the importance of hyperdiversity and oceanic culture—unconventional factors by Middle Eastern standards—little effort has been or is being devoted to the multidisciplinary approach that is needed to reconstruct the causes behind the ethnic amalgam of peoples who inhabit the Gulf basin, or the fact that they form a single cultural, economic, and historical unit. This unity applies to the Gulf's history, its oceanic culture, its innate mercantilist past and present, and its astonishingly active colonial history. The people of the Gulf increasingly dominated nearly all shores of the Indian Ocean for millennia, fostering many episodes of migration and the resultant ethnocultural heterogeneity of the Gulf itself and those other lands.

To understand the formation and evolution of the Gulf's unique culture and ethnic diversity, a basic knowledge of several interrelated fields, including geography and a history of the Gulf's seafaring past and present, is therefore necessary. A historic pattern that closely connects the Gulf to South and Southeast Asia and East Africa, but excludes it from the rest of the Middle East, will readily emerge. Such a pattern will then clarify the reason behind the marked dearth of Middle Easterners in the Gulf expatriate community and, instead, the abundance of peoples hailing from the far rim of the Indian Ocean and the China seas.

Such a review should also clarify two interrelated puzzles: how and why Southeast Asia, East Africa, southern India, and an overwhelming majority of island worlds in the Indian Ocean have become Muslim while no Muslim armies ever reached those faraway shores; and why the vast majority of the "guest workers" in the Gulf at present are from the oceanic world of south and southeast Asia. It should also clarify why the largest Islamic state in the world is a lush archipelago in Southeast Asia (Indonesia); and how and why such cultures as the Swahili have come to use the Iranic Zoroastrian calendar and observe the Now Ruz festival of the new year on the vernal equinox.[3] It should also help us better understand "exotic" facts such as the observance of the annual Shi'i festival of Ashura (tenth of Muharram) in seventeenth-century Siam/Thailand where Gulf families dominated the country's administration; or the oddity of a Shi'i state in seventeenth-century Cambodia.

The imprint of the Gulf is found in all of these, but the reverse is likewise true. The peoples of these distant lands came to settle in the Gulf and have imparted their genes and cultures to the local pool.

THE NATURAL SETTING AND SOCIOCULTURAL BOUNDARIES OF THE GULF BASIN

With little difficulty one may argue that the Persian Gulf–Gulf of Oman basin has not been historically a part of the Middle East at all,[4] and that the present connection is tenuous and in fact transitory. The Gulf basin is indeed isolated environmentally from the rest of the Middle East as well. (Map 2.1)[5] Thanks to the decisive natural geographic boundaries, the sociocultural boundaries of the Gulf world can be set with little difficulty. The first rise of the Zagros mountains forms the clear northern boundary. Only at two spots—at Laristan and at Jiruft—do the high Zagros recede from the coast for an appreciable distance, allowing for a good number of agricultural communities to live within the Gulf world. Elsewhere, the mountains hug the coast closely, providing some fresh water but not much flat arable land. To the south, as soon as the last oases peter out into the sands of the Empty Quarter, the Gulf world ends abruptly. In southern Iraq, the marshes—what the Sumerians called "the Sealand"—completes the circuit of the Gulf world boundaries. What went on within this isolated realm only seldom affected the immediate outside or was affected by it (Map 2.2).

NORTHERN GULF

The Gulf is hemmed in on its eastern and northern sides by the high Zagros range that towers up to 17,360 feet at Mount Dena, 15,120 feet at Zardakuh (both at the northern extremities of the Gulf), and 11,420 feet at Hazar (above the Strait of Hormuz),[6] all only between 60 and 80 miles inland from the Gulf coast.[7] Because of the Zagros, contact from the east and north—i.e., from Persia/Iran to the Gulf—has been limited, and often minimal for long stretches of time. Various Iranian governments, from ancient times to the present, have taken from the Gulf what wealth they could extract in episodes of sporadic occupation of the coastal region by force. They have given little in return to the region directly, except for providing some of the final markets for the goods that transit through its waters. As history has shown, the oceanic world of the Gulf could be conquered from the Iranian plateau but not held for long, rendering the endeavor costly and transient.

Such expansion of central Iranian authority into the Gulf has been unusual enough to be heralded with fanfare by any dynasty that has attempted it. The conquest of the port of Cameron and the islands of Qeshm and Hormuz from the Portuguese by the Safavid king, Abbas I, in the early sixteenth century, is celebrated as a major event in Safavid history. Abbas was so impressed he renamed Cameron as Bandar Abbas, "Port Abbas." The similar ephemeral attempt by the Afsharid monarch, Nadir Shah, in the eighteenth century likewise lasted a short time. Meeting with the resistance of the local elite, it ended in failure despite the great expense incurred by the Iranian treasury.[8]

The Gulf basin has never been a natural appendage of the high Iranian plateau. When conquered, it has split away at the slightest sign of weakness of the central Iranian government. Iran and its culture have always been continental, with little or no prowess in seafaring or maritime conquest. The Gulf, on the other hand, is an oceanic culture and adept in defusing attempts for domination from the interior by taking its defenses to the sea. It is a mistake automatically to include the Gulf basin—even the northern half of it—in the domains of any premodern Iranian state. Only on brief occasions is such inclusion warranted. The cultural contacts between the two, although more common, have been of the nature of an external influence, not exchanges among kin.

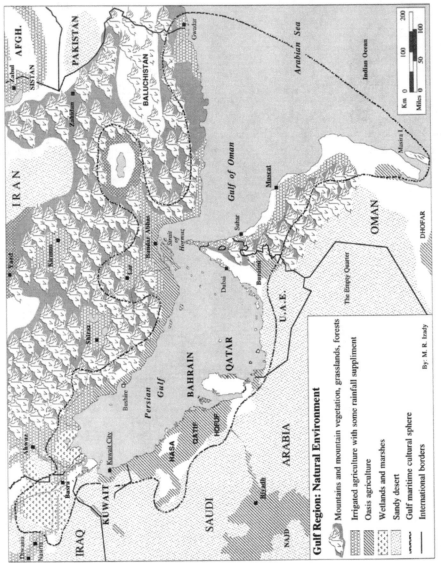

Gulf Region: Natural Environment

- Mountains and mountain vegetation, grasslands, forests
- Irrigated agriculture with some rainfall suppliment
- Oasis agriculture
- Wetlands and marshes
- Sandy desert
- Gulf maritime cultural sphere
- International borders

By: M. R. Izady

Map 2.1

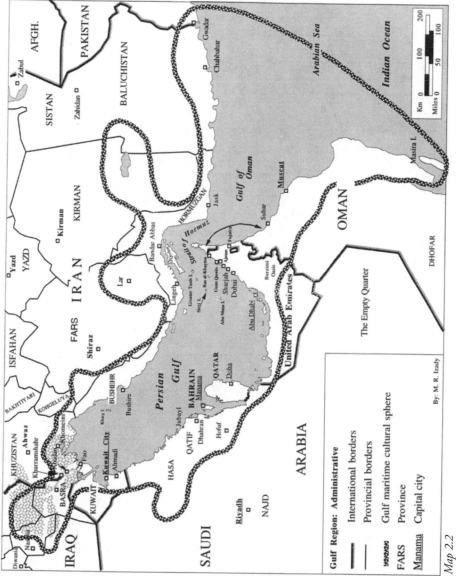

Map 2.2

SOUTHERN GULF

To the south and west of the Gulf basin is located the Rub al-Khali, "The Empty Quarter," and the similarly inhospitable deserts of Najd. The sands of Najd and the Rub have historically proven to be at least as much an insulator of the Gulf basin on the south as the Zagros on the opposite side of the Gulf. The political connection between the Gulf basin and the interior of Arabia has ranged from marginal to negligible. The cultural connection of the Gulf with the Arabian interior has been as tenuous as with the cultures of the Iranian high plateau.

At the head of the Gulf, this isolation is completed by the extensive marshes of southern Iraq, which cut it off from the arid Mesopotamian plain—environmentally and socially. Only the conduit of the Tigris-Euphrates rivers that cuts through the marshes allows for commercial and human contact between the Gulf and Mesopotamia. This contact has been rather intensive at times, such during the later Sumerian and early Abbasid periods. Nevertheless, the Mesopotamian world and the Gulf basin have never merged or come close to a merger.

THE GULF BASIN: ITS HISTORY AND CULTURE

In this splendid relative isolation, the Gulf society created a unique culture around that inland sea, using it as its farm and market, its highway, and its refuge. The sea-oriented Gulf people readily radiated into the vast expanses of the Indian Ocean to secure their livelihood and ambitions. They set up commercial settlements on the oceanic islands and along the coastal stretches of eastern Africa, southern India, southeast Asia, and the island worlds of Indonesia and the Philippines, not to mention southern China. They brought Judaism and Christianity to India by the third century, giving rise to the still-surviving and numerous Nestorian Christian community of the Malabar Coast of southern India.[9] In the ninth century, Zoroastrian settlers from Hormuz and Minab also came to settle in the commercial ports in Gujarat, India. They became the seed from which has grown India's modern Parsee (Zoroastrian) community.[10]

After the seventh century, and the advent of Islam, it is to the efforts of the ocean-faring society of the Gulf that is owed the creation of the most populous Islamic society on earth: Indonesia, which contains roughly as many Muslims today as there are Muslim Arabs. The Gulfis, if we may use the English translation for the local term *khaliji*, brought their culture, their beliefs, their languages, and their lifestyle to create the far-flung Islamic societies around the Indian Ocean and southern China. In return, they brought into the Gulf basin various peoples from these faraway lands, adding more diversity to the religions, languages, and races found there. The locals and the diverse immigrants were all, however, bound together by the elements of lifestyle based on oceanic commerce. Regardless of one's racial or cultural background, adopting the Gulf ethos of oceanfaring mercantilism meant a welcome inclusion in that society. Despite all these other diversities, the Gulf people formed a coherent society for thousands of years. The stories and accounts surrounding the seaborne exploits of the Gulfis is famously reflected in the tales of Sinbad the Sailor.

The commerce-oriented Gulf society continued to enrich itself financially and culturally. But in its long centuries of active promotion of international maritime trade in the Indian Ocean basin, it created much the same economic and cultural riches for nearly all societies with which it came into contact and interacted.

BUSINESS ETHOS OF THE GULFIS

An interesting outcome of this intensive commerce and commercialism was the emergence of a business mentality and hyperactivity similar to the phenomenon known today as "workaholism" and an obsessive drive for the accumulation of wealth just for the sake of itself. Medieval commentaries on this abnormal behavior among the Gulfi merchants is plentiful.

One of the earliest Islamic geographers, Abu'l-Qasim b. Ahmad Jayhâni, reports in A.D. 932 on an acute case that had led to the rare mental disorder of geophobia. He writes:

> There in Siraf, I was told there was a merchant who engaged in trade for forty years in the Indian Ocean and never set foot on dry land. Whenever they approached land, he would send out his lieutenants to accomplish whatever business there might be and bring aboard what was needed. If there appeared to be a problem with the ship, he would move into another, but never stepping onto dry land. In that forty years his wealth amounted to forty million [gold] dinars, and yet, whoever saw him could not tell him apart from his sailors.[11]

Istakhri in A.D. 957 further clarifies the demeanor of the Gulfi merchants when he too visits and reports from the famously affluent port of Siraf[12] in the northern Gulf:

> Sea trade is the source of the great wealth of the inhabitants of Siraf. In there I saw people who each had four million [gold] dinars or more, with some having far more. Despite this, their attire could not be differentiated from that worn by their employees.[13]

Muslih al-Din Sa'di, one of the foremost Persian poets of all times, enhances our knowledge of the hyperactive commercial culture of the medieval Gulf when he records in his *Gulistân* (13th century) an account of his encounter with a workaholic merchant on the island of Kish in the Gulf which by the eleventh century had overshadowed Siraf:[14]

> A rich merchant, who I heard had one-hundred-fifty camel loads of merchandise and forty slave retainers, invited me one evening to his abode on the Isle of Kish. All evening long he did not rest, mumbling instead incoherent words that: "my such and such a shareholder is now in Turkistan, and such and such a business in India. This is the deed for such and such a property; and such and such a deal is contingent on this and that." Sometimes he would say: "I am considering moving to Alexandria where the air is fair;" then would he say: "Nay, the Mediterranean is a turbulent sea!" "Well, Sa'di," he addressed me finally, "I have but one journey left ahead of me. If that is accomplished, I will rest for the remainder of my life in one place." "And which journey would that be?" I asked. "I shall carry Persian sulfur to China," he began, "which I hear musters a great price. Then, Chinese porcelain I will bring to Byzantium; carry Byzantine brocade to India; Indian steel to Aleppo; Aleppan mirrors to Yemen and Yemenite batik to Persia. Thereafter, I shall retire from commerce and settle down in a shop." Truly he spoke so much of this obsession of his that he ran out of words. . . .[15]

The same is echoed at the opposite end of the Indian Ocean when the sixteenth-century Siamese Muslim poet, Hamza Fansuri, admonishes the business-obsessed Gulfi and Southeast Asian merchants in Ayutthaya, Siam:

> Give ears, oh ye traveling merchants;
> cease being obsessed by what is *harâm*.[16]

> Forever you are counting your money;
> > forever stringing it, fearing its loss.
> Back and forth you run like a startled beast;
> > dizzying your beloved with the whirl.
> Give up this running, give up this world;
> > cease being a stranger to your own soul.[17]

This lucrative "obsession" was to continue unhindered among the Gulfis and their merchant allies until the arrival and later the domination of the Indian Ocean by the European fleets.

In many respects and in view of this long and exclusive social, economic, and even psychosocial history, the Gulf people richly deserve the designation of nation. This is despite the pluralism—linguistic, religious and racial—that existed and exists within the Gulf community. The underlying sociocultural and economic bonds between various segments of that society is stronger than what is found among neighboring nations. It is not hard to recognize and honor these bonds that form this nation of the "Gulfis."[18]

THE HISTORICAL PROCESS OF ETHNIC AND CULTURAL DIVERSIFICATION

For the period ending in the tenth century, the Iranic influence is most perceptible in the Gulf culture, whereas the Arab element comes to the fore after the tenth century. The overseas colonies and trading posts the Gulfis established around the Indian Ocean bear this mark. Sinbad is an Iranic name; so is *bandar* ("moorage, port," rendered as *banda* in Sumatra), dhow/dhaw (<*dhawraq*, a lateen-sail vessel), typhoon (<*tufoon*), *nakhoda* (skipper, captain), *shahbandar* ("port master," rendered as *siahbanda* in Malaya and Sumatra), *bar* ("coast," as in Zanzibar, and Malabar), *khwar* ("wetland, bay," rendered as *khawr, hawr,* or *khor* in Arabic), *palawan* (a Muslim "saint") etc.

The Chinese sources often record the presence of the *Possu*, "Persians" in relatively large numbers in various parts of coastal China and Southeast Asia in the seventh and eighth century. The Persian ships were visiting Chinese ports by 671, and their first colony was set up on the island of Hainan (opposite Hong Kong) in the year 747/48.[19] Ten years later, the Possu are reported to have raided Canton itself. In this raid we first hear of the "Ta-Shih," who accompanied the raiding Possu. Ta-Shih is, of course, the Chinese rendition of *Tazi*, the Persian word for an Arab.[20]

This Iranic primacy was mostly due to the demographic boom on the Iranian plateau and the northern side of the Gulf for many centuries prior to the sixth century A.D. Population movement within the Gulf itself was consequently from north to south. People brought, in addition to their genes, their culture (religion, language, habits) to the southern side of the Gulf. Zoroastrianism and many mystery cults prevalent on the plateau found strong footholds in the southern Gulf. The mystery cults such as Mazdakism/Khurramism and the Carmathian movement came to dominate Hasa/Ahsa, Qatif, Hufuf, and the Bahrain archipelago, becoming the foundation on which the modern dominant Shi'ism (standard and anomalous) of that region is built.[21] The same beliefs spread around the Gulf's commercial world in the Indian Ocean, becoming the roots for the surviving religious communal tendencies among the Yemenite highlanders and those in East Africa.

It should be noted at this point that the area of Hasa/Ahsa, Qatif, Hufuf, and the Bahrain archipelago was jointly known as the Bahrân coast in earlier times, which subsequently evolved to the "Bahrain" coast in the official records and literature. In the parlance of the inhabitants, the change to the official name did not occur until a few decades ago, and then only partially.[22] To avoid the inevitable confusing of the old, much larger Bahrân/Bahrain with the modern island state of Bahrain, the ancient term Bahrân is revived and used here in reference to that entire coastal area and its island dependencies (Map 2.3).

As early as A.D. 110, a navigation manual, the *Periplus Maris Erythraei*,[23] provides an account of the brisk trade between the western and northwestern Indian Ocean.[24] Colonies of Arabs, Persians, and other Iranic peoples of the Gulf "founded everywhere on the [East African] coast and islands commercial settlements in pre-Islamic times, centuries before Muhammed."[25] Instrumental in this expansion was the Iranic Barzangi (later, Zangi/Zangana) dynasty,[26] originally from the Shiraz area but dominant in the Laristan-Shabankara region of the northern Gulf coast and the Strait of Hormuz. Having come under military and commercial pressure from the nascent Sasanian dynasty of Persia, the Barzangis directed their resources to strengthening the Gulf's overseas settlements, as well as founding many new ones.

In East Africa, many colonial cities were founded in the Zanzibar archipelago and later, on the mainland, under the tutelage of the Barzangis/Zangis. The port cities of Zanzibar and Manda founded in the archipelago soon were rivaled and surpassed by port cities like Mombassa, Malindi, Brava, Mogadishu, Kismayu, and, of course, the Barzangi colonial capital of Kilwa south of modern Dar-es-Salaam. Kilwa became the nucleus of a Gulf empire in East Africa, better known as the "Kilwa Empire," that stretched from the Horn of Africa to northern Mozambique and included Gulfi settlements on the Comoros and Madagascar.[27]

The entire coast of East Africa came to be called after the dynasty, Barzangi-bar, "the Barzangi coast" evolving to Zagibar for short, whence "Zanzibar."[28] From this also comes the term *zangi* or *zanji/zinji* for a native African black in the Middle Eastern languages. Africa itself even came for a time to be known to the Middle Easterners simply as the Zanj/Zinj.

The establishment and expansion of the independent Kilwa Empire in East Africa was the direct reaction of the Gulfis to the political and military pressure placed on the Gulf basin by the energetic early Sasanians. The first Sasanian emperor, Ardasher I, took an active role in extending his control over the commercial southern sealanes. He subdued and confined the Barzangi domain to the immediate coastal lands between Siraf, Jask, and Musandam peninsula. He then attacked the principality of Bahrân, laying siege to its capital of Hagar (ca. 229 A.D.). The long siege ended when the Bahrâni prince/king, Sanatruk,[29] threw himself from the wall of the fortress.[30] He then moved on the neighboring port of Hatta/Khatt (modern Qatif, Saudi Arabia). Taking it, he rebuilt it closer to the shore and renamed it Pâniyât Ardasher ("Founded by Ardasher").[31] In the reign of his successor, Shapor I, Sasanians moved on Mazon (the southern shores of the Strait of Hormuz and vicinity) where they annexed both Suhar and Muscat.

This put an end to the Gulf's independence for a few decades, but this was regained after the death of Shapor I in A.D. 272 and held on to for the next three centuries.[32] The respite from Sasanian pressure came to an end in the mid-sixth century, when the resurgent Sasanians reconquered the Gulf and even wrested the Yemen from the Ethiopians (ca. A.D. 573).[33] This effectively cut off the Gulfis in East Africa for a few decades from their Middle Eastern routes and trade.

In the threatening shadow of the Sasanians in Persia, a new Gulf elite appeared to replace the Barzangis who had fully acclimated to East Africa. This new elite, by acknowledging Sasanian suzerainty, went on to fill the gap in the sea trade left by their Barzangi kinsmen whose relationship with the Sasanians remained hostile. They quickly

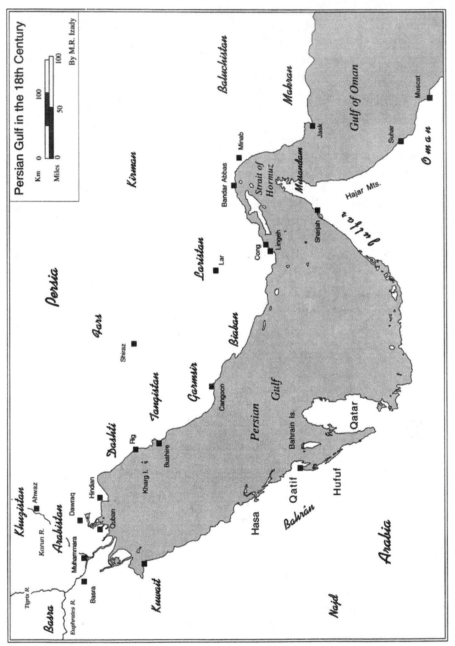

Map 2.3

evolved to become the rivals of the Barzangis, now that they both were vying for the same markets. They were exceptionally successful in their rivalry.

By the middle of the fourth century A.D., the new Gulf elite was challenging the Barzangis even over the control of the sealanes in the western half of the Indian Ocean.[34] This process left to the Barzangis only the west African coast and its immediate sea lanes.[35] The Gulf commercial world had spilt, with Barzangis dominating East Africa while the new Gulf elite under nominal Sasanian suzerainty fanned out into the rest of the Indian Ocean.[36] By the middle of the sixth century A.D., even western Indian Ocean commerce had decisively passed under the dominance of this new Gulf elite.[37] With the help of the Sasanian infantry, the Gulfis invaded and occupied the Yemen, ending the commercial rivalry of the Ethiopians and the Barzangis who were egged on by the Byzantines hoping to get a foothold in the Indian Ocean trade via the Red Sea. The port of Ma'alla (Aden) had been taken by 578 and the Gulfi corsairs stood guard at the Strait of Bab al-Mandab.[38]

In conjunction with trade, the new Gulf elite became instrumental not only in the further spread of Zoroastrianism, but also Nestorianism into the Indian Ocean basin. Nestorianism was a particularly Persian form of Christianity free of Byzantine control or influence.[39] The list of attendants of the synod of 410 includes one with the unlikely title "Metropolitan of the Islands, Seas and Interior of Dabag, Chin and Machin" (Indonesia, China, and Southeast Asia).[40] The seat of this Nestorian Christian expansion was the port of Rev Ardasher/Reshahr (pre-Islamic Bushehr/Bushehr <Beh Ardasher) in the northern Gulf.[41] The port city of Khatt (modern Qatif) served as the seat of the Orthodox bishop.[42]

Despite continual loss of maritime commercial ground, these mixed old Iranic Barzangi colonies from the Gulf continued their existence in East Africa until the early Islamic era. Between the eighth and ninth centuries, new commercial ports at Mogadishu, Brava, and Manda had been added to the other local port cities by the Gulfis. The brisk international commerce continued to enhance the prosperity and cultural and technological development of all parties involved. Further south, however, the Kilwa fortunes were under attack from the interior of Africa. The massive movement of the Bantu tribes from West Africa toward the Indian Ocean coast was reaching its apex at this time. The wealth of the port cities was attractive enough to the incoming Bantu chiefs to carry out incessant attacks on them.[43] The shortage of funds due to their dwindling access to commercial seaways had steadily undercut the Barzangis' ability to strengthen their fortifications and hire mercenaries for defense. This finally ended their ability to survive in the African milieu. While the ports to the north did manage to withstand the pressure, those farther south were eventually overwhelmed and destroyed.[44]

The Bantu adversity, however, was short-lived. Within two hundred years from its start in the ninth century, the violent tide had subsided. East African commerce was quickly restored to its "pre-Bantu" days, with new waves of Gulfi mercantile operations expanding south once again, to Mozambique. The difference was that during the time when Gulfis were experiencing their difficulties with the Bantu attackers, the Yemenite merchants had expanded their dominance over the Benadir ports and settlements. An Arabic broken plural of the Persian word, *bandar,* "moorage," "port," Benadir describes the modern Somali coast, from Kismayu to Mogadishu). They did not retreat when the Gulfis returned to take up the business they had left in East Africa earlier.

The role of the Yemenites in including the Hadhramis in the Gulf mercantile world was integral. The geographic proximity of the south Arabian coast to the Gulf had involved its peoples in the commercial oceanic activities of the Gulfis very early in time. The overwhelming demographic, technological, and economic superiority of the Gulf, however, routinely reduced the merchant mariners of the Yemen and other coastal communities of the Gulf of Aden–Red Sea to a subsidiary status. In this relationship, they were similar to other Gulf client communities and states around the Indian Ocean rim. Only when the Gulf's fortunes waned could these states and communities strive for a more prominent and lucrative position in the region. At any other time, their settlers, merchants, and mercenaries worked through the Gulfi channels for mutual benefit.[45]

At this juncture in time the Arabian element itself was on a steady increase in the Gulf at the expense of the Iranic peoples such as the Persians. This was fueled by positive climatic changes leading to agricultural/herding prosperity, and thus demographic gains. These trends culminated in the advent and explosive expansion of Islam, the "Arabian religion." Therefore, not just in their far-flung colonies but in the Gulf itself, the ethnic and cultural setting was going through a steady change. The Iranic dominance of the Gulf activities in the Indian Ocean soon began to wane after the advent of Islam, being gradually diluted by an increasing Arab element in the composition of the Gulfi elite per se. The process was, however, long, and the Arab element did not outweigh the Iranic until the sixteenth century.

THE SECOND WAVE OF GULFI SETTLEMENT IN EAST AFRICA

Less than two centuries after the demise of the Barzangis in East Africa, a new wave of Gulfis arrived to retrieve the markets there beginning in the late tenth century. This time, it was a joint endeavor by a Gulf elite that traced their background to the Persians and the Shabankara Kurds of the Shiraz region in southern Iran. East African traditions and chronicles, numismatic and architectural evidence, statements of the European traveler Joao De Barros, and the reports of Muslim travelers and geographers imply that after the Barzangis, another "Shirazi" dynasty moved to East Africa, established the Zanj Empire and ruled there for more than 500 years, from 980 to 1513.[46] The founder, Ali ibn Hasan, ruled over the whole coast from Lamu in the north to Sofala in the south, if not farther.[47] Thus the modern elite and many citizens of the Zanzibar archipelago, those of the Swahil,[48] and even to some extent in the Benadir coastal regions of East Africa call themselves "Afro-Shirazi," including the main political party in Zanzibar today. This has been also to distinguish them from the Omani-Baluch elite who arrived after the mid-seventeenth century and who were viewed as being lower in trade knowledge and bloodline. To this was artificially attached, in a very un-Gulfi way, a religious coloring.

The Shirazis arrived in large numbers and added heavily to the settlements at Pemba, Zanzibar, Lamu, Pate, Mafia, and the Comoro (Qamara) Islands (Map 2.4). East African ports like Mombassa, Lindi, Lamu, and particularly the new Kilwa now gained the stature of major Indian Ocean ports and commercial emporia. The new Shirazi dynasty rebuilt Kilwa Kisiwani ("Kilwa on the Island") in royal grandeur, and proceeded immediately to snatch the lucrative African gold business from the then-Yemenite-dominated port of Mogadishu. From the thirteenth to the fifteenth century, Kilwa became the sole gold capital of East Africa, controlling nearly all the gold produced in the interior of Africa in the Zambezi-Limpopo basin, brought to the port of Sofala for transportation. Metals (including gold and copper), ivory, tusks,[49] and mangrove poles became the standard issue of Africa in the lucrative international commerce. Cotton fabrics, steel blades, china, and glassware were imported in return.

The wealth of the Shirazi Kilwa was fabled in its own time. The great Kilwan palace of Husuni Kubwa (thirteenth-fourteenth century), of which the impressive ruins survive today, has more than 130 apartments and was for long the largest building in the entire sub-Saharan Africa. The expansion of the Jami Mosque in the capital as well as another palace, the Husuni Ndogo, all were financed at this time with the great profits from Kilwa's monopoly on the gold trade. The architecture of these buildings is strongly Gulfi, resembling the great buildings in Siraf, Basra, and Kish, with raised and painted calligraphic inscriptions for decoration. The amount of Chinese Sung and Ming dynasties porcelain found in the ruins speaks further of the wealth of the city and its close interconnection with the commerce of the oceanic world.

Gulf commercial activities worked their way into the interior of Africa via the major river networks such as Zambezi and Limpopo, bringing out slaves and indentured workers from the Bantu interior. Many of these took up residence in the Gulf itself. Local African chiefs-turned-kings benefited and prospered from the income, know-how and culture that was brought by the Gulfis. The Shona kingdom in the Mozambique is an example of what evolved out of this exchange.

The Gulf merchant marine, although most prominent in the Indian Ocean basin, did find it necessary to cooperate—after the usual initial confrontations caused by the conflict of interests—with the client states and/or allies and the commercial activities of the other cultures around the basin. These local interests were gradually and organically incorporated into the Gulfi network by liberal intermarriage between the Gulf merchant families and the local elite, followed by task allocation to the involved group. The resulting genetic diversity overseas sooner or later reflected itself back in the Gulf as well. By the fourteenth century, in fact, a new society and "ethnic" group had emerged on the East African coast and the islands, made up of dozens of independent port-states and sultanates, which were genetically a hybrid of African, Aryan, Semitic, and Austranesian elements, who were Muslims in faith and spoke a hybrid language made of a Bantu substructure, with an Arabic, Persian, and Malay vocabulary and superstructure. This they aptly named Ki-Swahili ("that of the coasts").

During the fifteenth century and the eve of the arrival of the Europeans, various Shirazi dynasties were ruling from Mombassa, Malindi, Zanzibar, Pemba, and, of course, Kilwa. Many other lesser places along the coast also had Shirazi rulers. Only the important port of Pate had a non-Shirazi ruler in the Nabahani family from Oman, who exerted strong influence in the neighboring port of Pemba too.

CONTACTS WITH SOUTH AND SOUTHEAST ASIA

Many Africans colonists were brought by the Gulfis into South and Southeast Asia via the established sea routes, where they came to populate many islands and add to the ethnic and racial diversity. The inhabitants of the Andamans[50] and the Nicobars, off the coast of Burma, Aeta in the Philippines, Semang in Malaysia, and the Negroid elements of New Guinea and Melanesia can trace at least some of their genetic ancestry to these resettlements. The resulting Negrito population has given a distinct character to the islands.[51] Centuries earlier, the Southeast Asians had been brought in the opposite direction under the auspices of the Gulfis and their allied merchants to provide the labor and populate the island worlds off the east and southeast coast of Africa, such as Madagascar and the Comoros. The district of Dhofar in Oman and the neighboring southern Yemen also received a substantial Austranesian (Indonesian, Malay, Melanesian) population at this time, which still forms an important genetic component of the local population.[52] The Austranesian demographic component in the entire southern seaboard of the Arabian Peninsula, from R'as al-Hadd southeast of Muscat to Aden and the island

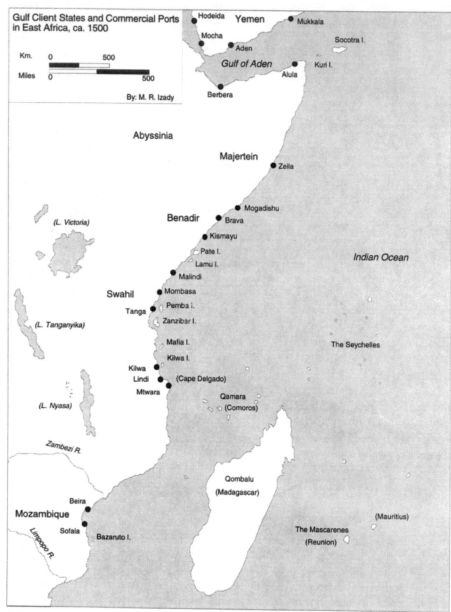

Gulf Client States and Commercial Ports
in East Africa, ca. 1500

Km.   0 ————— 500
Miles 0 ————— 500

By: M. R. Izady

Hodeida
Yemen
Mukkala
Mocha
Aden
Socotra I.
Gulf of Aden
Kuri I.
Alula
Berbera

Abyssinia

Majertein
Zeila

(L. Victoria)
Benadir
Mogadishu
Brava
Kismayu
Pate I.
Lamu I.
Malindi
Swahil
Mombasa
Tanga
Pemba i.
Zanzibar I.

Indian Ocean

(L. Tanganyika)

Mafia I.
Kilwa I.
Kilwa
Lindi
(Cape Delgado)
Mtwara

The Seychelles

(L. Nyasa)

Qamara
(Comoros)

Zambezi R.

Qombalu
(Madagascar)

Beira
Mozambique
(Mauritius)
Sofala
Bazaruto I.
The Mascarenes
(Reunion)

Limpopo R.

Map 2.4

of Socotra is hard to miss even today. At some point, the Austranesian settlements may have stretched to the Musandam peninsula and the environs of the Strait of Hormuz.[53]

The Africans brought by the Gulfis to settle in the Middle East per se gave rise to a large community at the head of the Gulf, where they ultimately set up a state of their own in southern Mesopotamia. This "Zanj/Zinj" state emerged from the Zangi/East African mercenaries brought into the region by the Gulfis to cater to the security needs of the caliphate in Baghdad. Like the other ethnic mercenaries in the hire of the caliphate (the Khurasanis, the Turks, the Daylamites), the Zanj seized the opportunity to grab power on their own. The contribution of the Zanj to the ethnography of the upper end of the Gulf has been obvious in the strong African features found presently among the inhabitants of the marshes, from Nasiria on the Euphrates to Fallahiyya/Shadgan on the Jarahi/Marun.

Settlers were also brought from peninsular India for settlement in the region. The Sasanian sources mention the arrival of Indian communities of sugar cane farmers into lower Khuzistan and Obole/Basra region to establish what became the first commercial cane sugar production area, not only in the Gulf but the entire Middle East. The important district and port of Hindian/Hindijan in southeastern Khuzistan still retains the memory of this early settlement of the region by Indians brought in via Gulfi enterprise and vessels.

It is not clear if these Indians are the same as those who later staged an episode of rebellion against the Baghdad caliphate and who are known as the Zutt. These Indian sugar cane farmers brought into the Gulf had come from the lower Indus/Sindh river region and were recognized as Sindhi in their ethnic identity by the earliest Islamic authors.[54] In more recent times they have come to be known as the Jati.[55] Presently in the Gulf, the Zutt are found only in Oman, where they form a gypsy folk grouping and continue to call themselves the Zutt.[56]

The commerce with India, the Malay archipelago, the Philippines, and south China was expanded, and new colonies were established. Although there are records of Chinese junks trading with East Africa in the seventh century, it was the Gulfis who dominated the cross-oceanic commerce between East and Southeast Asia and the Middle East–East Africa. The strong early presence of the Gulfis in southern China was followed as usual by the intermarriage and Islamization of many Chinese elite in southwest China proper (in the Pearl River basin) as early as the late tenth century (Map 2.5).[57]

The southeast Asiatic expansion by the Gulfis entailed direct competition with the local commercial classes that included Indians, Malayo-Indonesians, and the Chinese. Knowledge of how the Gulfis succeeded in gaining supremacy in that populous and technologically sophisticated region is scanty. But by the advent of Islam and the demise of the Sasanians, the Gulf commercial empire ruled supreme in the markets of south and southeast Asia and had established strong positions on the Chinese mainland. By 1010, Muslims formed a substantial population of Canton (Guangzhu) on the Pearl and soon after, at Zaitoon (Xianmen) on the Taiwan Strait. The presence of the Gulfis in some numbers in China, however, was not limited to the coasts. As early as the seventh and eighth centuries, the Gulfis had ventured into the waterways of China, forming settlements at major Chinese river ports.[58] Tien Sien King, who plundered Hang Chou on the Fuchung River (at the mouth of the Grand Canal) in 760, reputedly slaughtered "thousands" of Possu and Ta-Shih (Persian and Arab) settlers.[59] For economic reasons, all foreigners were expelled from China in 878 but returned soon, starting with the Gulfis themselves.

The port of Champa/Phonrang on the southern Vietnamese coast similarly contained a large Muslim presence as early as 1030. Piggybacking on the successes of the Gulfi merchants, Islam then spread into the island worlds of Southeast Asia. Pasai on

Sumatra become the earliest major Muslim port city in the Malayo-Indonesian archipelago by 1290, followed by Trengganau on the lower Malayan peninsula by 1300.

These came to form the first major spice and commodity trade monopoly in the ninth century via their allied Indian traders operating from Java. By the twelfth century the Gulfis had penetrated all the island worlds of Southeast Asia. Scores of Muslim dynasties incorporating local and Gulfi bloodlines and the Islamic religion had spread from the Philippines (Mindanao and Luzon) to Brunei, Aceh, Java and the Malay Peninsula. By the fifteenth century, the Gulfis and their allied dynasties had near total economic control of the Southeast Asia and Indian Ocean trade.[60] Their regional headquarters were located at Melaka/Malacca, which became the terminus for the trade in the Malayo-Indonesian archipelago, and at Bandar Seri Begawan in Brunei (on Borneo Island) that served as the *entrepôt* of the South China Sea trade. Both had been established as cities circa 1450 under the aegis of the Gulfis and their local allies. In the Philippines, Gulfis had proffered Islam as the religion of the elite, and soon it was embraced by the populace in the Sulu Archipelago, Palawan, Mindanao, and western Luzon.[61] Manila had become an important Muslim port by 1550.

This dominance was to last for about 1,000 years until A.D. 1500. The numbers involved in population exchange between the Gulf and South and Southeast Asia have been important. The geographical nomenclature with Iranic and Semitic roots that peppers southeast Asia—not to mention the family names of the Muslim populations there—is the telltale sign of the Gulf's once dominant position in the area.[62]

After the fall of the Shirazi dynasty—the last to arrive in Africa with an Iranic ethnicity—to the Portuguese in 1513, the Arabs, particularly those from Oman and Hadhramawt, came to dominate Gulf commerce with East Africa, albeit under the later clientship or suzerainty of various European colonial powers. The Portuguese, Germans, and the British successively ruled and divided the area into various colonial domains beginning in the seventeenth century. The dominance by Middle Easterners of the area nevertheless continued under European colonial regimes, albeit in an ever-shrinking form.

As expected, the East African Muslims were Shafi'ite Sunnis (as the pre-sixteenth-century Persians and the Sunni minority in Yemen), and remain so to this day. When in the course of the eighteenth century the Omani sultan arrived to dominate the East African coast, the old elite were often resistant to intermarry and mingle freely with the Omanis who were (and remain) Ibadis. The Baluchi troops of the Sultan of Oman gained the upper hand in the Swahil (late eighteenth century) and Benadir (1828) regions. They too were shunned by the local elite for intermarriage, as they found them not only poor in the knowledge of trade but also Hanafite Sunnis in their faith.

The Gulfis continued introducing new ethnic settlers into East Africa during the Omani phase of its domination. Baluch and Afghans (Pashto) mercenaries, Kurdish Naqshbandi mystic preachers,[63] Indian Bohra merchants, and Malayo-Indonesian "wives" continued to stream into East Africa aboard Gulfi ships or those of their associates. The Africans meanwhile streamed out into the Gulf and other ports around the Indian Ocean. The process continued until the anti-white revolution of 1964 violently removed the last vestiges of nonnative, Iranic-Arabian domination from their first, and ironically last, bastion: Zanzibar. This revolution resulted in the violent disempowerment and expulsion of most of the Arabian, Iranic, and Indic elements from the Zanzibar archipelago.[64] (Map 2.4)

ARRIVAL OF THE EUROPEANS

The first Europeans to arrive on the shores of the Gulf as conquerors since ancient times were the Portuguese. In 1487–88, Bartolomeu Dias rounded the Cape of Good Hope

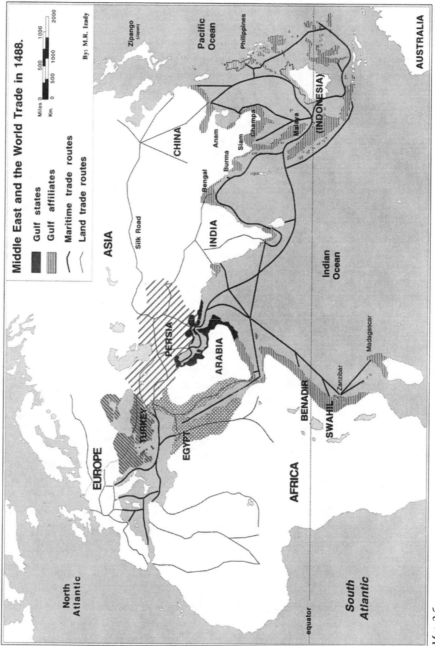

Map 2.5

for the Portuguese crown. This prompted Spain urgently to seek an alternative route to the markets of the East that culminated in the dispatch of Columbus in 1492 to find a westward route.

Although much has been made of the Ottoman "blockage" of international commercial movement between East and West that supposedly prompted the exploration for a direct sea route into the Indian Ocean basin by the European commercial empires, in reality no such thing existed when the Cape was rounded. When Dias circumnavigated the Cape, the Ottoman domains were limited to western Anatolia and the Balkans. Eastern Mediterranean seaports, from Egypt to Syria and to Tarsus in Cilicia, were under rule of the Egyptian Mamluks who depended on transit revenues and technological know-how. The Mamluks maintained close contact with the Gulf elite and shared their strategic interest in keeping the European merchant marines out of the commercial sea lanes of the Indian Ocean. When Europeans arrived in the Indian Ocean, they intended to maximize their trade profits by cutting out the Gulfis and their allied "middlemen."

Ten years after Dias's expedition, the Portuguese fleet under Vasco da Gama circumnavigated Africa and arrived in the Indian Ocean. Benefiting from his Iberian and North African Muslim pilots, da Gama was intent on presenting his exploratory force as friendly to the Muslim sea powers in the region. Da Gama rounded the Cape of Good Hope on November 22, 1497. He stopped in various well-established commercial Muslim ports in Mozambique. Presenting himself and his force as Muslims from Andalusia, he received fresh pilots from the sultan of Mozambique who guided them northward to Mombassa and Malinidi. From there, da Gama received his first Gulfi pilot, Ibn Majid. Foolishly believing in his ruse, Ibn Majid led da Gama's force eastward to India on the well-established Gulfi fast searoute. They arrived in Calicut after only 23 days, on May 20, 1498, and were welcomed by the local sultan, Zamorin, who also took them to be Muslims. Having been finally discovered through their own blunder,[65] the Portuguese failed to obtain a trade treaty, were speedily dismissed, and had to face hostility from the sepoys and lascars of local Gulf merchants. Abandoned by their Gulfi pilot, da Gama and his crew took three months to cross the ocean back to Africa. He lost one of his three remaining ships and nearly half of his crew.[66]

Only six months after da Gama's return to Lisbon in September 1499, another fleet under Pedro Alvares Cabral set out to repeat his voyage.[67] After rounding the Cape of Good Hope, Cabral prospected Madagascar and Mozambique and eventually arrived in 1500 in India where he established a trading factory at Cochin on the Malabar coast. The hostility toward these outsiders by the merchants led to a riot in which many of Cabral's men were massacred. Fearing a decisive failure in those formative years of his commercial adventure, King Manuel of Portugal had da Gama return to the Indian Ocean in 1502, heading an expeditionary force of 20 ships. On the East African as well as on the Indian side of the ocean, the Portuguese naval power met with decisive success. It sunk vast numbers of Gulfi and local ships, and struck alliances with disgruntled groups all around the ocean. This second mission was an astounding success, and the year 1502 marks the beginning of a speedy end to the commercial dominance of the Indian Ocean by the Gulfis and their allies, and the opening of its fabulously lucrative trade to the Europeans.

The defeat of the Gulfis and their fleet in the Indian Ocean by the Europeans was due solely to their inferiority in firepower, and even this not by much. The Gulfi ships were in fact superior in design and flexibility to those of Portugal or Spain, despite the fact that those two European fleets had modeled their ships on Gulf dhows.[68] It was the shorter range of artillery aboard the native vessels in the Indian Ocean—only by some tens of yards—that gave the upper hand to the European invaders. As early as the thirteenth century, seaborne artillery played an important role in Indian Ocean warfare, which pioneered the use of heavy artillery and many other forms of firearms. In nearly every important port taken by the Portuguese they found vast numbers of locally produced artillery and other firearms, some weighing over seven tons.[69]

Despite the wide availability and large caliber, not many of the native cannons had the range and maneuverability of the European pieces, and thus failed their defensive role. The sheer weight of the larger pieces made them practically stationary on land and very difficult to maneuver at sea.[70] The Gulfis soon brought Ottoman artillery experts as far east as Aceh, Banten, and Brunei to cast more nimble and powerful artillery. Their success was immediate but not long lasting.

By the 1550s, in response to the increasingly lethal Portuguese show of force through their ever-larger and heavier-armed warships, there was a shift toward large fleets of enormous galleys in the Gulf and eastern Indian Ocean, capable of carrying great numbers of artillery pieces. By 1600 not only Aceh but also Banten, Johor, Pahang, and Brunei could put a hundred or more armed galleys into battle. The same was true of other Gulfi-allied states in South India and beyond. The famed Acehnese galley, the "Terror of the Universe"—apparently the largest wooden ship of all time—carried over 100 heavy artillery on its 110–yard-long hull, which it used with devastating effect in 1629 on the Portuguese holed up in Malacca. This trend, Pierre Manguin has convincingly argued, contributed to the decline of the great trading junks and dhows that had previously ruled the seas.[71]

These new vessels did in fact succeed in checking and in many instances reversing previous Portuguese advances, but they proved ineffectual when faced with the Dutch and British heavy warships that arrived in the area in the early 1600s. The damage caused to the merchant shipping and commercial ship construction by this militarily induced shift in design and appropriation of materiel, however, wreaked havoc with the long-distance ocean commerce of the Gulfis and the allied states.[72]

Francisco de Almeida, the first Portuguese viceroy for its new possessions in the Indian Ocean basin, arrived in the area in 1505. On the way, Almeida captured the old Barzangi imperial capital of Kilwa, followed by the major gold-exporting port of Sofala in southern Swahil (modern Mozambique). Failing to capture Mombassa in the Benadir, his forces destroyed it and moved on to establish his headquarters at Diu on the strategic tip of Kathiawar peninsula in Gujarat, India. A force sent out under the command of Afonso de Albuquerque and Tristao da Cunha in 1506 continued north along the coast of East Africa, taking what it could and destroying what could not.

If the Portuguese were to dominate the commerce of the Indian Ocean, it was obvious that the Gulf itself had to be subdued. Albuquerque took the island of Socotra at the entrance of the Gulf of Aden in 1506, and then headed north to the Gulf of Oman and the Persian Gulf. He overwhelmed the defenses of the island of Hormuz and captured it in 1507 after the emir of Hormuz retreated to Minab on the mainland.[73] Muscat fell in the following months. Both these gains, however, were temporary, and these major ports had to be reconquered by the Portuguese. The war now became bloody, as it became a matter of life or death for the old commercial elite of the Gulf and their allies and dependencies, from Sofala, Mozambique, to Cebu, Philippines. In 1508 Almeida's son was defeated and killed by the sheer number of an expeditionary force made up of the best elements of the Gulf fleet and included naval elements sent from every commercial outpost of the Gulf in the entire Indian Ocean basin. Even a Mamluk navy from Egypt had joined the grand alliance, lured by the Gulfi money and a promise of admission into their oceanic commerce. But the Portuguese superiority in artillery still proved to be the decisive factor when the grand fleet was met by Almeida off

Diu in 1508. It was wiped out.[74] This was exactly ten short years after the passage around Africa into the Indian Ocean by Vasco da Gama in 1498.

The defeat of 1508 was so complete that Afonso de Albuquerque, the viceroy who replaced Almeida in the same year,[75] sought and achieved the more ambitious policy of complete control of all Indian Ocean traffic. This was done by a massive naval expedition that resulted in the second and more lasting capture of Hormuz and Muscat, as well as the port of Cameron (Gambrun/Jarun, modern Bandar Abbas) on the mainland, along with nearly all islands located in the Strait of Hormuz in 1512. The Gulf had been militarily neutralized. As the new viceroy, Albuquerque captured Goa in 1510, making it the new capital of the Portuguese commercial empire in the Indian Ocean. He then went after every Gulf outpost in the Indian Ocean and beyond.[76]

It was not, however, just the Portuguese threat to the Gulf's commercial world in the Indian Ocean that the Gulfis had to worry about. In the Gulf itself, the rise of Safavid power and its designs on the region was an equally threatening factor to the welfare of the native commercial elite. The first Safavid king, Isma'il, had dispatched ambassadors to Albuquerque at Goa for a possible military and commercial alliance only months after his defeat at Chaldiran by the Ottomans. To the Safavids, the Portuguese were the only natural allies against the Ottomans that could be found in the area. But their prestige took an immediate dive when in 1515, the emir of Hormuz managed to expel the Portuguese. Albuquerque's envoys met with Isma'il's representatives at Minab, signing a treaty by which Portugal, in return for Persian neutrality vis-à-vis the Portuguese interests in the Gulf, would help Persia in its pacification of Baluchistan and the imminent Safavid land expedition against Bahrân.[77] Some promises were also made to help the beleaguered Safavid king against the Ottomans.

Upon neutralizing the Persians, Albuquerque retook Hormuz in late 1515. He then organized a girdling chain of coastal forts around the Indian Ocean of which the linchpins were Hormuz, Goa, and Malacca.[78] Only a few outposts remained of what until a decade earlier amounted to a Gulfi oceanic empire.[79] By 1520, all the outposts of the Gulf commercial world had been overrun by the Portuguese, some of them with the help of Gulfi pilots themselves. In fact, the Gulfis' homeland was in the process of being nearly fully taken over by the Portuguese as well.

Finding the Safavid king enmeshed with domestic problems and threatened by the Ottomans, the Portuguese took practically all the islands and ports in the Persian Gulf and the Gulf of Oman and much territory in between, including Bahrân, Cameron, Cong-Lingeh,[80] and Jask. The Safavid monarch's reaction to this was nil, as his sovereign pretensions to the Gulf were no less tenuous than those of the Portuguese.

A general uprising of the Gulfis against the heavy-handed domination of the Portuguese had begun in earnest in 1520, lasting until 1522, and spread to many former Gulf outposts around the Indian Ocean as well.[81] The bloodiness and persistence of the uprising convinced the Portuguese that they would not be able to conduct commerce in peace if they persisted in excluding the Gulfis from their commercial interests in the East. After four years of sea and land combat, the Portuguese ultimately reached a modus operandi, allowing the Gulf merchant fleet to resume operation in the Indian ocean trade under Portuguese supervision, and later in equal cooperation.[82]

Both Gulfis and the Portuguese being ocean-trading people, gradually a strong bond of mutual interest developed between the waning power of Portugal and the reviving power of the Gulf elite following the general uprising of 1520–22. By the start of the seventeenth century, the two had become strongly intertwined in the basin of the Indian Ocean. The arrival of other European sea powers in the Indian Ocean pushed the Gulfis and the Portuguese even closer to one another. With the blessing of the Portuguese, the Gulfis fanned out again throughout their former trading posts. Returning to Southeast Asia, the Gulfis and their local Muslim allies gained control of nearly all of Java by 1528. The strategic port of Sunda Kelapa on Java was seized from its Hindu-Buddhist princes by the Gulfi-supported sultan of Bantam, and was aptly renamed *Jakarta,* "victory." The building block for the final Islamization of Malaya and the Malayo-Indonesian archipelago was thus laid.[83]

Far from opposing this Islamization process, the Portuguese limited their Christian missionary activities to Flores, Timor, and other small far eastern islands in the archipelago outside the Gulfis' sphere of interests. The prosperity resulting from the entente lasted for nearly 100 years until it came unraveled by the defeat of the Portuguese, whose power in the East came to be quickly replaced by the other European states who rushed into the lucrative markets of the Indian Ocean trade.

OTHER EUROPEAN POWERS

The first attempts were made early in the sixteenth century and came from a fully unexpected direction: a Spanish fleet arriving via the Pacific by rounding South America. It did so under the command of a Portuguese captain, Ferdinand Magellan, who landed in the bustling commercial outpost of Cebu in the Philippines in April of 1521. A few months later, the Spaniards had arrived in the Moluccas and clearly inside the commercial sphere of the Gulfis and the Portuguese. The Spaniards, busy with their colonization of the Americas, limited their ambitions to the Philippine archipelago alone, the conquest of which they had achieved piecemeal by 1571, when the major Muslim port of Manila fell to their hands. The Muslims were given the choice to convert or move. The Muslim presence in the largest Philippine island of Luzon had reached its apogee.

The Spaniards did not, on the other hand, trouble or bother the Muslim southern and western islands in the archipelago (such as the Mindanao, Sulu, and Palawan archipelagos) that fell more strongly within the sphere of Gulfi-Portuguese naval protection.[84]

The Dutch and the British broke into the Indian Ocean trade after the start of the seventeenth century. Direct access into the Indian Ocean had been secured by the British only in 1591 and by the Dutch in 1595. In the next half century, the British had replaced the Portuguese in India, while the Dutch had done the same in Southeast Asia.

The British East India Company (chartered 1600) and the Dutch East India Company (chartered 1602) were to penetrate the virtual Iberian monopoly of the European sea trade with the East. The Dutch were the more successful ones. By concentrating on specific and rather limited objectives, the Dutch achieved much more than their relatively limited resources should have permitted. Thus, contrary to their Portuguese counterparts, they did not start their adventure with the aim of dominating the entire Indian Ocean or attacking the Gulf and the militarily stronger western Indian Ocean. Instead, they directly broke into a single trade, namely that of spices, and for that, they went for the primary producer of the spices, namely the Malayo-Indonesian archipelago.[85]

The arrival of the Dutch and the British coincided with the revival of the might of Safavid Persia. The new king, 'Abbas the Great, had already vanquished his Central Asian enemies and his armies were heading for an equally crushing victory against the Ottomans. His country's traditional overland trading routes with the West having been blocked by the Ottomans, he needed a commercial outlet through the Gulf and, of course, could use the still ample wealth of the Gulf for his endless military operations.

In 1600, the Safavids had already subdued the Shabankara Kurdish emirs of Laristan and Cong-Lingeh. In 1601, their general, Allahvirdi, carried out an expedition against

Bahrain on the far side of the Gulf.[86] The Shabankaras were the strongest remaining native military forces in the Gulf and traced their ancestry to the old Barzangi royal house noted above.[87] Like most other Gulf entities, the Shabankaras had been enjoying a lucrative and mutually satisfactory relationship with the Portuguese for nearly four generations, and did not see the Safavids as "liberators" of the fellow Muslim Gulfis but for what they really were: continental plunderers who were there to take and not to give to the Gulfis. Then came the turn for the emirate of Hormuz.

Allahvirdi's two-pronged land attack on the port of Cameron on the one hand, and Hasa and Bahrain on the other, succeeded in gaining the latter for the Safavids.[88] Bahrain and the Bahrân region had been under a joint Gulfi-Portuguese control for nearly a century. Two years later in 1602, the envoys of King Philip II of Spain[89] arrived at the court of the Safavid Shah Abbas, asking for relief for Cameron and restoration of Bahrân to the Gulfi-Portuguese functionaries as a sign of friendship between the two empires.

Allahvirdi had constructed a fort near Cameron, calling it after his sovereign, Fort Abbasi, from which he kept up pressure on the Portuguese at Cameron and Cong. The siege of Cameron was lifted. Meanwhile, Bahrân managed to expel the Safavids and regain its independence. In a short time, she was to throw her lot with the emirs of Hormuz who were to become strong allies of Portugal in reaction to the Safavid's destruction of the ancient Shabankara emirs of Laristan and Cong.

The full attention of the Safavid monarch was now directed toward his protracted wars with the Ottomans, which were not to end until his final victory in 1619. Being an astute strategist, however, Shah Abbas never let the pressure on the Gulf fully subside or permit the Gulfis and the Portuguese to rebound. Smaller operations against the Gulf were conducted almost ceaselessly. The pressure on Port Cameron, for example, was never relaxed, although no success was forthcoming from sporadic attacks on its fortifications. In 1612 the operation against Cameron was placed under Allahvirdi's son, Imamquli, who finally succeeded in taking the port city in 1614. He destroyed the Portuguese fortress, and to punish the local Gulfis for their pro-Portuguese "infidel" sympathies, he looted the city and set fire to the trading houses of the Gulf merchants.

The hostility the Persian invader aroused in the city and among the influential Gulf families forced him to move the administrative offices of Cameron for safety to the nearby Fort Abbasi. In time, Fort Abbasi became the nucleus for Port Abbas (Bandar Abbas), which replaced Cameron altogether. The prosperous districts of the Bahrân were also taken by the Safavids at this time in 1614 from the emir of Hormuz and his Portuguese allies. These events marked the beginning of the end for the Portuguese role in the Gulf world and, ultimately, the Indian Ocean.[90]

Sensing that a major military operation against the Gulf by the Safavids was inevitable,[91] much of the Portuguese and Gulfi fleet and resources had been diverted to the environs of the Strait of Hormuz by 1619, leaving the rest of the Indian Ocean exposed. The time seemed opportune for the Dutch under Jan Pieterszoon Coen, who took Muslim Jakarta in the same year. Fortifying and naming it Batavia, they made it the capital of the Dutch East Indies.[92]

The Portuguese had become ever more dependent on the cooperation and material support of the Gulfis, considering that Portugal had had no monarch of its own since 1580 and that it also needed to maintain some minimum military and naval protection for her vast possessions around the Indian Ocean and the world. After the demise of the Shabankara emirs of Laristan, the emirs of Hormuz had become the most powerful native force in the Gulf.[93] Under pressure from the earlier Safavids, the emirs had moved their centuries-old capital from old Hormuz (below Minab) on the mainland to a small and barren island in the middle of the Strait of Hormuz, which they renamed the island of Hormuz. Under the Safavid ground attacks, by 1614, the emirs had lost control of the vital districts of Bahrân, which provided much food, timber, and men to the island emirate of Hormuz (the Bahrain archipelago had already been taken by the Persians in 1602). Only the large island of Qeshm had remained under the control of the emirs, and it was vital to their survival. The strategic location of the island emirate in the middle of the Strait of Hormuz, nonetheless, rendered its control of paramount importance to all contending parties.

The Safavids gained the support of the British through threats and lucrative promises to provide the sea contingent for attack on the Portuguese and the emir of Hormuz. Having only recently arrived in the area, the British were fearful of their sea rivals such as the Dutch. Meanwhile, he who underestimated the power of the Spanish or the diminished Portuguese navies at this time did so at his own peril. Furthermore, an amicable relationship existed at the time between Phillip III of Spain and James I of Britain. A combination of carrots and sticks offered by the Safavids finally convinced the British East India Company to undertake the operation.

In 1621 the British warships arrived on the scene, soundly defeating a large Portuguese fleet off Port Jask in the Gulf of Oman. There they were given port facilities and "factories" (trading headquarters) by the Safavids as their reward.

Under the protection of two British warships, Imamquli crossed the Clarence Strait[94] and seized Qeshm (January 23, 1622). This deprived Hormuz of its primary source of drinking water.[95] The sultan of Oman was successfully cowed by the Safavids into breaking his liaison with the Portuguese and avoided the impending catastrophe awaiting the emir of Hormuz. The combined Persian and British forces took Hormuz on April 22, 1622. Three thousand Portuguese captives were handed over to the British by the Persians in accordance with their original treaty of alliance. A general massacre of the native Gulfis of Hormuz was then ordered by the Safavid general, Imamquli. The heads of the most important victims—the leading Gulfi merchant elite—were pickled and carried to Fort Abbasi, and thence to Isfahan for the delight of the Persian court.[96]

The center of British operations in the Gulf basin was transferred from Jask to Cameron/Bandar Abbas, and their mercantile houses replaced those of the Portuguese. To counter the British, nonetheless, the Dutch were given the island of Hormuz and the ruined Portuguese fort for their commercial and naval headquarters in the following year (1623). Aggressively, the Dutch pushed for and received concessions in Bandar Abbas itself to rival the British. The British star, however, was rapidly rising, and eventually eclipsed Dutch fortunes in the Gulf and most everywhere else.

The Portuguese remained holed up in their stronghold of Muscat for another two decades until 1650, when they were finally expelled from the area by the Omanis, who had no more use for them.

It is doubtful if much Portuguese blood ever entered the veins of the Gulfis. Although Gulfis intermarried liberally with the followers of all creeds, they were the ones who took brides from other communities, rather than giving them. The Portuguese present in the area were obviously nearly totally male, and intermarriage between Muslim women and non-Muslim men is not allowed by the Koran. What genes were exchanged must have been largely illicit, and thus minor.

The occupation of these important Gulf trade ports translated into a windfall of wealth for the Safavids, most tangibly visible in the construction boom that engulfed the new Safavid capital of Isfahan. Having alienated if not killed most of the Gulfi merchant elite, the Safavids either by choice or necessity placed the international trade for Persian goods largely in the hands of the Armenian merchants in their capital, whose vast community had been earlier resettled there between 1605 and 1620.[97] For about three-quarters of a century, the Armenian merchants of Isfahan reaped enormous, although fleeting, profits that would have normally gone to the Gulf merchants and emirates. For the first and the last time, Armenians came to settle in the Gulf basin and add one more element to the ethnic and cultural diversity of the region. Meanwhile, the Armenian quarter in the Safavid capital, built from scratch, fast became the wealthiest Armenian community in the world. The Armenian mercantile involvement in the Gulf, although diminishing, nonetheless lasted until the end of the Zand period in Persia. As late as 1754 an Armenian contingent of merchants is found among those invited by the Dutch to augment the mercantile activities at their newly founded trading post at Kharg (see below). The Armenians are still found today in many Gulf ports, including Khurramshahr, Abadan, Bandar Abbas, Dubai, Manama, and Sharjah. Their role in the traditional cross trading of the Gulf is minor, with most marketing their technical expertise instead of trading skills.

The wealth that was gained by their taking of the northern Gulf merchant ports whetted the appetite of the Safavids for more. They embarked on a program of full domination of the Gulf trade through military occupation of the area. To accomplish this, it was necessary to annex the sultanate of Oman and the Portuguese-held port of Muscat on the one hand, and the Dayrid emirate of Basra and southern Khuzistan on the other. Both of these attempts, however, resulted in failure. In the case of Oman, the Safavids lacked the necessary fleet and faced hostile native Gulfis if they attempted a land march from their base at Qatif. They approached the British for naval support of their land forces to take Muscat and the rest of the sultanate of Oman. The British asked in return for the island of Hormuz as well as the right to maintain a battle fleet in the Gulf. The Safavids refused, and the plan unraveled. The last Safavid attempt on Basra in 1628, meanwhile, coincided with the death of Shah Abbas I, and immediately evaporated.

No other attempt was made in those two directions by the later Safavids. Gulfis had succeeded in resisting a total military occupation and domination by this most energetic Persian dynasty in centuries.

EXPANSION OF THE GULFIS

THE GULFIS IN SOUTHEAST ASIA

Under constant pressure from Persia, the energy of the Gulfis had decisively shifted away from their home base to East Africa and South and Southeast Asia. An entire class of traders and ruling families moved to those destinations, sparking a renaissance of Gulf influence. It is doubtful whether vast communities such as those of Indonesia, Malaysia, the Maldives, and the Malabar coast of India would have been so thoroughly Muslim if adverse events in the Gulf at this time had not pushed out so many influential Gulfis into those distant communities. Thus, the wind of Islamization in Southeast Asia reached typhoon force at this time, succeeding in converting over half of the entire population of the region to Islam within a mere 125 years up to 1725. A wealth of Southeast Asian Muslim scholars, writers, and poets writing in Malay emerged at this time.[98]

In 1596, for example, the Dutch commented on the mix of merchants greeting them in Banten (at the northwest end of Java) as follows:

> The Persians, who are called the Khorasanis in Java, are those who usually earn their living in [precious] stones and medicines . . . The Arabs and Pegus[99] are the ones who mostly conduct their trade by sea, carrying and bringing merchandise from one city to another,

and buying up much Chinese merchandise, which they exchange against other wares from the surrounding islands, and also pepper, against the time when the Chinese return to buy. The Malay and Klings [Muslim south Indians] are merchants who invest money at interest and in voyages and bottomry.[100] The Gujaraties, since they are poor, are usually used as sailors.[101]

Banten had been established in the 1520s as a Muslim port-state by one of the nine Muslim walis of Java, Sunan Gunung Jati, who established it after having vanquished the Hindu kingdom of Pajajaran in that island. He had secured the help of a Gulfi fleet for the purpose after having personally visited the Gulf on the way to Mecca and back. To avoid clashing with the well-established Acehnese westward commerce, the new sultanate of Banten concentrated on the spice trade of the South China Sea and China herself. This rather harmonious and traditional apportionment of the market between various interest groups and the elite in the Gulf is a phenomenon seen in nearly all Gulfi allied states around the Indian Ocean. The Makassar sultanate of Gowa and Tallo that was converted to Islam in 1605 and incorporated into the Gulf commercial world expanded its commerce and dominion south and southwestward from its home base in Celebes/Sulawesi into Buton, Sumbawa, and Timor—all to avoid any clashes with the sultanates of Banten, Aceh, Burunei, and Cebu. Only in the relatively short period of 1610–69 following the death of the founder of the sultanate did an atypical internal rivalry between Makassar and others ensue in contrast with the usual harmony in apportionment enforced all over the Gulf oceanic world.[102] In Mindanao (the southern main island of the Philippines), "even ethnic groups known in the eighteenth and nineteenth centuries for their fragmentation or statelessness tend to remember the age of commerce as a time when they were politically unified under strong kings."[103]

The riches brought by the commerce made for a common bond between the elite of every group within the realm of these oceanic mercantile states. Much was gained—or lost—depending on the forfeiture of traditional ethnocultural rivalries and the channeling of the resultant energy into the competitive commercial world. Those who did not invited poverty and fractiousness (Map 2.6).[104]

It was not only in the island worlds of Southeast Asia that the Gulfis' influence and fortune were expanding by leaps and bounds. On the mainland in Siam, Cambodia, and Burma Gulfis who fled from the Safavid-induced distressed conditions in the Gulf came to dominate the economic and political scene for centuries to come, with their influence reaching its zenith in the late seventeenth century. In Siam, the Persian influence reached its peak in the 1670s.[105]

The Gulfi upper class soon found that some of the local elite were willing to seize political power and establish local Muslim emirates under their aegis—a process already well advanced in the island worlds off their coast. Within a short time, Muslim emirs were ruling Siam, Cambodia, and neighboring states. David Wyatt has shown that the four most powerful official families from 1610 to the fall of the Ayutthaya dynasty in Siam in 1767 all derived from able Gulfis and their seafaring allies, brought into the commercial branches of government in the seventeenth century—from Persian, Brahman, Chinese, and Mon origins respectively.[106] As early as the 1540s, Persian, Indian, and Malay Muslims had been numerous in Ayutthaya Siam and were especially influential in the Siamese port of Tenasserim (now in Burma) on the Andaman Sea.[107]

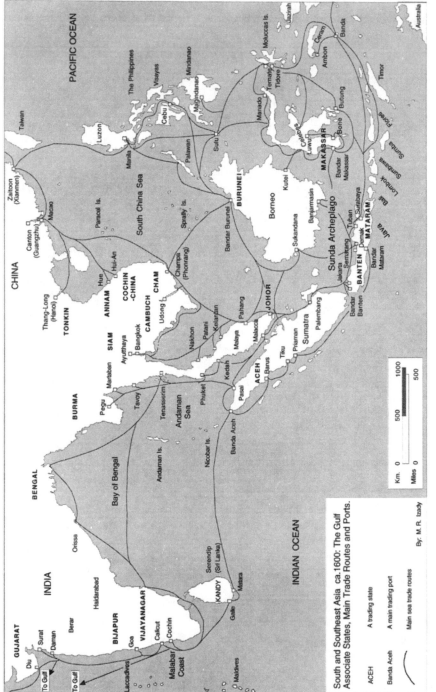

South and Southeast Asia ca.1600: The Gulf
Associate States, Main Trade Routes and Ports.

By: M. R. Izady

ACEH — A trading state

Banda Aceh — A main trading port

—— Main sea trade routes

Map 2.6

The largest Muslim group in mainland Southeast Asia was drawn from the Shi'is from among the Persians, Bahrâni Arabs, Indians, and even Azeris. Local conversions likewise became mostly into the Shi'i branch of Islam. The Siamese Muslim poet, Hamzah Fansuri, learned his mysticism among the Shi'i Gulfi community at Tenasserim.[108] Many works of history in Persian and local languages were produced at this time in Malaya, Burma, Siam, and Cambodia by the Gulfi immigrants, including the *Tâj al-salâtin* by Bukhari al-Jawhari[109] (1603) and *Kashti-i Sulaymân* by Ibrahim ibn Muhammad (1668).

During the long reign of King Prasat-thong (1629–56), the Shi'is reached a new height of power in Siam and dominated most of the political and commercial posts in the kingdom. According to a local Persian chronicle, Prasat's son Narai used to visit Persians "regularly. He took great pleasure in their social and table manners, food and drink."[110]

These Gulfi settlers succeeded in persuading Narai to attempt to seize the Siamese throne in 1657. The Persian community proved crucial in his success. During their annual Shi'i public procession and ceremonies of Ashura (tenth of Muharram) that ran in the major thoroughfares of the capital and were attended by the highest state dignitaries, the Persians approached the new ruler who had just replaced Prasat-thong and dispatched him with multiple gunshot wounds.[111] Narai was immediately declared king.

As might be expected, the Persian Shi'is were rewarded handsomely during the 33 years of Narai's reign (1656–88), including the tightening of their monopoly on many commercial and political-diplomatic activities. Among these was one Aqa Muhammad Astarabadi, better known by his Siamese title, Okphra Sinnaowarat, who arranged for a Thai embassy to be sent to the Safavid court of Persia in 1668. Astarabadi filled the Siamese army with Persian, Arab, and Indian Shi'i officers.[112] By 1670, the governors of all major ports were in the hands of these Gulfis: Tenasserim and Mergui governed by Persian Shi'is; those of Phuket and Bangkhli by Indian Shi'is, and Bangkok by a Shi'i Azeri.[113]

In concordance with the age-old maxim of *cujus regio, ejus religio* (whose kingdom, his religion), the ultimate aim of the Persians and other Gulfis was the conversion of the rulers, on whom they could place high hopes for establishment of new and thriving Muslim sultanates in the heart of mainland Southeast Asia.[114] In Siam, although thousands of influential Thai families converted,[115] the royal house remained faithful to Buddhism. Had the conversion of the king to Islam been achieved, Siamese history could have followed a very different course. Disillusioned by Narai's refusal to convert, the Shi'is staged a coup in 1686, in which they nearly succeeded in seizing the palace. With the help of armed Europeans in the capital, the king put down the coup, and the fortune of the Gulfis in Siam took a quick downturn, never again to rise to that prominence.

In addition to the well-entrenched Shi'is, Siam was receiving thousands of Muslim refugees from the war-torn island archipelago to the south where the Dutch and British warships were wreaking havoc. The Sunni aristocracy of many sultanate and emirate port cities were streaming into the better protected mainland from the onslaught. The Muslims from Champa (southern Vietnam) and Cambodia also entered into the relative safety of Siam.

Champa was perhaps the earliest locale on mainland Southeast Asia to be settled by the Gulfis as early as the eleventh century. This was largely due to geography: on the delta of Mekong River, Champa is on the direct sea route from the Indian Ocean into the South China Sea and China. The port of Champa/Phanrang (northeast of modern Saigon) had been the headquarters of the Gulfi merchants and their Southeast Asian Muslim allies for centuries when the port city was selected as the capital of the Cham kings in 1471.

Together, the influence of the Muslim merchants and the fortunes of Islam made rapid advances following this favorable change. By the late sixteenth century, conversion was a routine event.[116] Although the Cham royalty remained Hindu until about 1607, they encouraged conversion to Islam among their nobility for commercial reasons. The kingdom had been made into a Vietnamese vassal by 1611. This change resulted in no perceptible negative impact on the Gulfis' influence or Islam's popularity.[117] By the 1670s, the bulk of the population and the Cham royalty itself was Muslim.[118]

The Muslims from Champa were streaming upriver into Cambodia from the Mekong Delta, looking for trade, influence, and better security than was found under the Vietnamese suzerainty at Phonrang.[119] By 1642, a new king of Cambodia, Cau Bana Cand Ramadhipati, had taken the throne. He found the Muslims the only powerful and organized group he could count on for effective support. The following year, he converted to Islam and took the throne name of Sultan Ibrahim. He then proceeded to set up a Muslim sultanate in Cambodia on the Malay model,[120] becoming the only Shi'i monarch of Southeast Asia.[121]

Exposed to Vietnamese predation, Sultan Ibrahim finally lost his throne to a protracted Vietnamese invasion in 1658–59, invited in by the disenfranchised Cambodian Buddhist elite and monks. The rise of Islam in Cambodia and the Mekong delta was thus halted, leaving only Siam to continue with its Gulfi experience for another half century.

OMANI EXPANSION

Between 1650 and 1700, the European domination of Indian Ocean trade had become nearly complete. Not only was the Gulfis' commercial and political influence in Southeast Asia being phased out, but everywhere else too they were suffering. This included the Gulf area itself. Many of the commercial, political, and family relationships between the Gulf and other communities around the Indian Ocean were progressively curtailed or severed altogether. By 1800, only some low-key connections with south India and the Swahil-Benadir (East Africa) were still being maintained by the Gulf. The exchanges with Southeast Asia had become a trickle. Population exchanges followed the same course, with the receding flow limited to solely those with the Swahil.

After their calamitous defeat at the hands of the Persians and the British at Hormuz in 1621, the Portuguese lost the confidence and assistance of the Gulfis, not only in the Gulf itself but across the entire Indian Ocean basin. The Gulfis were in need of relief from the great distress placed on them by the Persian military and Armenian commercial advances, and the Portuguese were unable to defend themselves, let alone the Gulfis.

The split between the Portuguese and their Gulfi allies in Southeast Asia made both of them ripe for easy picking by the Dutch, who went after their trading posts with gusto. But first they had to fight off the British and their East India Company, who having basked in the limelight of the victory at Hormuz, were intent on breaking into the spice trade by taking some of the same unprotected commercial outposts of the vanquished. They were not as lucky when facing the Dutch.

In 1623, the Dutch massacred the English traders who had established shops at Ambon/Amboina in the previous year. The vacuum that was created by the virtual demise of the Portuguese and the eclipse of Gulfi power enticed the Dutch to rush to fill it. The paramount strategic port of Malacca had been taken by the Dutch in 1641.[122] On the western side of the Indian Ocean, the Dutch had taken many ports in Madagascar by 1630, and in 1652 proceeded to establish the port and the colony of the Cape[123] in what grew to become Dutch South Africa.

Violently expelled from Southeast Asia by the Dutch, the British now concentrated on the Indian subcontinent, where they had established a commercial base at Surat in

1612. Their inroads into the Gulf during their alliance with the Safavids was itself also a useful step in that direction.

Lacking an effective fleet of their own, a fact exacerbated by their foolish alienation of the Gulfis, the Safavids now felt apprehensive about unopposed British expansion into the western Indian Ocean and their increasing domination of the Gulf sea routes. Three short years after the fall of Hormuz and the near total routing of the Portuguese from the Gulf basin,[124] the Safavids had invited them back (1625). They were granted port facilities at Cong, along with permission to pearl off Bahrain as a counterbalance to the rising influence of the English and the Dutch.[125] The local Gulfis, whose expertise and historic interest in maritime commerce and their bonds with similar communities around the Indian Ocean would have made them valuable allies if pursued, were meanwhile ignored or actively suppressed by the myopic Persian (and, later, Ottoman) administrations. The pressure forced many of the Gulf elite to do what they had done under similar circumstance during the long centuries of Sasanian pressure in the third to seventh century A.D., and noted before: they moved to East Africa, coastal India, and Southeast Asia.

Nearly fifty years earlier, in 1650, the Omanis had booted the Portuguese out of Muscat and immediately started harassing them on the Swahil coast of Africa and beyond. They instigated many successful local rebellions in the Swahil against the Portuguese between 1660 and 1687.[126] In a quick blitz in 1698–99, the Omanis moved into East Africa in force, establishing their power over a thousand miles of coast, from Mombassa to Port Mozambique. The strategic port of Zanzibar fell in the same campaign. Now at the end of the seventeenth century, under protracted attacks led by the Omanis and the local rebellions, the Portuguese were quickly and permanently eliminated from all their possessions in East Africa north of Cape Delgado. Only Mozambique and its rich gold fields remained in their hands until 1975.

Many port-states, such as Mombassa and Kilwa, broke away and reasserted their political and commercial independence after the 1740s. The sultan of Kilwa had commenced commercial and political exchange with the Europeans, signing a treaty with the French in 1776 to provide them with slaves needed for the coffee plantations in the Mascarenes (Mauritius and Bourbon/Reunion islands). Other ports followed suit.

Under Nadir Shah, Persians attacked and conquered much of the northern Omani seacoast in the course of the 1740s—a feat that evaded the Safavids. Nadir reduced the Ya'rubids at Suhar into vassalage. The east African Gulfi and local merchant and political elite quickly took the opportunity to challenge the Omani predominance in East Africa. But by 1749 the Persian yoke had been thrown off, and a new dynasty of Bu-Sa'idis had emerged in Oman under the leadership of Ahmad ibn Sa'id. The dynasty still rules Oman. The Bu-Sa'idis, who later adopted the title of sultan, reestablished the Omani claim over Zanzibar and Pemba in East Africa. The most important Afro-Shirazi port of East Africa, Kilwa, had fallen to them by 1785.

The Omani star reached its zenith under the reign of Sa'id ibn Sultan (1806–1856), who swiftly brought under his firm rule all East African Gulfi and Swahili colonies from Mogadishu to Cape Delgado (west of the Comoro Islands). When he learned that the experimental planting of cloves in East Africa had shown promise, he grasped the opportunity to establish large clove plantations on Zanzibar and Pemba around 1818 and imported slaves from the mainland to work them. He then expanded the spice plantations to the Gulf itself, bringing experienced African spice farmers and slaves to settle in the Minab-Jask region where he founded new plantations. These Africans came to form tight farming communities and retain their African culture, language, lifestyle, and art and architecture to the present day.[127]

The spice and commercial business boomed, and the proceeds were used by Sultan Sa'id to regain lost control over the mainland ports, such as Mombassa, which was subdued and regained from the rival Mazruis in 1837. Commerce with the United States was established and expanded at an astonishing pace. Large scale importation of American cotton cloth was paid for by exports of spices, ivory, cowries, hides, coconut oil, sesame, copal and other local animal and plant products. By 1856 and the death of Sa'id, the United States and France each were importing over half a million dollars worth of goods from the Swahil (approximately $155 million each in 2001 dollars). Exports to British India were even higher.

The solid hold and the great wealth enticed Sultan Sa'id to move, in 1840, the Omani court from Muscat to Zanzibar, declaring it the capital. In an interesting reversal, the Omani were now overseeing their interests in the Gulf itself from their African capital in Zanzibar.[128] They retained the ruling title to Zanzibar until 1964. Knowledgeable about the benefit of maintaining relations with the sea powers of the world, Sa'id established treaties with the United States (1833) and France (1844). Sa'id also strengthened his ties with Great Britain (which already had port rights at Muscat), giving it the Kuria-Muria islands in the Arabian Sea (1854) in return for its help in snuffing out the rising Wahhabi threat to Oman.

The Omani successes at this time are undoubtedly due to the strong personality, wit, and energy of Sultan Sa'id. He maintained a well-disciplined corps of Baluch marines and Omani levies. He invested heavily in construction of ships and maintained a shipshape navy. In the field of diplomacy he was astute and kept a very good working relationship with the British without losing his freedom of action to them.

This was shown clearly in 1824. Fearing Sa'id's attack on their wealthy port of Mombassa, the local rebel Mazrui sultans asked the resident British functionary, Captain W. F. Owen, for protection. On his own initiative, Owen raised a British flag over the city. As soon as London found out about the move, orders were issued to pull down the Union Jack immediately and leave Mombassa to its own devices, to stand or fall to Sa'id—which it did in 1826.

At this same time, Sa'id also took Bahrain, Bandar Abbas, Jask, Chahbahar, Gwadar,[129] and a number of other important locales in the Gulf itself for Oman, some by force, others by purchase or lease from Persia. He encouraged sizable settlement of the Indian merchants and traders in East Africa, where they established large caravans running into the interior of Africa. This became the source of heavy involvement of the Indians in such East African countries as Malawi, Uganda, Zambia, Tanzania, Somalia, and Kenya. A substantial number of Indians also arrived as settlers in the Gulf per se at this time, becoming the ancestors of the modern "native" Indian population of Oman and the UAE (to be distinguished from the expatriate workers who arrived after 1965).

Upon his death in 1856, the British helped divide the sultanate between his two sons, with East Africa going to Majid (r. 1856–70) and the Gulf areas to Thuwayni (r. 1856–66). The Bu-Sa'idis remained in power in their shrinking East African domain, which became a British protectorate between 1890 and 1963, and were finally overthrown in a coup in 1964.

During this Omani period in East Africa's history, a new wave of settlers from the Gulf arrived, while a goodly number of Africans were settled in the Gulf areas in return. These included all ethnic elements in the Gulf, from Arabs to Persians, Baluchis, Kurds, and even Pashtos and Qashqa'is. The influential Mazrui family of Mombassa, who, as seen above, came successfully to challenge Omani suzerainty and dominated that port between 1746 and 1837, are a good example of this intermixture. The Mazruis were originally from Minab and Jask coasts, southeast of Bandar Abbas, where they are known as the "Mazari." Ethnically, they were largely Baluchi with Persian admixture before moving to Oman along with other Baluchi warrior clans in the hire of the Imam of Muscat. They became an influential clan in Oman, were arabicized, and eventually moved to Mombassa in East Africa.[130]

PRESSURE ON THE GULF
BY THE REGIONAL POWERS

The steady decline in the Gulf's ability to defend itself was not just against world-class empires. By the middle of the seventeenth century and the comprehensive disruption of the Gulf's economic base by the Safavids, the Gulfis gradually lost the ability to fend off even the marauding Bedouins coming out the wastes of Najd, Nafud, and the Badiya (of southern Iraq). Of all Gulf states, only Oman was to emerge from this new menace whole.

At the head of the Gulf, the Chaub (Banu Ka'b) tribe of Bedouins[131] settled on the deltaic lands of the Tigris-Euphrates-Karun river system. In time, the Chaub were assimilated into the Gulf milieu, converting to Shi'ism (the most common religion among the Arabic speaking Gulfis—then and now) and absorbing the maritime culture of the Gulf.[132] The Chaub became a formidable local sea power, which at one point during the reign of their emir, Salman, in the 1760s was able to defeat and capture a British East India fleet sent to challenge their dominance over the Shatt al-Arab and Basran commerce.[133]

It is hard to say who was inhabiting the area of southern Khuzistan before the Chaub arrival. The existence of many archaic Iranic toponyms—some pertaining to maritime activities—are markers pointing to the Iranic ethnicity of at least an appreciable portion of the old inhabitants. The Afshar Turcomans also dominated the area politically from the eleventh to the seventeenth century.[134] They must have been present in some numbers to maintain such dominance. Survival of Turkic features in the local Arabic and Persian dialects in Khuzistan and the immediate highlands as well as Turkic toponyms is evidence in support of this assumption.[135] It must be remembered, however, that the deltaic tidal flats and marshlands (Persian *khwar*, Arabicized into *khawr, hawr,* and *hor*) of southern Khuzistan were still under the waters of the Persian Gulf until about the beginning of the tenth century.[136] The territories south of Ahwaz were and still remain largely a combination of wetlands, tidal flats, and marshes, reminiscent of the better known marshlands of southern Iraq. Because of this "sealand" quality, both these areas have been integral parts of the Gulf world.

In time, the Chaub arabicized all the inhabitants of the wetlands and marshes—a triangular area between the southern suburbs of Ahwaz and the rivers Zohreh and the Shatt al-Arab. By the eighteenth century, the area aptly came to be known as "Arabistan"—the "Arab state" in Persian.[137] From their successive capitals at Port Quban (on the Gulf), Dawraq, and Fallahiyya (on the Marun/Jarrahi River), the Chaub spread their influence and settlements east to Hindijan. Some Chaub settlers ventured as far as Bushehr. They built up and expanded the village of Hafar at the confluence of the Karun and the Shatt al-Arab, to become subsequently the important port city of Muhammara (Khurramshahr, after the Persian annexation in the 1920s), rivaling Basra.[138]

On the southern side of the Gulf, the push by the Najdi Bedouins into coastal areas and settlements had begun somewhat later than the Chaub settlement at the head of the Gulf. The Najdis tried and succeeded in capitalizing on the declining Gulf societies in the early part of the eighteenth century, and one by one overran the Gulf's old centers of population—north and south. By the 1780s, the Najdi shaikhs and chieftains were ruling nearly every port and population center in the southern Gulf, from Kuwait to Ras al-Khaimah. Only the Sultanate of Oman—thanks partly to its overseas sources of income and mercenaries, and partly to the natural barrier of the Al-Hajar/Jebel Akhdar range—escaped being overrun and settled by the Najdi hordes.

In the northern Gulf, the coastal areas came under pressure in the seventeenth and eighteenth century from both the seaborne Najdi Sunnis and the Luri-speaking Shi'i tribes of the Iranian highlands. Introduction of the modern Persian dialect of Luri diminished and eventually replaced many older Iranic languages spoken by the native Gulfis, from Jask on the Gulf of Oman to Hindijan at the head of the Gulf. Only in secluded areas such as the island of Qeshm and the Musandam Peninsula of Oman (the Kumzar region) can one still hear such languages being spoken. The older form of Persian, oddly, can be found spoken, not so much in the northern Gulf, but among the communities in Qatif, Qatar, and the Emirates. These Persian speakers are Sunnis (as most Persians were until the middle of the sixteenth century). It is only in the Iranian sector of the Gulf where the Persian speakers are as often Sunnis as Shi'is—a situation unparalleled elsewhere in the state of Iran.[139] These are known as the 'Ajam in the southern Gulf to distinguish them from the "Irani" settlers who have arrived in the past few decades.[140]

The Omani sultans turned Bandar Abbas into a crown residence, where they spent a portion of each year. Under the rule of the second Qajar monarch of Persia, Fath 'Ali Shah, Persian administration was gradually extended to the northern coast of the Gulf between Bushehr and Lingeh. The sultan's possessions on the northern shores of the Gulf, however, were wrested only in the third and fourth quarters of the nineteenth century during the reign of Nasir al-Din Shah. Bandar Abbas had been taken in 1868, while Persian troops seized Jask and Chahbahar between 1872 and 1880. Oman itself, along with its other far-flung possessions along the coasts of northwest Indian Ocean, had acknowledged British supremacy in 1798.[141]

As noted earlier, in the heyday of their power, the Omanis had brought a large number of East African farmers (from Somalia, Djibouti, and the Kenyan and Tanzanian coasts) to settle the coastal regions between Gwadar, Jask, and Bandar Abbas, as well as the Julfâr coast, Musandam peninsula, and Dhofar. Although influenced by the local traditions, these remain authentic pieces of Africa in the Gulf, particularly on the Iranian coast.[142] In Julfâr and Oman proper, settlers from Africa, coastal India, and the Malay archipelago largely inhabit the Musandam peninsula, down to the ports of Ras al-Khaimah and Sharjah. The modern Shihuhs are an amalgam of these diverse early settlers.[143] The Indian Liwatis/Sindhis, Za'b, and Ali also were settled in the Musandam-Julfâr region. Along with the Shihuhs, they still constitute the bulk of the native population of the region, where the Arabic-speaking fellow Gulfis are in a minority. These Indians are largely Shi'is, while some still practice Hinduism.

Large communities of Baluchis have also come to settle in Oman, some dominating entire villages and locales in that area. The present Baluch population settled there after the return of the sultan from Zanzibar and his domination of the Makran coast. An Omani presence on the Makran coast did not completely end until 1958 when the Sultan finally negotiated the sale of the port of Gwadar to Pakistan for £3 million. The Baluchi tribal warriors who have little or no connection to Oman's internal feuds and elite proved to be the ideal body to form the praetorian guards for the Omani sultans and subsequently for many other Gulfi rulers. They still retain that special function today.

The Najdi Bedouins, meanwhile, have since the eighteenth century cut a swath out of the northern Gulf coast, claiming perhaps one half of all Arabic-speaking inhabitants on that side. In this period, Najdi Shaikhs such as Rahmah ibn Jabir (at Bushehr, Qatar, and Dammam) and the Jasimis (Qawasim) from the Julfâr coast (present UAE) extended their control to many ports in the northern Gulf region, competing for dominance with the local elite.[144]

BASRA AND THE GULF

For centuries Basra had managed to remain outside the direct administration of the neighboring Ottoman and Persian empires, much as Oman had. Basra paid its dues and "gifts" to Isfahan, Shiraz, or Istanbul as the political winds changed direction, but meanwhile retained her precious freedom of commercial action. The reasons behind Basra's final loss of independence arose from a complicated chain of events.

In August 1759 in the course of the Seven-Years' War (the "French and Indian Wars" in the American historical lexicon), the French bombarded the British headquarters in Bandar Abbas and, occupying the port city for 15 days, looted the British trading houses. As a result, the British moved their headquarters to Basra in 1763. Earlier, the Dutch had done the same with satisfactory results.

Seeking complete freedom of action, in 1753 the Dutch authorities in Basra under the direction of the Prussian Baron Kniphausen attacked and took the island of Kharg (northwest of Bushehr) from the emirate of Rig.[145] Possessing sources of fresh water, the island could well support the Dutch who built a fort as their independent headquarters there. The Dutch were proven too optimistic about their power and freedom to act in the Gulf. Thirteen years later, in 1765, the legendary "pirate" Mir Muhanna of Rig launched a successful attack on Kharg. Taking the island, Muhanna killed many Dutch and took many more captive. This ended unceremoniously and abruptly the 150–year presence of the Dutch in the Gulf and northwestern Indian Ocean.

The British in India were asked unsuccessfully by the Zands to provide the naval force for a joint strike against Mir Muhanna at Kharg. The Zands were trying to cut into the lucrative sea commerce of the Gulf, having learned from the Safavids what there was to be gained. Karim Khan Zand finally procured enough local dhows from his vassal Gulfi emirs to chase Muhanna off to Basra, where he was killed by the emir of that port city.

Karim Khan encouraged the British to return to Persian territory later in the same year. The local Gulfi ruler of Bushehr, Sheik Sa'dun, was incensed by this action of his suzerain in Shiraz and showed his annoyance by mistreating the British. By 1769, the British had gone back to Basra a second time, complaining of both Sheik Sa'dun and other local emirs who had rendered that part of the Gulf unwelcome to the outside maritime powers.

Following the second relocation of British interests to Basra, Karim Khan set out once and for all to extinguish Basra and Oman as rival trading posts hindering his plans for the commercial domination of the Gulf. He had already turned Nasr Khan bin Madhkur, the emir of Bushehr and Bahrain, into his vassal ruler (wali), but his 1766 attempt on Oman had met with failure (due to an outrage committed by his admiral, Zaki Khan, against the family of the Mu'ini emir of Hormuz, Shaikh Abdallah). In April 1775, he sent 30,000 troops toward Basra, being supported by a seaborne force sent by his vassal, Nasr Khan bin Madhkur. Sulaiman Aqa, the emir of Basra, asked for and received help from the Chathirs of Khuzistan and a seaborne force sent by the sultan of Oman. After 13 months of siege, Basra was taken by the combined forces of the Zand troops and the Gulfi seamen under the Madhkurid wali (May 1776). Upon the news of the death of Karim Khan (March 2, 1779), Basra was evacuated and restored to Sulaiman Aqa, who acknowledged Ottoman suzerainty once again but maintained its virtual independence.[146]

It is worth noting that the most recent Iranian territorial claim to the Bahrain islands was based on its rule by the Madhkurid dynasty of Bushehr who acknowledged Iranian suzerainty. Bahrain had been taken from the Hawilas (the Arabs who had returned from the Iranian coast to the southern, Arabian coast; see below) in 1752 by a joint operation of the Madhkurid emir of Bushehr and the Za'abi shaikh of Rig. Nasr Khan bin Madhkur died shortly after Karim Khan Zand, and his son tried unsuccessfully to avoid being sucked into the chaos and dynastic succession dispute that engulfed Persia. The Zand crown prince, Lutfali, sought support from the Gulfi emirs against the Qajar pretender, Agha Muhammad. The emirs of Rig threw their lot in with him, while Bushehr refused to interfere. Thus, Lutfali and the Rigi forces marched on Bushehr. The emirate of Bushehr was already suffering from the costly and ultimately futile expedition against Basra under the Zands, and this new belligerency further sapped the energies of the Madhkurids. Bahrain and Qatar were rapidly and permanently snatched from the dominions of the emirs of Bushehr (and, by extension, from Persia/Iran) by yet another, newer wave of nomadic invaders from Najd that also engulfed all other ports and emirates of the southern Gulf (except Oman) and threatened the rest as well.

THE NAJDI WAVE

The new wave of Najdi Bedouins into the Gulf basin was propelled by the zeal of a new puritanical religious movement, which in time introduced Wahhabism into the Gulf milieu. By 1744, the preacher Muhammad ibn Abd al-Wahhab (1703–92) received support from the most powerful chieftain of Najd, Ibn Saud. A quasi-messianic zeal and the prospects for plunder drove the Wahhabis to attack all corners of the Gulf world. By 1801, they had even seized Karbala in Iraq, the holiest Shi'i city, giving it to a sustained massacre and looting followed by the defiling of the shrines of al-Husain and al-Abbas. They evaporated into their desert refuge before any local government could react. The lines had been drawn, and the mutual loathing between the Shi'is and the Wahhabis has never subsided since.

Although a latecomer to the Gulf scene, Wahhabism was nevertheless carried by Gulfi vessels to the far corners of the Indian Ocean in the nineteenth and twentieth centuries, where Wahhabi teachings played a role in the history of Muslim Africa, India, and Indonesia. Prior to the ascendancy of the Wahhabis, most Sunni Arabs in the Gulf basin followed the Maliki school.

The greatest political achievement of Wahhabism proved to be its conversion of the tribal chieftains of the house of Saud. From 1763 to 1811 the Saudis expanded to bring under their control most of the Arabian peninsula, and they threatened the holy cities of Mecca and Medina with the same treatment they had meted out earlier to Shi'i Karbala. This brought out the energetic khedive of Egypt, Muhammad Ali, who pushed them back all the way to Najd and brought an Egyptian army to the very shores of the Persian Gulf for the first and the last time in history (1811–1818).

Following this setback, the Saudis slowly regained between 1821 and 1833 a good part of the territories they had overrun before the appearance of the khedive. The reemergence of Ottoman power in the area after 1847–48 meant a long period of dormancy for Wahhabism and the Al-Saud until the collapse of the Ottoman power in 1917. The House of Saud facilitated that collapse by supporting the British who were fighting the Ottomans in the course of World War I.[147] In 1932, Ibn Saud established the kingdom of Saudi Arabia, incorporating the entire Hasa, Qatif, and Hufuf (the old Bahrân) coast of the Gulf and its large Shi'i majority population. The Saudis denied any recognition of the Shi'is in the kingdom, which in addition to those in the Gulf basin also include the Zaidi Shi'is of Ta'if and the Imami Shi'is of Medina and Jidda.

The sparsely populated Kuwait had been already taken in the late seventeenth and early eighteenth centuries by the Najdi clan of Bani Utub, from whom sprang in 1756 the modern Sabah family of rulers in that state. Given the vacuum created by the death of the emir of Bushehr, Bahrain was taken over by the Bani Utub as well. The ruling Khalifa family of Bahrain claim to have sprung from the same tribe in Kuwait, which they left to settle in Qatar in the 1760s, before seizing the Bahrain archipelago and its predominant Shi'i community in 1783–85. The Bani Utub of both Kuwait and Bahrain are largely the followers of the mainstream Maliki school of Sunni Islam. This is because during their rise to power, Wahhabism was still in its infancy. Not so for Qatar. The Najdi Al-Thani takeover of Qatar by the mid-nineteenth century was late enough for the dynasty to have embraced Wahhabism before its arrival, and it remains a Wahhabi house today.

All other ports and emirates of the southern Gulf that were seized in succession by the various Najdi Shaikhs, from Kuwait to Fujairah, now boast of a dynastic connection with one another by strong blood lines. The last local Gulfi ruling elite to fall were the Jasimis (Qawasim) of the Julfar coast (modern UAE) in 1805. Various Najdi Shaikhs each took over a commercial port from the Jasimis. The Al Bu-Falah tribe had already dominated Abu Dhabi by 1760, culminating in the port's detachment from the Jasimi's jurisdiction in the 1790s under the leadership of the Nahyan house who then built the port. In time, the important commercial port of Dubai also fell, this time to the Najdi Falasah in 1833. Then, Ajman went to the Na'imi house of the Kharayban and Umm al-Qawayn to the Mu'ala house of the Wahhabi Alis. Only Sharjah and the largely non-Arab Ras al-Khaimah remained in the hands of the illustrious Jasimis, where they remain today. In Fujairah, the Sharqi clan practices Shafi'ism, which may indicate a conversion of this Najdi clan to that school from its original Malikism that predominated among other Najdis prior to the advent of Wahhabism in the mid-eighteenth century.[148]

By this time, virtually all the southern Gulf coast, from Khuzistan to the borders of Oman, had fallen to the Najdi tribal chieftains who ushered in Bedouin culture, beliefs, and genes from the interior of Arabia. The Najdi Shaikhs remain the ruling elite all over the Gulf states except Oman. (The northern half, of course, remains under Iranian and Iraqi domination). All of these are Sunnis, often representing a Wahhabi minority group in their respective states (in Bahrain, Qatar, and in four out of seven emirates within the UAE), and enjoy close family kinship with one another and the Saudi royal family. Only the barrier of the Jebel Hajar-Jebel Akhdar range prevented the Najdis from overwhelming Oman proper and kept the old Omani traditions and the ruling elite in place. This is apparent even in style of accouterment of the rulers. Sultan Qaboos of Oman stands out in his native attire when participating with the other modern Gulf rulers in diplomatic events.[149] The sultan is also the only Arab leader sporting a Persian name.[150]

For all practical purposes, most Bedouins in the Gulf have acclimated to the Gulf culture and maritime lifestyle. They have also picked up Gulf Arabic replete with centuries of exposure to other languages, such as Persian. Some others have lost the Arabic altogether. A definite linguistic boundary can be drawn around the Gulf by this particular Gulfi Arabic alone. It matches astonishingly well with the boundaries of the Gulf cultural world proposed in this work. The domain of this particular Gulf Arabic in which the reflex *y* replaces standard Arabic *j/jh,* and the initial *k* becomes *ch* (and replete with non-Arabic sounds such as *ch* and *p*),[151] includes (1) the Shatt al-Arab, lower Karun, parts of Euphrates below Nasiriyyah, and the banks of the Marun/Jarrahi rivers around Fallahiyya/Shadigan; (2) all the ports in the region, including the major cities of Basra, Muhammara/ Khurramshahr, Ma'shur/Mahshahr, Abadan, and Fao; (3) the southern parts of the wetlands and marshes of the Hor al-Huwaizah, Hor al-Hammar, and Hor al-Azim; (4) the territory of Arabistan (south of Ahwaz Ridge, from Amarah to Hindian/Hindijan); (5); Kuwait; (6) Hasa-Qatif-Hufuf; (7) Bahrain; (8) Qatar; and (9) the Emirates.[152]

In the Gulf today, the Arabic-speaking Sunnis and the Persian-speaking Shi'is should largely trace their background to this period of Gulf weakness that allowed for the invasion and settlement of the Bedouins since the seventeenth century. The older population, however, shows the reverse, being Shi'i and Ibadi (if Arabic-speaking) and Sunni (if Persian- and Baluchi-speaking). The Arabic speaking Sunnis and Persian-speaking Shi'is are the relative newcomers to the Gulf.

Many Sunni Arabs of the northern Gulf have come back to reside in the emirates, Qatar, Bahrain, and Hasa-Qatif-Hufuf, following the Persian occupation, but particularly after the recent oil boom. They are known as the Hawila ("the returnees") in the southern Gulf.[153] The Hawila under Shaikh Jabbara were in fact ruling Bahrain when the forces of Nadir Shah of Persia arrived to secure the islands temporarily for the Persian crown in 1736.[154]

END OF AN ERA

The Persian design for dominating the Gulf never fully receded after the Safavids launched it with gusto in the seventeenth century. To avoid being overwhelmed by the rising power of Persia under the new Qajar dynasty, the Khalifas of Bahrain formally conceded piecemeal to British colonial hegemony and "protection" in 1861. The choice for British protection was a natural one. After the expulsion of the French from the Gulf in 1763, followed by the booting out of the Dutch from their last stronghold at Kharg Island two years later, the British had been left the only—and the overwhelming—European power in the Gulf and western Indian Ocean. Emulating the Khalifas of Bahrain, the Qatari al-Thani family too came to place themselves under British protection in 1868. Under the Jasimis, the Julfâr coast held out for some time against the British domination. They fought back the only way available to them: raiding British merchant ships, which to the British translated as piracy. Julfâr and vicinity came to be known in the British lexicon as the "Pirate Coast."[155] At the end, however, resistance to the British became too costly and eventually impossible.

It was only during the short revival of Ottoman militarism in the latter part of the nineteenth century that part of the Gulf's oceanic world finally gave up its independence of action and was absorbed into that continental empire.[156] With Prussian help, the rebuilt Ottoman military swept away the independent and/or autonomous emirates of Kurdistan, Mamluk Iraq, and the emirate of Basra. The Ottomans even pushed southward to include for the first and the last time, Kuwait, Hasa, Qatif, and Hufuf, obtaining suzerainty even over Qatar. It was, however, only Basra that lost all vestiges of its autonomy for good. Others maintained their local rulers and emerged later to become the present ruling houses of Kuwait, Qatar, and Saudi Arabia. On the northern shores, by the late nineteenth century, all the emirates and autonomous entities had been swept away by the Persian government in Tehran, excepting the resilient emirate of the Chaub, which survived as walis of Arabistan into the 1920s and the time of Shaikh Khaz'al.[157]

The Gulf was in decline economically, demographically, and politically, and nothing seemed able to prevent or even slow that process. The progressive domination of all trade routes and markets of the Indian Ocean by the Europeans was steadily severing the lifeline of the Gulf: oceanic trade. Safavid and Afsharid violence wrought on the Gulf society was just an extra factor in its decline. The declining wealth and population meant an even less effective defense on the part of the Gulf. It was not just the empires of the Persians or the Europeans who could and did come to conquer the Gulf world; as we have seen, even the once-inconsequential Bedouins of Najd could attempt at a successful takeover of the Gulf basin.

MODERN TIMES AND THE REVIVAL OF
THE GULF'S OLD SOCIOECONOMIC PATTERNS

The discovery of vast petroleum deposits in the Iranian sector of the Gulf basin in the early twentieth century proved a prelude to similar discoveries in other parts of the Gulf. By 1965, every state or dependency in the Gulf had learned of the immense wealth under its soil or seas. A new "windfall" wealth had arrived, and this time it did not depend on favorable winds.

In many ways, the income from oil resembles the former source of wealth that had made the Gulf a worldly and prosperous region. During the heyday of its ocean trade, Gulfis manufactured little of their own. They bought goods others produced and sold them where they were needed, making a handsome profit as middlemen. Their prowess was in being excellent businessmen, deal-makers and, of course, great navigators. Modern oil-driven wealth is likewise due to nothing that the Gulfis manufacture themselves, but in dealing with what others—in this case, nature—has provided as the exchange commodity. The Gulf is overflowing with wealth yet again, and many of the old patterns could resume.

The oil-generated wealth has also revived the old trading instincts of the Gulfis, with the revival of many port cities as great centers of commercial exchange for goods and credit, not just for the Middle East, but far beyond. From China to Egypt, from India to Russia, trade, goods, and laborers are once again flowing into the Gulf.

The windfall wealth in the Gulf has led to an explosion in the demand for comfort, privileges, and the trappings of affluence. After centuries of economic and demographic decline, the Gulf could not answer its needs locally for labor to design, construct, and maintain the new amenities and facilities. What is fascinating is the composition of the expatriate workers who were brought into the Gulf.

The first Gulf state to develop an acute need for expatriate laborers was Kuwait. Exposed to the Nassirite pan-Arabist calls of the 1950s and 60s, Kuwait had little choice but share the new wealth with fellow Arabs. Against its own best judgment and Gulfi instincts, Kuwait invited in Arabs from elsewhere in the Middle East, most importantly from among the Palestinians (a political gesture), Egyptians, and Lebanese (due to the need for Arabic-speaking teachers, nurses, and physicians). Kuwait became the only Gulf state to have a majority of its expatriates from the Arab world until, of course, the unfortunate events of 1990–91. Ever since, Kuwait has joined the other Gulf states in having a vast majority of its expatriate workers from the same old oceanic states and former comrades-in-commerce around the Indian Ocean and the South China Sea.

The Gulf now has a cultural and ethnic composition similar to what could be postulated for medieval times, when the genetic and cultural bonds were strongest with the communities around the Indian Ocean rim. A cursory look at the ethnic composition of the expatriate workers in the Gulf should substantiate this long-lasting connection.[158]

Figure 2.1 Points of Origin of the Inhabitants of the Gulf Arab States in 1990

Point of Origin	Native	Indian Ocean Rim	Continental Mid East	Other
Bahrain	47%	17	3	33
Kuwait	27%	36	30	7
Oman*	73%	21	1	5
Qatar	27%	42	11	20
Saudi Arabia*	65%	23	11	1
UAE	20%	66	10	4

Note: Figures for the native population of Saudi Arabia are inflated. A figure of 40–50 percent native is a much likelier estimate. For Oman, a 60–65 percent native figure is likewise a more accurate estimate.
Source: The Central Intelligence Agency, *Atlas of the Middle East* (Washington: United States Government Printing Office, 1993), 14.

The tacit support, in word and deed, given by the Palestinians and some other Middle Eastern expatriate workers (such as the Jordanians) to the Iraqi invaders of Kuwait was illuminating to the Kuwaitis. They had uncharacteristically relied on continental Middle Easterners—particularly their "fellow" Arabs—to fill job openings in the sprawling economy of Kuwait instead of following the traditional Gulf method of turning to the communities and markets of the Indian Ocean rim. The same applied to the Saudis when the 1.5–2 million Yemenite expatriates expressed a similar joy at the crossing of the Iraqi forces into Saudi Arabia at Khafji in the winter of 1991. Both Kuwait and Saudi Arabia immediately expelled these Middle Eastern expatriates in their massive numbers. Their positions have been safely filled since 1991 by others from the Indian Ocean rim.

The share of the expatriates in the local labor force is even larger than their share of the total population—and expectedly so. They are imported for the express purpose of providing labor, not bringing in or creating large families of their own with non-laboring children. I have derived the ratio between native and expatriate inhabitants using the representation of the two in the labor force as the base. At present (2001), my estimate of the point of origin for the inhabitants of the Gulf reveals that the single most important change is of course in the drastic reduction of the continental Middle Easterners and the increase in those hailing from the Indian Ocean rim.

Figure 2.2 Share of Expatriate Workers in the Labor Force of the Gulf Arab States in 1990

	Point of Origin	
	Native	Expatriate
Bahrain	43%	57%
Kuwait	16	84
Oman*	31	69
Qatar	18	82
Saudi Arabia*	30	70
UAE	15	85

Source: The Central Intelligence Agency, *Atlas of the Middle East* (Washington: United States Government Printing Office, 1993), 14.

Contrary to common belief, the increase in the native population does not lead to a reduction of the numbers of expatriates, but in fact to its increase for at least the next two decades when the new generation can be expected to enter into the labor force. The extraordinary birthrates among the native population going through its own "baby boom" phase demands even more schools and hospitals, larger homes, playgrounds, teachers, nannies, public servants, and more labor in the service industries. All these will have to be imported—funds permitting—until such time when the birth rates drop and their baby boomers mature to occupy the jobs presently filled with expatriate labor.

Figure 2.3 Points of Origin of the Inhabitants of the Gulf Arab States (2001 Estimate)

| | | Point of Origin | | |
	Native	Indian Ocean Rim	Continental Mid East	Other
Bahrain	45%	24	3	28
Kuwait	24%	53	13	10
Oman	61%	34	1	4
Qatar	28%	49	9	14
Saudi Arabia	42%	48	5	5
UAE	18%	68	10	4

Note: Other includes American, Canadian, European, and Slav.
Source: All estimates are my own and are based on the labor to inhabitant ratio gathered from the local and American government sources.

The exceptions to this are of course the northern, or Iranian and Iraqi, sectors of the Gulf where settlers from the interior of those countries have readily satisfied the need for workers. In Iran, waves of various Iranian nationalities had remade the ethnic composition of the oil and import province of Khuzistan, but particularly its southern coastal region that was known as Arabistan until three generations ago. The new or vastly expanded ports of Abadan, Khomeini (formerly Shahpour), Khurramshahr (formerly Muhammara), and Mahshahr (formerly Ma'shur) contain large numbers of Persians, Azeris, Armenians, Kurds, and other Iranian nationals, in many cases outnumbering the locale Gulfis altogether. In Iraq, the Sunni Arabs and Kurds from central and northern Iraq have filled in whatever labor gap existed in the Basra-Fao area—an otherwise predominantly Shi'i Gulfi community. A large number of Africans brought to work in pre–Gulf War Iraq were from Arabic-speaking North Africa and the interior, and not from East Africa with which the Gulf had a historical connection. These, at any rate, nearly all left Iraq in the aftermath of the Gulf war. The Western expatriate workers in the Iranian and Iraqi sectors of the Gulf have always been negligible numerically, although highly visible in their sensitive expertise and positions.[159]

CURRENT LINGUISTIC, RELIGIOUS AND RACIAL DIVERSITY

It is nearly impossible to find a Gulfi who does not speak at least two languages. A necessity for sea trade, multilingualism has been a tradition in the Gulf. Often it is difficult to determine the native language of a given Gulfi due to the great intermixture of the speakers of various tongues through marriage or intensive exposure. It is very common to find an "Arab" Emirian having a Persian mother and speaking that language as his "mother tongue" but introducing himself as an Arab and speaking Arabic in all but the most intimate discourse at home. This phenomenon is rampant on both sides of the Gulf.

The two major families of languages present in the Gulf basin are Indo-European and Semitic, with each boasting roughly 45 percent of the population. Other language families including Turkic, Bantu, Ethiopic, and Somali, make up the residual population (Map 2.7).

Of the Indo-European group, the Iranic branch is the only one present among the indigenous Gulfis, with the minor exception of the Indic-speaking Liwati and Za'b of Musandam Peninsula and Ras al-Khaimah. A vast number of speakers of the Indic branch are now present as expatriate workers from Pakistan, India, and Bangladesh, dwarfing the older, native Liwati and Za'b in their multitudes.

The speakers of the Iranic languages are primarily the Persians. These, however, might have only barely formed the majority in this linguistic group in the Gulf prior to 1950. Persians are found in dense concentrations in the port cities of the northern Gulf, from Minab in the east to Bandar Abbas, Lingeh, Bushehr, and all the way to Bandar Daylam in the northwest. The countryside between Daylam and Bushehr and between Lingeh and Minab also is primarily Persian speaking. Only between Bushehr and Lingeh do the Arabic speakers predominate. Persian-speaking communities are also found in many islands of the Gulf, dominating the largest (Qeshm) and boasting around a fifth of the native inhabitants of the most populous (Bahrain). The very large Persian presence in the port cities of Khuzistan consists of recent arrivals who should properly be counted as expatriates.

The Baluchi-speakers form the second largest group, predominating in the entire northeast sector of the Gulf, from Minab to Gwadar (and further onward into Pakistan, to the western districts of Las Bela and Karachi). Baluchis are also found in pockets in Oman, from the Musandam peninsula to Muscat. Other Iranic languages, such as the Bashagirdi group (numbering nearly a dozen languages), are found spoken in the north-central Gulf, from Bashagird region to Qeshm and Kumzar in Oman. Others, found only in very small areas, pepper the northern rim of the Gulf, running along the Zagros mountains, but particularly in the county of Laristan.

In contrast to the multiplicity of the Indo-European family, Semitic languages are represented in the Gulf by only two (and very unevenly): Arabic and Aramaic. Arabic is the language most spoken as the first by the native Gulfis, perhaps by twice as many as the second most spoken, Persian. It is the state language in seven out of eight states that now share the Gulf. Only Iran, of course, has Persian as its official language. This Arabic hegemony, however, is of relatively recent date. As late as the mid-seventeenth century, Persian was still the dominant language among the Gulf communities, which is easily attested to by the dearth of Arabic words and wealth of Persian words among the Muslim communities of the Indian Ocean rim.[160] The strong cultural and commercial interaction between these communities and the Gulf, as noted before, ceased afterward. Only East Africa retained its close relationship with the Gulf after the seventeenth century, and there the Arabic influence has largely replaced the older, Persian influence. A cursory review of Swahili language shows an older, more evolved Persian body of vocabulary, superimposed by a newer, less evolved, and pristine Arabic: all telltale signs of the linguistic shift in the Gulf itself after the seventeenth century. The other Semitic language spoken in the Gulf is Aramaic. In the form of its Mandian dialect, it is used by an eponymous ethnic group in the wetlands and marshes of northwestern Gulf, in the Basra and Khuzistan regions.

Among the more exotic languages are those introduced from Africa and the Indian coasts. Representatives of many important African families of languages, such as Bantu,

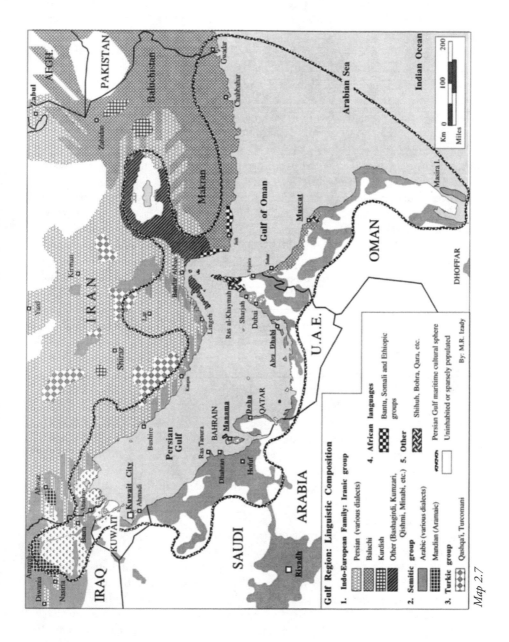

Gulf Region: Linguistic Composition

1. Indo-European Family: Iranic group

Persian (various dialects)

Baluchi

Kurdish

Other (Bashagirdi, Kumzari, Qishmi, Minabi, etc.)

2. Semitic group

Arabic (various dialects)

Mandian (Aramaic)

3. Turkic group

Qashqa'i, Turcomani

4. African languages

Bantu, Somali and Ethiopic groups

5. Other

Shihuh, Bohra, Qara, etc.

Persian Gulf maritime cultural sphere

Uninhabited or sparsely populated

By: M.R. Izady

Map 2.7

Somali, and Ethiopic, are found in compact communities on both sides of the Strait of Hormuz, in Iran, Oman, and the UAE. On the Iranian side, these communities remain relatively isolated and economically undeveloped, allowing for their African culture, language, religion, and genetic makeup to remain pristine. Some African villages there still retain their African names (such as Bunji) or ersatz African names (such as Zangian). Many more Africans were settled in the past centuries as far up the Gulf as Bushehr. Although none is now to be found linguistically African, the African cultural and genetic influence is readily discernible among the population there.[161]

On the Omani and Emirian coasts, these Africans are often referred to by pre-politically correct authors with the epithets "wild" and "fierce."[162] There, these Africans seem to have incorporated a Negrito[163] population from the Malayan archipelago that was settled there prior to or after the arrival of the Africans and south Indians.[164] These have mixed to form the anomalous native groups that predominate in the Musandam peninsula, Ras al-Khaimah, and parts of Sharjah.[165] Further up the Gulf, Africans are also found as villagers on the eastern Qatari coast.

Austranesians and Dravidians are also to be found mixed with the South Arabian/Himyarite elements in the highlands of Dhofar and the adjacent southern Yemen and the island of Socotra. Here, an ancient South Arabian, Himyaritic language, largely incomprehensible to a speaker of modern Arabic, is spoken by a plurality of the people. It is not clear if the Mahra and the Qara who populate the south Arabian coastal regions bordering on the Arabian Sea are also settlers from the period when the island of Madagascar and Natal coast of southern Africa came or were brought to be settled by the Malayo-Indonesians (ca. 500 B.C.), or whether they came later in late medieval times when the contact between the Gulf and Southeast Asia had reached a new height. By their appearance, these are clearly Austranesian peoples,[166] although most now speak Himyari, both in southern Yemen and Dhofari half of Oman. The Qaras predominate in the highlands of Dhofar. Many are also found in Salalah, the provincial capital. The Akhdam, found in the same areas as the Mahra, are Ethiopic and Somali in their culture, but few still speak the language.

There are also to be found many groups of Turkic speakers in the Gulf world, though less so now than centuries earlier. The areas occupied by the Arabic-speaking Chaub in southern Khuzistan were for centuries the domain of the Turcoman tribes of Afshar/Evshar. In the past three centuries, the Afshars of Khuzistan have been totally assimilated to form the composite ancestry of the present-day Arabic-speaking Chaub and Chathir inhabitants of eastern and southern Khuzistan. Turcomans are found in pockets now largely in the Laristan area, in the district of Khonj and the townships of upper, middle, and lower Tarakima ("the Turks"), and just inland from the coast in the district of Kangoon in the county of Bushehr. In Khonj, the Turcoman tribes of Nafar, Inanlu, and Baharlu predominate. The Turkic population of the Tarakima townships are largely Qashqa'i in speech. For centuries, some Qashqa'i tribes of Fars province in Iran have used the warmer regions in the Gulf basin, particularly the hilly regions in the counties of Bushehr and Laristan, for their winter camps, and these are most likely the settled, "Gulfi" Qashqa'is. Their main tribal body, however, remains outside the Gulf world. Above Bandar Abbas toward Kirman are, on the other hand, some smaller Turkic-speaking Turcoman groups, such as the Afshars, Gudari, and Qaragözlu. Like the Qashqa'is in Bushehr and Laristan, these spill over into the Gulf world from a larger concentration of the same tribes in Kirman. In Bahrain and the lower Gulf, many representatives of these Turkic groups are to be found today. None speak Turkic, but they retain their former Turkic clan names as their modern surnames.

Religiously, the Gulf is as diverse as linguistically. Altogether Shi'i Islam boasts the largest Gulf community overall, although both Sunnism and Ibadism lay claim to very large minorities (Map 2.8).[167]

Shi'ism predominates on the coast of Saudi Arabia. It has done so much longer than Persia/Iran has even been Shi'i. The same is true of the Bahrain archipelago, where approximately three-quarters of the population is Shi'i. Both of these two very old Shi'i communities, however, are now ruled by Sunni ruling houses. In the case of Bahrain, the Sunni rulers and their affiliate Najdi bedouins can trace their history of arrival back only to the eighteenth century, as noted above. Their rule over the Shi'is remains viable only through force. The same is true in Saudi Arabia, where Shi'is are unacknowledged nonentities in that officially Wahhabi state. The Iraqi sector of the Gulf is also overwhelmingly Shi'i, with only the desert district of Zubair that borders on Kuwait being Sunni. The Shi'i belt around the upper Persian Gulf that begins at Bahrain continues up into Iraq and down the Iranian coast to Bandar Abbas and Minab on the Strait of Hormuz. Only in two locales is this continuous Shi'i belt that surrounds the Persian Gulf for three-quarters of its circumference broken by the presence of Sunni-majority communities: at Kuwait and Laristan.

The Kuwaiti entity appeared in the largely uninhabited coast that existed between Basra and Hasa.[168] As seen, a small group of Najdi shaikhs took over the tiny fort ("kuwait" is the Arabic diminutive for the Persian "kad/kud/kut/" a fortified town, a fort) on the coast in the mid-eighteenth century. Following the discovery of large oil deposits under Kuwaiti soil in the twentieth century, the area grew by hundreds of thousands of people, deliberately selected to be largely Sunnis by the ruling government of Kuwait. Being sandwiched on three sides by a multitude of Shi'is, Arabic speaking and otherwise, Kuwait would have been a largely Shi'i community just like Iran, Iraq, and the Hasa, had there not be a deliberate attempt to prevent it. As a result, today, Shi'is form only small (and largely unwelcome) minority of the Kuwaiti population.

The Laristan region on the Persian coast of the north-central Gulf is, contrary to Kuwait, a Sunni district of great antiquity. The population is largely Persian speaking, with many other Iranic, Arabic, and Turkic dialects also being spoken. Although a large Shi'i minority exists in Lar (to include all the Turkic speakers in the area), the Sunni, Persian heritage of Lar goes back to the time when Persia/Iran was herself primarily a Shafi'ite Sunni land. The conversion of that country to Shi'ism was completed under the Safavids. But because the Gulf world is outside the cultural and natural realm of the Middle East, the Persian-speaking Gulfis have managed to retain their old Sunni heritage. Nowhere else in Iran/Persia has this been a possibility. Until the time of the Safavids, it was the Persians in the Gulf region who were largely Sunnis (all of the northern coasts of the Gulf) and the Arabs largely Shi'is (from Bahrain to Hasa to Iraq to Khuzistan).

Presently, in addition to Kuwait and Lar, only the sparsely populated UAE and the Qatar peninsula have a Sunni majority in the Gulf. Altogether, Sunnis form no more than 25 percent of the population of the Gulf cultural world, despite the fact that six out of eight governments there are Sunni controlled. In addition to Shi'i Iran, the other non-Sunni-dominated state in the Gulf is, of course, the historic sultanate of Oman. There, the Ibadi form of Islam predominates.[169]

True to form, only the Gulf could have provided the liberal atmosphere for this third branch of Islam to have survived centuries of persecution elsewhere and thrive. As early as A.D. 932, the geographer Jayhâni reports the area to have been predominantly Ibadi.[170] Once found in communities across the length of the Middle East, the Ibadis— known as the *Khariji*, "apostates," to their Sunni and Shi'i adversaries, and the *Ahl al-Surâh*, "People of Rectitude/Frankness" to the fair-minded authors of the time—were

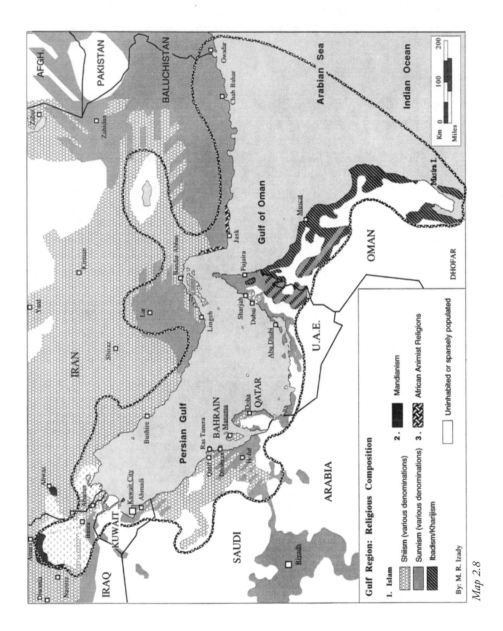

Gulf Region: Religious Composition

1. Islam

☐ Shiism (various denominations)

☐ Sunnism (various denominations)

☐ Ibadism/Kharijism

2. ☐ Mandianism

3. ☐ African Animist Religions

☐ Uninhabited or sparsely populated

By: M. R. Izady

Map 2.8

hunted down to extinction everywhere else in the Middle East. They have survived only "outside" the Middle East: in the Vale of Mzab oasis in the heart of the Sahara Desert of Algeria and the Gulf. The Omani community of Ibadis is far greater in number than the Mzabite community of the Sahara. While the Ibadis of Mzab have always felt under siege by the non-Ibadi Muslims around them, the Omani Ibadis have lived a peaceful, organic life with other Gulfis of various ilk for centuries, stretching to the present day.

Not all of Oman of course, is Ibadi in religion. In the detached Musandam peninsula, mainstream Sunnis are found alongside Ibadis and Shi'is in the towns and countryside. In the peninsula, however, the traditional African practices and the remnants of Hinduism are found alongside Islam, being practiced by the Shihus and the Za'b. West of the Jebel Akhdar mountains facing the Empty Quarter of Saudi Arabia, Wahhabi Sunnis predominate among the Bedouin tribes of that sparsely populated region. In Dhofar, the Qaras in the highlands likewise remain mainly African animists with a thin Islamic veil covering their African and other animistic beliefs. On the coasts, Islam of both Sunni and Ibadi forms has the stronger hold.

The Mandians of the Basran and Khuzistan wetlands are, like the Ibadis of Oman, a case study in traditional tolerance found in the Gulf world. Known as the Sabaeans to the ancients (and mentioned in the Koran as one of the five "Peoples of the Book"), Mandians were once numerous in the Middle East. With the draining of the wetlands by the Iraqi state in the past few decades,[171] the survival of the Mandians is now being seriously threatened after 2,000 years of residence in their last refuge. Many have dispersed into the southern Iraqi cities. It is too soon to declare them finished, but their chances of survival have been drastically compromised.[172]

The Jewish and Christian communities of the Gulf are nearly extinct, particularly the Christians. As already noted, however, Christianity and Judaism were spread by the Gulfis aboard their vessels to the Malabar coast of South India, Southeast Asia, and southern China. There exist remnants of these two communities in all those locales, but no longer in the Gulf itself. The Christians seem to have ceased to exist by the end of the seventeenth century along with the once thriving Zoroastrian community on the northern coast. The Gulfi Jews left for Israel after the creation of that state. The Christian, Jewish, and Zoroastrian communities of the Gulf at present are all expatriates.

The practice of Zâr, or "voodoo," in the Gulf is of particular interest. It is a part of the animistic beliefs of the native African community of the Gulf, but has spread among many Muslim communities as well. From Bushehr to the borders of Pakistan, Zâr is a part of the folk faith-healing among the Persians, Arabs, and particularly the Baluch, in addition to the Gulf Africans.[173]

CONCLUSION

Far from being a creation of the petroleum industry and an unstable community of nouveaux riches, the Gulf boasts an ancient and dazzling history of multicultural, entrepreneurial, and internationalist grandeur marked by astonishing stability. Nor is the Gulf's predominant urban culture with glittering port-states a new phenomenon fueled by oil. Ancient and medieval "glittering" port-states such as Siraf, Oboleh, Hormuz, Tiz, and Suhar are just the forebears of the likes of modern Kuwait City, Manama, Dubai, and Muscat. Gulfi affiliates around the Indian Ocean rim, from Zanzibar and Mombassa to Malaya and Brunei offer prosperous modern evidence of the old Gulf international connections and influence. The modern glittering shopping malls of Dubai, Sharjah, Abu Dhabi, Kish, Manama, and the like are just a modern version of what centuries ago the commercial centers such as Hormuz, Cong, Cameron, Basra, Siraf, Khat/Qatif, Suhar, and Muscat must have looked like.

At a closer look, even the judicious international investment portfolios of the Gulfis' newfound wealth is reminiscent of their former astute business tradition. Even in bringing the United States to help in their defense, the Gulfis are just repeating what they used to do when threatened by local Middle Eastern powers centuries ago: invite in and pay faraway powers to ensure their survival.

The hyperdiversity of the Gulf inhabitants is in itself a matter of celebration rather than concern. Having drastically reduced the number of Middle Eastern expatriate laborers in favor of Asians and Africans, the Gulf is as stable socially as anywhere else. There is nothing that binds the diverse expatriate workers together except for their expatriate working status in the Gulf. They belong to myriad ethnolinguistic groups, nationalities, religions, and cultures, from nearly every corner of the earth. In their overwhelming multitude, they have in fact imparted a sense of solidarity to the native Gulfis. The Gulfis' shrinking share of the total population of their states has necessitated binding together the native Gulf elements in order to maintain their cumulative leading position at the helm of their own respective countries.

Except for Saudi Arabia where, just as in Iran and Iraq, the Gulfis have been incorporated into a much larger non-Gulf state and form a discontented Shi'i minority in the staunchly Wahhabi society, everywhere else stability and moderation of action are and will continue to be the hallmarks of the Gulf's society and politics. The wealth and freedom of commercial action have not created a new Gulf but revived what the Gulf and Gulf society used to be.

NOTES

1. An episode of intermarriage between the fair-haired Christian men taken captive from an invading Ottoman army in the nineteenth century and the Arab Dhafiri Bedouin tribe (in modern Saudi Arabia's Gulf coastal area) is a good example of the ease with which the people in the Gulf basin intermarried. The descendants of these marriages remain known as the Ansârs ("Christians"), although they seem to be now Muslim in faith, while retaining their lighter complexion. See B. Ingham, *Arabia: Traditions of the Al-Dhafir* (London: Kegan Paul, 1986).

2. The third, bona fide branch of Islam after Sunnism and Shi'ism, Ibadism survives today mainly in Oman and in the heart of the Sahara Desert. For more detail, refer to notes 169 and 170, below.

3. John Middleton, *The World of the Swahili, An African Mercantile Civilization* (New Haven: Yale, 1992), p. 12.

4. Middle East is defined here as the area bounded by Egypt, Iran, Turkey, and Yemen on its four cardinal directions.

5. B. Ingham is confounded to note in his study of the linguistic geography of the head of the Gulf that "Although not an easy statement to substantiate, it seems that in many ways communications between the Persian coast of the Gulf and the Arab side are easier than between the Persian coast and the interior of Iran." The reverse should have been a matter of concern, as can be seen in this study. (Bruce Ingham, "Ethno-linguistic links between southern Iraq and Khuzistan," in K. McLachlan, ed., *The Boundaries of Modern Iran* (London: UCL Press, 1994), p. 98.)

6. The Strait of Hormuz is geographically defined to be the sea passage bound at the entrance by a line running from Cape Kuh on the Iranian coast of Baluchistan to Cape Diba, north of Fujairah, UAE. The exit is bound by a line connecting Cape Shaikh Mas'ud in Musandam (Oman) to the island of Hengam (Iran). The narrower

Clarence/Khusran Strait (between the island of Qeshm and the Iranian coast) is geographically a part of the marine passageway designated as the Strait of Hormuz.

7. Both Dena and Zardakuh are high and cold enough to support extensive permanent glacier fields, forming a formidable barrier between the Iranian plateau and the Gulf basin.

8. Failing to obtain the needed expeditionary fleet from the Gulf merchants, Nadir Shah was forced to construct his own by transporting lumber at great expense from the Caspian forests to the Gulf. The short Iranian occupation of portions of Oman and the Julfâr coast (present UAE) ceased immediately after his assassination in 1747. The name "Ras al-Khaimah" (Cape Tents) apparently designates where the Afsharid forces under admiral Latif Khan maintained a makeshift tent headquarters.

9. Hormice C. Perumalil and E. R. Hambye, eds., *Christianity in India* (1973).

10. The medieval Gujarati-language *Qisa-i-Senjan* ("The Tale of Senjan") records the history of this Zoroastrian migration from the Gulf coast to India.

11. Abu'l-Qâsim b. Ahmad Jayhâni, *Ashkâl al-'Âlam,* ed. F. Mansuri (written ca. A.D. 932). Only the original Persian trans. by 'Abd al-Salâm al-Kâtib is extant (Mashhad: Astan-i Quds, 1990), pp. 120–21.

12. Jayhâni declares Siraf to be the richest city in the entire land of Fars (*Ashkâl,* p. 58).

13. Abu-Is'hâq Istakhri, *Masâlik wa'l-Mamâlik,* the original eleventh century Persian translation, ed. I. Afshar (Tehran: Ilmi, 1989), p. 121.

14. Fallen first to strong earthquakes, Siraf was taken over by the emirs of Kish sometime in the middle of the 11th century. Ibn Balkhi in his *Fârsnâma* (finished in A.D. 1116) gives details of this along with a brief but unique account of the political and commercial rivalry between the two Gulf ports in the eleventh century. (Ibn Balkhi, *Fârsnâma,* ed. A. Behrouzi (Shiraz, 1343/1964), pp. 179–80.

15. Muslih al-Din Sa'di, *Gulistân,* ed. M.A. Foroughi and A. Gharib (Tehran: Iqbal, 1983), chapter "On the Virtue of Contentment," pp. 98–99.

16. An Islamic shariah term, meaning divinely forbidden. It is not clear to what "forbidden" thing Fansuri is referring. It cannot be mercantilism, since the Prophet Muhammad himself and his wife Khadija were both merchants. A Sufi master himself, he may consider the obsession with worldly assets that prompted this ceaseless business traveling to be detrimental to the true faith.

17. Hamzah Fansuri, *Asrâr al-'arifin,* in Naquib Al-Attas, *The Mysticism of Hamzah Fansuri* (Kuala Lumpur, University of Malay Press, 1970), the Malay text, poems pp. 94–96.

18. There are terms that outsiders used and use to refer to all Gulf people together as a group. In Iran they are called the *Bandari,* which in Persian means "those of the sea ports." The term *Swâhili,* meaning "those of the sea coasts," is the Arabic counterpart to the Persian term for the Gulfis. The same name is still being applied to the communities in East Africa established and developed by the Gulfis, namely the Swahili language and people.

19. Sharaf al-Zamân Tâhir Marwazi even makes note of a colony of Shi'i refugees from the Umayyad persecutions populating an island in the Pearl River, south of Canton. *China, the Turks and India,* ed., Vladimir Minorsky (London, 1942), viii.16.

20. And for Muslims in general, in the first Islamic century.

21. In A.D. 932, Jayhâni provides a valuable early report on the Bahrân/Bahrain coast and its society: "Bahrain is a district of Najd, with its capital at Hajar. It produces plenty of fruits . . . many dates and has plenty of springs. It is located on the coast of the Persian Gulf. Most of its inhabitants are Carmathians, may God's curse be upon them. It has plenty of villages and the tribe of Mudhir is found there. After Mecca and Medina, no city in Arabia is larger than Hajar" (*Ashkâl,* p. 46). A valuable eyewitness account of this process is provided by the traveler, geographer, and Isma'ili propagandist, Nasir Khusraw (d. 1088), who visited Bahrân and the neighboring regions (1046 to 1052), in his *Safarnâma.*

22. The geographical name Bahrân is of pre-Islamic origin. The city of Hagar/Hajar served as its Sasanian provincial seat (J. Marquart, *Erânshahr nach der Geographie des Ps. Moses Xorenac'i* [Berlin, 1901], p. 42; Anon., *Shatrastânhâ-i Erân,* ¶ 52, ed. J. Markwart/Marquart (Rome,

1931), ¶ 52). The Bahrain archipelago itself was known as Der to the Sasanian sources and Dârin to the early Islamic writers. The Qatar peninsula (formerly an island) was the Sasanian Meshmahik (Marquart, 1901:43). The Shi'i majority inhabitants of Bahrain still call themselves the Bahrâni ("Bahârna" in the Arabic broken plural form). See Henny Harald Hansen, *Investigations in a Shi'a Village in Bahrain* (Copenhagen: The National Museum of Denmark Ethnographic Series, Vol. XII, 1968), p. 22. Those of Hasâ/Ahsâ and Qatif (on the Saudi coast) seem to have largely ceased using the term at present. As late as the 1950s, however, the population in Qatif and Hufuf still called themselves the Bahrâni/Bahârana. See James H. D. Belgrave, *Welcome to Bahrain,* 3 ed. (Manama, 1957), 37; and R. Hay, *Sultanate and Imamate in Oman.* A Chatham House Memorandum (London, 1959), p. 91. The name of the island nation of Bahrain is a derivative of this old geographical name, and not the Arabic compound *bahrain,* "two seas," as is often maintained today.

23. A rather short manual by an anonymous traveler, *The Periplus Maris Erythraei,* "Roundabout the Indian Ocean" provides a concise description of trading ports in the Indian Ocean basin, including East Africa and the Persian Gulf. See *The Periplus Maris Erythraei,* trans. and ed. Lionel Casson (Princeton: Princeton University Press, 1989).

24. *Periplus,* p. 38

25. Richard Reusch, *History of East Africa* (New York: Ungar, 1961), pp. 33, 49.

26. The pre-Islamic Persian sources (as well as the early Islamic Arabic sources) record the name in its metathetic form as Badhrangi.

27. Population movement induced by the Gulfis was not restricted to in and out of the Gulf basin. It is fascinating to note that arrival in Madagascar of the Malay-Indonesian people, who dominate that island to the present day, is traceable to the period of brisk trade and settlements introduced by the Gulfis in the area and documented in the *Periplus.* The first arrival of the Malayo-Indonesians on the island dates to the first century A.D. Their route passed southern Oman and Hadhramawt, where many groups with Austranesian connection still remain today, and the East African coast. P. Verin, *The History of Civilization in Madagascar* (1986).

28. In many Iranic languages, a dark-complexioned person is still referred to as *siyah Barzangi,* "black African," i.e., using the older, more complete form of the name, not in the truncated form of "Zangi/Zanji."

29. The prince's name is a Parthian one. This may be a telltale sign of a close association of the region with the Parthian Federation that the Sasanians under king Ardasher had just overthrown in A.D. 226.

30. J. Markwart/Marquart, *A Catalogue of the Provincial Capitals of Eranshahr, Pahlavi Text, Version and Commentary* (Rome, 1931), p. 103.

31. Ibid.

32. For a review of the Sasanian engagement in the Gulf and Indian Ocean commerce see David Whitehouse and Andrew Williams, "Sasanian Maritime Trade," *Iran* 11 (1973), pp. 29–49.

33. It is at this time that the Sasanian sources make the unique reference to the Persian Gulf as the Gulf of the Arabs. "[King] Ardasher appointed Oshak as the margrave of Hagar in the Gulf of the Arabs." Anon., *Shatrastânhâ-i Erân,* ¶ 52, ed. J. Markwart (Rome, 1931). Hagar served as the capital of the Sasanian province of Bahrân.

34. Gervase Mathew, "The East African Coast until the Coming of the Portuguese," in Roland Oliver and Gervase Mathew, eds., *History of East Africa* (Oxford: Oxford University Press, 1963), p. 99.

35. The cultural remains include Zoroastrian fire temples in East Africa, and possibly in southern China in the Pearl River delta. Sasanian sources, including rock inscriptions and textual records, speak of the Barzangi house having served an important Zoroastrian function as custodians of the great temple of the goddess Anahita at Stakhr/Persepolis. It is hard to believe that such religious vestiges were not transplanted by the Barzangis to their East African domains.

36. The rather scanty numismatic evidence on exhibit at the Beit al-Amani Museum at Zanzibar city is evidence of this split. The museum holdings include four Parthian and one

Sasanian piece from the mint at Ctesiphon. The Sasanian piece is that of Ardasher I, the founder of the dynasty. No numismatic evidence for the subsequent 430 years of Sasanian rule after Ardasher has been found so far in the Barzangi-dominated East Africa. All this, nonetheless, gave a definite Iranic coloring to the earlier maritime trade in the Indian Ocean which is apparent in the archaeological remains.

37. Procopius, *History of the Wars,* trans. and ed., H. B. Dewing (Cambridge: Harvard Loeb Classics, 1932, reprint 1992), I.xx.11–12.

38. Whitehouse and Williamson, 1973: 44. Also, S. Smith, "Events in Arabia in the Sixth Century A.D.," *BSOAS* xvi (1954), pp. 425–68.

39. The Egyptian author Cosmas writes of the island state of Ceylon/Sri Lanka: " . . . the island has also a church of Persian Christians who have settled there, and a Presbyter who is appointed from Persia, and a Deacon, and all the apparatus of public worship . . ." Cosmas Indicopleustes, *Christian Topography,* ed. Montfaucon, in Migne, *Patrologia Gaeca* LXXXVIII, p. 336–38, trans. J. W. McCrindle (London: Hakluyt, vol. xcviii, 1897), p. 366.

40. Alphonse Mingana, "The Early Spread of Christianity in India," *Bulletin of the John Rylands Library* X (1926), p. 455.

41. "Ishoyahb's letter to Simon, metropolitan of Rev Ardeshir," in O'Braun, *Corpus Scriptorum Christianorum Orientalium: Scriptores Syri* II.xii.182.

42. J. Marquart, 1901: p. 42.

43. In response to these attacks from the interior, the East Africa ports, including those on the islands off the coast, hurriedly threw up strong stone protective walls. These became the standard "stone towns" that are still the hallmark of the region. The most important of these to survive is found at Manda on the Kenyan coast, dating to the ninth century, with stone blocks weighing up to a ton. Even in these hard-pressed times, Manda was maintaining close trading connections with the Gulf, with the grand port of Siraf near modern Bushehr its main trading partner. These African stone towns were ruled by powerful local merchant families that were hybrids of the Gulfis and the emergent local elite, with an increasing Yemenite element occurring toward the north.

44. Under attacks from the native population, the Barzangis met a violent end in East Africa when their capital of Kilwa fell and nearly 2,000 of its inhabitants were eaten by the native attackers. The Periplus had aptly named that coast as the land of the "Anthropophagea" a thousand years earlier.

45. For an account of the Hadhrami participation and contribution to the Indian Ocean mercantile world, see Ulrike Freitag and William G. Clarence-Smith, eds., *Hadhrami Traders, Scholars and Statesmen in the Indian Ocean, 1750s–1960s* (Leiden: Brill, 1997). This work needs to be treated with care, as it attempts to place the sparsely populated, resource-limited Hadhramawt ("Abode of Death") near the center of the mercantile world of the Indian Ocean, by discounting the paramount contribution and the leading role of the Gulfis, as well as the Southeast Asians, southern Chinese, coastal Indians, and East Africans.

46. Reusch, pp. 91–215; Mathew, pp. 102–106.

47. Reusch, p. 107.

48. Broken plural of the Arabic *sahil,* "coast," describing the area from Lindi to Mombassa and Malindi on the Tanzanian and Kenyan coasts.

49. The ivory of hippopotamus tusks is ideally suited for inlay work, being whiter and less prone to splitting than elephant ivory, and was most desired by the workshops of the Middle East.

50. Lidio Cipriani, *The Andaman Islanders,* ed. and trans. by D. Tayler Cox (1966); Vishvajit Pandya, *Above the Forest: A Study of Andamanese Ethnoanemology, Cosmology, and the Power of Ritual* (1993); A. R. Radcliffe-Brown, *The Andaman Islanders* (1922; repr. 1964).

51. The resulting Negrito population of Andaman, Nicobar (now extinct), Malaysia, Philippines, and New Guinea. The Negrito's physical traits include a male height of under five feet, dark brown to jet black skin, tightly curled or frizzy black hair, and full lips, all pointing to the direction of Africa. These traits are unique in Southeast Asia and not found in any other group in the region. See I. H. N. Evans, *The Negritos of Malaya* (1968).

52. In A.D. 932, Jayhâni reports of the inhabitants of Shahar, the capital of Mahra/Dhofar, to be speakers of "non-Arab tongues ('*Ajami*)" (*Ashkâl,* pp. 50–51).

53. In 1964 and prior to the flood of expatriate workers, S. Bruk and V. Apenchenko linguistically classify and enumerate the following for the ethnolinguistic groups in the British colony of Aden (subsequently, South Yemen) in a total population of 1,210,000: Arabic 1,100,000; Indic (Gujarati, Punjabi, Hindi/Urdu) 30,000, Somali 27,000; Bantu, 15,000; Malayo-Polynesian, 2,000; Hebrew 2,000; and Iranic (Persian), 1,000. For Oman, in a total of 565,000, they list: Arabic, 500,000; Iranic (Baluchi, 20,000; Persian, 15,000); Indic (Hindi/Urdu, Sindhi, 10,000; Gypsy 2,000); and Bantu, 10,000. For Trucial Oman (subsequently, the United Arab Emirates), in a total of 85,000, they list: Arabic, 75,000; Iranic (Persian, 3,000; Baluchi, 2,000); Bantu, 2,000; Indic, 1,000. For Qatar, in a total of 55,000: Arabic 45,000; Bantu, 6,000; Persian, 1,000. For Bahrain, in a total of 152,000: Arabic, 130,000; Persian, 9,000; Indic (undefined), 4,000. *Atlas Narodov Mira* (Moscow: Akademii Nauk, 1964), pp. 161, 163, 164. On the greater Yemen (the present-day republic of Yemen), the *Encyclopaedia Britannica* (s.v., Yemen, "the People") provides the following ethnolinguistic classification: "Ethnic minorities include the Mahra, a people of possibly Australian origin who occupy the eastern border areas of former South Yemen (as well as the island of Socotra) and who speak a variant of the ancient Himyaritic language. In the (northern) Tihamah, immigrations from Ethiopia and Somalia have occurred since World War II. There is a clear African admixture in a distinct social group known as the Akhdam, who perform menial tasks; some anthropologists consider this group the closest thing to a caste in Yemen. In the far north, there are still small remnants of Jewish communities, while in the area of Aden and the eastern regions of the former South Yemen there are distinct Indonesian as well as Indian elements in the population (attributable to economic and political ties extending back over two millennia)."

54. See, e.g., Jayhâni, *Ashkâl,* p. 58 and p. 138.

55. Etymologically, Jât is an evolution of Zutt.

56. *Encyclopaedia Britannica,* s.v., Oman, "the People." In 1964 Bruk and Apenchenko (*Atlas,* p. 165) count two thousand Indic-speaking "gypsies" for Oman.

57. This area of China still contains, perhaps, a third of the Muslim Chinese population. The pre-Revolution figures, provided largely by Western Christian missionaries, breaks down the Muslim population into the northern (Middle East–influenced) and southern (Gulf-influenced) groups. Samuel Zwemer in 1908 gives a breakdown of 3,500,000 southern Chinese Muslims against 15,100,000 northern ones, excluding Chinese Turkistan/Xinjiang (*The Moslem World* [New York: Presbyterian Board of Foreign Missions, 1908], p. 91). The southern Chinese Muslims include adherents from the dominant Han, but also the Miao, Yao, and various Yunanise groups.

58. Whitehouse and Williamson, 1973: p. 46.

59. Ibid.

60. A very valuable economic history of the Gulfis' involvement in the Indian Ocean prior to modern times is K. N. Chaudhuri, *Trade and Civilization in the Indian Ocean: An Economic History from the Rise of Islam to 1750* (1985).

61. Cesar Majul, *Muslims in Philippines* (Quezon City: University of Philippines Press, 1973), *passim;* B. H. M. Vlekke, *Nusantara: A History of the East Indian Archipelago,* rev. ed. (1959).

62. The examples are many. The names of the Malabar coast of India and the Nicobar islands off Burma parallel Zangibar/Zanzibar off Africa. The Palawan islands in the Philippines is likewise a Gulf nomenclature. It is fascinating to note that the older, largely geographical names are Iranic, while the newer, family names are Semitic (Arabic) in their majority.

63. Kurdish Naqshbandi Sufi preachers found their way in large numbers all over the commercial network of the Gulfis at this time. From Dutch Indonesia to German East Africa and British Somalia and Kenya, Kurdish Naqshbandi Sufi masters met with an extraordinary success in conversion. Their impact and association last to this day.

64. Many Gulfi females were obliged to marry the native revolutionary leaders to gain safety for their families to remain and work in the Zanzibar archipelago.

65. Having rashly revealed their true identity when unexpectedly encountering representatives of the ancient Nestorian Christians of the Malabar coast, they were quickly discovered for who they really were.

66. The unquestionably best source on this first epoch-making voyage by da Gama remains the journal by an unknown eyewitness to the voyage. See E. G. Revenstein, trans. and ed., *A Journal (by an Unknown Writer) of the First Voyage of Vasco da Gama, 1497–1499* (1898; repr. 1963). Also, Gaspar Correa, *The Three Voyages of Vasco da Gama, and His Viceroyalty,* ed. Lord Stanley of Alderley (1869; repr. 1963); Henry Hart, *Sea Road to the Indies* (1950; repr. 1971); and G. K., Jayne, *Vasco da Gama and His Successors, 1460–1580* (1910).

67. Da Gama had shown that the fastest and easiest way to round Africa was to sail southwest from Portugal to enter and benefit from the south Atlantic, counterclockwise ocean currents. This would of course bring one to a stone's throw of the as-yet undiscovered South America. Cabral tried to follow da Gama's method. However, he sailed too far westward, which brought him to land on the Brazilian coast of South America on April 22, 1500, which he duly claimed for Portugal. From Brazil, he sailed southeast, crossing the Cape of Good Hope, and entered the Indian Ocean. (William B. Greenlee, *The Voyage of Pedro Alvarez Cabral to Brazil and India* [1938]).

68. The Portuguese and Spanish caravels were replicas of the Gulf dhows, in general proportions and particularly their sails. Columbus's three caravels are examples of this. The invention of the lateen sail in the Gulf and its introduction into the Mediterranean in the ninth century revolutionized sea transport. By the virtue of their speed and tonnage, the Gulf craft were superior to the European ships that faced them at the beginning of the sixteenth century. By hull flexibility—dhows could be beached without any damage—the Gulf craft were far more adept at port calls where no natural harbor or port facilities were available. They can anchor—in fact, "land"—on ordinary sandy beaches. Such was not a possibility with the rigid-hull caravels. It was in the field of maneuverability (due to the Nordic rudder) and longer range of their firepower that the European warships surpassed those of the Gulf.

69. For a short but thorough review of the history of the native artillery and other firearms in the basin of the Indian Ocean, see Anthony Reid, 1993, pp. 219–33.

70. The superiority of range and maneuverability over the native artillery was best demonstrated by Vasco da Gama himself. On his second voyage he engaged and destroyed every opposing fleet he encountered. In the waters between the Laccadive islands and the Malabar coast, his artillery sunk a fleet made up of the Gulfis, Gujaratis, and the Malabaris without sustaining any serious damage to his fleet. He kept his distance from the native warships far enough to bombard them, but remained outside the range of their artillery. The same came to be repeated at various ports and in various naval engagements, from Hormuz to Manila, from Malacca to Mombassa.

71. Pierre-Yves Manguin, "The Vanishing Jong: Insular Southeast Asian Fleets in Trade and War: 15th–17th Centuries," in Anthony Reid, ed., *Southeast Asia in the Early Modern Era* (Ithaca: Cornell University Press, 1993), pp. 197–213.

72. Pierre-Yves Manguin, "Late Medieval Asian Shipbuilding in the Indian Ocean: A Reappraisal," in *Moyen Orient et Océan Indien* 2, ii (1985), pp. 1–30.

73. For a valuable treatment of the history of the emirate of Hormuz until the arrival of the Portuguese, see Jean Aubin, "Les princes d'Ormuz du xiie au xve siècle," *Journal Asiatique* 241 (1953), pp. 77–141. The article also contains Persian extracts of Muhammad Shabânkâr'i, *Majma' al-ansâb,* treating the later history of the emirate of Hormuz to the fifteenth century

74. R. S. Whiteway, *The Rise of Portuguese Power in India, 1497–1550,* 2d ed. (1967).

75. Returning to Europe, Almeida attempted to gain one more victory for Portugal over the Gulfis by defeating the forces of their ally, the sultan of Mozambique. He lost his life in an encounter with the Khoikhoin warriors on March 1, 1510.

76. The strategic port of Malacca north of Singapore that commanded the commerce of the Malayo-Indonesian archipelago and the passage into the South China Sea was taken in 1511. Most of the rest of the Gulf outposts in Southeast Asia followed suit in the course of the following year, beginning with the fall of the Moluccas (or the "Spice Islands," to

include Ambon, Buru, and Ceram) in 1512. The outpost at Macao at the mouth of the Pearl and opposite the paramount Chinese port of Guangzhu/Canton—where Gulfis had been present since the sixth century–was taken in 1513. Among the major ports, only the Sultanate of Brunei (on Borneo) and the Sultanate of Aceh (on Sumatra) survived this initial Portuguese onslaught, and thus flourished as the most powerful local entities well into the second half of the seventeenth century. Only by 1888 did Brunei need to acknowledge European suzerainty in the shape of a British protectorate. Aceh never did.

Now a small oil-rich nation on Borneo island, Brunei remains an extension of the Gulf world in many astonishing respects. As in the Gulf states, over 40 percent of the population of Brunei are hired expatriate workers who are systematically denied—as in the Gulf—assimilation into that society through citizenship. (See, D. S. R. Singh, *Brunei, 1839–1983* (1984); N. Tarling, *Britain, the Brookes, and Brunei* (1971); D. J. M., Tate, *The Making of Modern Southeast Asia,* 2 vols. (1977–79). The same is true of Malaysia (30 percent Chinese, 20 percent Indian, and other expatriates), and Singapore, 95 percent Chinese expatriates. Although the number of expatriates in Indonesia is small (5 percent and shrinking), it has caused many ethnic riots there nonetheless.

77. 'Abbâs Iqbâl Âshtiyâni, *Târikh-i mufassal-i Irân* (Tehran: 1940), p. 678.

78. Colin McEvedy, *The Penguin Atlas of Modern History* (New York: Penguin, 1972), pp. 16–17. Albuquerque originally tried to control the Red Sea–Gulf of Aden outlet as well by taking the port of Aden. The desolate island of Socotra at the entrance of the Gulf of Aden proved too desiccated to support even an outpost there. The main cause for abandoning the idea, however, was an age-old one: prior to construction of the Suez Canal, little commercial traffic used the Red Sea route, so it was not worth the cost of fighting to establish and defend a series of outposts in the Red Sea–Gulf of Aden basin.

79. For a good review of the events, see C. R. Boxer, *The Portuguese Seaborne Empire* (1969); K. M. Matthew, *History of the Portuguese Navigation in India* (1987); and particularly, S. Subrahmanyam, *The Portuguese Empire in Asia* (1993).

80. Located five miles east of Lingeh, Cong was for long the main port of the area before the rise of Lingeh in the past three centuries. A. Faraji et al., eds., *Jughrafiya-i mufassal-i Iran* ("A Detailed Geography of Iran"), (Tehran: Shirkat-i chap u nashri-i Iran, 1988), vol. 2, p. 1251. For general historical purposes, the two ports may be treated as one.

81. *Cambridge History of Iran* (1986), vol. 6, p. 381.

82. Iqbâl Âshtiyâni, ch. 13, *passim.* As Iqbâl puts it, two factors had led to this Portuguese blunder. One was the ease with which the stupendous initial victories were gained. It falsely convinced them of the Gulfis' military inferiority as much as their own seemingly invincible navy and politics. They saw no need to share anything with the former masters of the Indian Ocean trade, nor did they regard them worth the worry. This quickly proved to be an illusion. Second was the inexperience, incompetence, and corruption of the Portuguese governors who took over at Goa and the affairs of their Indian Ocean possessions after the death of the able Afonso de Albuquerque in 1515.

83. The Portuguese kept their stronghold at East Timor for centuries afterward, until the 1970s.

84. A freak incident in 1580 had, meanwhile, placed the Spanish king on the throne of Portugal as well, making a rivalry even less necessary. Philip II of Spain had claimed and obtained the Portuguese crown in 1580 after the death of King Sebastian in Lisbon. This Portuguese-Spanish crown merger lasted until 1648. Despite this merger, the Spanish and Portuguese commercial and political elite, and thus their overseas empires, remained legally and actually distinct throughout the period of their crown union.

85. W. P. Coolhaas, *A Critical Survey of Studies in Dutch Colonial History* (1960).

86. Iqbâl Âshtiyâni, p. 678.

87. Ibid.

88. Ibid., p. 679.

89. See note 84 above. Although Spain and Portugal remained commercially distinct throughout their crown union, Spain did speak for Portugal's interests diplomatically.

90. One of the best sources of information on the Portuguese involvement in the Gulf and the Indian Ocean remains the classic by Charles D. Ley, ed., *Portuguese Voyages, 1498–1663* (1947; repr. 1977).

91. By now, Shah Abbas had vanquished all his foreign enemies and was at the height of power.

92. Some years earlier in 1607 and 1608, the Dutch had attacked and looted the gold-rich port of Sofala in Mozambique with little opposition from the Portuguese or the Gulf fleet.

93. Jean Aubin, "Les princes d'Ormuz du xiie au xve siècle," *passim.*

94. See note 6 above.

95. Among the British left dead by the assault on Qeshm lay William Baffin, the celebrated navigator who piloted two expeditions searching for the "Northwest Passage" around the top of North America. Baffin Bay and Baffin Island in northern Canada are named after him.

96. Iqbâl Âshtiyâni, p. 684.

97. Accounts of Armenian merchants of Isfahan breaking into the Indian Ocean trade for the first time at this occasion are illuminating. Alien to the commerce of the southern seas, the Armenians were filling the shoes of the Gulfi merchants—from southern India to the Philippines and East Africa—who had momentarily lost their position or lives to the Safavid onslaught. For a brief but useful history see G. Bournoutian, *A History of the Armenian People* (Costa Mesa, California: Mazda, 1994), vol. 2, ch. 14.

98. Among the most famous are Hamzah Fansuri, Syamsuddin (Shamsuddin) Samatrani, Nurruddin Raniri, and Abdurra'uf Singkili.

99. The Burmese, particularly those from the coastal south and specifically the city of Pegu.

100. From the Dutch word *bodermerij,* it is a contract by which a ship is hypothecated as security for repayment of a loan at the end of a successful voyage.

101. Anthony Reid, *Southeast Asia in the Age of Commerce: 1450–1680* (New Haven: Yale University Press, 1988–93), vol. 2, pp. 66–67.

102. The best source is David Bulbeck, "A Tale of Two Kingdoms: The Historical Archeology of Gowa and Tallock, South Sulawesi, Indonesia," a doctoral dissertation, Department of History, ANU, Canberra, Australia, 1992. Other sources include Charles Boxer, *Francisco Vieira de Fiueiredo: A Portuguese Merchant-Adventurer in Southeast Asia, 1624–1667* (The Hague: Nijhoff, 1967).

103. Adrian Vickers, *Bali: A Paradise Created* (Ringwood, NSW, Australia: Penguin, 1989), 46–53. Also, see "Thomas Dias, Letter from Melaka, 18 November 1684," in F. de Haan, "Naar midden Sumatra in 1684," *Tijdschrift voor Indische Taal* 39 (1897): pp. 336–57.

104. Some lines from an Acehnese epic, *Hikayat Pojut Muhamat,* succinctly summarize this Gulfi dictum across the commercial world of the Indian Ocean:

> While you stay here in the palace, my Lord, [the rival] Jumaloy Alam is in Kampung Java . . .
> My Lord collects the dues on the forest products: ten percent of the resin, ten percent of rattan,
> And when the vegetable-grower has harvested well, he brings to you onions and ginger.
> The duties on the sea commerce is collected meanwhile by Jumaloy Alam;
> And he rakes in, over and over again, thousands upon thousands of bahars.
> My Lord is content when he has enough to eat; he does not pursue riches

The sultan of Aceh who is addressed by these pointed lines seems to have taken note. His sultanate became one of the most successful trading partners in the Gulfis' commercial oceanic alliance. Pocut Muhamat, *Hikayat Potjut Muhamat: An Acehnese Epic,* trans. G. W. J. Dewers (The Hague: Nijhoff, 1980), pp. 60–61.

105. For a review of the role and history of the Gulf Persian elements in Siam and the neighboring Southeast Asian states, see Jean Aubin, "Les Persan au Siam sous le regne de Narai (1656–1688)," *Mare Luso-Indicom* 4 (1980).

106. David Wyatt, "Family Politics in Seventeenth- and Eighteenth-Century Siam," Papers for a conference on Thai studies in honor of William J. Gedney (1986), as noted in Anthony Reid (op. cit., 1988–93), vol. 2, p.121.

107. The French ambassador was impressed by the magnificence of one of their houses, which he was allotted in 1685 after the owner had been disgraced (Jean Aubin, 1980: p. 124).

108. Hamzah Fansuri, *Asrâr al-'arifin*, in Naquib Al-Attas, *The Mysticism of Hamzah Fansuri* (Kuala Lumpur: University of Malaya Press, 1971), the English text. As his name implies, Fansuri's roots were from the port city of Fansur in Java.

109. Bukhari al-Jawhari, *Tâj al-salâtin*, ed. Khalid Hussain (Kuala Lumpur: Dewan Bahasa dan Pustaka, 1966). A French translation is available by Aristide Marra, *Makhota radja-radja, ou la couronne des rois* (Paris, 1878).

110. Anthony Reid, 1993: p. 190.

111. Ibrahim ibn Muhammad, *Kashti-i Sulaymân* (1668), translated from Persian as *The Ship of Sulaiman* by J. O'Kane (London: Routledge, 1972), pp. 77, 95–97.

112. Anthony Reid, 1993: p. 191.

113. Dhiravat na Pombejra, "Crown Trade and Court Politics in Ayutthaya during the Reign of King Narai: 1656–88," in J. Kathirithamby-Wells and J. Villiers, *The Southeast Asian Port and Polity: Rise and Demise* (Singapore: Singapore University Press, 1990), p. 134.

114. Ibrahim ibn Muhammad, 1668: pp. 98–100.

115. Guy Tachard, *A Relation of the Voyage to Siam, performed by Six Jesuits* (London, 1686: reprinted Bangkok, 1981), pp. 214–15.

116. Gabriel Quiroga de San Antonio, *Breve y verdadera relación de los successos del Reyno de Camboxa* (1604), in A. Cabaton, ed., *Brève et véridique relation des événements du Cambodge* (Paris, 1914), p. 124.

117. Cornelis Matelief, "Historische verhael vande treffelijcke reyse, gedaen naer de Oost-Indien ende China," (1608), in *Begin ende Voortagangh* (1646), p. 120, as noted in Anthony Reid, 1993: p. 189.

118. Pierre-Yves Manguin, "L'introduction de l'Islam au Campa," *Bulletin de l'École Française d'Extreme-Orient* 66 (1979), pp. 269–71.

119. This coincided with a period of great political instability and dynastic warfare in the country, inviting much foreign intervention in that rich land. The Muslim minority emerged from this civil disturbance as the most important military and financial force in Cambodia.

120. Anthony Reid, 1993: p. 189.

121. He "commanded the nobility to follow his example, and made much fuss about mass public conversion of the elite. "[Sultan Ibrahim] said to the ministers, mandarins and royal servants of all service groups, "You must all enter the religion of Allah. Anyone who refuses to enter must leave the royal service." Fearful of royal authority, the dignitaries and all the mandarins agreed to all embrace the religion of Mahomet. . . . The ministers, the mandarins, and all the royal servants all participated, without exception, in the ritual of cutting the foreskin . . . When the king returned to the august royal palace, he ordered, "The king and the members of the royal family must wear a long tunic and always insert a kris in it." *Chroniques royales du Cambodge (de 1594 à 1677)*, trans. Mark Phoeum (Paris: l'Ecole Française d'Extreme-Orient, 1981), p. 190.

122. K. Glamann, *Dutch-Asiatic Trade, 1620–1740*, 2d ed. (1981). In the same year the Dutch won a monopoly on trade with Japan through the island of Dejima (off Nagasaki), when the Tokugawan government expelled the Portuguese and all other Europeans from Japan (except, of course, for a single famous building on an island in Nagasaki harbor).

123. The modern South African state centered on Cape Town.

124. Muscat did remain Portuguese until 1650.

125. Iqbâl Âshtiyâni, p. 684.

126. This strategy was not new. In a three-year period between 1586–89, the Swahili elite had orchestrated an attack on the Portuguese position by the Zimba (a Bantu horde) from inland and the navy of Ottoman Egypt by sea. The Egyptian navy raided the Portuguese positions as far south as Mombassa. Neither attack, however, succeeded in dislodging the Portuguese.

127. Numerical estimates are provided later in this paper. In 1892, G. Curzon gives an interesting account of the Makran Coast African inhabitants when he observes: "There is also throughout the country a considerable admixture of the African element, due to the large importation of slaves from Muscat and Zanzibar. Some of the faces present a thoroughly negro type." *Persia and the Persian Question* (London: Frank Cass, 1966; a reprint of the 1892 original), vol. 2, p. 259. The British Naval Intelligence Division's *Geographical Handbook Series; Persia* (1945) contains an interesting photograph of one of these villages (Fanuch on the Kaur river) capturing its typical African round huts with conical thatched roofs (plate no. 89).

128. For the sake of brevity, the enduring internal power struggle in Oman between the Imam and the sultan has been overlooked here. The Ibadi Imam and the secular sultan in Oman are taken here to represent the same general Omani factor in the course of greater developments in the Gulf world. Only since 1741 when Muscat became the seat of the Bu-Sa'idi sultans (that led to the marginalization of the Imam in the interior of Oman), does the sultan become the primary or sole power in that land. See Rupert Hay, *Sultanate and Imamate in Oman*. A Chatham House Memorandum (London, 1959).

129. The Omani claim to an earlier ownership of Gwadar (through a benevolent Baluchi grant in 1784 of the port to the refugee Bu-Sa'idi, Sultan bin Ahmad) is tenuous at best.

130. H. A. Razmara, ed., *Geographical Dictionary of Iran* (Tehran: The Geographical Bureau of the Iranian Armed Forces, 1949–53), text in Persian) vol. 8, pp. 388–89. The Mazruis at present claim only Arabian descent, mixed with African blood.

131. An offshoot of the Banu Khafaja, the name of this group and dynasty appear in nearly all non-British sources before the twentieth century in the "corrected" Arabic form of Ka'b. This should be avoided. The group always referred and still refers to themselves in their own authentic, Gulfi Arabic dialect as the Chaub. To adulterate this in order to read the name as it would be in the deserts of Badiya and Najd is to wipe out centuries of Chaub history and the fact that they have become a maritime group and an integral part of the Gulf world, and are no longer the desert nomads their ancestors were. The same should be observed regarding the Chathir, Khazray, and Chinanah (in preference to Kathir, Khazraj, and Kan'anah). The switching of the initial *k* to *ch* by the Arabs in this area of Khuzistan may in fact be a legacy of the influence of the Afshar Turcomans, who for centuries dominated the region but are now gone completely. The tribal names of Chaub and Chathir are just the better-known examples. In the Afshar dialect of Turcomani (as also with some Azeri dialects that have been influenced by Afshars), this consonant switching is commonplace.

132. Ahmad Kasravi, *Five-Hundred Years of Khuzistan's History* (Tehran, 1951), pp. 150–68. Text in Persian.

133. John Perry, "The Banu Ka'b: An Ambitious Brigand State in Khuzistan," in *Le Monde iranien et l'Islam: Sociétés et Culture* (Paris: Centre de Recherches d'Histoire et de Philologie, École pratique des Hautes Études, 1971), vol. 1, pp. 131–52.

134. The history of the Afshar Turcomans in Khuzistan and their political dominance of the province and the surrounding regions is recorded in well-known historical texts. Rashid al-Din Fadlallâh (*Jâmi' al-tawârikh-i Rashidi*) records the history of the earliest of the Afshar rulers of Khuzistan, commencing with the energetic emir, Shimeli Käshtoghan (mid-twelfth century). Works of Ibn Athir (*al-Kâmil fi'l-târikh*), Hamdallâh Mustawfi (*Târikh-i guzida*), and Ahmad Ghaffâri *(Târikh-i jahânârâ)* successively record the subsequent centuries of the Afshars in Khuzistan to the mid-sixteenth century.

135. For example, the important oil town of Aghajari (aghach-äri, "woodman"), and the district of Byer Ahmadi ("hilly" Ahmadi).

136. In A.D. 932, for example, Jayhâni reports that the Tigris empties into the Gulf at Khishâb ("sweet water"), only six miles below Abadan (*Ashkâl-i 'Âlam*, p. 57). Presently, the Shatt al-Arab (a joint estuary of Tigris-Euphrates-Karun) empties into the Gulf southeast of Fao, about 45 miles below Abadan. See also M. R. Izady, "Roots and Evolution of Some

Aspects of Kurdish Cultural Identity in the Late Classical and Early Medieval Periods," Ph.D. dissertation (New York: Columbia University, Department of Middle Eastern Languages and Cultures, 1992), ch. 1.

137. The increasing number of Arab immigrants in the area eventually led to obsolescence of the ancient name of "Khuzistan" altogether. Until the nineteenth century, the hilly northern part of the province, north of the Ahwaz ridge, was still known by the old name. The steady settlement of that area by the Arab Chathir, Lam, and Harwan tribes finally led to the entire province becoming known as "Arabistan." The old name was officially revived only after 1925, and now applies to the entire province.

138. A very valuable assessment of the Chaub as well as the general history of the Gulf in the eighteenth and nineteenth century is provided by J. G. Lorimer in his *Gazetteer of the Persian Gulf, 'Omān and Central Arabia* (Calcutta, 1908–1915; reprinted, London, 1986), vol. 2, s.v., "Arabistan," pp. 115–65.

139. Laristan between Lingeh and Jahrum has a solid Sunni majority, although its population remains overwhelmingly Persian-speaking. The same is true of many similar communities inhabiting lands between major ports of the northern Gulf. Some very good sources of information on the topic include the aforenoted *Geographical Dictionary of Iran* (ed. H. A. Razmara, 1949–53); Mas'ud Keyhân, *Joghrafiya-i mufassal-i Iran* ("Detailed Geography of Iran") (Tehran: 1931–32); and particularly *Farhang-i âbâdihâ-i kishvar* ("Village Gazetteer of Iran") (Tehran: Central Bureau of State Statistics, 1968).

140. Bruce Ingham, "Ethno-Linguistic Links Between Southern Iraq and Khuzistan," in K. McLachlan, ed., *The Boundaries of Modern Iran* (London: UCL Press, 1994), p. 98.

141. Following the Conference of Berlin (1884–85) and the ensuing "Scramble for Africa," Zanzibar was forced to became a British protectorate in 1890. In 1892, the entire coast of Benadir in East Africa had been ceded by the sultan in Zanzibar: Britain took Kisimayu, while Italy got Adale, WatShaikh, Mogadishu, Merka, and Brava, which they included in their colony of Somalia.

142. See note 127 above.

143. Little solid research has been carried out on the non-Arab natives of the eastern and southeastern Arabian peninsula, leaving only conjecture as to their origins, racial and linguistic affiliation. B. Thomas, for example, using unscientific onomastic methods, claimed to have found most important ethnic groups in Oman already mentioned in the Book of Job in the Bible. Bertram Thomas, "The Musandam Peninsula and its People: The Shihuh," in Philip Ward, ed., *Travels in Oman* (London: Oleander, 1987).

144. J. B. Kelly, *Britain and the Persian Gulf* (Oxford: Clarendon, 1968, reprint, 1991), pp. 208–13.

145. Port Rig is 11 miles southeast of the port of Ganaveh on the road to Bushehr. It is located on the coast closest to the islands of Kharg and Khargo. The population is overwhelmingly Persian in speech and Shi'i in religion.

146. In gratitude, the Ottoman court also gave him the governorship over the province of Baghdad and he henceforth came to be known as Sulaiman Pasha (Ahmad Faramarzi, *Karim Khan Zand va khalij-i Fars* (Tehran: Sina, 1967), pp. 78–79). This was of course an empty gesture by all parties. The Ottoman control of Mesopotamia at the time was practically non-existent.

147. See, e.g., H. St. John Philby, *Arabia of the Wahhabis* (1928), and *Saudi Arabia* (1955); John Sabini, *Armies in the Sand* (1981); A. M. Abu-Hakima, *History of Eastern Arabia* (1988).

148. David Long, *The Persian Gulf: An Introduction to Its Peoples, Politics and Economics,* 2nd edition (Boulder, Colorado: Westview, 1978), p. 17.

149. The light turban worn by the sultan contrasts most markedly with the *kefiyyas* worn by all the Najdi rulers, from the Saudi king to the Kuwaiti, Bahraini, and Qatari emirs, and the emirs and shaikhs of the United Arab Emirates.

150. Qaboos is the Arabic rendition of the Persian name *Kavus/Kayos,* meaning a king, and is in fact a cognate of that English term (as well as German *könig,* Dutch *kining*).

151. As an example, the name of the ubiquitous Bedouin headdress, the *kafiyya,* is pronounced as *chapi* or *chapiyya.*
152. Bruce Ingham, 1994: p. 95.
153. Lorimer, *Gazetteer,* vol. 8, ii, p. 754.
154. John Perry, *Karim Khan Zand* (Chicago: Chicago University Press, 1979), p. 151.
155. This brings to mind an equally uncomplimentary marker that was placed by the Europeans on the proud Bugis of the Southeast Asian sultanates of Makassar, Tindor, and Ternate. The derisive English term "bogeyman" harks back to the fear that the Bugi seamen placed in the hearts of the European trade monopolizers.
156. On the East African front, Egypt had snatched the ports of Brava and Misimayu in 1875–76 from the Omani sultan of Zanzibar. The ports of Berbera and Zeila had already fallen to Egypt in 1874.
157. Britain then proceeded to force its suzerainty over all emirates on the southern half of the Gulf. Bahrain fully accepted British protection in 1861. All these actions, meanwhile, were viewed as null and void by the Tehran governments who regarded the Khalifas as illegitimate interlopers. The Iranian territorial claim was not to end until the UN-sponsored referendum of 1971 and the islands' independence. It is worth noting that until 1971, two seats were left empty in the Iranian parliament for the Bahraini representatives.
158. Much controversy surrounds demographic data for the Gulf countries, with the local governments overestimating their native population in relation to the expatriates. This would naturally lead to a picture of a more stable society than the reality warrants. In 1992, for example, the Saudi official census (as reported in the Dammam-based *Saudi Commerce and Economic Review*) lists a mere 27 percent of a total population of 16.9 million to have been expatriate, lowered to 25.2 in 1999. This figure seems more odd when realizing that the Kingdom employs over 700,000 expatriate chauffeurs alone! Using the local and official figures, Andrzej Kapiszewski of Jagiellonian University, Krakow, Poland, provides the following native to expatriate ratios for the following Gulf states (March 17, 1999, on Gulf/2000 cyber forum. This has been subsequently published in his work, *Nationals and Expatriates: Population and Labour Dilemmas of the Gulf Cooperation Council States* (London: Ithaca Press, 2001):

	Native	Other
Bahrain	61%	39%
Kuwait	34.5	65.5
Oman	72	28
Qatar	33	67
Saudi Arabia	69	31
UAE	24	76

Kapiszewski lists his sources for these figures to have been: for Bahrain—figures for June 1997, Central Statistical Organization, as quoted in *Gulf News* (October 28, 1997); for Kuwait—figures for June 1997, The Public Authority for Civil Information, EIU Country Report (3rd quarter 1997), p. 18; for Oman—figures for June 1997, Information and Documentation Center, Monthly Statistical Bulletin (March 1998), p. 2; for Qatar—1997 census data, as quoted in *Al Khalij* (April 20, 1998); for Saudi Arabia—author estimates based on different reports; for UAE—the total population, Ministry of Planning Data, *Annual Economic Report 1997,* breakdown for categories based on 1995 percentages.

In reality, only the sultanate of Oman has a native majority among all Gulf states outside Iran and Iraq, and will in all likelihood continue to be the only one for the near future.
159. A general survey of the Gulf states, including its history since the nineteenth century, can be found in Alvin J. Cottrell et al., eds., *The Persian Gulf States: A General Survey* (Baltimore: Johns Hopkins University Press, 1980).

160. East Africa is the sole exception, due to the continuing and uninterrupted presence of the Gulfis in that region until 1965.

161. The number of these Africans on the Iranian coast of the Gulf, who still speak various Bantu languages was estimated in 1964 by Soviet authors S. Bruk and V. Apenchenko to be around 10,000 (*Atlas Narodov Mira*, p. 163). Applying the average Iranian population growth rates, this figure should be over 40,000 at present. The celebrated *Geographical Dictionary of Iran* finds it too difficult to identify the language and religion of these African villages on the Gulf, and uncharacteristically provides no linguistic or religious information on the said villages at all (vol. 8, "Kirman and Makran," *passim*).

162. E.g., David Long, 1978:17, 19.

163. See note 51.

164. Who may have constituted the last inhabitants of the Gulf to speak a Malayo-Indonesian language.

165. Lorimer, *Gazetteer*, vol. 2, pp. 1805–10.

166. While Bruk and Apenchenko refer to these as Malayo-Indonesians (*Atlas*, p. 161), the *Encyclopaedia Britannica* (s.v., "Yemen: the People") does not hesitate to call them "Australians," i.e., of south seas' origin.

167. For a brief study of the Gulf Arab Shi'is, see Yitzhak Nakash, *The Shi'is of Iraq* (Princeton: Princeton University Press, 1994). Also, Rend Rahim Francke and Graham Fuller, *The Arab Shi'a: The Forgotten Muslims* (New York: St. Martin's, 1999), chs. on Bahrain, Iran, Iraq, Kuwait, and Saudi Arabia.

168. Jayhâni in A.D. 932 states: "The land between Bahrân/Bahrain and Abadan [i.e., the territory of modern Kuwait] is an uninhabited desert. The travel there is by sea" (*Ashkâl*, p. 53).

169. Ibadism came into existence at exactly the same time that Islam split into Sunnis and Shi'is over the question of succession to the Muslim caliphate between Ali and Mu'awiyya in the seventh century, just three short decades after the death of the Prophet Muhammad. Presently, small Ibadi communities are also found in many ports around the Indian Ocean where the Omanis came to settle and/or rule in the past 500 years, such as Zanzibar and coastal East Africa.

170. Writing on Oman, Jayhâni states: "The port of Suhar is the largest city of Oman, where much commerce takes place. No Muslim port on the Indian Ocean is more bustling or affluent than Suhar. I have heard its dependencies stretch over three hundred parasangs [1,200 miles]. The Ibadis (*Ahl-i Surâh*) predominate in that land. But, a dispute broke out between them and some of the elite of the Bani Sâma. One Muhammad al-Sâmi hailing from that tribe went to the [Abbasid] caliph, al-Mu'tadid, asking for support. He sent general Ibn Thawr with him who occupied Oman for al-Mu'tadid. Until this time, the treasury, mosques and the [appointment of] imams are all in the hands of the [Abbasid] caliphs" (*Ashkâl*, p. 51).

171. The largest draining took place in the 1990s when the Iraqi government accelerated the process to prevent the marshes from being used as a refuge by anti-government forces.

172. The Mandians are renowned silversmiths, and their wares are sought in the markets of southern Iraq and Iran. This may give them the economic impetus to hold their community together, now that their traditional lifestyle and habitat has been devastated.

173. A number of works in Persian are all that are available in print on Zâr. One of the best among these is Ali Riyahi, *Zâr u bâd u Baluch* (Tehran: Tahuri, 1977).

CHAPTER 3

THE EROSION OF CONSENSUS
Perceptions of GCC States of a Changing Region

IBRAHIM A. KARAWAN

In the Gulf, we are witnessing a stage characterized by an uncertainty in how the Gulf Cooperation Council (GCC) states perceive major regional changes. Policymakers and policy analysts in that region are not sure about the significance and implications of the latest developments in Iran, Iraq, or the Middle East peace process, or about the impact of nuclear tests in South Asia on the region. The regional setting remains a less understood component in the perceptions of the GCC countries than the two other levels that their ruling elites have to develop concrete strategies to manage, namely the domestic level and the international system level.

FISCAL CHALLENGES

With regard to the domestic level in these states, the main problem they face is that oil revenues remain insufficient to cover the growing costs of the cradle-to-grave welfare state to which they have become accustomed, leading to two conclusions. First, the era of what has been referred to as "surplus petrodollars," with unlimited goods provided by the state is basically over; and, second, the resultant situation can adversely affect the ability of these states to cope with the combination of internal and external claims on their oil-based financial resources (i.e., demands for higher social spending, greater military expenditures, lower budget deficits, and faster payment of external debts).[1]

Oil prices and, hence, oil revenues have tended to fluctuate rather sharply in the last few years. On June 22, 1998, after a meeting of GCC oil ministers, two states (Kuwait and the United Arab Emirates) decided to reduce their oil production by 170,000 barrels per day while Oman opted to cut its production by 20,000 barrels per day until the end of that year. After being hit hard by a slump in the world oil prices for which there was no immediate fix, GCC states started (also against the backdrop of a rapidly growing population) to look for ways to stop the downward trend in oil prices and enhance their oil revenues. Saudi Arabia, for example, decided to pursue austerity measures and an economic strategy of privatization.[2] The gap between Saudi oil revenues and estimated revenues in 1998 was around $3.4 billion, although by 2001, Saudi measures seemed to be working and a budget surplus of about $2 billion was predicted.[3]

After the price collapse in 1998, OPEC, which accounts for 40 percent of the world's oil, sought to keep prices in the middle of a $22 to $28 target range by manipulating output. It cut production in 1998 and 1999, raised it in 2000, and cut it again in 2001.[4] (Iraq's exports are not included.) Up to mid-2001, OPEC's strategy had been largely effective. But even with the significant increase of oil prices in 2000 and 2001, what has come to be called *tarshid al-infaq al-'am,* or "the rationalization of public expenditures" continued to be a component of state policy. In short, GCC states have faced similar fiscal problems that had a negative impact on their economic development, growth rates, and their ability to continue large-scale acquisitions of sophisticated weapon systems. Of course, the GCC states have faced these problems and constraints in varying degrees of fiscal intensity and political significance.

One challenge faced by the ruling elites in the GCC states is how to determine the sociopolitical order of importance of the fiscal demands that they encounter and what blend of economic and political criteria should guide such determination. A complex balancing act is needed to cope with these mounting pressures where short-term fixes do not seem possible. However, it would not be accurate to conclude that these regimes see themselves as "lame Leviathans" on the brink of collapse due to certain fiscal constraints.

Put differently, there is certainty about the fiscal challenges they face, but no clarity about the political implications of these challenges for domestic and regional stability. In fact, this applies to all Gulf regimes whether they are Arab or not. Determining the implications of having many educated but unemployed youth, particularly in the strategically located urban centers, is the political and the internal security concern that crosses territorial boundaries in the region. Also this is where the linkages between domestic and regional levels become relevant. Having these domestic problems on an ongoing basis can be more challenging for regimes if the regional setting becomes conflict-ridden in ways that can provide external backing to internal unrest or that necessitate allocating a greater share of the state revenues for military expenditures.

Due to these concerns, ruling elites of GCC states as well as other oil producing countries felt the urgency to do something in order to stop and reverse these trends. Saudi Arabia and Iran played a major role in reaching an agreement by OPEC countries to cut production significantly to boost oil prices and, hence, revenues.[5] Other GCC states agreed to adopt such strategy to reduce the stored amounts of oil and increase oil prices for their own collective good. It is not clear, however, whether the oil producers' compliance is assured in a sustained way, how long cuts in oil production should remain in force to achieve their intended results and before industrialized countries pressure the OPEC countries to increase production, and what sustained increases in oil prices are to be expected as a result of pursuing that strategy.[6] According to the UAE oil minister, Obeid bin Saif Al-Nasiri, GCC oil ministers, who meet up to six times a year, will be monitoring the situation to see what should be done to ensure that oil prices are stabilized at an acceptable level to producers and consumers.[7] In other words, while the strategy of reducing oil production has worked in the short run to increase the prices of oil, and the revenues of oil, other regional and global factors, some of which are political in the first place, can limit the sustainability of such outcome, and hence GCC states cannot count on the long term continuation of such a policy outcome.

CONSTRUCTIVE AMBIGUITY?

The features of the contemporary international system after the end of bipolarity and their impact for the Gulf region seem to have been settled. During the Cold War, the United States had enjoyed a certain primacy in the Gulf region, and it had let other international actors know what was permissible and what it was not going to allow them to do in that region. However, the Soviet Union was still there willing and able to make an appearance from time to time—directly, as during the early stages of the reflagging of Kuwaiti oil tankers near the end of the first Gulf war, or indirectly, a decade and a half earlier, through its military and political relationship with Iraq.

The clarity resulting from this systemic change at the top of the pyramid of the international system did not create certainty in the minds of GCC leaders regarding how the United States was going to translate its preponderance of power globally and regionally into a game plan to influence the main developments and actors in the Gulf.[8] Equally unclear was how the United States planned to manage its relations with the other main international actors in the post–Cold War era (France, Russia, and China) regarding developments in the Gulf (e.g., Iran and Iraq) after two wars believed to have been won by the United States (the Cold War against the USSR and the Gulf War against Iraq).[9]

Moreover, many are not certain if dual containment of Iran and Iraq remains the backbone of U.S. policy in the area. Has U.S. policy been undergoing a considerable shift that would make it more nuanced? What explains the incoherence in American policy toward Iran between 1998 and 2000? Statements by former president Clinton and former secretary of state Albright tended to be increasingly hopeful and perhaps even encouraging with regard to the political reformers in Iran led by Khatami. However, U.S. foreign-policymakers under Clinton insisted that the Islamic Republic of Iran remained the number-one sponsor of terrorism in the world, that Iran continued to pursue its efforts to produce weapons of mass destruction, and, hence, that U.S. sanctions against Iran must continue.

Many officials in GCC states are unsure whether the lack of American consistency is one actually centered on the principal policy objectives or just regarding particular policy means. Is it a deliberate reflection of what former U.S. secretary of state Henry Kissinger hailed before as an exercise in "constructive ambiguity?" Put differently, does this American incoherence reflect a lack of policy consensus among American foreign-policy makers with regard to what is strategically desirable or differences regarding what is politically feasible in order to maximize U.S. interests?[10]

Similar uncertainty concerning American intentions exists among ruling elites and political analysts in the Gulf region with regard to Iraq. The United States has been showing more signs that the overthrow of the Islamic regime in Iran is no longer one of its preconditions for improving American economic and political relations with Iran. Can U.S. foreign policy reconcile itself any time soon to a Baathist regime in Iraq with Saddam Hussein at its helm, if it can be proven that the objectives of the weapons inspection regime were met, depriving Iraq from access to the military means to threaten its neighbors? Given the insistence of Iraq on denying and defying any weapons inspection regime, what can be done in response? Can the new Bush administration implement successfully what it has called "smart sanctions"? According to what time frame? And should the GCC states endorse that untested concept at a time when sympathy with the suffering of the Iraqi people has been growing in the societies of the region? It should be noted that Saudi and Kuwaiti positions with regard to these sanctions have differed from those of other GCC states.

I have argued thus far that Arab ruling elites in the Gulf have been faced during a short time frame (particularly during the last years of the 1990s) with a set of regional changes that required responses or certain policy adjustments. They have had important policy choices to make, but the parameters of these changes and what should and could have been done were not always clear. Two of these changes appeared obvious: domestically, the fiscal challenges facing these states were real and were not going to pave the way for an abundance without limits, and globally, the United States emerged as the only superpower left, and American hegemony, or the ability to act in a hegemonic manner, in the Gulf itself has become a fact of that area's life.

While the first change was a source of concern, the second, at least initially, was perceived by the ruling GCC elites as reassuring. Even with regard to these two domestic and international developments, the challenge of figuring out precisely what is to be done has remained uncertain for the regimes, and there is no consensus on how to act among the GCC countries as a whole.

Uncertainty has not been exactly a constant feature of elite perceptions in that region. When it comes to the regional setting, and to put this matter in historical context, sources of regional threats appeared compellingly clear to the GCC states at two critical junctures in their contemporary experience. The first emerged after the Iranian revolution in 1979. Needless to say, major revolutions, especially in the immediate aftermath of their triumph, are not inclined to see themselves as meant primarily for domestic consumption. On the contrary, they tend to see their experiences as relevant, if not necessary, for many other countries and perhaps for humanity as a whole. The Iranian revolution in 1979 was not an exception when it came to its interest in remaking the region in its own revolutionary image.

In light of efforts to bring about domestic political reforms in Iran and to improve Iran's relations with its Arab neighbors, there is no point in debating at any length whether Iran's leaders in the decade that followed their revolution tried to destabilize regimes in the surrounding countries, regimes that they deemed to be copies of the shah's regime and as such deserving of a similar fate. Needless to say, they pursued an interventionist policy, but it did not succeed. The presumed revolutionary spillover effects did not materialize, making the Islamic Republic of Iran not the pioneering model that was followed by many others, but an experiment that was not duplicated either in the Gulf region or beyond. If it were true, as some claim today, that leaders of Iran did not pursue in the early 1980s an interventionist regional policy, the significance of Iran's policy shift toward GCC regimes in the late 1990s would be greatly diminished.

The second moment that created more policy clarity and political certainty among the GCC states came with the invasion of Kuwait in August 1990. Once again, the expectation that state sovereignty, inadmissibility of territorial gains via conquest, sanctity of territorial borders of states, and principles of non-intervention in the domestic affairs of another country,[11] let alone a fellow Arab country, were shattered. This was done by a country that proclaimed itself, and had been declared by other Arab states (ironically including Kuwait itself during the first Gulf war), as "the sword of the Arabs."

Uncertainty regarding regional developments and actors is not a permanent feature in GCC states' perceptions of conflict and cooperation in the Gulf. There are particular historical moments when consensus has existed among the Arab states in the Gulf about their sense of confronting clear and present regional dangers. In such concrete situations, these dangers have acted as forces that cemented consensus among these states, which considered themselves actual or potential targets of these dangers and concluded that their interests could be seriously harmed if they did nothing in response to such regional threats.

During the last two decades we have witnessed developments that may be explained by the notion of the "erosion of consensus" in the Arab regional system.[12] In fact, instead of the GCC states' subsystem representing an exception from these developments, the unfolding trends in the region are likely to make GCC countries more of a representative sample than a deviant case within the Arab setting. This can have an important conceptual and policy significance. I shall elaborate on this point in the conclusion of this chapter. Now, I will identify four issue areas that illustrate the salience of these trends with regard to the "erosion of consensus" and point out briefly their manifestations, causes, and implications.

STATE OR REVOLUTION IN IRAN?

No other topic has kept the principal policymakers and analysts in the Gulf preoccupied since the election of Mohammed Khatami as president of Iran more than this one. The issue has centered on the question of who is in charge in Iran at this historical juncture: the state or the revolution? Is it those who want to live within the regional status quo or others who aspire to undermining it? Most rulers and analysts in the GCC countries agree that significant changes, and not just cosmetic ones, have been taking place in Iran. But have such political changes reached a stage where they could be truly characterized as irreversible? Is Iran trying to alter its broad strategy or merely its regional and international image? There is no single answer to these questions among GCC states and this has been manifested, beyond the few joint GCC official statements, in their divergent perceptions and state policies toward the Islamic regime in Iran.[13]

For almost a decade, Qatar and Oman have advocated improving the ties of GCC states with Iran. They have seen in recent reform-oriented developments in Iran a proof of the accuracy of their political judgments. Qatar, particularly since Shaikh Hamad bin Khalifa came to power in 1995, has developed strong relations with Iran. Moreover, Omani information minister Abdal-Aziz al-Rowwas called for the inclusion of Iran in future Gulf security structures. Even Kuwait, despite its close relations with the United States, has witnessed persistent questions about the "Iranian threat," a threat that many of the Omani elites have deemed as a reflection of a certain ideological outlook rather than one based on verifiable evidence.[14]

Saudi Arabia has maintained a more cautious approach. After many visits to Riyadh by top Iranian officials such as Hashemi Rafsanjani, Natiq Nouri, Kamal Kharrazi, and Mohammed Khatami, the Saudi interest in normalizing relations with Iran has been clearly but incrementally set in motion. It was important for Saudi Arabia that Iran by 1998–99 had shown a strong interest in establishing a sort of détente with Riyadh. From such a perspective, Iran has made most of the ideological and political changes that facilitated its rapprochement with Riyadh. Gone are the days when the Iranian leaders had insisted that "monarchy and Islam were mutually exclusive," or when they had stipulated that "the House of Saud was unfit for the custodianship of Islam's holiest shrines," or when they referred to the Saudi regime with disdain as "the government of the Hijaz."[15]

Despite the awareness by Saudi political elites of significant changes in Iran, they identify a certain dualism in the Iranian regime: on the one hand there is the reality of a tired and restrained Iranian state, but on the other hand there is the restlessness and ideological legacy of the Islamic revolution. Thus, there is no compelling Saudi interest to rush strategic cooperation with Iran, particularly if Riyadh wants to avoid "unnecessary damage and disappointment." While Saudi policymakers understand the desire of some in Iran's leadership to introduce greater changes and recognize that it is not in the interest of Saudi Arabia to antagonize a regional power like Iran while it is exploring its domestic reform and regional accommodation, they do not accept the notion of the end of Iran's Islamic revolution.[16] That is why Riyadh has been reluctant to accept proposals by Iran for significant economic cooperation with GCC states similar to an organization linking Iran, Turkey, Pakistan, and Central Asian republics.[17] Iranian suggestions of military cooperation with Saudi Arabia have been rejected by Riyadh, but an agreement about internal security matters with Iran was acceptable to the Saudi leadership and after long preparations it was signed in Teheran by Saudi interior minister Prince Nayef bin Abdel Aziz and his Iranian counterpart in April 2001.

Despite Saudi-Iranian rapprochement and also a few high-level visits exchanged with Iran,[18] Bahrain remains skeptical about the Iranian regime and stresses concrete actions rather than sweet talk or mere intentions.[19] For many years, Bahrain has accused Iran of attempting to foment unrest among the Shi'i community against the Al-Khalifa regime in Manama as well as maintaining territorial ambitions against the state of Bahrain. The reports of Syrian attempts at political mediation between Iran and Bahrain have been frequent, but no tangible success has resulted from such efforts.[20] The election of Khatami was perceived in Manama as a potential landmark, and the adoption of softer Iranian language toward the region was not missed. Whether the softer tone will actually be translated into a coherent, accommodationist, and sustainable policy no one is certain. Doubts about the distribution of political power and the shaping of the dominant ideology in Iran persist, and they tend to make the skeptics see Iran's position as reflecting a change in policy posture rather than a change in policy substance.

Consider, for instance, a widely read column in a Bahraini newspaper on the struggle for the soul of Iran. It stated the following: "It is about time for Iran to realize that the world faces a real, not an invented, problem dealing with it. Iran addresses the world with two tongues as well as with two orientations. . . . The problem is that each of those has its own foreign policy and its ways of dealing with the world: confrontation or dialogue? This produces, at the very least, doubts, suspicions and ambivalence."[21] In short, the irony boils down to this: the president who won 70 percent of the popular vote does not control the main instruments of state power, whereas those who lost most of that popular support do so. In light of that paradox, who will make Iran's regional policies?

Put differently, these perceptions in their essence reflect doubts about the viability of Khatami's position in the context of a political war of attrition against his camp within the Islamic regime in Iran. After all, frequent analogies made between Khatami and Gorbachev and references to him as "Ayatollah Gorbachev" are not particularly reassuring. These perceptions also reflect doubts about the predictability of the regime's behavior on the regional level. For instance, current struggles in Iran are seen as conflicts "between 'country' and 'revolution.' . . . The election of Khatami as president is an expression of a desire to move the revolution to a mature stage, but Iranians found themselves in a new situation dealing with two governments and two rulers. . . . The conflict between them will continue until the 'country' and the 'revolution' separate. What is unclear and unforeseen is the cost of this separation."[22]

The UAE also does not share with other leaders in the Gulf region their optimism about recent changes in Iran. For the leaders of the UAE, the ultimate test of any meaningful change in Iran's regional behavior would require Iran's relinquishing control over three islands it has occupied, conducting serious negotiations with the UAE over these islands, or accepting binding arbitration by the International Court of Justice. According to the foreign minister of the UAE, Rashid Abdallah Al-Na'imi, addressing Arab foreign ministers, "with the election of President Khatami, we felt hopeful and saw some opportunity for reconciliation. We have sought a peaceful settlement of the three islands issue, including by international arbitration, which led to an opening in Arab-Iranian relations. Now, the situation is getting worse as shown by Iran's military exercises and consolidation of its occupation of the Islands. Iran thinks it can, at the same time, maintain that occupation and enjoy good relations with the Arabs."[23] Oman sympathized with that UAE position despite its own good relations with Iran.

From the UAE perspective, no changes thus far in the domestic Iranian political scene have had significant impact on Iran's insistence on keeping its unilateral forceful occupation of the three islands. Despite Kuwaiti attempts to pursue an opening toward Iran, there is sympathy there too with the UAE position. Both the UAE and Kuwait have strong doubts about Iranian demands for the withdrawal of American troops from the Gulf and for ending joint maneuvers between GCC countries and the United States. Instead, Iran suggests that the GCC countries rely on a regional security system in which Iran would be the leading power. "If America is a global military power which Iran fears, then Iran is also a regional military power which Gulf states fear. . . . Iran wants GCC states to abandon their alliance with America to subject them to its unchallenged hegemony. . . . If we the Gulf Arabs had the freedom to choose between American protection and Iranian protection, would we choose the latter? Of course not."[24]

The UAE position regarding the islands has been supported for years by all the GCC States, members of the 6+2 (GCC states + Egypt and Syria), in the Damascus Declaration, and by the Arab League. Iran has consistently defied this consensus, so why should Arab states, whether in the Gulf region or in the Arab world at large, unilaterally change their stand toward Iran without linking that change to alteration of Iran's policy regarding the islands?[25] Thus, the UAE position is to make enlargement and acceleration of GCC states' political opening toward Iran contingent primarily upon significant change in Iran's position with regard to the islands. The best hope of the UAE to achieve that is to get GCC countries to engage in collective bargaining with Iran in support of its position and interests.

Saudi Arabia, on the other hand, argues that despite the importance of GCC coordination toward regional developments, each state remains the ultimate source of formulating its foreign policy. Others should not claim to have a veto power over each state's determination of desirable or attainable courses of action. From such a perspective, the old GCC position of holding periodic meetings to denounce Iran has basically led nowhere. It did not liberate any occupied land, did not isolate Iran, and did not stop GCC countries themselves, including the United Arab Emirates, from trading massively with Iran or from developing ties with Tehran. According to Riyadh, the election of President Khatami brought to Iran a new perspective and style that should be given in fact and not only in words, an opportunity to have a positive impact on Iran's regional relations.

An opening toward Iran can be useful, according to Riyadh, in making the oil policies of GCC states more effective and in counterbalancing Iraq after the sanctions regime comes to an end. According to the Saudi perspective, the GCC states should engage Iran and both sides should refrain in a sustained way from escalating regional tensions if a peaceful settlement of the islands issue is to be reached and if the future is to be different from the past. A mini-war of words has erupted as a result of these specific policy differences between the UAE and Saudi Arabia. Mediation by GCC member Qatar managed to diffuse this war of words, to reduce its intensity but not to undo the policy differences between Saudi Arabia and the United Arab Emirates regarding the best way to deal with Iran about *mas'alat al-Juzur*—the islands issue. By the summer of 2001, the UAE seemed to be interested in improving its political relations with Iran while not dropping its claim to the islands.

A POLITICAL REHABILITATION OF IRAQ?

Over the last few years great attention has been given to determining the impact of any significant and accelerated reentry by Iraq to the oil market on the financial and political interests of oil-producing countries in the Gulf, given Iraq's huge oil reserve base.[26] The partial increase in Iraqi oil production from 600,000 barrels a day in 1997 to 1.6 million barrels per day in 1998 was considered by analysts as a contributing factor to a downward trend in oil prices.[27] Since Iraq cannot be kept outside the oil market forever, the terms and the pace of its reentry into that market (as a major oil exporter) must be thoroughly explored and agreed upon by other exporters as well, particularly by the GCC members themselves. The concern with that issue surfaced again when Iraq threatened in June 2001 to withhold its 2 million barrels per day in response to deliberations to impose "smart sanctions" by the United States and Britain.

But the Iraqi oil export factor is not the only possibly divisive issue here. Political factors are likely to play a major role in determining the future of the sanctions regime. In other words, does Iraq still represent a source of military and strategic threat for the other countries in the Gulf? If so, what are the best ways to ensure that it will not menace some other regional actors in the future? How can that be ensured in light of the record of deceit and manipulation of information by the Iraqi regime? Finally, could the current strategy, based on the punishment and isolation of Iraq, result in deep bitterness on the part of the Iraqi people toward other Arab regimes who have been perceived as condoning harsh sanctions against them, thus threatening future relations after President Saddam Hussein is no longer in power?[28] Once again, no unified position or common foreign policy exists among the Arab states in the Gulf region (or outside it) with regard to this issue.

Some Arab intellectuals and policymakers in the Gulf region argue that the economic sanctions regime punishes the Iraqi people in a way that is unprecedented in its cruelty without bringing Saddam down. Shaikh Zayed, president of the UAE, has called since 1995 for the political rehabilitation of Iraq and has offered to host a comprehensive Arab summit in his country with Iraq's participation.[29] Newspapers in the UAE, Qatar, and Bahrain publish pictures of many deformed and undernourished Iraqi children and implore, even admonish the Arab world to take a stand and end the sanctions to relieve the suffering of the Iraqi people as the African states have done vis-à-vis the anti-Libyan sanctions. From time to time, these three GCC states have sent planes carrying food and medical assistance to Iraq. Moreover, they argue that the cruelty of sanctions did not achieve their objectives, namely weakening or bringing down the regime of Saddam Hussein.[30] They lament the lack of incentives, a road map, or a "light at the end of the tunnel" to encourage Iraq to cooperate with Western arms inspections. Until when, they ask, should the Iraqi suffering be allowed to continue? At what human cost? What kind of future neighbor will the Iraqi people become under the influence of such severe privation? Finally, would helping the Iraqi people entail a decision to violate the American-imposed sanctions?

According to such a perspective, Iraq's invasion of Kuwait was a crime, but Iraq has paid a very heavy price for it, and a reassessment of the dangers involved in continuing that severe punishment is warranted, particularly since Kuwait is now a free country that enjoys security and stability. Those who share that perspective want to rehabilitate Iraq even under Saddam's regime and to "open a new page by allowing it to return to the Arab fold."[31] They seek Iraq's rehabilitation to the Arab setting to counterbalance non-Arab powers, namely Iran, Israel, and Turkey, and also to strengthen Syria's position in its conflict with Israel.[32]

Others see that perspective as naive. A weaker and, in practice, divided Iraq cannot do much to tip the scales in the Arab strategic equation. An Iraqi regime that acquires considerable power will not represent a threat to those big three non-Arab countries but could pose a threat to its Arab smaller neighbors. Kuwait, they argue, is aware of the human suffering felt by the Iraqis, but the Saddamist regime is the main actor to be blamed because it has taken the Iraqi people as hostages to keep itself in power and has devoted its attention only to rewarding its security organizations, the pillars of its continuity in power. Iraq has to stop casting doubt over Security Council Resolution 844 on the demarcation of its border with Kuwait. A GCC meeting in June 1998 expressed "profound anxiety and dismay" over statements by Iraq's Deputy Prime Minister Taha Yassin Ramadan in which he raised doubts about the internationally recognized Iraqi-Kuwaiti borders.[33] Similar disturbing statements were made by the son of the president, Uday, in January 2001 in a letter to his father that was published and broadcast in Iraqi official media. Iraq must comply unconditionally with Security Council resolutions, particularly regarding the immediate release of the Kuwaiti prisoners suspected of being held in Iraq, and the return of Kuwaiti property stolen by the Iraqi military and security forces, and desist from "provocative and aggressive acts."[34]

From such a perspective, the immediate lifting of sanctions against the Iraqi regime would not only strengthen it but would also encourage it to engage in aggressive acts against other states in the region, as it has done before. Instead, apologizing for the invasion of Kuwait and strict compliance with the weapons inspection regime must be key requirements for ending or phasing out the sanctions regime. A strict linkage between these two regimes is crucial, and the key is "verifiability" or "verification" and not just nice words for public relations by Saddam. Kuwait and Saudi Arabia stress the necessity for Iraq to go beyond its claims of victimization and take a serious initiative by modifying its stands in a positive direction and stopping its familiar denial games and its gambling to regain confidence in the region and save its people.

Divisions have also erupted regarding the protracted weapons inspection regime, UNSCOM and after that UNMOVIC. For years the United States has maintained that the implementation of its task should not be subject to any negotiations with Saddam Hussein. Arab regimes in the Gulf agreed generally that Iraq had to abide by the UN weapons inspection regime, whether regarding its conventional weapons or weapons of mass destruction. When Saddam challenged UNSCOM, the United States and Britain responded with punitive military strikes. Some of the GCC states expressed concern about the repercussions on the domestic and regional levels of large civilian casualties in

Iraq resulting from the Western military strikes. But there was no unified stand among them with regard to granting or denying U.S. access to their military facilities to launch strikes against Iraqi targets.

HOW AND WHEN TO DEAL WITH ISRAEL?

Many analysts agree that developments in the Gulf region and the Arab-Israeli conflict or settlement are linked. But in what way and leading to what type of policies? There is no consensus among GCC states about these issues. Most of the policymakers and opinion makers in these states denounced Israeli policies under Netanyahu, Barak, and Sharon alike and insist on "no normalization before peace."[35] Against the backdrop of the Iraqi claims that Arab "subservience" to the United States has damaged the Palestinian cause and has benefited Israel, GCC states expressed "categorical rejection and condemnation of the Israeli decisions to extend the borders of Jerusalem and transform its demographic map as a violation of international law and legality."[36]

Qatar and Oman condemned Israeli policies, particularly under Netanyahu, but they have maintained the right to differ with other GCC and also Arab states regarding allowing Israeli prime ministers to visit these two countries or organizing Middle East economic conferences to which the Jewish state would be invited. By hosting a Middle East Economic Conference, Qatar adopted a position that the leaders of Saudi Arabia and the UAE from the GCC, as well as Syria and Egypt from the Damascus Declaration group, considered threatening to "the higher interests of the Arab nation."[37] According to these leaders, an Arab summit decided in 1996 to freeze bilateral and multilateral steps toward normalizing economic, political, or cultural relations with Israel as long as the peace process was stalemated, and Qatar's position violated that decision. From such a perspective, Israel's participation in the Doha Economic Conference made it necessary for Arab states who wanted to abide by the decisions of the Arab summit to boycott the Doha meeting; otherwise, they would be really sending Israel the message that it could have Arab normalization and occupy Arab lands at the same time.

While Saudi Arabia, Kuwait, Bahrain, and the UAE refused to go along the path of normalizing their relations with Israel (as recommended by the United States) before a comprehensive and just peace is reached,[38] Oman and Qatar did not want the club of *al-shaqiqat al-Kubrayat* (elder sisters), namely Egypt, Syria, and Saudi Arabia, to tell them how to formulate their policies vis-à-vis Israel and whether a total boycott or selective engagement of sorts represents a better strategy for them. One Qatari newspaper, *al-Watan,* addressed those in the Egyptian press who denounced Qatar for hosting the MENA conference (the previous one was held in Cairo) under the following titles: "We are your students and you are our teachers in normalizing relations with Israel,"[39] and "Arabism, Egyptian style."[40]

With regard to substance, Qatar responded to its Arab critics by insisting that it alone had the sovereign right to decide what to do about this foreign-policy matter. Qatar had committed itself to hold the economic conference in Doha, and such commitment should not be revoked due to any external pressures even under the ideological pretext of pan-Arabism. It did not ask other Arab states that wanted to boycott the Doha conference to attend against their own will. By the same token, these states could not coerce the state of Qatar to cancel a conference that it had agreed to host on its sovereign territory. This national right was exercised, without seeking permission from others, by Morocco, Egypt, and Jordan, and despite objections by Syria, Iraq, and Libya in the name of the so-called superior interests of the Arab nation. By holding the conference in Doha, Qatar did not indicate it had lost its interests in Arab and Islamic issues. Several months after the MENA conference, the crown prince of Qatar, Shaikh Jassim bin Hamad, issued a decision establishing the "Permanent Qatari Committee to Support Jerusalem"—the holy places as well as the Arab population in Jerusalem.[41] With the onset of the second Palestinian *intifada,* Qatar allowed peaceful marches to denounce Israeli policies in solidarity with the Palestinians.

Consider as well the position adopted by Oman's foreign minister, Yusif al-Alawi, during his meeting in Cairo with leading Arab nationalists from Egypt. Needless to say, those intellectuals were critical of the stands he had taken regarding *al-Sharq Awsatiyah* or Middle Easternism. He has identified Middle Easternism as an inclusive concept and economic framework that should and could accommodate all those who are interested in becoming part of its regional project, Arab and non-Arab alike (including Iran, Turkey, and Israel). In response to the familiar question about the need to wait until Arab-Arab conflicts are solved and Arab unity is achieved before making a move along this Middle Easternist path, the Omani foreign minister did not hesitate to characterize such an outlook as a recipe for endless inaction and stagnation and, thus, as part of the Arab problem, not of the Arab solution.[42] However, with the eruption of the Al-Aqsa *intifada* in the fall of 2000 and the coming of Sharon to power in Israel, such nonconformist stands became less common but they did not totally vanish, particularly when any prospects of peace negotiations emerge.

REJOICING IN PAKISTAN'S NUCLEAR PROMOTION?

The Arab Middle East is not the only subsystem with which the GCC states interact and have major political, strategic, economic, and demographic linkages. The Indian subcontinent is another such region. No wonder then that the overt nuclear proliferation in South Asia in May 1998 attracted considerable attention in the Gulf region.[43] In response to this proliferation, Arab analysts in GCC states discussed at great length the significance of that development for the region. Some of them have asserted that Pakistan's nuclear tests brought joy to the "Islamic street" and concluded that Pakistan's tests should be viewed as an occasion to rejoice because a fellow Muslim country had become member of a most prestigious club.[44] This club is open to only a select few states that acquire nuclear weapons, possess the means of delivering these weapons to their selected targets, and, by establishing a system marked by a balance of nuclear terror, are able to deter their enemies and attain international status and prestige.[45]

Not everyone on the Arab side of the Gulf has perceived the situation that way. One objection to—or at the very least, one reservation about—this enthusiasm for Pakistan's entry into that influential international club was made rather clearly by the defense minister of Bahrain. He had pointed out that Islam and Islamic organizations are not factors that could really influence how Pakistan's nuclear capability might be used. Rather, the national interest of Pakistan as interpreted and decided upon by the Pakistani leaders themselves (particularly in deterring threats by India) would be the decisive factor in that regard.

This position aims to remind those Arabs inside and outside the Gulf who became jubilant after Pakistan's nuclear tests that the assumption that nuclear weapons in the hands of Muslim Pakistan would strengthen Arab positions is without foundation.[46] Moreover, it can be argued that an Arab and Islamic glorification of the Pakistani nuclear bomb as an "Islamic bomb" does not help the Arabs and Muslims as much as it helps Israel who can refer to such rhetoric in lobbying the United States and Western audiences to warn against the nuclear dimensions or aspirations of a "green threat."[47]

Even for those who did not expect any extension of military power from nuclear Pakistan to Arab states, Pakistan, they argued, still had the "power of the example, the power of defiance" to offer the Arabs. Pakistan, which defied the threat of American sanctions and was a latecomer in nuclear research relative to India, was viewed from such a perspective as a model for the Arabs to follow if they were interested in bringing their prolonged *tawazun al-da'f* or "balance of weakness" vis-à-vis Israel to an end.[48] It is a model that illustrates the importance of political will and allocation of all necessary resources to achieve core national interest objectives.[49] Moreover, the failure of the international community, and particularly the United States, to prevent Pakistan from becoming overtly nuclear can encourage other regional powers, such as Iran, to conclude that the costs of defying nuclear non-proliferation regimes are acceptable and affordable.[50] According to this perspective, the game of dominoes that has started on the Indian subcontinent could slowly but surely move toward the Middle East.

Given that Israel is widely believed to be the only actual nuclear power in the Middle East, the success of other actors in gaining nuclear capability tends to be considered a positive development for deterrence purposes by adherents of this particular viewpoint.[51] However, much depends on who among the aspirants to join the nuclear club succeeds in achieving that objective. The proposition that a nuclear capability in the hands of any Arab state translates necessarily into a significant power for all Arab states, or that a Pakistani nuclear bomb becomes by definition an "Islamic bomb," is not generally accepted among policymakers and analysts in the Gulf region. On the contrary, it can be argued that nuclear weapons, if they are built in or around the region, are going to have a national—not transnational—signature and potential utilization.

In fact, some Arab analysts saw the nuclear proliferation in South Asia as a likely source of strategic instability leading more states in the region to try to become nuclear. Under these conditions, Iran could be expected to follow suit and develop its own nuclear capability. Israel, which has a significant nuclear arsenal, could take its nuclear weapons out of the proverbial basement to intimidate the Arab or Muslim countries and to impose its preferred set of political negotiating terms regarding the Arab-Israeli settlement. Thus, the strategic boundaries of the Persian Gulf region were expanded in light of the Asian nuclear tests in 1998.[52]

CONCLUSION

On May 26, 1981, the leaders of six Arab countries in the Gulf region, Bahrain, Kuwait, Oman, Qatar, Saudi Arabia, and United Arab Emirates, ended their summit meeting in Abu Dhabi by declaring the establishment of the Gulf Cooperation Council.[53] The main objective of this organization was to enhance cooperation, coordination, and integration between the member states. Meetings of the GCC states have tried to develop common foreign and security policies. The foundation period of the GCC was strongly influenced by the Iranian revolution, which threatened to destabilize the Arab regimes in the region and remake them in its own image. That stage also witnessed the outbreak of war between the two strongest states in the region, Iraq and Iran, a war that threatened to escalate and spill over into the region. In other words, the regional situation then was loaded with political and ideological threats as well as major military and strategic threats. Around these issues it was not difficult for the GCC states to reach a consensus.[54] However, around the four regional issues examined in this chapter, issues that deal with the question of who is a friend and who is an enemy in that region and how to deal with those actors, the consensus among the GCC states seems to be clearly eroding.

Three main points should be stressed in this conclusion. First, such consensus among the GCC states did not just vanish overnight. Rather, it has been eroding incrementally throughout the 1990s. The old expectation that GCC states would find it easy to develop common policies regarding regional issues and challenges due to their very similar economic, social, and political characteristics did not materialize. However, these states still agree regarding some regional developments that must be avoided, including partition or fragmentation of Iraq as a state and its potential destabilizing repercussions for their own national and regional security. They agree also about the need to coordinate their national policies against terrorism and political violence, as well as militancy in the name of Islam. In fact, the GCC states have established a sophisticated and complex system for data exchanges on threats to regime security in order to counter any political unrest or instability instigated from outside.[55]

Second, in the absence of conditions of compulsion or a house-on-fire image in international relations where a group of countries face a decisive or crucial threat to their national existence, the GCC states are, in fact, likely to develop quite divergent policies and different alliance preferences in dealing with external pressures, conforming to the overheated house image, according to the analysts of international relations. In the latter case, the external setting or structure does not confront these regional actors with the compelling conditions or an absence of alternatives that could lead to uniformity of state action and regional alliances. The relative weakening of military and ideological threats from Iraq and Iran has contributed to the erosion of the earlier consensus among the GCC states during the 1990s.

Third, there has been a growing trend in the region that may be summed up as the primacy of the state. Territorial state boundaries, even if they had started as artificial and drawn by the colonial powers, continue to be significant. Conflicts between states over these boundaries tend to have great influence over their relations, even among states that have considerable similarities, as is the case in the Gulf. In that region, state boundaries are important and popular identification with them remains unmistakable. Distinct state interests do persist and they often lead to different regional policies. For states involved with others in territorial conflicts or over external intrusion into their domestic affairs, the temptation to play balance-of-power games on the regional level becomes strong (e.g., the UAE and Bahrain's sympathy toward bringing Iraq back to the Arab fold to balance Iran). That is one more reason why relations at the regional level in the Gulf and the strategies to be pursued toward it remain the most fluid issues among GCC states.

NOTES

1. Gary Sick, "The Coming Crisis in the Persian Gulf," *The Washington Quarterly,* vol. 21, no. 2 (Spring 1998), pp. 196–98. According to Crown Prince Abdallah bin Abdel Aziz of Saudi Arabia in his comment on the first Saudi budget surplus in 19 years, "the increase in oil revenues will not slow down the program of economic reforms but will give us a greater flexibility." *Technical Review Middle East,* April 30, 2001, p. 24.

2. *al-Hayat,* July 3, 1998 reported a 10 percent cut in the budget of incomplete projects, and restrictions on filling vacant jobs in public enterprises in such areas as health, education and training. It is estimated that Saudi Arabia in 2001 and despite a significant increase in oil revenues still has over 12 percent unemployment, particularly among the educated

and the semi-educated young people, illustrating the difficulties in meeting their socioeconomic aspirations. See *Technical Review Middle East,* April 30, 2001. See also *The Middle East,* May 1, 2001.

3. *Middle East Economic Survey,* July 23, 2001.

4. Reuters (London), July 29, 2001 (online).

5. *al-Hayat,* March 24, 1999. On the improvement in the budgets of GCC countries in 2001, see *Gulf News,* February 4, 2001. Even with a significant rise in oil prices, the enhanced revenues will have to be used for paying off outstanding arrears to contractors, reducing vast domestic debts, military purposes, and possibly building foreign exchange reserves. According to the World Bank, "The windfalls from higher oil prices will be temporary, and the structural changes will need to be made to improve fiscal positions and increase the scope of private activity in domestic economies." For more, see *Technical Review Middle East,* April 30, 2001.

6. See a good analysis in "Augmenting the OPEC countries Budget Requires Moving Fast to Raise Prices," *al-Hayat,* March 1999 and also Ihsan 'Ali Bou Haliqah, "Oil is an Economic Commodity," *al-Majallah,* July 12–18, 1998, p. 51.

7. *al-Itihad* (UAE), June 8, 1999, p. 8. On pressures from the industrialized countries, particularly the United States, see *al-Hayat,* May 2001.

8. An analysis of these questions can be found in Richard Herrmann, "The Middle East and the New World Order: Rethinking U.S. Political Strategy After the Gulf War," *International Security,* vol. 16, no. 2 (Fall 1991), pp. 295–329; Abdullah al-Shayeji, "Dangerous Perceptions: Gulf Views of the U.S. Role in the Region," *Middle East Policy,* vol. 5, no. 3 (September 1997) pp. 1–13.

9. Philip Gordon, *The Transatlantic Allies and the Changing Middle East* (Oxford: Oxford University Press, 1998), chapters 3–4, and Robert Blackwill and Michael Sturmer, eds., *Allies Divided: Transatlantic Policies for the Greater Middle East* (Cambridge, MA: MIT Press, 1997).

10. John Duke Anthony, "The U.S.-GCC Relationship: A Glass Half-Empty or Half-Full," *Middle East Policy,* vol. 5, no. 2 (May 1997), pp. 22–41.

11. Michael Barnett, "Regional Security after the Gulf War," *Political Studies Quarterly,* vol. 111, no. 4 (1996–97), p. 600, and his "Sovereignty, Nationalism, and Regional Order in the Arab State System," *International Organization,* vol. 49, no. 3 (Summer 1995), pp. 479–510. See also George Joffe, "Middle Eastern Views of the Gulf Conflict and Its Aftermath," *Review of International Studies,* vol. 19, no. 2 (April 1993), pp. 177–99; and Ibrahim Karawan, "Arab Dilemmas in the 1990s: Breaking Taboos and Searching for Signposts," *Middle East Journal,* vol. 48, no. 3 (Summer 1994), pp. 439–44.

12. Ibrahim A. Karawan, "Arab Dilemmas in the 1990s," ibid.

13. For an Iranian perspective, see MEI Policy Forum, "Iran's Regional Policies," in *Middle East Insight* (September-October 1998), pp. 37–44, and Mahmood Sariolghalam, "The Future Of the Middle East," *Security Dialogue,* vol. 27, no. 3 (1996), pp. 303–17. On elite conflicts in Iran, see Mark Gasiorowski, "Power Struggle in Iran," *Middle East Policy,* vol. 7, no. 4 (2000), pp. 22–40.

14. Abdullah Al-Shayeji, "Dangerous Perceptions," pp. 2–3.

15. Ibrahim A. Karawan, "Monarchs, Mullas, and Marshals: Islamic Regimes?" *Annals of the American Academy of Political and Social Science,* vol. 524 (November 1992) pp. 104–11.

16. Ibrahim Karawan, "Saudi-Iranian Détente?" analysis of Saudi-Iranian relations posted on Gulf/2000 forum (Columbia University, March 1998).

17. This suggestion was made by Iran's assistant foreign minister for Arab and African affairs, Mohammad Sadr, and reported in the leading Arab newspaper, *al-Hayat*. For more, see "Iran's new government seen courting Arab rivals and Turkey," in *Mideast Mirror,* vol. 11, no. 171, September 4, 1997.

18. On the visit by Rafsanjani to Manama, see *al-Hayat,* March 5, 1998, p. 1.

19. *Akhbar al-Khaleej* (Bahrain), July 2, 1997, p. 7. See also a reference to statements by defense minister of Bahrain, Sheikh Khalifah Bin Ahmad Al-Khalifah, about Bahraini perceptions of Iranian threats to Bahrain's security and stability in *al-Hayat*, July 1, 1998. See also statements by Bahrain's foreign minister, Shaikh Mohammad Bin Mubarak Al-Khalifah, who attended the meeting of the Organization of Islamic States in which he said that Bahrain's relations with Iran must be based on nonintervention in the domestic affairs of each other and that "it must be evident that there are significant differences with Iran which must not be ignored. Rather, they have to be addressed frankly." *Akhbar al-Khaleej*, January 11, 1998, p. 3.

20. *al-Siyassa* (Kuwait), June 30, 1996, and *Al-Wafd* (Egypt), June 23, 1996), and *al-Watan* (Kuwait), June 11, 1996, and *al-Siyassa* (Kuwait), June 1996, p. 1, p. 8.

21. Sayyed Zahrah "Yawmiyat Siyassiyah" [Political Diaries], *Akhbar al-Khaleej*, December 10, 1997, p. 7.

22. Omran Salman in *Akhbar al-Khaleej* (Bahrain), July 14, 1999 and *al-Khaleej* (United Arab Emirates), July 30, 1999. See also statements by the late Sheikh 'Issa Bin Salman Al-Khalifa in *Akhbar al-Khaleej*, June 30, 1998, p. 3.

23. See the text of his statements in *al-Hayat*, March 1999. Conservative forces in Iran have reacted angrily to these statements. One of their newspapers (*Jumhouri Islami?*) has called the foreign minister's statements "rude" and "delusional." Furthermore, it argued that the policy adopted by the Iranian government to reduce tensions "does not seem to be fruitful vis-à-vis some small countries led by officials who accumulate weapons and support the presence of American and allied forces in the Gulf to threaten Iranian national security. They do not shy away from conducting joint military maneuvers with the Americans, however they escalate the situation when we exercise our right in conducting some military maneuvers and training." The spokesman of the ministry said, "The Islamic Republic is keen to improve its relations with the countries of the region but it maintains its right to conduct military exercises to defend its sovereign territory" and insisted that the three islands "represent an indivisible part of our land." See *al-Hayat*, March 1999.

24. See an article in *al-Watan* by the Kuwaiti commentator Mohammad Abdelkader al-Jassem. For more, see *Mideast Mirror*, vol. 11, no. 238, December 8, 1997.

25. See *al-Hayat*, March 1999. Since mid–1998, the patience of the United Arab Emirates with regard to "the visits diplomacy" by Iran seemed to be running out. Media circles close to the government wondered aloud about "occasional verbal moderation" by some Iranian leaders while other Iranian officials insisted that the islands were Iranian lands beyond any negotiations with the UAE. See a report in *al-Hayat*, July 13, 1998, p. 4.

26. Paul Stevens, "Oil and the Gulf: Alternative Futures," in Gary Sick and Lawrence G. Potter, eds., *The Persian Gulf at the Millennium* (New York: St. Martin's Press, 1997), pp. 93–94. See also *al-Hayat* June 5, 2001 and *al-Watan* June 3, 2001.

27. Joseph Kostiner and James Placke, "Low Oil Prices: Implications for the Gulf Monarchies," p. 1. On the impact of Iraqi oil, see F. J. Chalabi, "Iraq and the Future of World Oil," *Middle East Policy*, vol. 7, no. 4 (2000), pp. 163–73. On the Saudi readiness to produce enough oil to make up for most of the oil cut by Iraq in protest of American and British attempts to impose new sanction regime on Baghdad, see the statements of the Saudi oil minister in *al-Hayat*, June 3, 2001, p. 11, and *al-Hayat*, June 5, 2001.

28. See statement by the emir of Bahrain in *al-Hawadith*, April 19, 1998, p. 19. For more on the positions of Arab states in the Gulf, see Ghanim al-Najjar, "The GCC and Iraq," *Middle East Policy*, vol. 7, no. 4 (2000), pp. 92–99.

29. See *al-Hayat*, June 4, 1998, p. 3. According to Saddam Hussein's first deputy, Taha Yassin Ramadan, "the embargo against Iraq will not be lifted without a confrontation or a battle." *Al-Mushahid al-Siyassi*, May 17, 1998.

30. On approaching this issue conceptually, see Robert Pape, "Why Economic Sanctions Do Not Work," *International Security*, vol. 22, no. 2 (Fall 1997), pp. 90–136, and also by

Robert Pape, "Why Economic Sanctions Still Do Not Work," International Security, vol. 23, no. 1 (Summer 1998), pp. 66–77.

31. Sayyed Zahrah, "Al-'Awdah,"[The Return] Akhbar al-Khaleej, February 2, 1998.

32. See an editorial in Al-Khaleej (UAE) that portrays Iraq as the solution to most Arab, regional problems "Ba'd Tis' Sanawat?!" [After Nine Years?!], July 30, 1999.

33. Agence France Presse, June 28, 1998. The Iraqi News Agency, INA, responded by saying: "These [Kuwaiti] leaders today are working to reopen wounds and increase tensions and sow discord to serve the interests of the Americans and their Zionist allies." AFP, June 29, 1998.

34. al-Qabas (Kuwait), July 13, 1998. See also reports in al-Hayat, June 5, 2001 about Saudi official complaints against Iraqi armed incursions into Saudi territory that resulted in a few clashes and a number of casualties.

35. Statements by the Bahraini foreign minister to Akhbar al-Khaleej on January 11, 1998, p. 4. In response to American pressures, GCC countries lifted secondary and tertiary types of Arab economic boycott against Israel.

36. See, for example, "GCC Foreign Ministers Issue Statement at the End of Meeting In Riyadh," BBC Summary of World Broadcasts, June 30, 1998.

37. See the rationale for Qatar's position in the speech delivered by the emir at the Council of Foreign Relations in New York on June 10, 1997, p. 2. For a more recent example, see the Qatari suggestion in mid-May 2001 to host a summit meeting between Chairman Arafat of the Palestinian Authority and Israel's Prime Minister Sharon in Doha at a time when the Arab League had decided to sever all ties with Israel. See al-Hayat and al-Safir, May 13–17, 2001.

38. See on that position statements of Shaikh 'Issa Bin Salman Al-Khalifa in Akhbar al-Khaleej (Bahrain), June 30, 1998, p. 3.

39. Ahmed Ali, "Nahnu Talamidhukum wa Antum Asatithatuna fi Tatbi' al-'Alaqat ma'a Isra'il," al-Watan (Qatar), November 9, 1997.

40. See in particular Ahmed Ali, "al 'urubah 'ala al-Tariqah al-Misriyah," al-Watan, (Qatar) November 11, 1997.

41. al-Hayat, June 4, 1998, p. 3.

42. Mahfouz al-Ansari, "Halaqat Niqash Mahdudah wa Hadith min al-Qalb," [A Limited Discussion Forum and a Talk from the Heart], Al-Ahram, January 15, 1994, p. 6. After the Amman Arab summit conference in April 2001, Oman's foreign minister has insisted that Arab states should be expected to implement summit decisions according to their different perceptions and positions. See al-Hayat's coverage of the conference.

43. See by Magdy Omar, "India and Pakistan: a Nuclear Confrontation or Mutual Deterrence," in a leading newspaper in the United Arab Emirates, al-Itihad, July 1, 1998, and Tal'at Msalam, "The Implications of the Nuclear Race in South Asia on the Arab-Israeli Conflict," al-Itihad, July 19, 1998.

44. On the Pakistani calculations see Samina Ahmed, "Pakistan's Nuclear Weapons Program," International Security, vol. 23, no. 4 (Spring 1999), pp. 178–204, and S. Ahmed, "Security Dilemmas of Nuclear-Armed Pakistan," Third World Quarterly, vol. 21, no. 5 (2000), pp. 781–94.

45. Abdallah al-Shayji, "Tawazun al-Ru'b," [Balance of Terror] al-Watan (Kuwait), May 30, 1998, and article by Fawziya Abu Khalid in al-Hayat, July 1, 1988, p. 17.

46. Interview with the defense minister of Bahrain, al-Hayat, June 27, 1998, p. 4. See along similar lines al-Itihad (UAE), July 23, 1998.

47. See the article by Shafiq al-Masri in al-Hayat, June 18, 1998, p. 17.

48. See "India, Pakistan and Nuclear Explosions," al-Safir, June 27, 1998, p. 22.

49. al-Itihad, July 19, 1998.

50. The Iranian daily newspaper, Kar-va-Kargar, argued that "As one of the pioneering Islamist States, Iran's need for an 'Islamic bomb' is quite clear. . . . [It is] a vital necessity. . . .

Particularly because of the Zionist regime's proven hostility towards Iran." The newspaper has added that "Considering the nuclear capability of India, Pakistan, Kazakhstan and the Zionist regime, Iran's geopolitical situation demands a revision in this regard." *Reuters,* June 8, 1998.

51. Ibrahim A. Karawan, "The Case For a Nuclear-Weapon-Free Zone in the Middle East," in Ramesh Thakur, ed., *Nuclear Weapons-Free Zones* (London: Macmillan, 1998), pp. 184–93.

52. Gamil Mattar, "The Bomb has Brought India Back to the Map of the Gulf," in *al-Hayat,* May 24, 1998, p. 17. See also S. Sitarman, "Domestic Politics and Grand Foreign Policy Motivations of the Indian Nuclear Weapons Program," *Journal of South Asian and Middle Eastern Studies,* vol. 24, no. 1 (2000), pp. 57–74; and Fawzi Saloukh, "On India, Pakistan and the Nuclear Explosions," *al-Safir,* May 23, 1998, p. 22.

53. Hassan Hamdan Al-Alkim, *The GCC States in an Unstable World* (London: Saqi Books, 1994), pp. 42–47

54. Ralph Magnus, "The GCC and Security: The Enemy Without and the Enemy Within," *Journal of South Asian and Middle Eastern Studies,* vol. 20, no. 3 (Spring 1997), pp. 72–94.

55. Amitav Acharya, "Regionalism and Regime Security in the Third World: Comparing the Origins of the ASEAN and the GCC," in Brian Job, ed., *The Insecurity Dilemma* (Boulder: Lynne Rienner Publishers, 1992), pp. 159–61.

CHAPTER 4

A REGIONAL SECURITY SYSTEM
IN THE PERSIAN GULF

SAIDEH LOTFIAN

INTRODUCTION

This chapter explores the development of a new regional security framework for the Persian Gulf and discusses the sources and security implications of actual and potential threats that have to be considered in any study of the Persian Gulf security system.

In discussing the security regimes for this region, the author has three purposes: to describe the security dilemma of these states in a historical context; to examine the conflicting assessments of the regional balance of power with an emphasis on direct and indirect foreign military involvement; and to explore the essential steps toward ultimate development of a mutually beneficial regional security system for the six members of the Gulf Cooperation Council (GCC), Iran and Iraq.

This chapter also examines key assumptions about Persian Gulf security, starting with observations summarized in the following box. These assumptions underlie reasons for the increase in militarization of the region, its consequence of increasing instability and economic problems (particularly in view of the demographic characteristics and more importantly the age structure of the regional states), and the future of evolving regional interdependence. Finally, the trend toward greater regional cooperation is described and explained by the need to expand socioeconomic opportunities throughout the Persian Gulf dictating a general process toward regionalism, and by a renewed interest in "Islamic solidarity."

INHERENT INSECURITY PROBLEMS

The eight Persian Gulf states possess 3,926,063 square kilometers of land area, are in control of a large portion of the world's oil and gas resources, and have maritime jurisdiction over important waterways and trade routes.[1] The population of the eight Persian Gulf states in 1999 was approximately 122.8 million, of which an estimated 26.4 million live in the GCC states, 72.6 million were Iranians, and 23.8 million were

BOX 4.1

MAJOR ASSUMPTIONS ABOUT
THE PERSIAN GULF SECURITY SYSTEM

- The vulnerability of the five smallest littoral states of the Persian Gulf is such that they are not in a position to defend their territories by themselves in the event of a large-scale war.
- The three largest and most populous states (Iran, Iraq, and Saudi Arabia) have military aspirations to dominate the regional security system.
- Iraq's expansionist foreign policy is the main obstacle to building a long-lasting peaceful security system in the Persian Gulf for as long as Saddam Hussein rules.
- The reduction of the likelihood of future outbreak of wars and instability necessitates democratic reforms by the regional governments.
- A viable regional defense system is not feasible without direct involvement of major powers.
- As long as the regional governments do not show a commitment to solve their disputes peacefully, there is little that the major powers can do to advance regional security.
- A major cause of tension is the regional arms race, and as long as these states have oil income, they will continue to divert national resources to military buildup and arms imports.
- Given the oil wealth and the strategic importance for the major powers, the prospect of demilitarization in the region is unlikely.
- Long-term security in the Persian Gulf is contingent upon active participation of all regional states, the promotion of regional trade, closer political links, and respect for territorial integrity.
- A stable and favorable sociopolitical condition is associated positively with lower levels of regional disparities.

inhabitants of Iraq. The significant characteristic of the GCC population is the considerable number of foreign workers and non-natives who, by their presence, make the nationals of these states (notably Kuwait,[2] Qatar, and UAE) a minority in their own homeland.[3] Taking into account the non-national elements of the region's population, approximately 19 million foreigners (including refugees and guest workers) reside in the Persian Gulf. As a result, slightly less than 88 percent of the Persian Gulf population are nationals of the eight regional states, while the remaining 12 percent are non-nationals (based on the data presented in table 4.1 and table 4.2).[4]

Many low-income governments of the Middle East and South Asia (e.g., Egypt, Jordan, India, and Pakistan) consider the emigration of their citizens to high-income Persian Gulf states "as an opportunity for reducing unemployment, earning remittances and reducing demographic pressures."[5] The problem is that the majority of foreign workers intend to make the host countries their permanent home. The UAE leads with a 76 percent share of non-nationals in its population, closely followed by Qatar with a 75 percent share. In Iran, the non-indigenous group consists of a large number of refugees, and those seeking relief from economic needs. Over 3 million refugees have come from Iraqi Kurdish- and Shi'i-inhabited areas as well as war-torn Afghanistan. With a downturn in their economies, the Persian Gulf states have established restrictive cross-border regulations to check the influx of foreign workers and refugees.

Aside from the small native population, the vulnerability of the five smaller Persian Gulf states (Bahrain, Kuwait, Qatar, UAE, and Oman) is derived from geographic size, low industrial capacity, limited domestic markets, dependence on oil, uneven development, and other factors. Leaving aside the disadvantage of lack of strategic depth and lower natural resource endowments attributed to small geographic size, it may be easier for a small state (like the UAE) to grow faster than a state with a larger size and population (like Iraq). In 1998, the GCC states had a combined GDP of 237.4 billion U.S. dollars and an average GDP per capita of $9,003. Finally, a distinct character of the Persian Gulf states is that few people participate in politics and major decisions are made by traditional elites. In some cases, political participation is controlled or coordinated by the government. Pressure for broad-based political participation has often brought on increased repression. The transition to democratic rule is made possible by the emergence of a politically aware younger generation to which power will eventually be transferred. In 1999, over 45 million people (or 37 percent of the 122.8 million population) of the eight littoral states were between the ages of 13 and 32 years old. With over 40 percent, Saudi Arabia has the highest percentage of the younger generation in its population (see tables 4.1 and 4.2). In the long run, the Persian Gulf states will encounter serious unemployment problems for the multitude of young men and women with higher expectations than their parents had at their age. If not addressed, these socioeconomic problems could be disastrous for the entire region.

AREAS OF POSSIBLE CONFLICT

Here, I shall focus on the main sources of future conflict in the Persian Gulf: territorial and border disputes.[6] Nonetheless, external forces may exploit internal tensions in the Persian Gulf states for their own geopolitical gain. New security risks, emerging in these societies, stem from conflicts within states. The years ahead will provide great challenges to the decision-makers to find peaceful means to settle their centuries-old interstate disputes, and the manifold domestic conflicts. They will face increasing difficulty in applying the old tactics to new conflict situations.

The instability of national boundaries is particularly evident throughout the recent history of the Persian Gulf. There are many concurrent boundary and territorial disputes among the eight states over land and maritime areas. Some of these conflicts involve areas of considerable size, natural resources (such as oil, gas, and water) and strategic importance. The region has been the scene of great military activity and tensions in the latter half of the twentieth century. Many states in this region and the adjacent areas have been affected by the two devastating wars and continued permanent military preparation to confront the next crisis. Initial estimates of the costs of the Kuwait-Iraq war to the frontline states (Egypt, Jordan, and Turkey) as well as to the Palestinians and Pakistanis residing and working in Kuwait and Iraq were over $30 billion. Costs resulting from the UN embargo on Iraq included reduced trade and transport receipts, lost revenues earned from the Iraqi pipeline by Turkey, and the loss of worker remittances by other states. The European countries and Japan in large part covered these financial costs.[7] After the war, Kuwait was compelled to take the unusual step of getting a $5.5 billion loan to help compensate for huge resources devoted to the reconstruction efforts.[8]

Table 4.1 The Balance of Power in the Persian Gulf

Variable	Iran	Iraq	Saudi Arabia	Kuwait	Oman	Qatar	UAE	Bahrain
Total area, sq. km[1]	1648000	434920	1960582	17820	212460	11000	75581	620
Total boundaries, km	5440	3631	4415	464	—	60	867	0
Total coastlines, km[2]	3180	58	2640	499	2092	563	1318	161
Population, in thousands	72664[3]	23846	18000	2200	2213	681	2650	626
Young population, in thousands[4]	26804	8870	7518	631	735	159	575	192
	(37%)	(37%)	(42%)	(29%)	(33%)	(23%)	(22%)	(31%)
Population density per sq. km	44	55	9	123	10	62	35	1010
% nationals in population[5]	99.95[a]	100	73	35	73	25	24	63
Military personnel, in thousands[6]	545.6	429	105.5	15.3	43.5	11.8	64.5	11
	(350)	(650)		(23.7)				
Military participation ratio[7]	7.5	18	5.9	7	19.7	17.3	24.4	17.6
GDP, 1998, in billion $US	89	19	133	27	14.2	11.2	46	6
GDP per capita, 1998, in $US	5300	—	8500	13500	8300	19700	15400	8600
Total military expenditure, 1998, in billion $US[8]	5.8	1.3	20.9	3.4	1.8	1.3	3	.402
					(0.2)			(0.3)
Military burden, 1998, %[9]	6.5	6.8	15.7	12.6	12.7	11.6	6.5	6.7
Military expenditure per capita, $US	80	55	1161	1545	813	1909	1132	642
Military expenditure per sq. km area, in 1,000 $US	3.52	2.99	10.7	190.8	8.47	118.2	39.7	648.4
Value of arms imports, 1995–1999, in million $US at constant 1990 prices[b]	959	—	9231	2722	689	1134	3268	330
Nuclear weapons	0	0	0	0	0	0	0	0
Submarines	3	0	0	0	0	0	0	0
Main battle tanks	1345	2200	1055	167[10]	123	44	237	106
Amphibious	9	0	0	0	1	0	0	0
Combat aircraft	304[c]	130	432	76	40	18	99	24
Foreign forces[d]	0	1058	7000	1250	—	50 US	—	940 West
		UNIKOM	US & GCC	US & UN				

Table 4.1 (continued)

Notes: [1] Total area in square kilometers.

[2] Total coastline in kilometers. Iran has a 2,440-kilometer coastline on the Persian Gulf, and 740 kilometers on the Caspian Sea.

[3] Kurdish people make up about 7 percent of Iranian population, 20 to 25 percent of Iraqi population, and 20 to 23 percent of Turkey's population.

[4] Young population, in thousands, is total younger adult population between 13 and 32 years old. The figure in parentheses is the percent of these younger generations in total population.

[5] Percent nationals in population constitutes the percentage of the native people in the total population in 1999, as compared to the foreigners and non-national residents of the country.

[6] Military personnel, in thousands, is total active armed forces, and the figures in parentheses show reserve forces in thousands. About 30 percent of the UAE's active armed forces are expatriates.

[7] Military participation ratio is calculated by the formula: (total active military personnel / total population) x 1,000.

[8] Military expenditures in billion $US for 1998. The figures in parentheses show Foreign Military Assistance (FMA) received from the US government in millions of $US in 1998.

[9] Military burden is calculated by: (military expenditure / GDP) x 100.

[10] 218 M-1A2 will be delivered.

[a] Non-nationals residing in Iran are mostly war or economic refugees from Afghanistan and Iraq. According to the interior ministry, over 2 million foreigners in Iran have registered at 330 registration offices throughout the country since February 19, 2001. See, "1 m. more Foreign Nationals Report for Registration," *Iran News,* Wednesday May 9, 2001, p. 3.

[b] Data on arms imports are taken from the SIPRI Yearbook.

[c] Less than 50 percent of U.S. aircraft types are assumed serviceable.

[d] In Iraq, some 936 troops and 238 military observers from 33 countries (UNIKOM) are present. In Saudi Arabia, some 5,000 U.S. forces with short-term temporary duty (six months), some 600 British and 130 French forces were stationed in 1996. There is also a 7,000-strong Peninsula Shield Force (one infantry brigade) containing elements from all GCC states. In Kuwait, some 902 troops and 197 observers from 32 countries (UNIKOM) are present: 250 U.S. Army personnel and pre-positioned equipment for one armored brigade, 1,000 naval personnel, and some air force with aircraft detachments are stationed. In Qatar, pre-positioned equipment for one armored brigade was being assembled. In Bahrain, U.S. Air Force periodic detachments of fighter aircraft and support, 230 aircraft navy (Headquarter CENTCOM and Fifth Fleet) as well as 40 UK RAF (Southern Watch). In the UAE, the U.S. Air Force operates KC-10 refueling planes from Al Dhafra Air Base to sustain U.S. fighter aircraft covering the southern no-fly zone.

Source: *The Military Balance 1999–2000.* (Oxford and London: Oxford University Press; for the IISS, October 1999); "North Africa and Middle East," *Military Technology (MILTECH)* 17, 1 (1993): 137–65; and U.S. CIA, *The World Factbook 1994.* University of St. Louis Libraries, 1994. Björn Hagelin, Pieter D. Wezeman, and Siemon T. Wezeman, "The Volume of Transfers of Major Conventional Weapons," *SIPRI Yearbook: Armaments, Disarmament and International Security.* Oxford: Oxford University Press, for SIPRI, 2000, pp. 368–77.

Table 4.2 The Balance of Power in the GCC. Three Potential Gulf Security Systems, and Selected Peripheral Countries, 1999

Variable	GCC	PG 5	PG 7	PG 8	Turkey	Pakistan	Israel
Total area, sq. km[1]	2278063	317481	3491143	3926063	780580	803940	20770
Total coastlines, km[2]	7273	4633	10453	10511	7200	1046	273
Population, in thousands	26370	8370	99034	122880	65161	144350	6007
Young population, in thousands[4]	9810	2292	36614	45484	24367	52809	2092
	(37%)	(27%)	(37%)	(37%)	(37%)	(37%)	(35%)
Population density per sq. km	11.6	26.4	28.4	31.3	83	180	289
Military personnel, in thousands[6]	251.6	146.1	797.2	1226.2	639	587	173.5
	(23.7)	(23.7)	(373.7)	(1023.7)	(378.7)	(513)	(425)
Military participation ratio[7]	9.5	17.5	8.1	10	9.8	4.1	28.9
GDP, 1998, in billion $US	237.4	104.4	326.4	345.4	188	61	97
GDP per capita, 1998, in $US	9003	12473	3296	2812	6300	2400	18200
Total military expenditure, in million $US[8]	30802	9902	36602	37902	8400	4000	11300
	(0.2)				(22)	(2.5)	(3000)
Military burden, 1998, %[9]	12.97	9.5	11.2	10.97	4.5	6.6	11.7
Military expenditure per capita, $US	1168	1183	369.6	308.5	129	27.7	1881
							(2381)
Military expenditure per sq. km area, $US	13521	31189	10484	9654	10761	4975	544054
Value of arms imports, 1995–1999, in million $US at constant 1990 prices	17374	8134	18333	18333	6461	2873	2903
Nuclear weapons	0	0	0	0	0	10–15	100–300
Submarines	0	0	3	3	15	10	4
Main battle tanks	1732	677	3077	5277	4205	2320	3800
Amphibious	1	1	10	10	8	0	1
Combat aircraft	689	257	993	1123	440	389	459[a]
Foreign forces[b]	9240 West	2240 West	9240 West	10298 West	2800 West	UNMOGIP	0

(continues)

Table 4.2 (continued)

Notes: *PG 5* includes GCC members except Saudi Arabia. *PG 7* includes the six GCC members plus Iran. *PG 8* includes the six GCC members plus Iran and Iraq.

[1] Total area in square kilometers.

[2] Total coastline in kilometers. Iran has a 2,440-kilometer coastline on the Persian Gulf, and 740 kilometers on the Caspian Sea.

[3] Kurdish people make up about 7 percent of Iranian population, 20 to 25 percent of Iraqi population, and 20 to 23 percent of Turkey's population.

[4] Young population, in thousands, is total younger adult population between 13 and 32 years old. The figure in parentheses is the percent of these younger generations in total population.

[5] Percent nationals in population constitutes the percentage of the native people in the total population in 1999, as compared to the foreigners and non-national residents of the country.

[6] Military personnel, in thousands, is total active armed forces, and the figures in parentheses show reserve forces in thousands. About 30 percent of the UAE's active armed forces are expatriates.

[7] Military participation ratio is calculated by the formula: (total active military personnel / total population) x 1,000.

[8] Military expenditures in billion $US for 1998. The figures in parentheses show Foreign Military Assistance (FMA) received from the US government in millions of $US in 1998.

[9] Military burden is calculated by: (military expenditure / GDP) x 100.

[10] 218 M–1A2 will be delivered.

[a] The are also an estimated 250 combat jets stored.

[b] In Turkey, the NATO HQ Allied Land Forces South Eastern Europe (LANDSOUTHEAST), and HQ 6 Allied Tactical Air Force (6 ATAF) are located. Also for Operation Northern Watch, there are 230 personnel from the UK Air Force with six Tornado, and 3,034 U.S. military personnel. Israel has periodic detachments of F–16s at Akinci air base. On Turkish territory, the U.S. has installations for seismic monitoring.

Source: The Military Balance 1999–2000. (Oxford and London: Oxford University Press; for the IISS, October 1999); "North Africa and Middle East," *Military Technology (MILITECH)* 17, 1 (1993): 137–65; and U.S. CIA, *The World Factbook 1994.* University of St. Louis Libraries, 1994. Bjorn Hagelin, Pieter D. Wezeman, and Siemon T. Wezeman, "The Volume of Transfers of Major Conventional Weapons," *SIPRI Yearbook: Armaments, Disarmament and International Security.* Oxford: Oxford University Press, for SIPRI, 2000, pp. 368–77; and the author's calculations.

At the moment, regional military confrontations might be in abeyance, but the underlying causes of the past wars have not been addressed. From the highest to the lowest likelihood of occurrence, I shall briefly discuss four potential conflict situations in the Persian Gulf. They are 1) conflict over Iraqi territorial claims to Kuwait; 2) the Iran-UAE islands dispute; 3) the Iran-Iraq border dispute, and 4) territorial disputes among the GCC.

THE IRAQ-KUWAIT BOUNDARY DISPUTE

Given the history of animosity between Iraq and Kuwait, and the character of the Iraqi leader, Saddam Hussein, it is easy to understand why the Kuwaitis think that the border issue has not been permanently settled.[9] Despite the enforcement of the land and maritime boundary on January 15, 1993, based on the reaffirmation of Kuwait's sovereignty over the offshore islands of Warbah and Bubiyan, the problem of Iraq's territorial claims has not been resolved. The Iraqi regime initially refused to cooperate with the UN Commission charged with redrawing Kuwait-Iraq boundaries. In a sense, the instability of the Iraq-Kuwait joint border is of concern to the other Persian Gulf states. Beyond doubt, any Iraqi annexation of these islands for military purposes would be followed by a strong Iranian counteraction.[10] In August 1990, the Iranian government announced its support for the liberation of Kuwait. The then-president Ali Akbar Hashemi Rafsanjani declared that his country would "tolerate no alteration of political geography of the region"[11] and emphasized the sovereignty and territorial integrity of regional states. The government of President Mohammad Khatami has followed the same policy of opposing any effort aimed at changing the map of the region.

There remain two solutions for this uncertain situation. One entails maintaining a UN peacekeeping force (e.g., the UN Iraq-Kuwait Observation Mission or UNIKOM) indefinitely in the conflict-prone border areas, at least for as long as the regime of Saddam Hussein remains in power in Baghdad. The other is pressing for a democratic regime change in Iraq without further delay. The U.S. government has looked into the second option and has established contacts with the anti-government Iraqi National Congress (INC). The INC is an umbrella organization of Iraqi opposition groups formed in 1992. It includes the two main Iraqi Kurdish groups (the Kurdistan Democratic Party and the Patriotic Union of Kurdistan) as well as the Iraqi National Accord consisting of former Iraqi government officials. However, other opposition groups such as the Iranian-backed Supreme Council for Islamic Revolution in Iraq and the Iraqi Communist Party do not believe that a U.S.-backed resistance would succeed in overthrowing the Saddam regime.[12] Unlike 1953, when the U.S. government helped to topple the government of Premier Mossadegh in Iran through behind-the-scenes assistance, Washington has now shown a willingness to involve itself more openly in determining the new Baghdad leadership.

The case of Iran apparently has not provided U.S. decision-makers with valuable lessons for its future involvement in the internal affairs of Third World states. The main weakness of the U.S. plan to defeat Saddam Hussein by helping the Iraqi opposition groups to install a new regime in Baghdad is its foreign imposition. Any new regime would have a problem of legitimacy in the eyes of the Iraqi people who, like other Middle Easterners, are suspicious of foreign designs. Given the historical animosities of the rival factions forming the INC, moreover, the United States will find it very hard to work with this group. Still, time is on Hussein's side. For how long will foreign forces be willing and able to maintain the northern no-fly zone for the protection of Iraqi Kurds?[13] It is highly probable that if the Iraqi regime is left unchanged, it will repeat its indiscriminate attacks on its own people (starting with the ethnic and religious minorities), and create hundreds of thousands of Kurdish and Shi'i expellees and refugees. However, many observers are wondering whether war with one of his neighbors had not lost its value as a means of survival for the current Iraqi regime.

THE IRAN-UAE ISLANDS DISPUTE

It has been occasionally observed that naval strategy calls for Iran to block the Strait of Hormuz in the event of a war in the Persian Gulf. Hence, Iranian control of the three strategically located islands of Greater and Lesser Tunb and Abu Musa had been seen in light of Iran's desire to have a dominant regional power position. This leaves two major choices open to the two neighboring states: first, going to war over these three islands; or second, limiting the causes of armed confrontation through direct bilateral negotiation over their future status. Conscious of the cost of a war, neither side has demonstrated any intention to choose the first option. Iran's stance on the islands is that the dispute should be settled peacefully without the threat or use of military force.

Iranian papers have quoted official foreign ministry sources as saying, "Iran has always expressed readiness for resolving the current misunderstandings between Iran and the UAE in an atmosphere of trust . . . Iran has also announced that it is prepared to hold the negotiations anywhere."[14] For its part, UAE government officials have recognized Iran's need for self-defense capability. In May 1994, the crown prince of Abu Dhabi, Shaikh Khalifa Ibn Zayed Ibn Sultan Al-Nahyan, commenting on Iran's naval modernization program, stated: "Any country has the right to consolidate its forces, but without carrying out aggression or threatening others . . . We are bolstering our defenses to face all crises, but we believe stability in the Gulf will not be achieved through a race for acquiring advanced weapons."[15]

Beyond these explicit official statements, bilateral UAE-Iran trade statistics highlight the significance of economic interactions as a basis for broadening the common areas of interest. An official report released by the Dubai Customs Department revealed that Iran ranked first in trade partnership with Dubai in 1997.[16] Simple logic would suggest that a possible solution to the UAE-Iran island dispute would be the creation of a "mutual economic zone" in Abu Musa island where the two states have joint sovereignty. But politics in this region often defies logic. Realistically, the UAE-Iran islands dispute must be examined within the context of Arab-Iranian relations, particularly Iran-GCC ties. In a May 1999 informal one-day meeting in Jeddah of the GCC heads of states, UAE president Sheikh Zaid bin Sultan al-Nahyan decided not to join the other five leaders. This was interpreted to mean that the UAE government is eyeing Iran-Saudi rapprochement with watchful suspicion because it is afraid that Saudi Arabia may no longer support the UAE position on Abu Musa.[17] And yet, in an apparent effort to soothe UAE officials on the sensitive issue of the three islands, Qatari foreign minister Shaikh Hamad was reported as sympathetically saying, "We in Qatar consider this as an issue not only of the UAE but also as our issue. . . . We believe that Iran should hold negotiations with the UAE on resolving the issue through peaceful means or through arbitration. This is Qatar's firm position."[18]

At the conclusion of the twenty-first annual GCC Heads of State Summit in Manama on December 31, 2000, the six member states issued a statement that endorsed the UAE's request to take the island dispute to the International Court of Justice (ICJ) in The Hague.[19] Not surprisingly, Iran's foreign ministry spokesman, Hamid Reza Assefi, voiced Tehran's immediate objection to this idea by saying, "We regret that these countries unreasonably and out of international standards and regardless of neighborly amicable relations, have raised certain claims against the territorial integrity of the Islamic Republic of Iran and its territorial waters."[20] As to the suggestion of resorting to the ICJ to resolve the dispute, Iran's Deputy Foreign Minister Mohammad Sadr said, "Our position is clear. The Persian Gulf islands are an integral part of Iran's territory. . . . I don't think the issue will go to court. It is not a court matter."[21] Iranian officials have invariably announced their preference for direct negotiations with the UAE government as a means of conflict settlement.

Even though the role of third parties might facilitate conflict management, there is a more significant factor for peaceful resolution of a dispute. When territorial negotiations involve states with a background of hostility, reaching an agreement is more complicated because neither side trusts the other or has any faith in its expressed non-belligerence. Central to this conception is the idea that action shows one's intentions better than mere words. In order to have better understanding of interstate disputes, two factors must be considered: the history of animosity and the personality of leaders involved. The case of the Iran-UAE controversy over the islands does not constitute a protracted and historically long conflict, nor is it one that requires immediate attention by either side. A positive factor is the ascension of a moderate leader in Iran, known for his determination to reduce tension in Iranian foreign relations. Iranian politicians have tried to make it clear to their southern neighbors that Iran does not pose a direct threat to them and is not interested in territorial expansion. Even the presence of foreign forces in the region and military cooperation between the UAE (and the other GCC states) with the United States is not an obstacle to strengthening Tehran-UAE relations. There are close U.S. allies (such as Turkey) that have maintained neighborly ties with Iran within the framework of regional organizations (such as the Economic Cooperation Organization). In terms of naval power, the Iranian military presence in the Persian Gulf is now far less than it was before the revolution. Because of the inescapably high stakes involved for the two contiguous states, Iran's main military concern is the 1,456–kilometer land frontier with Iraq, where there have been periodic border clashes and a costly eight-year armed conflict starting in 1980.[22] This brings us to the discussion of the third probable conflict in the Persian Gulf in the near future.

THE IRAN-IRAQ BORDER DISPUTE

The irredentist ambitions of Baghdad in the southwestern Iranian province of Khuzistan are well known, as are its claims over the Shatt Al-Arab waterway (called the Arvand River by the Iranians), and joint border areas. A major security concern for Tehran is to deter further Iraqi military adventures in Iranian territories and persuade Baghdad to stop supporting and providing sanctuaries for the anti-government *Mujaheddin-i Khalq Organization* (MKO) based in Iraq. In the spring of 2001, the Iranian military launched missile and air attacks on the MKO bases inside Iraqi territory.[23] Compromise on this issue would appear to be ruled out, since what is in dispute is the internal security of Iran. This fact alone should be sufficient to call into question the proposition that Iran and Iraq might form an anti-U.S. alliance as a reaction to its dual containment policy.

Saddam Hussein tried to justify his September 1980 invasion of Iran by stating, "Iran has shore along the Gulf extending for hundreds of kilometers, while Iraq has only limited outlets, most important of which is the Shatt al-Arab."[24] The Iraqi move was a clear violation of the 1975 Algiers agreement signed by the two riparian states of the Shatt Al-Arab to end an enduring boundary dispute. However, some western commentators tacitly supported the Iraqi territorial claim over the Shatt Al-Arab. One author argued:

> For Iraq, the Shatt al-Arab is only one of its geographic vulnerabilities in the area. . . . Umm Qasr, the Iraqi naval base, lies on the border with Kuwait, and can only be reached by sea through a narrow passage between the Iraqi shore and Kuwaiti islands. . . . Iraq is also the only member of OPEC whose oil exports cannot reach the outside world without crossing foreign territory in the north (Syria, Turkey, and Lebanon), or without coming so close to Iranian territory in the south that it cannot be said to enjoy territorial security at all for its principal means of survival.[25]

Whatever the cause, the Iran-Iraq War has the unenviable distinction of being one of the most violent and lengthy wars of the twentieth century in the Third World with thousands of civilian and military fatalities, 2 million wounded, and millions of war refugees. There are palpable reminders of the deadly conflict. Since the end of the war, several hundred Iranians have been killed or injured from thousands of land mines planted along Iran-Iraq borders. In 2000, 1.8 billion rials were allocated to mine-sweeping operations.[26] Iranians feel they should remain attentive to risks associated with any signs of growing military power of Iraq, their old foe. The extent of the Iraqi threat is still uncertain. In reply to the question of whether "Iraq still maintains an operational missile force," UNSCOM[27] Executive Chairman Richard Butler stated: "Iraq does have a missile force of vehicles that can go *less* than 150 kilometers, and they are legal. With respect to a *prohibited* operational missile force . . . we can't say with certainty that they don't."[28] Once the UN sanctions are lifted, the Iraqi military may reemerge as a potential threat to Iran. It has to be remembered that the most serious Iran-Iraq confrontation is generally regarded as having arisen from what appears to have been Iraqi miscalculations of Iranian military power and their will to fight. Future misperceptions of each side's intentions by the other could be terribly harmful for regional stability.

TERRITORIAL DISPUTES AMONG THE GCC

Many GCC states have been embroiled in territorial and border conflict situations (e.g., Qatar vs. Bahrain, Qatar vs. Saudi Arabia, Oman vs. Saudi Arabia).[29] As with all territorial disputes, those on opposite sides of GCC disputes have strong feelings about their territorial integrity. During the fifteenth annual summit of the GCC heads of states in Manama, in December 1994, three of the principal GCC contenders, Bahrain, Qatar, and Saudi Arabia, demonstrated strong disapproval of the allegations made against them by their particular disputant.[30] The gravest dispute was the Bahrain-Qatar quarrel concerning sovereignty over the Hawar Islands located 1 kilometer from Qatar and 20 kilometers south of Bahrain, and the Dibal and Jarada shoals. In December 1995, the two tiny neighboring states were at the brink of a war. However, Bahrain and Qatar accepted a March 16, 2001 ruling of the International Court of Justice that endorsed Bahrain's sovereignty over the Hawar islands and granted the control of potentially resource-rich Dibal shoals and other territories to Qatar. At the time of this writing, the GCC states seem more responsive to changing political circumstances and show a determination to cooperate diplomatically to solve their border disputes peacefully.[31] The leaders of the UAE and Oman signed a border demarcation agreement, covering "the border sector extending from Umm Al Zumoul where the boundaries of Oman, the UAE and Saudi Arabia meet, to the east of Al-Aqeedat."[32] By the use of peaceful means of settling their disputes, the leading GCC allies have contributed to achieving and maintaining regional tranquility, which could promote economic development.

THE REGIONAL BALANCE OF POWER

Intensified regional arms acquisitions have made the GCC a primary trading partner of the major Western powers. To help the GCC states in their efforts to modernize their armed forces, European states (notably the United Kingdom and France) and the United States have focused their arms sales on them in the aftermath of the second Persian Gulf war. Military cooperation between the major powers and the Persian Gulf states assumes varied forms ranging from transfers of major weapon systems to the provision of advisers and military personnel. Obviously, economic factors have influenced their positions as arms suppliers. Political considerations, nevertheless, continue to play a substantial role in arms sales policies.

Iranian government officials have argued that the United States and its major allies have used a fictional "Iran threat" as an excuse to maintain their domination of the Persian Gulf. The United States has embarked on a massive military buildup in the region and tried to justify its military domination by pointing to Iranian aggressive policies and placing them in the context of Iran's foreign policy goal of exporting the Islamic revolution to other regional states. As examples of suspicious behavior, they call attention to Iran's military modernization program, its plan to complete the Bushehr nuclear reactor (as a way to acquire nuclear capability), its support for terrorism and its opposition to the Middle East peace process.

Some Iranians and others in the Middle East argue that the United States played a role in encouraging Iraq to invade Kuwait for two purposes: to create a pretext for stationing American forces in the Persian Gulf region, and gaining access to military bases; and to destroy Iraq's war-making capabilities. Now they are arguing that the United States tries to exaggerate the "Saddam threat" to justify the continued presence of U.S. military forces. Whatever the underlying causes of the Iraqi invasion of Kuwait, it is remarkable that in its wake many regional states sought to strengthen their military power position. Looking at the statistics presented in tables 4.1 and 4.2, the following facts are noteworthy. More than 37 billion dollars were spent in 1998 in the military budgets of the eight littoral states of the Persian Gulf. This represents nearly 11 percent of the GDP of these oil-rich countries. With $30.8 billion in military expenditures, the share of the six GCC member-states in regional defense expenditures is about 81 percent. Saudi Arabia's military budget is now one of the largest in the world and in 1998 its defense expenditures reached over 15.7 percent of GDP.

Saudi Arabia ranked as the number one recipient of major conventional weapons in the period 1992–97. For the five-year period of 1995–99, its aggregate arms imports equaled $9.2 billion U.S. dollars.[33] The Persian Gulf countries and the three proximate states of Israel, Pakistan, and Turkey accounted for almost one-third of the value of the world's arms imports in 1993–1997.[34]

Beyond the sheer volume of arms transferred to the GCC states, the arms export deals of the major powers are striking for three other reasons. One is that they entail payment of billions of dollars in cash or oil,[35] and the second is the degree of technical sophistication of advanced major weapons systems delivered to Saudi Arabia, the UAE, and Kuwait. Lastly, all five permanent members of the UN Security Council have been involved in arms sales to the Persian Gulf. The UAE and the United States are negotiating for a package of military sales including F–16 fighters, missiles, and radar systems for delivery in 2004. To promote arms sales, among other reasons, the United Kingdom opened a permanent defense attaché's office in Doha in July 1995. The United Kingdom Royal Air Force has taken on the task of training Qatari aircrews. And the two governments have signed a number of defense agreements, including a November 1996 memorandum of understanding for arms sales with an estimated value of about U.S.$830 million.[36] One unprecedented arms deal involved China and Saudi Arabia. In March 1988, the first report of the sale of the Chinese nuclear-capable DF–3 (or CSS–2) (*Dongfeng*, or East Wind) IRBMs, with a range of 1,800 to 3,200 kilometers, came out. The catalyst for this deal was the American government's rejection of the Saudi request to sell Stinger missiles and their launchers to the Arab kingdom. Some analysts have argued that Saudi Arabia got the short end of the stick by exchanging a considerable amount of money for an obsolete weapon system.[37]

Much has been written about Iran's military buildup and its hidden agenda to develop an offensive capability. One has to keep in mind the fact that in 1975, prior to the revolution, Iran ranked seventh among 140 countries, with $7.7 billion in military expenditures.[38] In 1979, Iran had over 600 high-performance combat jets and various helicopters supplied by the West. More than 20 years after the revolution, this large country has 304 jet aircraft, of which fewer than 50 percent are assumed serviceable. As an observer noted, "Iran is building an air force, not rebuilding one."[39] Compared to this, the six GCC states had a total of 689 top-of-the line combat aircraft in 1999, and had placed orders for more aircraft with the United States, United Kingdom, and France.

Most concern has been centered on the long-range missile capability of Iran and Iraq, because this can threaten countries outside the region (e.g., Israel) as well as the U.S. forces in the Persian Gulf. As a result, the United States is providing financial aid to Israel for the development of an anti-missile defense. Iraqi missile attacks against targets in Saudi Arabia and Israel had negligible military impact. However, a key question often raised in strategic studies is whether Third World host countries willing to permit their territory to be used by U.S. military forces for either deterrence or war-fighting invite hostile retaliation against their own populations. Saudi lack of confidence in U.S. resolve and ability to shield Saudi Arabia from Iraqi attack contributed to an initial reluctance in Riyadh to request U.S. intervention after Iraqi troops captured Kuwait.

In Turkey, there was domestic criticism of President Ozal's handling of the crisis. Foreign ministry officials were concerned that Ozal's hardline stance toward Saddam Hussein could drag Turkey into a direct confrontation with Iraq. The important issue was whether Ankara should permit the U.S. Air Force to use the NATO airbase at Incirlik, located about 500 kilometers from the Iraqi border, which is now home to about 55 U.S., French, and British air force jets flying patrols over the no-fly zone that covers the Kurdish region of northern Iraq. General Necip Torumtay's resignation, and the replacement of retired General Kemal Yamak, the president's national security adviser, signaled sharp differences among the Turkish decision-makers concerning Turkey's support for the coalition forces. If Iraq had launched Scud missiles at Ankara or other cities in the territory of its northern neighbor, Ozal might have shifted his position from support of U.S. war efforts to a more neutral stance in the crisis.[40]

One can conclude that unrestricted exports of high-technology weapons systems, and particularly long-range missiles, will be accompanied by higher levels of uncertainty in times of crisis. In economic terms, these arms imports are definitely unprofitable; they are neither capital goods nor consumer goods. As such, they deplete national resources without generating needed goods and services for the public. The only public good they are supposed to produce is security against foreign attacks. However, the question is how much is enough for the defense of states, which need their scarce national resources for the development of the civilian sectors of their economies. It is widely believed that one reason for Japan's economic miracle was that it limited its military expenditures, relying on the United States to protect it. By contrast, a heavy defense burden and the ill-usage of national resources is assumed to be a reason for the breakup of the Soviet Empire.

Another trend is a marked increase in the size of the armed forces of the Persian Gulf states. In 1999, there were over one million regular military forces in the region. The GCC's military personnel amounted to 251,600, bringing the alliance's Military Participation Ratio (MPR) to more than nine. This meant that there were about ten soldiers and officers in every 1,000 population of the southern Persian Gulf. In descending order, the sizes of regular military forces of the eight littoral states were (in thousands): Iran (545.6), Iraq (429), Saudi Arabia (105.5), UAE (64.5), Oman (43.5), Kuwait (15.3),[41] Qatar (11.8), and Bahrain (11). The 1999 MPR of these states were from the highest to the lowest as follows: UAE (24.4), Oman (19.7), Iraq (18), Bahrain (17.6), Qatar (17.3), Iran (7.5), Kuwait (7.0), and Saudi Arabia (5.9). (Refer to tables 4.1 and 4.2.)

REGIONAL SECURITY ARRANGEMENTS

In the following section, I provide a brief account of major security arrangements, some of which have been put into practice in the Persian Gulf since the end of the 1991 war. Some are derived from the standard framework in existing literature on regional security systems as they relate to the Persian Gulf; others indicate gaps in that literature.

THE STATUS QUO
(A U.S.-SUPPORTED REGIONAL SECURITY FRAMEWORK)

The vulnerability of the five smallest littoral states of the Persian Gulf is such that they are not in a position to defend their territories in the event of a large-scale war. If a state is incapable of defending itself, the obvious option is to search for a powerful ally. Two crucial events, the 1979 Iranian revolution and the Iraq-Kuwait crisis, brought about a marked change in the nature of U.S. military relations with the strategically situated Persian Gulf states. The United States was transformed from a close Iranian ally to the leading Iranian adversary and became militarily active in the southern Persian Gulf. During the Iran-Iraq War, the United States put its own flag on eleven Kuwaiti tankers starting in mid–1987, and provided naval protection for them. Immediately after its liberation, Kuwait decided to sign ten-year bilateral defense agreements with the five permanent members of the UN Security Council.[42]

As noted earlier, the two larger northern Persian Gulf states, which have been subjected to the U.S. dual containment policy, are the main challengers of the U.S.-

dominated regional security framework. According to some analysts, the major reason for Iran's opposition to the presence of foreign forces is that these forces are viewed "as a potential rival that would dilute Iran's otherwise important regional role. This role is expected to increase as a potential counterweight for Iraq."[43] Whatever the reason may be, the Iranian government has adamantly protested the U.S. military buildup in the region, and consistently calls for the removal of all foreign military forces there. It has been noted that the United States and other great powers have historically attempted to maintain and secure access to Persian Gulf resources and markets for themselves and their allies and often to keep out their rivals. Consequently, arms trade agreements, technical assistance, military aid, and advisers have been offered to the regional states. Iranian government officials in particular have shown a sensitivity to the deployment of American naval forces in the waters of the Persian Gulf, and the military basing strategy of the United States aimed at gaining access to a network of air bases and port facilities in the area. Since the end of the Desert Storm and Desert Shield operations, Iranians have complained that foreign military involvement in the region makes cooperation on security issues among the Persian Gulf states more difficult.

The Iranian political and military elites have expressed similar perspectives on the security implications of the foreign military presence for the regional states. During the September 1996 U.S. military buildup in the Persian Gulf—a consequence of the Iraqi armed intervention in Kurdish-inhabited northern Iraq—the then-commander of the Islamic Revolutionary Guards Corps (IRGC), Major General Mohsen Rezaie, was quoted as saying: "[I]f the slightest problem breaks out for us or the slightest pressure is exerted on us, we'll disregard all restrictions and become engaged in conflict with the United States throughout the Persian Gulf."[44] His successor as commander of the IRGC, Rahim Safavi, has made similar statements.

In his talks with visiting Saudi defense minister Prince Sultan Ibn abd al-Aziz in Tehran, the supreme leader of Iran (*Rahbar*), Ayatollah Ali Khamenei, underscored Iran's eagerness to promote cooperation with Saudi Arabia but condemned "the destabilizing presence of foreign forces" in the Persian Gulf.[45] Speaking during the Iran-Taliban crisis, President Khatami offered an identical sentiment by calling the presence of American forces in the Persian Gulf a source of crisis and security concern for others. He added that "it is surprising that the Americans express concerns about the measures taken to ensure the safety and security of our eastern borders. Undoubtedly, we are more concerned about regional security than the Americans."[46] Following along a similar line of reasoning, Iran's Foreign Minister Kamal Kharrazi stated:

[W]e believe the presence of forces outside our region will not help to strengthen regional security, but will in itself serve as an element of tension. Existence of crises provides an excuse for the presence of these forces. . . . Their presence will turn the region into a military barrack, cause greater instability, lead to proliferation of conventional and non-conventional weapons, pollute the environment and in the long run impede political, social and economic development of the countries in the region. . . . We have consistently believed that security in the Persian Gulf cannot be "imported," and the accumulation of a huge arsenal of weapons will not help improve the security situation.[47]

In a message to the eleventh annual Persian Gulf International Conference in Tehran, President Mohammad Khatami expressed the same sentiment. He said, "As long as we define the Persian Gulf region just as an energy resource, the destructive presence of alien forces would continue and improper domestic rivalries would overshadow peace and stability in the region."[48]

To most Iranian government officials, the Persian Gulf has basically been turned into an American-dominated body of water in the post–Cold War era. The head of Iran's Environmental Protection Organization has claimed that the Persian Gulf, a shallow body of water, can no longer bear the burden of the presence of American forces and their military exercises. The level of water pollution in the Persian Gulf is 47 times more than that of the open seas, and a leading reason is the presence and frequent passage of U.S. military naval vessels.[49] Officials have also expressed concern over the potential for nuclear accidents or incidents in the Persian Gulf involving U.S. nuclear-powered attack submarines.[50] Whether or not foreign forces have introduced nuclear weapons in this region is a question that remains to be answered. The U.S. government does not provide any information about its nuclear deployments. In September 1995, the commander of the USS New Orleans Amphibious Ready Group (ARG), Captain Richard Ormsbee, was asked whether his naval vessel, which called at the UAE port of Jebel Ali, carried any nuclear weapons. He replied, "U.S. government policy does not allow us to disclose such information. I can neither confirm nor deny any nuclear capabilities on board."[51]

A country's power position can be enhanced by having distant bases in strategic locations, required to maintain a credible combat capability for unilateral or multilateral intervention to deal with political crises and conflict situations in the region. However, it is also evident that the United States has plans to expand its influence in the area, to confront the expansionist policies of its adversaries, and to sell military equipment to its local allies for the twin purpose of strengthening their relative power positions and to improve U.S. trade balances with the oil-rich regional states. Nevertheless, the cost of supplying and protecting American forces could be prohibitive without the contribution of the regional governments.

The naval military vessels are to be used in the event of a war with Iran or Iraq, and are often involved in military exercises with the GCC forces. As mentioned above, it is argued that the creation of the GCC in 1981 was a reaction to the Iranian revolution and the Iran-Iraq War. Times have changed. The Iranian government has begun to adopt a less ideological and more interest-oriented foreign policy approach to its relations with Europe and the GCC.

If it is the perception of shared threats that creates commonality, then the Arab-Iranian détente and an eventual regime change in Iraq tend to make the GCC as a purely defensive alliance impractical because of a lack of common enemy. Mandel maintains that the concept of alliance has changed significantly in the new security environment of the post–Cold War era. He points to "more emphasis on cross-cutting interdependence in alliances, as opposed simply to reliance on one core power, due to diffusion of types of essential power in the international arena." He also asserts that "a successful alliance is one which is regional rather than global, single-purpose rather than general all-purpose."[52] Obviously national and regional realities dictate reliance on unilateral initiatives, regardless of alliance formation, to confront security threats.

A major change will come about after the United States starts a gradual withdrawal of its own forces in the Persian Gulf. While Washington has indicated that such a change in U.S. foreign policy is unlikely for the time being, as any student of the history of great power involvement in this region can tell us, the permanent stationing of foreign forces in this region is improbable. To keep Iran and Iraq in line, and to maintain U.S. influence in the region, however American troops in the Persian Gulf will not be withdrawn soon. Indeed, the U.S. Central Command (CENTCOM), responsible for U.S. security interests in this region, also assumed responsibility for all U.S. planning and operations in Central Asia on October 1, 1999.

A NEW PERSIAN GULF SECURITY SYSTEM

The weakness of the status quo is that not much attention has been paid to democratization of the regional states. Does democracy in the Persian Gulf really matter to the foreign powers? Mernissi argues, "[D]emocracy in the Arab world would have meant an intolerable increase in unpredictability in the oil and arms markets. The enlargement of the political theatre, to allow Arab citizens to express their free will through twenty-two parliaments of Arab states, would have introduced a high level of uncertainty."[53]

What is changing in these societies is the consciousness not only of governments but also of peoples as they insist on expanding into new areas of social change. Why should we focus only on elite attitudes? Note that it is not the belief systems of the leaders that are necessarily involved, and that the change in foreign-policy attitudes of the Persian Gulf states may be even greater if foreign-policy attitudes of the masses are taken into account. We need to generate data about the beliefs of the public in the Persian Gulf regarding their countries' foreign-policy posture. We should explore questions of what state-society relations will be like in the coming years in each of the eight Persian Gulf states, what lies ahead for the reformists, how we might build bridges between the governments and the disillusioned public, and what will be the role of foreign powers in democratization. Whatever the final conclusions from a balanced assessment of all these questions, it is clear that the present system (i.e., the GCC plus direct foreign military presence plus the American policy of dual containment) with its exclusionary approach to regional security is no longer a viable security arrangement. National needs and conditions of all states in a region must be considered for designing a regional security system. A central deficiency of the U.S.-dominated regional security system is the failure to acknowledge the vital interests of the northern Persian Gulf states.

The second shortcoming of the status quo is that after the United States established itself as the principal power balancer in the Persian Gulf, no major efforts were undertaken to encourage democratic change. The U.S. forces stationed in a GCC state may not be much help to a besieged regime. Actions taken by foreign forces may not succeed in reversing a popular uprising or a coup d'état, even if they could have been undertaken. It is difficult to assess the potential reliability of the United States as an ally under a variety of circumstances. Will the United States support governments in times of crisis? GCC political leaders are aware that it is risky to get too close to foreign powers militarily. The experiences of the shah of Iran in 1979 and Iraqi King Faisal in 1958[54] remind them that the regional regimes with strong backing of the United States were overthrown. American policymakers have long been accused of inability "to deliver on their projects and promise."[55] Conversely, U.S. administrations have been criticized for supporting Third World leaders for longer than was justified in terms of their support among prominent segments of their own societies. From the standpoints of the Persian Gulf elite, too much confidence in foreign powers—and dependence on them—is not prudent.

As discussed above, the GCC-based security system was initially a consequence of a general fear of Iran's Islamic fundamentalism and Iraq's resurgent territorial ambitions. Fear of Iran and Iraq's military power and their probable impact on regional security has preoccupied defense planners in the GCC. Neuman, who has studied the impact of foreign military assistance in developing areas, concludes:

> New weapons that have promised enhanced capabilities often have burdened the Third World recipient with requirements for infrastructure and for maintenance, logistical, and operational skills that are rarely available. . . . Modern weapon transfers to Less Developed Countries' combatants have not, therefore, translated into short-term military power and have instead increased the combatants' dependency upon long-term training in operational and maintenance techniques and the donors that can supply them.[56]

Lack of weapons standardization and cost-saving joint purchase of weapons, as well as differences in the perceived external threat (Iran or Iraq, or other states), have made the goal of close multilateral military cooperation unreachable by the GCC. The fact that GCC interactions are dominated by Saudi Arabia may provide the basis for the formation of a subsystem composed of the five smaller GCC members. However, this development is less likely because of the high level of systemic vulnerability in the event of an open crisis.

According to Qatar, Saudi Arabia occupies a dominant position in "the command structure and manpower" of the Peninsula Shield.[57] Based on the 1999 data presented in tables 4.1 and 4.2, Saudi Arabia possessed 86 percent of the total area of the GCC, 68 percent of the GCC population, 42 percent of the GCC military personnel, 56 percent of the alliance's GDP, 68 percent of GCC total military expenditures, 53 percent of its arms imports in 1995–1999, 61 percent of its main battle tanks, and 63 percent of the GCC combat aircraft in 1999.

Relationships between Iran and the GCC could not be termed neighborly and cordial until the early 1990s. Although some trade ties developed during the late 1980s, foreign policy objectives were not revised to allow for cooperation in substantive matters. The situation changed drastically after the election of Iranian president Khatami in May 1997. Iranians have publicly declared that the main motive for this rebuilding of the armed forces is deterrence, and not the pursuit of regional hegemonic power. Iran's rearmament must be seen as the basis of the self-reliance component of its overall national security policy. The other major component has to do with regional cooperation, particularly with the Persian Gulf and the ECO states. In January 1998, Iran's Minister of Defense Admiral Shamkhani tried to reassure the GCC by declaring that "Iran's military power was no threat to the Islamic states and other countries which did not threaten Iran's independence and territorial integrity."[58]

The trend toward greater democratization of Iranian politics may explain the apparent logic of the change in the attitudes of the GCC toward its northern neighbor. It may also be pointed out that the change in question is also a product of the commitment of the GCC states to allow more citizen participation in formulating state policy. On the issue of creating and/or sustaining the institutions of democratic governance, it has to be understood that unless the regional governments utterly fail to catch the train as it passes, they should be able to avoid the breakdown of the political and social order in their respective countries.

Regional suspicions regarding Iranian military designs in the Persian Gulf have been diminished by a series of high-level visits by government officials of the GCC to Tehran, attesting to the mutual interest in improving their bilateral and multilateral ties. These official visits and favorable statements assume more significance in view of the existing U.S.-Iran antagonism. Khatami told Saudi defense minister Prince Sultan in Tehran that expansion of bilateral Iran-Saudi ties would benefit "not only the region but also the entire world."[59] In this meeting, he reiterated Iran's willingness to sign a defense pact with Saudi Arabia, covering the establishment "of a joint Muslim defense force" to deter mutual enemies.[60] Earlier, Iran's defense minister, Admiral Shamkhani, had voiced his thoughts concerning Persian Gulf security. He stated, "the current regional context requires special security measures and a new defense system. We think that the best way to realize this objective is in military cooperation between Iran and Saudi Arabia."[61] For political and security reasons, Saudi Arabia rejected Iran's proposal for a bilateral military alliance, but the two governments agreed to exchange military attachés. The dominant view in Tehran was that in spite of Saudi initial rejection of this Iranian initiative, Iran should seek to persuade the Persian Gulf states to join a broader defense organization. Khatami's insistence that the expansion of ties with the GCC states is a top priority in Iran's foreign policy agenda is one of the reasons for the signing of a security pact between Iran and Saudi Arabia on April 17, 2001. This agreement is aimed at fighting terrorism, organized crime, and drug trafficking.[62]

A combination of factors presently prevent Iraq's participation in the multilateral talks among the Persian Gulf states: continued UN sanctions, Iraqi policies toward its Kurdish minority, the U.S. foreign policy posture, and Iraqi territorial demands that both Iran and Kuwait consider to be totally unacceptable. Iraq has remained the focus of regional concerns about the use of military force in an inter-state war situation in the Persian Gulf, and therefore a real threat to the prospect of a stable security environment. It is possible that unless Iraqi leaders are given a viable alternative, the Baghdad regime may soon be forced to once again employ offensive policies to change the political geography of the region.

An integration of several subsystems (e.g., GCC, ECO) could also be considered. However, inter-regional cooperation among the subsystems of the Persian Gulf, the Red Sea, and Central Asia may remain limited for some time, and would require the formation of a security system for the entire Middle East.

CONCLUSION

The crucial point is that assessing the costs and benefits of regional integration and cooperation in all areas will continue to induce the Persian Gulf states to proceed slowly but steadily toward more cooperative policy choices. So far there have been many indications that the Iranian and the GCC governments recognize the need for maintaining closer economic and social ties. There is little evidence that an integrated defense system will soon be created by the littoral states of the Persian Gulf. However, the effect of a general change in the security environment may even push the Baghdad regime to adopt pragmatic foreign policies toward its neighbors.

One has to consider the role of elite personalities in interstate relations. Like elsewhere in the developing world, the national security of the Persian Gulf states has been closely linked with the security and interests of ruling classes. However, new major players have come into power in Iran, Bahrain, and Qatar. The traditional elite may have concluded that regional cooperation might help them to consolidate the legitimacy of their political system. They have realized that they should seek common stances regarding regional and international issues.

Perhaps I am wrong in discerning an undercurrent of belief among the Arab and non-Arab elite in the region that the time is ripe to look for areas of possible cooperation, to unmask common interests suppressed by competing ideologies, and to redefine basic needs and realistic goals to the point at which strategies of peaceful conflict resolution can be developed and applied to all cases. To the extent that such a view among regional elites exists, it probably stems from the need for further initiatives to confront the security challenges of the twenty-first century Persian Gulf. Demographic changes outlined in this chapter, coupled with socioeconomic problems, make it all the more imperative that all involved parties focus their attention on a combination of cooperative efforts to avoid many of the pitfalls of war.

I have to stress an important point that is often forgotten in the debate over the feasibility of arms control in the Middle East, particularly as it relates to the verification problem in the case of the so-called rogue states like Iran and Iraq.[63] And that is that the security concerns of all regional states must be taken into account. While we advocate a policy of military modernization for the purpose of deterrence and defense for the GCC, we cannot ignore the fact that any new major military purchase and acquisition of military equipment would be watched closely by the larger northern Persian Gulf states.[64] Indeed, we should expect Iran to react by following suit in order not to fall behind in the regional arms race. The repeated Israeli threats to attack the Bushehr nuclear reactor upon its completion changed the Iranian policy of a unilateral cap on long-range missiles. The development of a long-range missile capability by Iran must be seen as an attempt to deter Israeli military attacks rather than as a policy of regional expansionism against Iran's smaller neighbors in the south.

Weapons of Mass Destruction (WMD) arms control discussions have focused primarily on when Iran or Iraq will acquire nuclear capability and long-range ballistic or cruise missiles. Many Middle Eastern states contend that it is equally important to discuss when Israel will sign the Nuclear Non-Proliferation Treaty (NPT) and adopt a declared nuclear posture. The focus should not be exclusively on the transfer of weapons of mass destruction and technology with application in nuclear fields. Arms control efforts should also concentrate on the transfer of high technology conventional weapons to the region.

Regional efforts to reach an agreement to limit arms should be encouraged by the major powers. Reducing existing armaments, as a step in the direction of arms control, in a geographic area of significant economic and political interest is an agonizing task but not an unattainable one. Part of the effort would be directed toward preventing the placement of WMD in the region, and eventually to establish a nuclear free zone in the Persian Gulf to reduce the devastation of war and accidents.

One possibility is that the Persian Gulf states press forward to create a maritime Zone of Peace as a first step in regional disarmament. They need to secure an international agreement under which the five permanent members of the Security Council as well as Pakistan and India would be required to stop sea deployment of nuclear weapons in the region. In practice, however, this initiative requires considerable adjustment of attitudes and behavior of regional and extra-regional actors who have an interest and a stake in the stability and economic prosperity of the Persian Gulf.

What is needed is greater mutual trust and confidence to bring about an alteration in the perceptions of the regional states in order to change their security doctrines and foreign policy attitudes toward each other. Hence, an alternative approach to encouraging greater regional stability is provided by the literature on confidence-building measures (CBMs). There are numerous areas of common interest (e.g., seabed mining; conservation of living maritime resources; protection of the Persian Gulf ecosystem, which requires long-term planning; the issue of a nuclear-free Persian Gulf) that could become bases for regional cooperation. Specific CBMs (cooperation in areas like search and rescue, marine environmental protection programs, piracy, and drug control) developed for the Asian Pacific may be applied to the Persian Gulf.[65]

Of course, it is unrealistic to assume that arms control and other CBMs will eliminate the causes of conflicts. Unless steps are taken to protect the legitimate security interests of the states concerned, there is no hope for the maintenance of lasting regional peace. This leaves the Persian Gulf states with two options. The first option requires continued reliance of the weaker states on major external powers to deter aggression by the stronger states. The second option is limiting the chances of regional armed conflicts through regional cooperation.

In regards to regional integration, I would assert that first the economics of oil, despite the emergence of the Caspian Sea in the international oil market, has increased the region's political and strategic significance; and second there is a need for a more concerted regional approach to dealing with the regional conflict situation and overwhelming insecurity problems caused by the nature of present regimes in the Persian Gulf. The fact is that continued conflictive relations between neighboring states have resulted in diversion of resources mainly for deterrence. The resources saved due to the relaxation of tension could be applied to development projects needed to solve the threatening social and economic problems. As resources diminish, governments will find it increasingly difficult to augment their revenues by collecting more taxes, since they cannot find enough high-income citizens to tax. The lack of public confidence in government is well justified by the past performance of the regimes in power. The people cannot be blamed for having a skeptical view of governments that do not tolerate any popular opposition.

The Persian Gulf states must formulate their foreign policy by paying increased attention to the establishment of closer economic links, particularly in relation to controlling international oil prices, foreign investment and environmental protection. Long-lasting peace can never be achieved if economic, political, and ethnic inequalities remain in evidence in the region. Regional states should adopt action-oriented norms, which would guarantee initiatives indicating the sincerity of each initiating side to work toward regional peace.

NOTES

1. The Persian Gulf is a nearly landlocked epicontinental basin with an area of 239,000 square kilometers. It is 990 kilometers long and 338 kilometers at its widest stretch. The Strait of Hormuz, its narrowest point, is 56 kilometers across. The deeper water (up to 80 meters) is off the Iranian coast. "Appendix A. The Persian Gulf," in Alvin J. Cottrell, ed., *The Persian Gulf States: A General Survey* (Baltimore: Johns Hopkins University Press, 1980), pp. 541–43.

2. According to official Kuwaiti figures, by the end of March 1999 the population of this small Persian Gulf state amounted to 2.3 million, of which only 792,743 were Kuwaitis. See *Kuwait Times*, Monday, May 3, 1999.

3. The labor-importing GCC states are apparently changing their immigration policies to deal with security and political issues associated with the growth of foreign workers. The UAE government considers the problem of illegal and clandestine workers, and unauthorized entry into its territories as a national security problem with adverse socioeconomic effects. See "Immigration law violations threaten national security," *Khaleej Times*, May 10, 1999; and Onn Winckler, "The immigration policy of the Gulf Cooperation Council (GCC) states," *Middle Eastern Policies*, vol. 33, no. 3, July 1997, pp. 480–93.

4. The percentage of nationals in the total population of the Persian Gulf states from the smallest to the largest is as follows: UAE (24 percent), Qatar (25 percent), Kuwait (39 percent), Bahrain (68 percent), Saudi Arabia (73 percent), Oman (73 percent), Iran (97 percent), Iraq (99 percent). Afghan and Kurdish refugees of Iraq constitute about 3 percent of the population of Iran, whereas fewer than 1 percent of the Iraqi residents may be non-nationals. Of the 24,397,400 population of the GCC, only 15,680,732 are nationals and the remaining 8,746,668 are foreigners. Refer to tables 4.1 and 4.2 in this chapter, and for a discussion of migratory movements in the Southern Persian Gulf region and the demographic changes in the GCC, refer to Nadji Safir, "Migratory currents in the Middle East," *Development,* 1, 1993, pp. 23–27; J. S. Birks, "The demographic challenge in the Arab Gulf," in B. P. Pridham, ed., *The Arabian Gulf and the Arab World.* (London and New York: Croom Helm, 1988); and Gawdat Bahgat, *The Gulf Monarchies: New Economic and Political Realities* (London: The Royal Institute for the Study of Conflict and Terrorism, February 1997).

5. Myron Weiner and Rainer Munz, "Migrants, refugees and foreign policy: prevention and intervention strategies," *Third World Quarterly,* vol. 18, no. 1, 1997, pp. 25–51, p. 25.

6. Prior to the Iranian revolution of 1979, there was no disagreement over the name of the Persian Gulf. For a while there has been a question of whether the Persian Gulf should be called by other names (e.g., the Iranian Gulf, the Arabian Gulf, the Islamic Gulf, the Persian-Arabian Gulf, Al Khaleej Al Arabi, Khaleej-e Farsi, or the Gulf). It is not my intention to raise the issue of whether historical, geographical, or other factors should determine the name of this body of water. For an excellent discussion, see C. Edmund Bosworth, "The Nomenclature of the Persian Gulf," in Cottrell, ed., *The Persian Gulf States,* pp. xvii-xxxiv; reprinted in *Iranian Studies,* vol. 30, no. 1–2, Winter-Spring 1997, pp. 77–94.

7. John Murray Brown. "World Bank to release $200m loan for Turkey," *Financial Times,* October 4, 1990; David Buchan and John Wyles, "EC plans aid for frontline countries," *Financial Times,* September 8, 1990; and David Housego, "Pakistan seeks help to ease Gulf shocks," *Financial Times,* September 14, 1990.

8. "Market Briefing—Kuwait," *Jane's Defense Weekly,* July 29, 1995, p. 17.

9. Recently, Saddam Hussein's eldest son, Uday, called on the Iraqi National Council to change the map of Iraq to include Kuwait as Iraq's nineteenth province. See "Uday Reclaims Kuwait as Part of 'Greater Iraq'," *Arabia.com,* January 15, 2001.

10. Ewan Anderson and Jasem Karam. "The Iraqi-Kuwaiti Boundary," *Jane's Intelligence Review,* vol. 7, no. 3, 1995, pp. 120–21; and Harry Brown, "The Iraq-Kuwait Boundary Dispute: Historical Background and the UN Decisions of 1992 and 1993," in Clive Schofield, ed., *IBRU Boundary and Security Bulletin,* vol. 2, no. 3, October 1994, Durham, UK: University of Durham, pp. 66–80, pp. 75–77.

11. As quoted in R. K. Ramazani, "Iran's foreign policy: both North and South," *Middle East Journal,* vol. 46, No. 3, Summer 1992, p. 400.

12. "Washington upbeat about Iraqi opposition,*" Al-Ahram Weekly,* Internet edition, April 15–21, 1999,.

13. There are reports indicating a change in the attitude of Turkish politicians toward the no-fly mission over northern Iraq based at Incirlik Air Base. See Terry Boys, "As Turkey renews Iraq Ties, Operation Northern Watch Future is Cloudy," *Stars and Stripes,* January 19, 2001. Available at http://www.pstripes.com/jan01/ed011901j.html

14. "Kharrazi to visit UAE," *Iran News,* May 9, 1998, p. 1.

15. Francis Tusa, "Trapped between the forks: Gulf states watch Iraq, Iran closely," *Armed Forces Journal International,* no. 131, July 12, 1994, pp. 28–30.

16. "Iran ranks first in trade partnership with Dubai," *Iran News,* May 9, 1998.

17. "UAE Sheikhs worry about thaw in Iran's ties with Arab neighbors," *Tehran Times,* May 10, 1999, p. 1.

18. "Qatar plan to raise islands row with Iran," *Khaleej Times,* Internet edition, May 4, 1999, http:.

19. "UAE Praises Outcome of GCC Summit on Isles," *Emirate News Agency (WAM),* January 3, 2001. http://www.wam.org.ae/2001/Jan/03/352787.html.

20. "Iran Rejects PGCC Communique over its Persian Gulf Islands," *Iran News,* Tuesday, January 1, 2001, p. 1.

21. "Iran Rules out Court for Islands Dispute," *Iran News,* Thursday, January 11, 2001, p. 1.

22. For an assessment of Iran's threat perception and security policies, see Saideh Lotfian, "Threat Perception and Military Planning in Iran: Credible Scenarios of Conflict and Opportunities for Confidence Building," in Eric Arnett, ed., *Military Capacity and the Risk of War: China, India, Pakistan and Iran* (Oxford: Oxford University Press for SIPRI, 1997), pp. 195–215.

23. In protest over the launching of Iranian missile attacks against the MKO bases near Iraqi cities on April 18, the Iraqi government decided not to participate in an international conference on the Palestinian issue, which was organized by the Iranian parliament on April 24, 2001. See "Iraq Refuses to take part in Tehran's Conference on the Palestinian Intifada," *ArabicNews,* April 23, 2001. Available at http://www.arabicnews.com/ansub/Daily/Day/010423/2001042318.html.

24. Saddam Hussein, "Address to the Nation," Baghdad Radio, September 28, 1980, reported in *FBIS, Middle East and Africa,* September 29, 1980, as quoted in John W. Amos, II, "The Iran-Iraq war: conflict, linkage, and spillover in the Middle East," in Robert G. Darius, John W. Amos, II, and Ralph H. Magnus, eds., *Gulf Security into the 1980s: Perceptual and Strategic Dimensions* (Stanford: Hoover Institution Press, 1984), p. 52.

25. Claudia Wright, "Implications of the Iraq-Iran War," *Foreign Affairs,* vol. 59, 1980/1981, pp. 275–303, quoted by John W. Amos, II, op. cit., p. 52.

26. "Iran Demines 765 Regions along Border with Iraq," *Iran News,* Sunday, April 29, 2001, p. 2.

27. UNSCOM (UN Special Commission on Iraq) was formed pursuant to Security Council Resolution 687 (1991) for the purpose of onsite inspection of Iraqi capabilities to develop weapons of mass destruction including chemical and biological weapons.

28. "Disarming Iraq: Butler speaks out," *Middle East Insight,* September-October 1998, pp. 7–12, p. 10.

29. Graham E. Fuller and Ian O. Lesser. "Persian Gulf Myths," *Foreign Affairs,* vol. 76, 3, 1997, pp. 42–52.

30. Andrew Rathmell. "Threats to the Gulf—Part 1," *Jane's Intelligence Review,* vol. 7, no. 3, 1995, pp. 129–32.

31. See "Bahrain and Qatar both Proclaim Victory in Border Disputes," *Arabia.com,* March 16, 2001. Available at http://www.arabia.com/article/0,1690,News/41986,00.html

32. "Way cleared for UAE-Oman full border accord," *Khaleej Times,* Internet edition, May 3, 1999; and "UAE and Oman sign border pact," *Bahrain Tribune,* Internet edition, Thursday, May 3, 1996 and "Border agreement annexes signed," *Observer,* Internet edition, May 5, 1999, http: //www.omanobserver.com.

33. Siemon T. Wezeman and Pieter D. Wezeman, "Transfer of Major Conventional Weapons," in *SIPRI Yearbook: Armaments, Disarmament and International Security* (Oxford: Oxford University Press for SIPRI, 1998), p. 300; and Bjorn Hagelin, Pieter D. Wezeman, and Siemon T. Wezeman, "The Volume of Transfers of Major Conventional Weapons," *SIPRI Yearbook: Armaments, Disarmament and International Security* (Oxford: Oxford University Press, for SIPRI, 2000) pp. 368–77.

34. For an excellent discussion of GCC military expenditures, sources of weaponry for these states, and data for major weapons systems in their inventories for the 1981–1985, and 1985–1986 periods, see Erik R. Peterson, *The Gulf Cooperation Council: A Search for Unity in a Dynamic Region* (Boulder and London: Westview Press, 1988), pp. 195–201.

35. A good example of such an arms package is the Al-Yamamah agreement between the UK and Saudi Arabia. It is a £15 billion deal involving the transfer of "120 Tornado combat jets, as well as more than other 200 aircraft and helicopters, mine-hunters, weapons, training and facilities, including a full-scale air base." See Victor Mallet and David White, "Saudi pride acts as small print in BA's arms deal," *Financial Times,* December 14, 1989.

36. "Qatar boosts defense capabilities," *Jane's International Defense Review,* 1, 1997, p. 9.

37. Yitzhak Scichor, "A Multiple-Hit: China's missile sale to Saudi Arabia," *Sun Yat-Sen Center for Policy Studies (SCPS) Paper No. 5,* National Sun Yat-Sen University, Taiwan, April 1991, pp. 1–2, and 13.

38. Ruth Leger Sivard, *World Military and Social Expenditures, 1977.* (Leesburg, VA: WMSE Publications, March 1977), p. 15.

39. As quoted by David Silverberg and Francis Tusa, "Shadow over the Gulf: Iran is preparing, but for what?" *Armed Forces Journal International,* September 1995, p. 24.

40. Michael Ellis and Jeffrey Record, "Theater Ballistic Missile Defense and U.S. Contingency Operations," *Parameters,* 122, 1, Spring 1992, pp. 11–26, p. 18.

41. With the exodus of many expatriate soldiers mostly from Egypt, Pakistan, and Palestine, the January 1992 size of Kuwaiti armed forces was reduced from 16,000 to 5,000. The Kuwaiti government has started recruiting more military personnel among Egyptians, Pakistani, and Bedoons. See Peter Lewis Young, "Gulf and South West Asian Security Issues," *Asian Defense Journal,* 23, 12, 1993, p. 28.

42. Since the end of the 1990–1991 war in the Persian Gulf for the liberation of Kuwait, as a security measure this tiny state has concluded a number of defense and military pacts with the Big Five. The Kuwaiti government has signed: (1) a ten-year defense agreement with its major western ally, the United States, on September 19, 1991, covering military technical assistance, and the right to pre-position U.S. equipment in Kuwaiti territory; (2) four pacts including a ten-year defense agreement with its former protector, the United Kingdom, on February 11, 1992, covering technical assistance, joint exercises, and arms sales; (3) two military cooperation pacts with France on August 18, 1992 and October 13, 1993; (4) technical and security cooperation agreements with Russia, including two pacts signed on February 16 and on November 29, 1993 for arms sales, the exchange of information, and joint maneuvers; (5) a military cooperation agreement with China for technical assistance for the reorganization of Kuwaiti armed forces on March 24, 1995. A good discussion of these topics is in Jacques de Lestapis, "Striking a strategic security balance," *Jane's Defense Weekly,* July 29, 1995, pp. 23–24; and Tony Banks et al., "Buying security from the West," *Jane's Defense Weekly,* March 28, 1992, p. 534.

43. Shahram Chubin, "Iran and the Gulf crisis," *Middle East Insight,* pp. 30–35, p. 35. A similar argument is presented by Ramazani concerning Iran's resentment toward British domination in the Persian Gulf in the nineteenth century, particularly after the United Kingdom decided to place Bahrain Island under its protection. See Rouhollah K. Ramazani, *The Persian Gulf: Iran's Role* (Charlottesville: University Press of Virginia, 1972), pp. 15–18.

44. During the crisis, the United States had deployed 30,000 military personnel, 25 warships, and more than 200 strike aircraft in the Persian Gulf. See James Bruce. "Iran warns of 'massive war' with USA in Gulf," *Jane's Defense Weekly,* October 9, 1996, p. 25.

45. "Leader blasts foreign military presence in Persian Gulf," *Iran News,* May 5, 1999, p. 1.

46. "Khatami: Amrica mansha-e bohran ast," *Kayhan,* September 10, 1998, p. 1.

47. Statement by Kamal Kharrazi, foreign minister of the Islamic Republic of Iran at the Eighth Persian Gulf Seminar, *Regional Approaches in the Persian Gulf,* Tehran, IPIS, February 24–25, 1998.

48. "President Urges Removal of Alien Forces in Persian Gulf," *Iran News,* Monday, January 8, 2001, pp. 1 and 15.

49. *Salaam,* July 28, 1997, p. 1; and *Ettela'at,* September 29, 1997, p. 2. There are empirical studies supporting the view that higher military expenditures and arms production have an adverse impact on environmental quality; see, for example, Robert E. Looney and David Winterford, "The environmental consequences of Third World military expenditures and arms production: the Latin American case," *Rivista Internazionale di Scienze Economiche e Commerciali,* vol. 40, no. 9, 1993, pp. 769–86.

50. The Iranian government has been concerned about pollution control and preservation of the marine environment in the Persian Gulf. Even before the establishment of regional pollution control measures, Iran had taken the lead in establishing such regulations for its territorial waters and the limits of superjacent waters of its continental shelf after signing the International Convention for the Prevention of Pollution from Ships in November 1973. This convention identifies "special areas" that require more restrictive protective actions, and the Persian Gulf has been recognized as a "special area." See Charles G. Mac-Donald, "Iran's strategic interests and the law of the sea," *Middle East Journal,* 34, 3, Summer 1980, pp. 302–22, pp. 319–20.

51. Jebel Ali is the UAE port where a small amount of U.S. prepositioned naval equipment is maintained. See "US naval ships berth at Jebel Ali," *Khaleej Times,* September 10, 1995, p. 3.

52. Robert Mandel, *The Changing Face of National Security: A Conceptual Analysis* (Westport, CT: Greenwood Press, 1994), pp. 30–31.

53. Fatema Mernissi, "Palace fundamentalism and liberal democracy: Oil, arms and irrationality," *Development and Change,* 27, 1996, pp. 251–65, p. 261.

54. In July 1958, the coup-makers seized Baghdad, killed King Faisal and his premier, and put an end to monarchical rule in Iraq.

55. Volker Perthes, "Security perceptions and cooperation in the Middle East: the political dimension," *The International Spectator,* vol. XXXI, no. 4, October-December 1996, p. 56.

56. Stephanie G. Neuman, *Military Assistance in Recent Wars* (New York: Praeger, 1986, for the CSIS Washington Papers), p. 89.

57. Philip Finnegan. "Shifting alliances shake Gulf unity—Gulf Cooperation Council schisms spoil chance of NATO-like joint force," *Defense News,* December 12–18, 1994, pp. 1, 44.

58. "Shamkhani says Iran's military power no threat to other countries," *Kayhan International,* February 1, 1998, p. 1.

59. "Tehran, Riyadh discuss regional developments, security, religion," *Iran News,* May 4, 1999, p. 1.

60. "Khatami for military alliance with Riyadh," *Khaleej Times,* Internet edition, May 4, 1999.

61. "Iran calls for defense pact with Saudi," *Bahrain Tribune,* Internet edition, April 30, 1999.

62. *Iran News,* May 13, 2001, p. 1.

63. An important point to be made here is that Iran is a signatory of major arms control agreements like the Biological Weapons Convention, Chemical Weapons Convention, Comprehensive Test Ban Treaty and Nuclear Non-proliferation Treaty. Also, the Tehran government has submitted data for the UN Arms Register, and it has participated in CD talks on Transparency in Armament (TIA). "By exaggerating the potential threat of Iran to the GCC and Israel, U.S. security policy makers make a deterrence strategy more attractive to Iran." See Eric Arnett, "Reassurance versus Deterrence: Opportunities to Expand Iranian Participation in Confidence-Building Measures," *Security Dialogue* (Oslo), December 1998.

64. In November 1993, Deputy Foreign Minister Ali Mohammed Besharati expressed the official view that "our neighboring countries are signing military pacts with big powers one by one, and strengthening their military arsenals; so why can't we replace the weapons we lost during the eight-year imposed war [with Iraq]," as quoted in James Wyllie, "Iran—Quest for security and influence," *Jane's Intelligence Review,* vol. 5, no. 7, July 1993, p. 311.

65. Practical CBMs classified in three categories for the Asia Pacific include

Category or Basket 1: Dialogue on security perceptions, including voluntary statements of defense policy positions; participation in the UN conventional Arms Register; enhanced military contacts, including high-level visits; exchange between military academies, staff colleges, and training; observers at military exercises, on a voluntary basis; cooperative approaches to sea lines of communication, beginning with exchanges of information and training in such areas as search and rescue, combating piracy, and drug control.

Category or Basket 2: Further exploration of a regional arms register; regional security studies center/coordination of existing security studies activities; major defense publications, such as defense white papers; maritime information databases.

Category or Basket 3: Notification of major military deployments; maritime surveillance cooperation.

For details, see Paul Dibb, "How to begin implementing specific trust-building measures in the Asia-Pacific region," *The Strategic and Defense Studies Center (SDSC) Working Paper No. 228,* Canberra, July 1995, p. 7.

CHAPTER 5

ON THE PERSIAN GULF ISLANDS
An Iranian Perspective

JALIL ROSHANDEL

Nowhere on the globe will you find as many border disputes as among the Persian Gulf countries. For this reason the number of clashes, incidents, and renewal of claims is very high. Only shortly after the Iraqi occupation of Kuwait, in August 1990, a dispute between Saudi Arabia and Yemen over border territories thought to contain oil was revived. In the 1992 Khafus incident, Saudi Arabia occupied the southern part of Qatar. It would not be surprising if tomorrow morning CNN announced that Iraqi troops had occupied Warba and Bubiyan islands or something completely unexpected happened between two other states in the region.

In the Arabian peninsula, British colonialists drew the borders in desert areas. These borders have never been clearly demarcated, and their existence was largely limited to maps. Their significance increased greatly during the second half of the twentieth century, creating disputes which periodically escalated. Saudi Arabia and Qatar and Qatar and Bahrain, for example, have had all sorts of oil- and gas-based border disputes.[1] So far the GCC has not been able to solve any of these disputes over territory. In the upper part of the Persian Gulf, such disputes helped initiate two major wars between Iran and Iraq, and Iraq and Kuwait. From a conspiracy-theory point of view (which has a lot of support in Iran today), the current state of affairs may be regarded as a British-made scenario.

The islands issue between Iran and the United Arab Emirates (UAE) is more precisely between Iran and Sharjah over the island of Abu Musa and between Iran and Ras al-Khaimah over the Tunb islands. Although they are usually referred to as disputed islands, the dispute over Abu Musa is actually settled, taking into consideration the Memorandum of Understanding (MOU) agreed upon in 1971. This "gave Iran full jurisdiction over the range of hills on the northern side of Abu Musa, where it could maintain a military presence . . ."[2] At least theoretically there should not be a dispute over ownership of the islands, but perhaps on the application of the memorandum. What is puzzling is how a supposedly settled dispute can be the subject of conferences and scores of articles and papers.

To review the environment in which the dispute came to a head, it is useful to turn back some pages of history and return to the early 1970s, when the British Empire withdrew from the region and permitted the local shaikhdoms to attain independence. A hundred years of British colonial presence limited social and political development there. Except for Bahrain, none of the emirates had a single political party, labor union, or free mass media. The ruling power was mainly a tribal inheritance with the decision-making process under the control of the shaikh or amir. The rulers consisted of shaikhs' sons, brothers, close family members, and all those who favored the status quo and agreed with whatever was decided by "His Majesty" and were against what he seemed to be against. No development in its Western sense, except economic development, could have been expected.

British control over the lower Gulf territories began in 1820. The emirate of Sharjah was created only in 1856. When in 1903 the British seized Abu Musa and the Tunb islands from Iran and gave them to the Qasimi tribal entity of Sharjah, Ras al-Khaimah was not considered to be an emirate and only achieved trucial status in 1921. Half a century later, in 1971, the United Arab Emirates was formed as a regrouping of seven small lower Gulf emirates.

For the British stability meant whatever guaranteed their interests. When the shaikhs of Abu Dhabi, Ajman, Dubai, Fujairah, Ras al-Khaimah, Sharjah, and Umm al-Qaywayn decided to create the United Arab Emirates, nationalist Arabs outside the region from Algeria to Aden and Baghdad protested their decision because they thought it might perpetuate the status quo. For them the status quo meant the British presence, which in fact guaranteed the shaikhs' rule. Such was the environment when in 1971 the Abu Musa issue was first settled between Iran and Sharjah.

This paper will not review the details of general territorial and border disputes existing in the region but will instead focus on the three islands. The geographical and geopolitical contexts in which such disputes occur are of great importance; if such disputes existed elsewhere they would not have the same significance or be the subject of such concern. By examining the existing records and history of claims and counter-claims, two facts are evident:

- Despite long-conflicting claims to the islands, it was only during the period of British control and with their help that the islands became part of Sharjah or Ras al-Khaimah; and
- Iran, in light of its historical claims over the islands, occupied them in 1971. This action resulted both from the power vacuum resulting from British withdrawal from the Persian Gulf, and arrangements justified through a face-saving Memorandum of Understanding.

The United Arab Emirates was created only a few days after this arrangement in 1971. Most Iranians are convinced that the three islands belonged to Iran long before the UAE emerged as a nation-state in 1971. Some find a direct link between Iran's acquisition of the islands and the independence of Bahrain. According to this view, the arrangement was in part to compensate Iran for recognizing Bahrain's independence. Such a belief reflects the state of affairs in the late 1960s and early 1970s. At the same time, it demonstrates how difficult and complex the settlement of territorial disputes is in general and in this region in particular. The difficulties impeding a settlement of maritime boundary disputes between Iran and its Arab neighbors are immense.[3]

This paper will try to define the Arab perception of Iranians or Persians, which to a great extent is at the core of the existing mistrust. Understanding this perception may help to clarify the positions taken by both sides. Then we will consider the "islands question" from both sides and focus on the often-forgotten story of why the issue has come up in the way it has, while trying to explore what course the representation of the issue has taken. We will then briefly examine the 1971 Memorandum of Understanding and the environment in which it was formulated as the only possible way to satisfy both sides' expectations. Finally, six possible scenarios regarding the future development of the conflict will be presented and the likelihood of each will be assessed. The conclusion will contain some policy implications for decision-makers.

ARAB PERCEPTIONS OF IRAN

To understand the relations between Iran and its Arab neighbors, one should consider that there are really two different patterns of behavior and two distinct perceptions. I do not intend to make a distinction based on Arab and Persian or to use the earlier terminology "Arab" and "'Ajam," but in fact such a distinction exists.

The ancient Persians were the only "superpower" of a region larger than the Middle East of today, and almost all urban and populated centers of the Arabian peninsula, directly or indirectly, were under their control. At that time Arabs had no ill feelings toward the Persians and even needed them for their security. Arab perceptions of Iran changed after the emergence of Islam. When Islam entered into Iran, the old-time rivalries and competition reappeared and the word "'Ajam" came to mean "the Persians."

When the Shi'i minority acquired power in Iran in 1501 and the majority of the population converted to this faith, the differences between Arab and Persian and Shi'i and Sunni were accentuated. This competition created historical, political, and cultural tensions and even a literally different people, where the Shi'is were always the minority in the Islamic world and Sunnis the majority. The state of political relations between the two peoples has depended to some degree on the perceptions formed over the centuries.[4]

The relationship between the Iranian monarchical regime and its Arab neighbors was predicated on the notion of Iranian nationalism against Arab tribalism. Islam was not considered as a commonality and point of agreement unless the shah was giving a formal speech. By the 1970s, the shah didn't want to be the "brother" of his neighbors but, with U.S. support, the dominant power of the region. This element has played an important role in the making of Arab perceptions about Iran and the Iranians. They knew the shah was not a friend of the Arabs, but he had enough power to counter the Iraqis and that to them was admirable. The shah was the symbol of Shi'ism against Sunnism, but at the same time he was the only power in the region that could fight against communism. By using his military and police power to suppress communism in Iran, and supporting Arabs in their struggle against local leftist movements, he gained Arab confidence that he would not be a threat to them.

THE ISLANDS

Though some Iranians may not have heard of the three islands, to many others their strategic significance is very clear. In 1971, one could find some very carefully premeditated texts in the media saying that Iran had occupied its three Persian Gulf islands and the shaikh of Sharjah welcomed the troops. The location of the islands on the tanker route near the entrance to the Strait of Hormuz, critical for international oil transportation, together with their strategic significance for Iranian security, highlights their importance.

Ownership of the islands became the subject of diplomatic controversy between Persia and Great Britain when the Persian government tried to establish a customs post on Greater Tunb in 1904. In fact during a critical period preceding the Constitutional Revolution in Iran (1906–11), the British tried to take advantage of the problems facing the Qajar government and establish greater influence over the Persian Gulf.[5]

On November 30, 1971, the date the islands were returned to Iran, the population of Greater Tunb was around 240 people. In 1992 there were 400 people living on the island. The population consisted mainly of Iranians coming from Bandar Lingeh and Arabs of the Bani Yas tribe from Dubai.[6]

Abu Musa is a small island located at a distance of 45 kilometers from Sirri Island, 46 from Greater Tunb, 44 from Lesser Tunb, and 64 from Sharjah. Different sources have given various figures for its surface area, from 7 to 22, 66, and 90 square kilometers.[7] This island has other names in local dialects, such as Bu Mouf and Gap Sabz (Big Prairie), which suggests that freshwater reserves existed there in the past. Abu Musa was the name given to the island hundreds of years ago, so that a change of name, as in the case of the Shatt al-Arab, seems improbable.[8]

The population of the island, according to Iranian sources in 1992, was around 2,200 of whom 470 were non-Iranian, mostly from Sharjah, and the rest being Iranian citizens.[9] Richard Schofield, the well-known British scholar who has worked extensively on border disputes, gives a higher number for the Arab population that he believes to be "on the order of 600 people."[10] Iranian scholar Pirouz Mojtahed-Zadeh believes that "Abu Musa's permanent population of 600 is made up of Iranians of Lingeh origin and Arabs of Sharjah origin from the Sudan tribe of the village of Khan in Sharjah."[11] According to other sources in 1992, the population of Abu Musa was 500 Arabs and 2,500 Iranians, and many Arabs of the island are reported to have Iranian origins.[12] A recent article in the journal of Iran's Revolutionary Guard Naval Forces notes that "there are 2,000 Iranians and 405 citizens of Sharjah (the UAE). Some of these native Arab-UAE inhabitants of Abu Musa island are in fact from India, Pakistan and Egypt."[13] Today there are three residential areas on the island, two made up of Iranian residents and a third of Arabs, mostly from Sharjah. To enter the Arab residential area one needs special permission, and no Iranian has the right to enter without such permission.

The population of the island consists of government employees, teachers, fishermen, and shopkeepers. There are few facilities for entertainment, and local flights connect the island to Bandar Abbas only three times a week. There are two wharves on the island used by both the Iranian and UAE-administered parts, which in itself holds potential for daily friendly contact between the two sides. Two units of freshwater equipment provide drinking water for the two parts. The production of electricity for the island is less than adequate. The Mubarak oil field offshore produces 10,000 to 17,000 barrels of oil per day, the income of which is equally divided between Iran and the UAE. Buttes Oil and Gas Co., the concession for which was granted by Sharjah and endorsed by Iran in December 1971, produces the oil, which is considered to be the best quality oil of the Persian Gulf. Abu Musa's deposits of red iron oxide are also well known.

Greater Tunb is situated southwest of Qeshm island, 50 kilometers from Bandar Lingeh and 70 from the emirate of Ras al-Khaimah. The name "Tunb" is taken from the

Tangestani dialect of the Persian language. (The word "Tunb" in the Persian language has been defined as a mound, and the superficial features of the two islands are visible in the form of a series of hillocks, which has been the cause of the definition in Iran's geographical dictionary.)[14] It is also called Tunb Gap (greater Tunb or greater hill; the word Tunb means hill in Tangestani), as well as Tunb Mari (hill of snakes). It has an almost circular shape with a dry and sandy surface of about 12 square kilometers. In the northern part of the island there are small hills of around 50 meters' height, but the southern part is level and, like the eastern part, the most suitable area for ships to approach. Tunb has always had a hot and humid climate. Its strategic and defensive role is very important for Iran.[15]

Lesser Tunb is an uninhabited, rectangular-shaped, partly rocky island, 35 meters in elevation at its highest point. Lesser Tunb is of secondary significance from a strategic point of view. It is situated at a distance of 50 kilometers from the Iranian port of Lingeh and 92 kilometers from Ras al-Khaimah. The Tunbs, before their occupation by the British, were administratively part of Bandar Lingeh and the Iranian authorities of Lingeh appointed governors of the islands.

TWO VERSIONS OF ONE EVENT

Between 1971 and 1992 the Memorandum of Understanding regulated relations between Iran and the UAE over Abu Musa, and a good level of cooperation existed. Iranians were sensitive about any unusual event around the island. Any increase and decrease in the population, where shared administration was agreed upon, was continuously monitored. Lessons learned from Bahrain in the 1960s showed how, according to a calculated plan, the number of Arab immigrants could be increased on the island and exceed the number of inhabitants of Iranian origin. (During the period of British interference in the affairs of the region they tried to change the population pattern by restricting Iranian visits while encouraging Arabs to travel and immigrate to Bahrain.) A similar plan could work in the case of Abu Musa to separate it from Iran.

In 1992 there were indications that the UAE was trying to change the population pattern of Abu Musa island in this manner. This was one of the main reasons for the resurrection of the dispute. Abu Musa is not a tourist island. Its very limited facilities can hardly satisfy the needs of its scanty population. Many Arabs reside there only because they get paid for it. The UAE therefore invites Arabs (non-UAE subjects) to live on the island in order to increase the number of residents.[16] Pirouz Mojtahed-Zadeh interprets the story as follows: "Reports from military sources in Tehran say that without the permission of the Iranian Government, the United Arab Emirates were busy building new establishments in the non-military part of the island. It seems that with the agreement of certain Arab countries, a number of non-native Arabs are to become residents on the island in order to gradually put Iranian sovereignty of the island under doubt."[17]

According to local Iranian officials, some eight months before the 1992 events they noticed such hidden activities. A Dutch sailor carrying military equipment and guns was discovered in the vicinity of Abu Musa, and it was after this that the Iranian authorities proposed issuing security passes to non-nationals visiting the island. The UAE authorities refused and sent two other boats carrying people without such passes. Both parties, while reporting the event in the light of their own interests, have conveyed the basic story of what happened. According to the Iranian newspaper *Jomhouri Islami:*

One morning (August 22, 1992) a boat with 104 people of Emirate and non-Emirate nationality (mostly Indian, Bangladeshi . . .) was refused entry to the island. According to what has been said in the media, the UAE was quite aware of the result of such a mission and therefore a number of ambulances, helicopters, foreign journalists and photographers were present at the Khalid port in Sharjah to cover their return some 48 hours later. The refusal of their entry to the island and the return to Sharjah was widely publicized and it was connected to the previous event of April in which a group of non-national employees of the emirate of Sharjah were also prevented from entering the island.

It should be noted that both Sharjah and Iran use the existing wharf on the Sharjah-administrated part of the island. The former has no border facilities and uses Iranian facilities. The newspaper continues: "Before approaching the coastline in the boat the people were told that Iran would neither let them in nor would it allow an immediate departure. 'The Iranians will not even give you food and water during the stay at the border, and in case of an attempt to return to Sharjah it is quite possible that Iranian soldiers will shoot at you from the coastline'. But it was not true and the Iranians gave them food, water and medical aid before they were returned to Sharjah."[18]

If this Iranian version of the event is correct, then it is understandable why those ambulances, helicopters, journalists, and photographers were gathered on their return to Sharjah. The publicity concerning the identity of these people has apparently convinced even well known scholars. Richard Schofield writes:

> Then came the well-publicized incidents of April and August 1992, which seemed to suggest that the MOU was unworkable or, at best, in need of renegotiation. In April the Iranian authorities prevented a group of non-national employees of the emirate of Sharjah (a group comprised of Pakistani, Indian and Filipino laborers and technicians and, also, non-UAE, principally Egyptian-Arab teachers) from entering the Sharjah-administered part of the island. The dispute intensified with reports on August 24, 1992 that Iran had refused entry to a large party of over 100 third-party nationals. These were mainly Egyptian teachers and their families, many of whom had originally been denied entry to Abu Musa back in April.[19]

Schofield's assertion no doubt is based on the documents available to him, but ever since the event I could not find an answer to the question of the relationship between 470 non-Iranian people (or 600 if we accept Schofield's figure) with "over 100 third-party nationals . . . mainly Egyptian teachers and their families." There is no proportion between the number of the population and the number of teachers and their families.

What justifies this sudden increase of population if we do not take Iranian warnings about a "security problem" seriously? According to Iranian sources, some armed men had already been arrested in the vicinity of the island just before this event and the Iranian authorities claimed the "U.A.E was tempting Arab families with huge salaries to take up residence on the island in order to disrupt the population balance."[20]

Looking at the event impartially, it seems that the story is not really important. Perhaps an escalation of the problem could have been avoided if both parties had contacted each other and explained the necessity of such an unusual move. The fact that both Iran and UAE (on behalf of Sharjah) are mutually administering the island and their subjects are living on the same island—albeit in different and divided locations—is itself a problem-creating process. Clashes and similar events are unavoidable unless other solutions can be found. An exchange of information in the case of irregular events, which might have created confidence and avoided disputes, was not explored or foreseen in the MOU. Then-Foreign Minister Ali-Akbar Velayati attributed the event to "misjudgments of junior Iranian officials," but tried to find acceptable ways of returning to the previous situation.

This event proved that some differences still exist in the interpretation and application of the MOU as well as in the way each party considers best to follow up its national interests. The visions and perceptions each side has created over the years differ from that of the other and have created expectations beyond what was intended by their actions. The action of each party should have been regulated by the MOU but it has not. It is for this reason that Iran has consistently expressed its acceptance of the MOU and its willingness to carry out negotiations and discussions on that basis.

Both in the Arab world, including the UAE, and to some extent in the Western media, there was more coverage of the event than necessary. The issue of sovereignty was raised and efforts were made to place in doubt the efficacy of the MOU. It seems that through publicity and by using unlimited Arab economic resources and Western academic support, efforts were made to create a big crisis on a small island. As was said by then-Iranian Deputy Foreign Minister Abbas Maleki, "the volume of press coverage is bigger than the island itself."[21]

THE MEMORANDUM OF UNDERSTANDING

As already mentioned, the Tunbs and Abu Musa, according to political scientist Asghar Ja'fari Valdani, belonged to Iran until 1903. They were previously administered under the Iranian port of Lingeh, a city itself part of Fars province. This led to many years of negotiation between Iran and Britain, ending with the 1971 agreement. In fact this was designed as a face-saving arrangement, and nothing beyond the coexistence of the UAE and Iran in Abu Musa was meant at the time. In a speech aired on Radio Sharjah on November 29, 1971, Shaikh Khaled ibn Muhammad al-Qasimi, shaikh of Sharjah, announced that he had signed the letter of agreement in order to maintain the interests of the citizens of Sharjah as well as for continued friendly and fraternal relations with Iran.

Dabiri argues that the objectives of the MOU were twofold: "to accommodate Iran's sovereignty over the island of Abu Musa on the one hand, and to do this through a face-saving formula for the shaikh of Sharjah on the other."[22] However, he admits that in the preface to the MOU, it is stated that "neither Iran nor Sharjah has abandoned its claim to Abu Musa or recognized the other's claim."[23]

Using Arab references Schofield has also quoted the same clause, but in a slightly different version: "Neither Iran nor Sharjah will give up its claim to Abu Musa nor recognize the other's claim." The slight difference in the above text may be because of its translation into Persian and a second translation from Persian into English. The English text of the MOU as published in Patricia Toye's edited volume does not seem to be the original. It is typed on a piece of white paper with no letterhead or signature, while all other correspondence published in the same volume has the Iranian royal emblem or other relevant sign and signatures.[24] If there were many other disputes remaining from the British colonial presence, the dispute over Abu Musa was apparently considered as resolved.[25]

I do not intend to enter into a legal interpretation of the contents of the memorandum, though there should not be a serious problem between the two states in case such an interpretation proves necessary. The agreement appears to be the only conceivable way to satisfy both sides' claims to full sovereignty and to start fruitful exploitation of the islands' resources. This also satisfied British and American oil and gas companies that proceeded with exploitation of the petroleum resources of Abu Musa and of the seabed and subsoil beneath its territorial seas.[26]

Britain's Foreign and Commonwealth Office had an important role in obtaining necessary confirmations from both sides and conveying the letters exchanged. Iran and Britain did not reach an agreement soon or easily; it took them months of negotiations. Therefore I contest the idea that the MOU "had been forced by Iran upon the Ruler of Sharjah on Britain's departure from the Gulf at the end of 1971."[27] "Sharjah was still a British protectorate at the time and in accordance with the terms of its special treaty of 1892 with Great Britain, it did not have the right to sign an official agreement or treaty with any foreign power except Great Britain."[28] For this reason the MOU could not be "forced by Iran upon the Ruler of Sharjah" or in fact upon Britain. All documents were exchanged through British diplomatic channels and not directly between Iran and Sharjah.

It should be recalled that there had been special treaties, or Exclusive Agreements, between Britain and the rulers of the Persian Gulf shaikhdoms who, willingly or unwillingly, surrendered parts of their sovereignty to the British government. These included the following rights:

a. The establishment of diplomatic or consular relations with foreign powers other than Britain;
b. The conclusion of treaties and agreements with foreign states, other than Britain, without its consent;
c. The cession or disposal of their territories by means of sale, lease, mortgage or other means, without the agreement of Britain;
d. The grant of mineral or oil concessions to foreign governments or to the subjects of such governments, without the consent of Britain.[29]

When Iran landed its troops on the islands, the British took no steps to halt the operation, although according to the said treaties they were responsible and could have acted. There are some more points that deserve attention:

- The shaikh of Sharjah stated in his speech to the people that "this letter of agreement conformed to the hopes and wishes of the people of Sharjah."
- During the final days of negotiations, the Iranian foreign minister wrote in an official letter to British foreign secretary Sir Douglas Hume: " . . . that nothing in the said arrangement shall be taken as restricting the freedom of Iran to take any measures in the island of Abu Musa which in the opinion of Iran's government would be necessary to safeguard the security of the island or of the Iranian forces . . ."
- The receipt of the letter was acknowledged and Lord Hume responded that "the contents of the letter had been communicated and made clear to the Shaikh of Sharjah."[30]
- The MOU was reached through Iran's undertaking to make "semi-annual contributions of £750,000 Sterling on 21 April and 21 October of each year [i.e., £1.5 million annually], beginning in 1972."[31]
- Then-Minister for Foreign Affairs Abbas Ali Khalatbari, in a letter to Shaikh Khalid Bin Muhammed Al-Qasimi, Ruler of Sharjah, states: "The Imperial government of Iran will regard itself as entitled to terminate or suspend payments under the said agreement if Your Highness takes any actions inconsistent, in Iran's view, with friendly relations between Iran and Sharjah."[32] This letter was also conveyed through British authorities to the ruler of Sharjah.

The MOU was, and perhaps still is, the only practical way of getting out of a stalemate in bilateral relations between Iran and its Arab neighbors in the Persian Gulf. Both the national and the international context in which it was reached, the power and weakness of the local players, as well as the shrewdness and influence of external players, should not be forgotten.

THE CONTEXT

At the time the problem of Abu Musa was solved there were two major regional powers in the Persian Gulf, namely Iran and Saudi Arabia. Iran was considered the most important, and its willingness to assume the defense of the Persian Gulf against external threats after the British departure provided it with a significant role in the region. Regarding the disputed islands in the Strait of Hormuz, John Duke Anthony wrote in 1975:

> . . . a substantial segment of Sharjah's population appears to have acquiesced in the Iranian occupation of the islands for the time being. This attitude stems partly from recognition that ending the occupation in the near future is unlikely and partly from the material benefits they stand to gain under the arrangement. Even in Ra's al-Khaymah, where there is continuing resentment against Iran for its occupation of the islands, there is acknowledgement of Iran's superior military power and recognition that the Iranians intend to remain on the islands for the foreseeable future.[33]

In fact the United Arab Emirates, with no dispute with its stronger northern neighbor, gained more from the status quo, and for several reasons the situation was favorable to it:

- Iraq, Egypt, and Syria recognized the political independence of the UAE.
- The UAE had appeared as part of a greater Arab homeland.
- A dispute settlement with Iran reduced negative external pressure that could jeopardize the stability of the confederation.
- For the UAE, Iran was a regional power supported by the United States and other Western countries, which would not destabilize the new nation or other Arab states of the Persian Gulf. On the contrary, it helped Oman to fight against a guerrilla movement threatening the country.

The Arabs of the Persian Gulf suspected the shah and his politics, but they needed him and so tolerated him. When in 1971, despite Arab world public opinion, the shah took control over Abu Musa and the Tunbs, the Arab emirates showed little negative reaction. Abu Dhabi and Ras al-Khaimah were under pressure to react against the event, but the shah was so powerful that such a reaction did not occur. The islands issue became a forgotten and cold issue when, later the same year, the UN Security Council adjourned consideration of the complaint already taken to it.

When the dispute reemerged in 1992, both Iran and the UAE operated in quite a different context from that of 1971. New hopes and expectations had been created.

- Soon after the 1979 Islamic revolution in Iran, many neighbors, including the UAE, feared a spillover of the Islamic movement.
- After the revolution, Iran assumed a new role in the region that could—even unintentionally—inspire some local Islamists. The UAE therefore felt threatened.

- Because of their massive assistance to Iraq during eight years of war with Iran, the Arab monarchies expected some direct or indirect retaliation by the Iranians.
- The new Islamic Republic of Iran was no longer protected by an external super-power; it had not lost the war to Iraq and by 1992 had survived 12 years of war, imposed isolation, and containment policy, and it continued to resist the American presence in the Persian Gulf.
- The tribal governing apparatus of the Persian Gulf shaikhdoms had experienced almost two decades of vicissitudes, and the domestic scene was no longer comparable to that of the 1960s or 1970s.
- Democracy, political participation, and political pressure groups were no longer unknown to the ruling families and their subjects. Though the emirates were and still are dependent on outsiders for their defense, they experienced a new alliance under the GCC.[34]
- In some emirates, power had passed to other members of the family who were more responsive to people's expectations.
- The money received from the export of oil, in addition to a better-functioning economy after the formation of the UAE, had created more self-confidence—if not arrogance.
- A new generation, many of them educated abroad, came back with doctoral degrees and new imported ideals alongside beautiful European cars.
- Royal decisions could not be made unmindful of public opinion as before.
- A foreign political, social, and military presence, stronger than that of the British, has penetrated the region. It has affected and in a sense infected the Arab states in all aspects. The UAE thought it could depend on such powerful protection.
- A second generation of the old British protectors equipped with new powers of scientific interpretation of their grandfathers' actions tried to find new explanations for the old points of disagreement on the islands issue.[35] Such efforts can still easily provide enough incentive to fight for what in fact is much less important than the difference the British have with the French in the English Channel.
- A very calculated propaganda, while exaggerating the destructive power of the Islamic Revolution, tried to magnify Iranian threats vis-à-vis its Arab neighbors. This was also used as an instrument to contain the Islamic revolution within Iranian territory.

In such an environment, a detonator was needed to set off an explosion, and inexperienced junior Iranian officials of Abu Musa provided that. A wave of anti-Iranian sentiment covered the Persian Gulf region and, from Abu Dhabi to Cairo, interpreted Iran's move as asserting full sovereignty over the islands, thus blocking any negotiation.

FUTURE SCENARIOS

By studying in depth the origins of the current situation and the changes in Iranian domestic and international policies, six different scenarios for the future are conceivable, though they do not share the same degree of probability. A brief outline of each of these scenarios has been provided in order to suggest ways to overcome the stalemate.

MAINTAINING THE STATUS QUO

This is a pattern to be followed reluctantly. Both parties are forced to continue in the present situation in order to avoid any unwanted confrontation. It is not, however, clear to what extent this can continue. From time to time there are hints of change, but irrational impulses directed toward each other halt any move toward final resolution. In some cases both parties have avoided entering a new phase on the issue.

For instance, in March 1999 the United Arab Emirates lodged a complaint at the Arab League over what it called a "provocative" action on the islands from the Iranian side. It is very interesting that according to the Emirati ambassador in Cairo, "the UAE views all past and future actions by Iran on the islands as undue provocations."[36] According to Reuters, the ambassador said his country was upset because "Iran had opened a municipality building and educational complex on Abu Musa." He apparently added that the UAE sees these practices as violations of the memorandum of understanding between the UAE and Iran . . . and a bid to consecrate the occupation and change the demographic state by force."[37]

The argument he enters into is very similar to that mentioned earlier, except that this time the same pattern was followed by the Iranians with a slight difference. In 1992, the UAE tried to introduce non-UAE nationals, while the current issue is in fact providing better conditions of life for the Iranians already living in the island. However, according to the same source, the ambassador "urged Iran to settle the dispute through bilateral negotiations or international arbitration."

Taking the current state of affairs into consideration, an effort to maintain the status quo is apparent. But this scenario will not resolve the problem. Such a tendency is completely understandable due to the highly volatile environment in the region. It is also possible that it will dominate relations between the two neighbors until the problem itself is forgotten or until no further necessity is felt to stir it up. This could be a scenario if both parties were willing to take sound and significant steps toward mutual cooperation and confidence building.

SOLVING THE PROBLEM THROUGH INTERNATIONAL DIPLOMACY

Both Iran and the UAE may not be open to such a solution for different reasons. The Islamic revolution in Iran has created a belief in self-reliance and independence. Turning to others to settle national issues contradicts the very essence of the revolutionary rhetoric that trumpets "Independence, Freedom, Islamic Governance." The desire to remain independent, especially in foreign policy, works against such an approach.

The UAE, too, may not relish exposing itself to the uncertainties of external intervention over a small issue for which there is sufficient local expertise. The UAE federal government, acting on behalf of the seven emirates, needs a domestic consensus before inviting London, Washington, Paris, or others to offer their suggestions. Both Iran and the UAE may face internal pressures from rival political factions and groups. A revival of Iranian claims to Bahrain, for example, such as occurred in the early years of the revolution, would jeopardize the security environment of the region.

Today, active international diplomacy may have some positive impact in the islands dispute, but such diplomacy depends a lot on an improvement of relations between Iran and other countries like the United States, the United Kingdom, and other major European states. As long as the United States maintains its extensive military presence and political influence in the region, it will be difficult for Iran to settle its disputes with the Arab countries. Overall it seems that there are many complexities at this level, and Iran is faced with three different issues of international diplomacy: relations between Iran, the GCC, Syria, and Egypt; relations between Iran and the European countries; and relations between Iran and the United States.

THE SEA OF BLOOD

For many decades, any attempt to solve regional problems through resorting to coercive means has produced more tension and led to the degradation of regional relationships. In December 1992, the GCC summit in Abu Dhabi called upon the Islamic Republic of Iran "to cancel and abolish measures taken on Abu Musa island and to terminate its occupation of the Greater and Lesser Tunb islands, which belong to the UAE."[38] Such statements only serve to escalate an atmosphere in Iran of feeling threatened by an Arab world backed by the United States. It also highlights the importance of the islands for Iranian national security.

It was in such circumstances that the image of a "sea of blood" came into being with former president Hashemi Rafsanjani's rather defensive and harsh declaration that "Iran is surely stronger than the likes of you." To dissuade any potential aggressor, he added: "to reach these islands one has to cross a sea of blood."[39]

Thus the notion of "the sea of blood" can be perceived as a possible scenario, the realization of which depends on many parameters including military preparedness and the political will of both parties as well as some regional and extra-regional supporters. While it is not categorically rejected, this remains one of the most improbable of the likely scenarios.

The idea of deterring shipping through the Strait of Hormuz can also be placed within the same context. Although the notion of closing the strait was first raised by Iran, it was at a time when Iran was faced with powerful international support for Iraq during their war. Iran itself is dependent on the continuous exportation of oil and other goods and commodities from its southern borders. It is true that "the greatest inhibition to a potential move by Tehran to try to close the Strait is the fact that Iran itself would be the party most gravely injured because Hormuz is the sole outlet for its oil, the lifeblood of its economy . . ."[40]

Iran's relations with its Arab neighbors, especially those of the Persian Gulf, have improved since President Mohammad Khatami was elected in May 1997. Perhaps the only issue that has upset neighboring states has been Iranian maneuvers in the Persian Gulf, which the Arab League has criticized. U.S. sources have often tried to raise alarms over an Iranian military threat to its Persian Gulf neighbors by emphasizing the idea of "the sea of blood." This scenario is certainly not in accord with the current state of mind in Iran or President Khatami's policy of détente in the region. Considering Iran's concerns over its vital interests in the Caspian Sea, it is clear that President Khatami would not risk opening fronts in two different directions: one, in the Persian Gulf, with the UAE, and another with Azerbaijan in the Caspian. On the contrary, rather than exposing himself to criticism by conservative hardliners, Khatami will try to solve both problems to strengthen his own power and credibility. In other words, the momentum has arrived to solve the problem with the UAE.

SOLVING THE PROBLEM THROUGH BILATERAL NEGOTIATIONS

This is not really an improbable scenario. Both Iranians and UAE officials have repeatedly urged the necessity of such an initiative. In fact it can go beyond negotiation and include practical steps such as reexamining the contents of the existing Memorandum of Understanding and reconsidering and updating it in order to comply with contemporary circumstances. But to enter into bilateral negotiation is a time-consuming process. Recent moves on the part of Iran, particularly after the new president took office in 1997, brought some hope in this regard.

In some cases significant results have been achieved through bilateral negotiation. When it comes to the Iran-UAE dispute, it seems that the political will exists, at least from the Iranian side, to overcome past problems, but the UAE centers of decision-making are not yet prepared for solutions. It is important to note that though the UAE is a federation of seven shaikhdoms, the islands issue relates to only two of them. It is quite possible that among the members of the UAE there is no consensus on how far to pursue their disagreement with Iran. Abu Dhabi and Dubai might be more militant in continuing the conflict, while others may have little incentive to act the same way.

Economic ties between the Emirates and Iran and through Iran with the Central Asian and Caucasian republics might be the main reason to dampen the conflict. After all, if the islands have a strategic importance for Iran, they may have lesser strategic and more economic significance for the Emirates. A potential lack of unity exists on certain issues such as the islands, and this is reflected in the relations of Arab states with Iran. After 1997 President Mohammad Khatami tried to change the basis of relations with neighbors, and the context of inter-Arab relations had to cope with the new orientation in Iranian foreign policy. This move has reduced Arab pressure on Iran and is likely to have a similar impact on UAE members.

Nevertheless, bilateral negotiations remain one of the most probable scenarios for which the domestic environment needs to be created. Both countries should be vigilant and avoid transformation of the dispute into other forms of hostility. In bilateral relations Iran should not seek to undermine the UAE because of its small size and military weakness. This is in fact a very dangerous development that can ruin any bilateral or regional solution. The UAE also should be warned that any attempt to broaden the disagreement over the islands can end up with the kind of international intervention that is absolutely against the interests of every country involved in the issue.

With the unannounced visit to Tehran of Shaikh Hamdan b. Zayed Al Nahyan, the UAE minister of state for foreign affairs, on July 23, 2001, the dispute over the islands entered a new phase. The visit took place less than one month after the UAE had renewed its call to Iran to resolve the dispute either through direct dialogue or international arbitration.[41] A few weeks earlier, the ministers of the GCC had invited Iran to submit the conflict to the International Court of Justice in The Hague.[42] Although upon his return Shaikh Hamdan denied discussing the islands issue, there is no doubt that it was raised. Rumors of possible Syrian involvement in facilitating this visit support our assumption that this scenario has a high degree of likelihood to solve this long-running dispute.

THIRD PARTY OR INTERNATIONAL ARBITRATION SCENARIO

To refer the islands issue to a third party or international arbitration has been one of the options the Arab states of the lower Gulf have pursued since 1992. It does not seem as easy as it may appear, given Iran's position on the issue. For instance, Iran does not feel a necessity to open a new file on the Tunbs, its sovereignty being justified on historical grounds. From a legal point of view, Ras al-Khaimah, supported by the British, had a temporary presence on the islands. Therefore recourse to arbitration is neither necessary nor relevant. In bilateral negotiations, whenever the UAE tried to initiate negotiations over the Lesser and Greater Tunbs, the Iranian delegation left the session. Iran has always stated its readiness for talks on Abu Musa but not on the Tunbs, and it has shown very little enthusiasm to refer to third party or international arbitration.

Iran's formal position rejects any mediation over the three islands and urges direct talks with the United Arab Emirates to resolve the dispute. Iranian authorities have expressed the necessity of direct talks between the two countries on many occasions. In the past, even UN secretary-general Kofi Annan has tried without success to bring the two sides together.[43]

One should distinguish between "third party" and "international" arbitration. Iran might accept a third party as the facilitator of negotiations, such as Syria or the UN secretary-general, but this depends a lot on who and what the third party is. At the same time Iran may not see the necessity of referring to international arbitration as long as all negotiation avenues are not closed. Nor does it seem logical to refer the issue to sources beyond the two countries as long as the two have not resumed negotiations and have not reached an impasse. Without entering into direct talks it seems irrelevant to invite third party or international organizations to intervene in the matter. However, the exception would be if relations improve between Iran and other Arab states of the region. Saudi Arabia, for instance, is a key ally of the UAE and can play a major role in the issue as a third party. The conclusion of an unprecedented security agreement between Iran and Saudi Arabia in April 2001 changed the regional dynamics, although it is too soon to say what effect, if any, this will have on the islands dispute.

LOOKING FOR A REGIONAL SOLUTION

On the regional plane two major levels should be distinguished from each other: first, a broader regional setting that can include greater Middle East players like Syria, Egypt, Jordan, and even Israel (which is probably not an option at present); and second, the Persian Gulf states, benefiting from the recommendations of other Arab countries.

One of the most feasible ways to move toward regional peace and tranquility seems to be at the regional level. The region—if such a concept can be rightly used for the Persian Gulf—is starved for integration and peaceful relations. It is within such a framework that efforts to find solutions for disputes can produce a tangible result. The Iran-UAE dispute is, of course, interrelated with many other issues in the region.

To overcome regional problems, one should seek regional solutions. At least during the process of conflict resolution, external intervention must be limited. The confidence-building process in the region is very fragile, and mistrust and pessimism dominate. Recent developments in Iranian foreign relations seem to involve a plan for regional integration. Iranian authorities have repeatedly tried to create an atmosphere of confidence among their neighbors, though this has not yet proved successful.

On several occasions the Khatami government has declared better relations with Arab neighbors, including Iraq, a top priority. Iran's attempt to transform its foreign policy pattern and replace it with a more rational one to prevent generating animosity and mistrust is described by Edmund Herzig as "Iran's regionalism." He emphasizes that in following a regional policy of defusing tension, Foreign Minister Kharrazi was the first to accord "top priority to relations with the GCC states." Herzig says: "Speaking at the 52nd UN General Assembly, Foreign Minister Kharrazi expressed the desire to 'turn a new page in relations' and 'undertake new initiatives in a more energetic fashion' [. . .] He held out an olive branch, saying: 'Let's be transparent. Let's sign a pact of non-aggression. Let's cooperate for economic development of the region.'"[44]

Other practical steps taken by President Khatami have reinforced new orientations in Iranian foreign policy. His visit to Syria, Saudi Arabia, and Qatar in May 1999 should be considered a turning point in Iran's relations with its Arab neighbors. Further and future developments of these relations can have a deep impact on the islands issue.

Though the Iranian parliamentary election of February 2000 may be considered a big step forward for the reformists, in very sensitive areas, like foreign policy, considerable progress remains to be achieved. The continuation of the power struggle and competition between the conservatives and the reformists work against any probable positive impact that President Khatami could have in reducing tension between Iran and the UAE.

Most of the Persian Gulf states, with the exception of the UAE, enjoy deepening relations with Iran. The Emirati journal *Khaleej Times,* which is close to official circles, has taken the lead in writing against Iran and defines Iran's position as "stubbornness and provocations."[45]

The *Khaleej Times* believes that "The fact that some Gulf countries put normalization and openness with Iran before the settlement of this issue [of the islands] does not serve the interests of the Emirates and will encourage Iran to maintain its occupation." The journal stressed that it expects other members of the GCC to show their support by "translating their solidarity with the Emirates into concrete action."[46]

Despite all controversies one should agree that there is the political will to review and improve feelings between Iran and the Arab World, and this can be achieved only in a regional context. On the realization of such a "rapprochement," a regional response to territorial disputes seems not improbable.

CONCLUSION

We have tried to view the disagreement over Abu Musa and Greater and Lesser Tunb in its regional and international context rather than merely as a bilateral dispute between the UAE and the Islamic Republic of Iran. The problem has been created by external players and cannot be solved on the national level only. Many factors play a role, including history (which I have not focused on in this paper), as well as geography and geostrategy. On another level, perceptions and misperceptions play an important role in the development of attitudes among the nations of the region. As the Indian researcher Shah Alam has noted: "Khatami's détente policy is intended to generate confidence among the Gulf states that Iran poses no threat to them politically or militarily. However, the growing Iranian military capability is perceived by the Gulf states as a threat. Iran's efforts will now be to prevent generating animosity and mistrust because it perceives the conflict with the Gulf states is not healthy for Iran."[47]

We have tried to show how this changing perception in Iranian foreign policy and its new approach toward its neighbors to the south can influence the dispute. At the same time we are well aware of the limits of legal interpretation and of the importance of positions taken in the past. For instance, it may well happen that any one of the involved countries will try to create special feelings about the islands—as is the case with the name for the Persian Gulf—among its people. In such a case the issue can soon be transformed into a matter of national dignity and pride fueled by emotion. In some circumstances the country that has created the emotion will not be able to control or change it.

Why the Iranians have taken the position they have is to some extent understandable if one realizes that the revolutionary government does not want to cede any territory that Iran controlled prior to the revolution. People will not support such measures and will perhaps interpret them as an inability to safeguard national interest and security. It is important to discover how the UAE position regarding the islands can be justified, since they had little reaction, if any, toward the 1971 Memorandum of Understanding. In fact the people of Sharjah or other emirates forming the UAE have not rejected the MOU. The structure of power and the state in the UAE is different from Iran, and any small concession from Iran might be enough to satisfy them and close the file for some time. Some are of the opinion that border disputes may reemerge at any time depending on the politico-economic conditions of the countries involved. So any settlement at this dispute can also be a temporary one.

It is necessary to consider the islands issue as part and parcel of regional politics and not only through the positions taken by Iran or the UAE; otherwise the region will have difficulty in finding solutions for its problems. For centuries, the politics of divide and rule has resulted in an atmosphere of mutual suspicion and lack of trust among the Persian Gulf countries. The problems of the region stem from without and not from within. It is time to benefit from the momentum created by Iran's revolution, which itself has moved into a more advanced stage in defining Iran's relation with the Arab world and the West.

President Khatami's approach toward Iran's Arab neighbors and his landmark visit to some of them have given a big boost to regional stability. He is the highest-ranking Iranian official to visit Saudi Arabia since Tehran's 1979 Islamic revolution. In this visit Khatami urged Muslim nations "to resolve disputes and tolerate their differences for the sake of regional security." Khatami emphasized that "security" is a goal for the Islamic *ummah* and necessitates avoiding issues related to ethnic sovereignty and border disputes. He said: "The Islamic *ummah* must settle disputes through dialogue and that would not allow its dependence on foreign powers."[48]

Iran is not capable of changing the root elements of the equation, i.e., its size and power as compared to the small vulnerable states of the Persian Gulf. What it can do is create a new environment of mutual respect, of cooperation rather than rivalry, and ease the tension.

Khatami's tour proved that the islands problem, if pursued at a regional level, might have some chance of solution. Direct negotiation with the UAE may still be among the possible scenarios, although the limits of such direct negotiation are known: the UAE wants to discuss the Tunb islands while Iran considers this as irrelevant and rejects any precondition to the negotiations.

The fact that the meeting of GCC foreign ministers in June 1999 and the GCC summit meeting in Muscat in April 2000 did not back the UAE's claims, suggests that Khatami's foreign policy is advancing toward a regional solution for the problem. Although the GCC summit in Bahrain in December 2000 did maintain that the islands belonged to the UAE, this only demonstrates that an immediate solution appears improbable. However, even after the GCC's unexpected support for the UAE claims Iran stressed that it was ready to hold talks. Rejecting the GCC resolution, Iranian foreign ministry spokesman Hamid Reza Assefi said in an interview, "The Islamic Republic says the islands are an integral part of its territory, but that it is ready to hold talks with the UAE to clear up any 'misunderstanding.' Iran cannot accept a committee set up by the six-member council without seeking any consultation from the Islamic Republic, and merely based on domestic mechanisms. The committee has always proved to be biased."[49] Though he called the final declaration "devoid of any realism" and said that it "lacks [a] spirit of cooperation," he said that "if the committee is making efforts to encourage us for consultation, we welcome it." Despite all the challenges made by both parties, it seems that a revision of the text of the MOU can satisfy the mutual interests of both sides and at the same time create a context for claiming victory over the other party.

To satisfy national sympathy and feelings created during the past decade or so, it is perhaps more useful to rely on third party intervention, provided that a regional player rather than an international one plays the role. Probably the dispute can be solved more easily if followed in a regional perspective in which Arab and Muslim countries can intervene and suggest their solution. This, too, has limits and depends on the future development of Iran-Arab ties on the one hand and Iran-U.S. relations on the other.

NOTES

1. Until agreements announced in June and July 2000 respectively, Saudi Arabia and Yemen and Kuwait and Saudi Arabia also had border disputes. The dispute between Bahrain and Qatar was decided largely in favor of the former by the World Court in March 2001 (*Financial Times,* March 17, 2001). Saudi Arabia and Qatar signed a border agreement on March 21, 2001 (Reuters, March 21, 2001, from Doha, online).

2. Geoffrey Kemp and Robert E. Harkavy, *Strategic Geography and the Changing Middle East* (Washington: Carnegie Endowment for International Peace in Cooperation with Brookings Institution Press, 1997), p. 96.

3. For a comprehensive and realistic study of Iran's maritime boundaries, see Pirouz Mojtahed-Zadeh, "Iran's Maritime Boundaries in the Persian Gulf: the Case of Abu Musa Island," in Keith McLachlan, ed., *The Boundaries of Modern Iran* (London: UCL Press, 1994), pp. 101–27.

4. For a realistic explanation of Arab perceptions toward the Iranians, see Mohammad Masjed Jamei, *Continuity and Change, an Introduction to . . . the Persian Gulf Shaikhdoms* [title translated] (Tehran: Pishgaam, 1998).

5. "Historical Roots of Iran's Ownership of Tunb Islands," *Tehran Times,* May 6, 1999.

6. Asghar Ja'fari Valdani, *A Historical Look at the Iranian Islands of Tunb and Abu Musa* (Tehran: IPIS, 1997), pp. 36–37.

7. *Ettela'at* [Iranian daily newspaper in Persian], Dec. 1, 1971, gives respectively 7 square kilometers for Abu Musa, 6 for Greater Tunb and 1.5 for Lesser Tunb. Other sources believe the area to be about 66 square kilometers: "Statistical Calendar of the Country, 1369," Tehran, Iranian Statistical Center, 1991, p. 11. According to *Kayhan* [Iranian daily newspaper], Abu Musa has an area of 22 square kilometers. But *The Economist Intelligence Unit* (EIU), Country Report, United Arab Emirates, which inserts Abu Musa information under UAE entry, No. 2. 1992, p. 6, gives 90 square kilometers as the area of the island.

8. Valdani, ibid.

9. Ahmad Sajedi, "One day in Abu Musa," *Jomhouri Islami,* no.3873, October 17, 1992 (25 Mehr 1371), p. 12.

10. Richard N. Schofield, "Border Disputes in the Gulf: Past, Present, and Future," in *The Persian Gulf at the Millennium,* ed. Gary G. Sick and Lawrence G. Potter (New York: St. Martin's Press, 1997), p. 143.

11. Mojtahed-Zadeh, p. 109.

12. Valdani, *A Historical Look,* pp. 36–37.

13. Mohammad Reza Kafash-Jamshid, "Gozaresh-i Safar Beh Jazayer-e Jonub" ["The report of travel to the islands in the south"], *Mahnameh-ye Khalij-e Fars* [Persian Gulf and Security Monthly], Autumn 2000, pp. 51–55 (quotation is on p. 52).

14. "Historical Roots of Iran's Ownership," op. cit.
15. Guive Mirfendereski's excellent essay provides a consolidated record of the islands' nomenclature, with a view to ascertaining their etymological origins. See "The Toponymy of the Tonb Islands," *Iranian Studies,* vol. 29, nos. 3–4, Summer/Fall 1996, pp. 297–320.
16. Valdani, ibid, pp. 37–38.
17. Mojtahed-Zadeh, p. 124, quoting from *Echo of Iran,* May 1992, p. 4.
18. Sajedi, op. cit.
19. Schofield, in *Persian Gulf at the Millennium,* p. 150.
20. Asghar Jaffari Valdani, "Unstable Borders in the Persian Gulf," *Iranian Journal of International Affairs,* vol. V, nos. 3, 4, Fall/Winter 1993–94, pp. 539–60.
21. Abbas Maleki (then Deputy Minister of Foreign Affairs in Education and Research), quoted in *Iran Focus* (November 1992), p. 2.
22. Mohammad Reza Dabiri, "Abu-Musa Island: A Binding Understanding or A Misunderstanding," *The Iranian Journal of International Affairs,* vol. V, nos. 3, 4 Fall/Winter 1993–94, pp. 575–83.
23. Ibid., p. 577.
24. Richard Schofield, op. cit., quoting from *Round Table Discussion on the Dispute over the Gulf Islands* (London: Arab Research Center, 1993), p. 14. The whole set of documents was released by the Iranian Foreign Ministry and published in the *Journal of Foreign Policy,* vol. 6 (1993), pp. 193–208. This journal is published by the Institute for Political and International Studies in Tehran.
25. Valdani, op.cit., p. 542.
26. As mentioned in the letter dated November 26, 1971, from Buttes Gas & Oil Co. to Dr. Eghbal, Chairman of the Board and General Managing Director, National Iranian Oil Company, in *Arabian Geopolitics* 2, Regional Documentary Studies, Series Editor: R. N. Schofield, *The Lower Gulf Islands: Abu Musa and the Tunbs,* ed. P. L. Toye, vol. 6, Archive Editions, 1993, p. 496.
27. Ibid., preface to vol. 1, p. v.
28. Mojtahed-Zadeh, op. cit., p. 120.
29. Hussain M. Al-Baharna, "The Consequences of Britain's Exclusive Treaties: A Gulf View," in B. R. Pridham, ed., *The Arab Gulf and the West* (New York: St. Martin's Press, 1985), p. 169.
30. Dabiri, op. cit., p. 578.
31. Paragraph 2 of the letter dated November 30, 1971, addressed to "His Highness Shaikh Khalid Bin Mohammed Al-Qasimi, Ruler of Sharjah," and signed by "Abbas Ali Khalatbari, Minister for Foreign Affairs" of Iran in: *Arabian Geopolitics* 2, Regional Documentary Studies, Series Editor: R. N. Schofield, *The Lower Gulf Islands: Abu Musa and the Tunbs,* ed. P. L. Toye, vol. 6, Archive Edition, 1993, pp. 499–501.
32. Ibid., p. 498.
33. John Duke Anthony, *Arab States of the Lower Gulf: People, Politics, Petroleum* (Washington: The Middle East Institute, 1975), p. 226.
34. Gulf Cooperation Council (GCC) is the official title, but as the name "Gulf" and its geographical location is not clear, it is converted into PGCC (Persian Gulf Cooperation Council) in Iranian texts.
35. For instance British scholar Richard N. Schofield, who has written extensively on the dispute, concludes that the Iran-Sharjah Memorandum of Understanding was a "forced compromise," while recognizing that Iran never surrendered rival claims. His colleague Patricia Toye was series editor of a six-volume publication of over 3,000 pages that present the British records of the dispute.
36. *UAE Complains to Arab League over islands dispute,* CNN interactive, March 1, 1999: http://cnn.com/WORLD/meast/9903/01/BC-UAE-IRAN-ISLANDS.reut/index.html.
37. Ibid.

38. *BBC Summary of World Broadcasts: the Middle East* ME/1573/A/7 (December 29, 1992), as quoted in Schofield, *Border Disputes in the Gulf,* p. 151.

39. *Middle East Economic Survey,* January 11, 1993, p. C3. Also quoted by Richard Schofield, op. cit., p. 151.

40. William L. Dowdy, "The Strait of Hormuz as a Secure International Waterway," in B. R. Pridham, ed., *The Arab Gulf and the West* (New York: St. Martin's Press, 1985), p. 169.

41. *Emirates Bulletin,* no. 12, June 27, 2001.

42. AFP, June 3, 2001.

43. *Iran rejects mediation, wants UAE talks on islands,* CNN interactive: http:www.cnn.com/WORLD/meast/9812/08/BC-IRAN-EMIRATES-ISLANDS.reut/index.html.

44. Edmund Hertzig, "Iran and its Regional Relations," in Rosemary Hollis, ed., *Oil and Regional Developments in the Gulf* (London: The Royal Institute of International Affairs, 1998), pp. 115–35.

45. *Khaleej Times,* April 29, 2000.

46. Ibid.

47. Shah Alam, "The Changing Perception of Iran Towards the Gulf States," Research Paper in *Strategic Analysis* (Journal of the Institute for Defence Studies and Analysis, New Delhi, India), vol. 24, no. 11 (February 2001), pp. 2085–96. The full text can be retrieved at: http:www.idsa-india.org/an-feb–9–01.html.

48. *Iran's Khatami calls for unity among Muslim nations,* CNN interactive, May 14, 1999. http:www.cnn.com/WORLD/meast/9905/14/iran.syria.reut/.

49. Interview of the Iranian foreign ministry's spokesman, January 1, 2001. The full text can be retrieved on the foreign ministry's web site: http://mfa.gov.ir/English/.

CHAPTER 6

THE ISLANDS QUESTION

An Arabian Perspective

HASSAN H. AL-ALKIM

The roots of the crisis between the United Arab Emirates (UAE) and its largest neighbor, the Islamic Republic of Iran, over the islands of Abu Musa[1] and Greater and Lesser Tunb[2] go back to the late nineteenth century. The dispute culminated, on November 30, 1971, in the Iranian seizure of the three islands. The continued Iranian occupation of the islands and Iran's adamant refusal to accept mediation or arbitration reveal Tehran's desire to be the paramount power in the Gulf subregion, and presents a dilemma for future UAE-Iran rapprochement. Although relations between Iran and the Gulf Cooperation Council (GCC) states have improved under President Khatami's administration,[3] the twenty-first GCC summit in Bahrain in December 2000 endorsed the UAE's position on the islands and decided to dissolve the committee that it set up in July 1999 to mediate between the UAE and Iran.[4] The Iranian reaction to the GCC decision was exaggerated and demonstrates Iran's desire to blame the GCC states for the state of tension in the region.[5]

Various scholars have treated the islands question differently. Iranian experts like Pirouz Mojtahed-Zadeh have tried to prove Iran's claim to the islands on the basis of non-factual information.[6] He argues that Iran has all the historical, legal, and geographical elements substantiating its claim and blames the British, as the external power, for cutting off the islands' connection with the mainland. Arabs like Mohammed al-Mahmoud, Abdul Wahab Abdul, Mohammed al Roken, and Walid al-Adhami argue that the Iranian claims are self-defeating and have no legal or historical grounds. Western scholars like Rosemarie Said Zahlan, Frauke Heard-Bey, David Poole, and Richard Schofield see the Iranian claims as questionable.[7]

The geographic location of the Gulf states has always been an important element in determining inter- and intra-regional interaction. This chapter endorses the importance of subregional cooperation and views the persistence of the islands question as detrimental to a new regional security policy. Security and stability in the Gulf area cannot be fostered through an arms race or dependence on foreign powers. Rather, regional security necessitates the pursuance of a policy of cooperation, coordination and possibly economic integration among the states of the region. This chapter first reviews Iranian claims to the disputed islands and Iran's objectives; it then focuses on the 1971 Memorandum of Understanding (MOU) before considering the development of bilateral relations, Iran's encroachment on Abu Musa, the posture of the GCC states, and Iran's regional policy.

THE IRANIAN CLAIMS

The Iranians consistently raise historical, legal, and strategic justifications for their occupation of the three islands. They view the islands question as a territorial problem, yet refuse to accept arbitration or recourse to the International Court of Justice (ICJ) as a means to settle the issue. Iran and Sharjah agreed to administer different parts of Abu Musa without settling the issue of sovereignty over the island, whereas upon the ruler of Ras Al-Khaimah's refusal to conclude a similar agreement, Iran landed its forces and the issue of the two Tunbs became one of occupation.

In the Arab view, except for sporadic Persian control the Gulf has been an Arab lagoon since the inception of the first Islamic state in the seventh century A.D. Between the early sixteenth and mid-twentieth centuries it came under European colonial rule under the Portuguese, the Dutch, the French, and finally the British.[8] Iran rarely succeeded in controlling the southern shore. Historical records confirm that these islands belonged to Ras al-Khaimah and Sharjah and were administered by the Qasimi family of the south for more than 200 years. The first documentary record shows that the Qasimi ruler of the south sent an official letter to the British Resident in 1864 expressing his sovereignty over Abu Musa and the two Tunbs. In 1871, the ruler of Ras al-Khaimah denied the people of Lingeh, an Iranian port on the Gulf, entry into Tunb island. In 1873, the ruler of Sharjah dispatched fifty armed men to regain Abu Musa from the Qasimi of Lingeh who, in 1877, endorsed the sovereignty of the Qasimi of Ras al-Khaimah over the Tunb islands.[9] The Qasimi of Lingeh recognized, in five letters, the sovereignty of the Qasimi of the south over Abu Musa and the two Tunbs.[10] The ruler of Sharjah, Salim bin Sultan, used to send his opponents to Abu Musa and was himself exiled to the island after he was deposed from power in 1883.[11] Although the Iranians confirm that the islands in the southern Gulf belonged in the past to the Qasimi of Lingeh, they refuse to accept the arrangements made between the two Qasimi factions.[12] According to a document published by D. W. Lascelles, British legal adviser, on September 4, 1934, Iran had not exercised de facto authority over the disputed islands for the previous 184 years.[13]

The first time the Iranians laid an official claim to the disputed islands was in 1904 when they dispatched their customs officer (of Belgian nationality) to Abu Musa island. They withdrew him upon the protest of Sharjah's ruler and failed to present the documents, requested by the British authority, to substantiate their claim. During the Anglo-Iranian negotiations in 1929–1930 the Iranian side repeated its claim to the three islands. A proposal was discussed that would have led to British recognition of Iranian sovereignty over the island of Sirri in return for Iranian recognition of Arab sovereignty over the three disputed islands. The Iranians, however, offered, in August 1929, to abandon their demand for Abu Musa on the condition that they make arrangements with the ruler of Ras al-Khaimah for the sale of the two Tunbs and control of the lighthouse. R. J. Clive, the minister in Tehran, supported the idea, but only if the lighthouse remained under absolute British control.[14] The British political agent, C. C. G. Barret, in

May 1930 presented the idea to the rulers of Sharjah and Ras al-Khaimah, but it was rejected.[15] In October 1930, the Iranians proposed to lease the two Tunbs for fifty years and again the idea was turned down despite initial British support.[16] Others argue that the ruler of Ras al-Khaimah accepted the offer but laid down rigid conditions that were unacceptable to the Persians.[17]

Moreover, Iran claims that it has more than 20 geographical maps that show the islands depicted in Iranian colors. This argument is negated on the following grounds:

- The Iranians are using unofficial maps drawn by the British between 1807 and 1897 for their use in the Gulf. They include a map presented to the shah in 1888 by Sir Henry Drummond Wolff, the British minister in Tehran,[18] but it is neither part of an agreement nor attached to an agreement between the two countries as an appendix. Another unofficial map offered as evidence by the Iranians is that of Lord Curzon in 1892.[19] The fact is, however, that this map, which appeared in his book, *Persia and the Persian Question,* is considered a private map[20] with no legal value and inadequate proof of authenticity.
- The authority in the case of the disputed islands is the British government, which pursued a consistent policy from the eruption of the crisis in 1903 until the second half of 1971 of recognizing that the islands belong to the emirates of Sharjah and Ras al-Khaimah.
- The British government recognized the mistake committed by the Foreign Office official and corrected it by its official stand that the islands belong to the Qasimi of the south.
- A private map published in Germany in 1864 (prior to the map used by the Iranians to prove their rights in the islands) shows that the three disputed islands belong to the Qasimi of the south.[21]

Political claims are not necessarily justifiable on legal grounds. Contemporary international law forbids the forcible acquisition of territory. Article 2/4 of the United Nations Charter calls on all members to "refrain in their international relations from the threat or use of force against the territorial integrity or political independence of any state, or in any other manner inconsistent with the purposes of the United Nations." The Iranians' use of force, at 2:30 A.M. on November 30, 1971, against the territorial integrity of the Omani Coast Emirates, then under British protection, violated the principles of the UN. Such an act is illegal and violates the principles of modern international law. On this ground, the Iranian occupation of the Tunbs is illegitimate and could be regarded, according to the principles of international law, as a crime.[22]

IRAN'S OBJECTIVES

The British decision to withdraw from east of Suez led to a new era in relations between Iran and Saudi Arabia. The new tendency was cemented with direct American involvement in the Arabian Gulf through its new subregional security doctrine based on the Twin Pillar policy. As a result of the Iranian-Saudi rapprochement, the shah relinquished his claim to Bahrain. He then renewed claims to the islands of Abu Musa and Greater and Lesser Tunb. Tehran's public claims to the disputed islands ensured that maximum attention was focused on the issue. Determined to play its self-appointed role as "policeman of the Gulf," Iran, having renounced its claim to Bahrain in the interest of good neighborly relations, would have found it very difficult to abandon its claim to the three islands. Iran was determined to seize the islands for the following reasons:[23]

- Freedom of navigation in the Gulf, at all times, was essential, because Iran, unlike Saudi Arabia and Iraq, depends totally on the Gulf as the only outlet for its oil exports.
- Iran needed to exploit its offshore oil resources and protect not only its extensive oil installations at Kharq island and elsewhere, but also its oil cargoes for the entire length of the waterway.

The Iranian authorities were manipulating the islands question for domestic and regional political gains by presenting it to the public as an issue of national sovereignty. On the one hand, Iran managed to divert local public opinion away from the major political, economic, and social domestic problems. On the other hand, it succeeded in using the question of the islands as part of its carrot-and-stick policy toward the GCC countries. Revolutionary Iran showed continuity with its predecessor in its claim to the three occupied islands.

The British orchestrated a memorandum of understanding between Sharjah and Iran but failed to persuade Shaikh Saqr bin Mohammed, the ruler of Ras al-Khaimah, to reach a similar deal. On November 1, 1971, Shaikh Saqr stressed his commitment to preserve the emirate's sovereignty over the Tunbs. He revealed Sir William Luce's proposal that Ras al-Khaimah cede sovereignty over the two Tunbs in return for annual payment of $2.7 million by Iran and a 49 percent share of the income from any oil discovery in their offshore waters, an idea he rejected.[24] The ruler of Ras al-Khaimah replied that he would not sell the islands for any sum whatsoever.[25]

In 1970, after the shah had decided to drop his claim to Bahrain, Iran reasserted a claim to the three islands and indicated that it would not recognize the UAE until it obtained control of all the islands.[26] On September 28, 1971, the shah proclaimed that "we need them; we shall have them; no power on earth will stop us."[27] After occupying the islands, the shah reiterated his country's position and claimed that he needed them to protect the entrance of the Gulf through the Strait of Hormuz.[28] Iran, however, has much more strategic territory than the disputed islands, notably Qeshm island and Bander Abbas controlling the entrance of the Gulf. The shah's insistence on the annexation of the islands may have emanated not so much from their strategic value or Iran's historical rights as from his desire to save face at home after he had relinquished his claim to Bahrain.[29] This was what made it difficult for him to sacrifice the islands for better relations with the Arab states in general, and the Gulf states in particular.

Britain's new attitude was not consistent with its earlier policy. In the early twentieth century, the British had resisted Iran's claim to the islands and continued to regard them as indisputably Arab.[30] However, recognizing the importance of Iran as a regional power and keen to honor its historic pacts with the seven Omani Coast Emirates (today comprising the United Arab Emirates), Britain was convinced that an Anglo-Iranian agreement should be reached. Hence, once it became clear that they were unable to work out a deal acceptable to both parties, the British attitude became favorable to Iran. On leaving Tehran for the Omani Coast Emirates on November 17, 1971, Sir William Luce (a former British Political Resident in the Persian Gulf who had been appointed a special representative to find a solution) said, "Iran and Britain have sorted out their differences over the Tunbs and Abu Musa. The shaikhs can now form their federation."[31] Anthony Cordesman argues,

Britain, which saw the Shah as the principal future source of stability in the Gulf, was not prepared to make an issue of the matter and made an arrangement with Iran that would allow it to occupy the islands immediately after the British departure. The evidence is uncertain, but the presence of a British carrier in the immediate area during the Iranian occupation, and a number of British actions, indicated British complicity in the Shah's invasion.[32]

The continued Iranian occupation of the three islands reveals their desire to play the role of policeman of the Gulf. This was clearly revealed in statements issued by officials of the governments of both the former Pahlavi regime and the Islamic Republic. Abolhassan Bani Sadr, the first president of the republic, stated in March 1980:

Evacuate [the islands]? Who is going to take them? To whom do the islands belong? Not to anyone. . . . In the south there is Abu Dhabi, Qatar, Oman, Dubai, Kuwait, Saudi Arabia . . . to us these states are connected with the United States and are not independent. At the end of the Gulf there is the Strait of Hormuz through which oil passes. They [the Arab governments] are afraid of our revolution. If we allow them to have the islands they will control the Strait. In other words the United States would control the waterway. . . . Is it possible to give such a gift to the United States? . . . If all of them, the littoral states of the Gulf, were independent, we would have returned the islands to them.[33]

THE MEMORANDUM OF UNDERSTANDING

Due to Iranian pressure and the British desire not to engage in a new confrontation with Iran, a British-sponsored Memorandum of Understanding (MOU) was concluded between Iran and Sharjah over the island of Abu Musa. The memorandum stated:[34]

1. Sharjah agrees to the stationing of Iranian troops in the northern part of Abu Musa, Iran having full jurisdiction over them. The Iranian flag will fly there.
2. Sharjah will maintain jurisdiction over the rest of the island, with Sharjah's flag flying there.
3. Both Iran and Sharjah recognize a 12–mile zone of territorial waters around the island.
4. Revenue derived from oil exploration, on and offshore, will be divided equally between Sharjah and Iran.
5. Iran will pay Sharjah £1.5 million a year, until the emirate's annual receipts from oil total £3 million a year.

Iran, failing to reach an arrangement with Ras al-Khaimah over the Greater and Lesser Tunbs, decided to send its troops on November 30, 1971, and to occupy them by force. The outcome of the unbalanced confrontation between the Iranian forces and the Ras al-Khaimah police force was the death of four of the Ras al-Khaimah policemen and three Iranian soldiers and the deportation of the Arab people of Greater Tunb to Ras al-Khaimah.[35]

THE DEVELOPMENT OF BILATERAL RELATIONS

The British decision to withdraw east of Suez was welcomed by Iran. The shah's imperial regime was determined to maintain the upper hand in Gulf affairs. In the changing circumstances that followed the British departure, Iran, in search of regional security, sought to coordinate its policies with Saudi Arabia. The shah, in the autumn of 1968, paid an official state visit to Riyadh in which the two sides agreed to delineate their maritime border. The visit was followed by the shah's decision to relinquish his claim to Bahrain. He then, however, asserted a claim to the islands of Abu Musa and the Greater and Lesser Tunbs. British documents released in January 2000 and published in the newspaper *Al-Khalij* revealed Saudi complicity in the matter,[36] which is substantiated by the fact that the Saudis "merely expressed regret over the incident."[37]

Iran recognized the UAE on December 4, 1971, but diplomatic relations were not established until December 23, 1972. The first two years of UAE-Iran relations were somewhat cool. Nevertheless, cooperation was sought in matters of economy, culture, health, and defense. Relations were strengthened through intergovernmental contacts. Shaikh Zayed said on March 19, 1975, "we are very anxious to promote good and traditional relations with Iran," and he paid two state visits to Tehran in 1975 and 1977. On his first visit Shaikh Zayed announced that his trip was intended to mark the beginning of an era of closer cooperation that would benefit the region. However, relations between the two countries have never been stable.[38]

The new Gulf policy adopted by the Iranian revolutionary leaders led to speculation among concerned parties that the islands question might be resolved. It was thought that Iran might give back the three disputed islands in exchange for the UAE's assurance that it would not grant sanctuary to any more members of the shah's former regime.[39] Shahriyar Rouhani, Khomeini's representative in Washington, gave the impression that Iran might hand back the three disputed islands.[40]

The UAE heard with optimism the announcements in early 1979 by the revolutionary leadership in Iran that all agreements made by the former regime would be reviewed and possibly abrogated.[41] It gave strong grounds for hope that the islands question would finally be settled. The new hope, however, did not materialize in anything concrete. It has been suggested that the UAE's refusal to extradite former Savak collaborators led Iran to halt all efforts to improve relations.[42] In June 1979 Ibrahim Yazdi, then foreign minister of Iran, denied that Iran was ready to hand back the islands to the UAE.[43]

The islands question did not prevent the development of relations between the UAE and the new Iranian government. The two countries maintained diplomatic ties on an ambassadorial level, and a series of messages and official visits were exchanged. The UAE was quick to recognize the revolutionary government and Ambassador Issa al-Ruhaimil returned to Tehran on March 4, 1979. The UAE, in support of the new government, criticized U.S. policy toward Iran. The message of Ayatollah Khomeini conveyed by PLO leader Yasir Arafat to UAE officials was encouraging: the abandonment of the shah's expansionist policy would mean a review of all policies and agreements, including those concerning the disputed islands. Iraq's revival of the islands question at the outbreak of the Iran-Iraq War, in the fall of 1980, complicated the issue further and led the Iranians to reassert their claim to the islands.

IRAN'S ENCROACHMENT ON ABU MUSA ISLAND

Since the early 1980s Iran has been violating the MOU and has pursued a policy of gradual encroachment on Abu Musa. Since 1983, it has based surface-to-air missiles in the Gulf islands and used Abu Musa as a base for speedboat attacks on shipping and oil installations.[44] A crisis first erupted in April 1992 when Iranian authorities prevented a group of expatriate workers from entering Abu Musa. The crisis escalated in August 1992 when the Iranian authority on the island, demanding Iranian entry visas, turned back a passenger ferry with 110 Arab schoolteachers and their families returning after their summer vacation.[45] The feeling in the UAE in particular and among the Gulf states in general is that with the defeat of Iraq in 1991, the Iranians were trying to see how far they could assert themselves as the new dominant regional power.[46]

In 1999 the UAE claimed that Iran's militarization of Abu Musa was threatening its security, its oil fields, and shipping via the Strait of Hormuz, through which one-fifth of the world's oil supply passes. The United States made similar claims. (However, satellite images of Abu Musa released in early 2000 showed no evidence that the island had been turned into an "unsinkable aircraft carrier" capable of closing the strait during a crisis.)[47] The Iranian development program in Abu Musa included a road network, a 4–kilometer airstrip, port facilities, and agricultural projects. Iran also did not hesitate to interfere in the daily lives of the citizens of the island by preventing them from constructing new buildings or renovating old ones, closing their businesses, and requiring Iranian permits before launching new businesses.[48]

The new Iranian policy in the Arabian Gulf subregion raised fears about Tehran's other ambitions in the area. Iran could claim sovereignty over the oil fields and oil reserves within the 12–mile zone constituting the islands' territorial waters—although production there is already shared as set out in the MOU.[49] In a further provocative step, it was announced in November 1996 that a branch of one of the Iranian universities would be opened in Abu Musa.[50] The Iranian authorities in 1998 also organized a tour to the southern islands, including the three disputed islands, for Arab students studying in Iran.

During a meeting of the two sides in Abu Dhabi on September 27–28, 1992, and in Doha in 1995, the UAE delegation presented their Iranian counterparts with several demands.[51] Iran had to:

- Terminate its military occupation of the islands of Greater and Lesser Tunb;
- Commit itself to observing the provisions of the 1971 MOU with respect to the island of Abu Musa;
- Refrain from intervening in any way or under any circumstances or under any pretext in the UAE's exercise of its complete jurisdiction over its sector of Abu Musa;
- Revoke all steps or measures which it imposed on the UAE government organs on Abu Musa and on the citizens of the state and on expatriates who work there;
- Indicate a suitable framework to resolve the question of sovereignty over Abu Musa within a specified period of time.

Shaikh Sultan Bin Zayed, UAE deputy prime minister, reiterated the UAE position in a recently published article. He pointed out that the UAE is determined to settle the islands question peacefully and not let it spoil relations between the two countries indefinitely. "Negotiations cannot go forever, and if the UAE and Iran cannot resolve the islands dispute bilaterally, then there should be no reason not to seek an impartial ICJ decision."[52]

THE GCC AND IRAN'S REGIONAL POLICY

Competition among the major subregional powers (Iran, Iraq, and Saudi Arabia) for hegemony threatens to overwhelm the smaller states of the lower Gulf.[53] The absence of a balance of power among the Gulf states (see below) has inspired their policies toward both each other and the outside world. Iran's relations with the Arab littoral states demonstrates the complexity and multidimensional aspects of Arab-Persian interregional relationships. "On the one hand, the connection includes cultural and social ties as well as active and substantial trading links. On the other hand, the relationship faces mutual distrust and misperception."[54]

Prior to 1979, Saudi Arabia and the small states of the lower Gulf cooperated with Iran to check the Ba'thist Iraqi government's threat to their security. They seized the opportunity of the Iran-Iraq rapprochement after the 1975 Algiers Accord to maneuver between the two regional powers to protect their national interests. Saudi Arabia, in particular, "endeavored to use Iraq to frustrate the shah's schemes to institutionalize his hegemonic aspirations through a Gulf collective defense pact, and to use Iran to check Iraq's aspiration to become the center of an alignment of the Arab countries of the Gulf."[55]

Revolutionary Iran since 1979 posed a threat of a different nature to the conservative Gulf states. After the fall of the Shah, Saudi Arabia and the Gulf states shared a common apprehension of the new Iranian regime.[56] The new government also posed a challenge to Saudi Islamic legitimacy. Hence, the source of regional threat shifted from Iraq to Iran, causing a change of regional alliance from an Iranian-Saudi axis to an Iraqi-Saudi axis. This was manifested in the Saudi support of Iraqi war efforts and promotion of a policy of reintegrating Egypt into Arab politics. On the international level, their pro-Western policy prudently coincided with a cautious improvement of relations with the USSR.[57]

The Iran-Iraq War furnished the conservative Arab Gulf states with an opportunity for both checking the new Iranian threat and excluding Iraq from any future regional security arrangement. On the one hand, the Arab states of the Gulf supported Iraq's war efforts politically and financially. Their contribution to the Iraqi war effort was estimated at $200 billion. Saudi Arabia alone paid more than $25 billion.[58] Kuwait and Saudi Arabia allocated 300,000 barrels of oil per day for Iraq to compensate for the decline in the latter's oil production due to the destruction of its oil installations. Saudi Arabia permitted Iraqi construction of a pipeline to carry 1.5 million barrels a day of its oil to the Red Sea to avoid the Iranian blockade.[59] The secretary-general of the GCC, Abdullah Bishara, justified the GCC states' support of Iraq on the basis of maintaining the status quo in the region.[60]

On the other hand, once it became clear that Iraq was unable to win a quick war, the GCC states pursued a dual policy toward Iran. While they continued to support the Iraqi war efforts, some of them began to strengthen ties with Iran. As a result, the Iranian ambassador to the UAE assumed office in October 1982, and quiet payments to Iran started to take place.[61] The Saudi fear of Iranian retaliation against the GCC states' oil installations, because of Iraqi bombardment of its oil installations, led them to export refined petrochemical products to Iran to make up for the shortage.[62] The GCC states turned down the Kuwaiti request for a collective measure to deter the Iranian attacks on Kuwaiti vessels and left Kuwait to decide on the feasibility of any alternative that might meet its requirements.[63]

Iraq's preoccupation with the war helped the Saudis bring the Gulf security organization under their aegis. The Iran-Iraq War led to renewed impetus for Saudi Arabia and its neighboring small Gulf states to increase cooperation not only for mutual defense and security, but on a broad spectrum of political and economic issues. The outbreak of this war paved the way for a leading Saudi role among the GCC states within OPEC and AOPEC. Simultaneously, Saudi Arabia took advantage of the Iraqi pursuit of the war to conclude a delineation of borders agreement in 1985. The agreement was sealed during King Fahd's official visit to Baghdad in March 1989, the first for a Saudi monarch since the Iraqi revolution.

Since the fall of the shah, the states of the lower Gulf have expressed a common apprehensiveness of the new Iranian government.[64] Iran's foreign policy is not minimalist and continues to be bellicose.[65] There is a persistent element of ambiguity about Tehran's foreign policy objectives which emanates from the dualism within the revolution.[66] "The triumph of the revolution in Iran confronted the Saudis with a critical threefold problem: it turned Iran from a strategic shield to a major threat; it placed the Kingdom in the middle between two mutually hostile regimes in Baghdad and Tehran; and it presented an immediate danger to vital navigation in the Gulf."[67] Other equally distressing activities and policies include:[68]

1. Iran's continued occupation of the islands of Abu Musa and Greater and Lesser Tunb;
2. Ongoing Iranian programs to develop a conventional military arsenal and to acquire weapons of mass destruction, including nuclear weapons;
3. Iranian sponsorship of extremist groups and covert operations around the world;
4. Iran's active role in attempting to destabilize Arab Gulf governments; and
5. Iran's attempt to dominate the Gulf region as the sole hegemonic power.

Revolutionary Iran showed continuity with its monarchical predecessor in its ambition to be the region's paramount power.[69] Anwar Gargash, an Emirati analyst, argues that despite the great shift from a monarchic to a revolutionary republican system, Iran's goals in the region have neither shifted nor changed; rather, the new Iranian government poses a threat of a different nature to the Arab Gulf states.[70] Until Khatami's election, Iran sought to use Shi'i communities sprinkled throughout the region to achieve its aims.[71] Shi'is in the GCC countries were active during the Iran-Iraq War in supporting Iran, some by collecting donations, while others arranged arms deals for Tehran, acting as a third party or a broker to overcome the arms embargo imposed against Iran.

Despite the GCC states' arms purchases, they view the Iranian military buildup and its policy to acquire nuclear capability with great suspicion.[72] Since the end of the Iran-Iraq War in 1988, Iran has pursued a policy of making up for its losses, which were estimated at 40 to 60 percent of its military arsenal.[73] The Iranian government adopted a 15–year military buildup program with emphasis on air defense. In a step to enhance its manpower, in 1998 the armed forces were increased to 545,600, plus 125,000 for the Revolutionary Guard and reserves estimated at 350,000. Defense expenditures amounted to $5.8 billion.[74] The significance of the Iranian rearmament lies in the fact that it ordered equipment designed to take control of waterways. Under a 1995 defense agreement, Russia agreed to supply Iran with one Kilo-class submarine, 160 T–72 tanks, 600 armed personnel carriers, and a number of munitions including anti-ship mines, cluster bombs, and long-range torpedoes. Russia had previously provided fighter aircraft and surface-to-air missiles.[75] Iran also produces its own armaments.[76]

Such a military buildup will enable the Islamic Republic to:[77]

1. Secure its position as the regional superpower in the Gulf;

Table 6.1 Elements of Power among the Gulf States, 2000

Elements	Bahrain	Kuwait	Oman	Qatar	Saudi Arabia	UAE	GCC	Iran	Iraq
GDP	$6bn	$27.0bn	$14.2bn	$11.2bn	$133bn	$46bn	$225.4bn	$89bn	$19bn
Growth	-2.8%	-14.0%	-7.0%	11.5%	-10.8%	-5.6%	—	1%	12%
Inflation	-0.2%	1%	-5.7%	2.6%	-0.2%	3.1%	—	30%	45%
Debt	$2bn	$9.0bn	$3.9bn	$8.6bn	$22bn	$13bn	$56.8bn	$21.9bn	$23bn
Population	.626m	2.2m	2.2m	0.681m	18m	2.65m	24.3m	72.6m	23.8m
Air force	11,000	15.300	43,500	11,800	105,500	64.5	208,143.5	545,600	429,000

Source: The Military Balance 1999–2000 (London: International Institute for Strategic Studies, 2000, pp. 129–49).

2. Gain leverage over the United States, believing it can follow the North Korean example by trading nuclear capability for economic support; and
3. Use its power to blackmail neighboring Arab Gulf states into increasing oil quotas and participating in foreign investment opportunities in Iran.

Iran, in a bid to establish its dominance over the region, installed Silkworm missile batteries on Abu Musa with which it could control the entrance to the Gulf, a fact acknowledged in November 1996 by the Iranian navy commander, Ali Shamkhani.[78] (However, satellite images of Abu Musa, published in *Jane's Defense Weekly,* refute suggestions that it has been fortified militarily and poses a threat.[79] According to *Jane's,* "the most remarkable aspect about Abu Musa is its lack of major military infrastructure and fortification, despite the fact that it has been under Iranian occupation for 29 years.")[80]

The alliance between Iraq and the GCC countries was short-lived. The unsettled border dispute between Iraq and Kuwait and the increased oil production by both Kuwait and the UAE prompted the Iraqi government to adopt a hostile posture toward these states. Saddam Hussein, in the Revolution Day speech on July 17, 1990, branded Kuwait and the UAE as stooges for America by keeping oil prices low.[81] Iraq exerted pressure on Kuwait by mobilizing an armored division on the latter's border. The Iraqi invasion of Kuwait on August 2 forced the GCC countries to change their foreign policy orientation from an alliance with Iraq to an alliance against Iraq. In addition to the fact that Iran was enjoying good bilateral relations with Oman and excellent trade links with the UAE, the changing regional environment prompted a new GCC perception of Iran. The Iraqi invasion opened a new venue for a GCC-Iran rapprochement. Iran, though it refused to join the American-led coalition against Iraq, was quick to denounce the Iraqi move and called for the restoration of Kuwaiti sovereignty. The Iranian policy toward the Kuwaiti debacle was welcomed by the GCC countries and paved the way for closer cooperation between Iran and the states of the lower Gulf. Such tendency was enhanced by other variables, including Khatami's accession to power, Fahd's ailing health and Crown Prince Abdullah's gradually assuming power in Saudi Arabia, the violent change of leadership in Qatar, and the peaceful transition of power in Bahrain. However, despite all the positive developments in GCC-Iran relations, the islands question continues to hinder the process of regional cooperation.

On the subregional level, Saudi Arabia and the states of the lower Gulf face a triple security problem: Iran, Iraq, and Yemen. Maintaining warm bilateral relations with these states is the appropriate option. In fact, relations between the GCC states and the two main subregional powers, Iran and Iraq, have never been stable. Iran's perspective on Gulf security is based on the idea that it is the responsibility of the littoral states. The Iranian authority believes that there are three states of significant importance for any Gulf security arrangement—Iran, Iraq, and Saudi Arabia. Thus, any arrangement that does not coincide with this perspective would not be acceptable to Iran, which explains Iran's opposition to the Damascus Accord[82] and the U.S. doctrine. The Iranian perception of Gulf security differs from that of many local scholars on both sides of the waterway. Both sides need to search for common ground to secure mutual interests and achieve regional stability. Iran, driven by its national interests, on the one hand would have to support the confidence-building process among the states of the Gulf and the Arabian peninsula on the basis of a new security formula (6 + 3): the GCC countries, Iraq, Iran, and Yemen.[83] On the other hand, such an initiative would ultimately require Iran to yield to the logic of wisdom and accept the fact that the settlement of the islands issue in a way that would honor both sides' rights and territorial integrity would be a milestone on the road toward regional integration.

CONCLUSION

The islands question clearly constitutes the main problem hindering a normalization of relations between Iran and the UAE, and indeed between Iran and the GCC. The reformists in the Iranian ruling elite are keen to promote Iran's national interests but must work within its ideological constraints. Thus Reza Safavi, the Iranian commander of the Revolutionary Guard and a member of the right-wing faction, criticized Khatami's new regional policy toward the GCC states in general and the UAE in particular. He stated that the issue of the islands should not be left to the politicians to deal with. He added that the islands question should be left to the military since its responsibility is to protect national sovereignty and territorial integrity.[84]

The Iranian occupation of the islands has not prevented the development of relations between the two sides on all levels. The UAE recognized the Iranian occupation as a fait accompli it could not prevent; however, it did not cede its claim to sovereignty over the islands.[85] The UAE, as a mini-state aware of the imbalance of power with Iran, and in the absence of a deterrent force, whether regional or international, opted for a low-profile policy on the issue. It pursued a policy of peaceful coexistence with Iran, hoping that the development of good relations would inevitably lead to the settlement of the remaining problems.

The crisis can be brought to an end through negotiations to reach a peaceful settlement that would satisfy both parties. A judicial settlement by the International Court of Justice (ICJ) would not be an alternative unless its verdict is binding. This requires both parties to agree in advance to take the case to that court. Iran, however, probably due to the fact that it lacks the legal and historical evidence that could prove its ownership of the islands, is adamant in rejecting any form of arbitration. It has consistently refused to settle the issue of the two Tunbs by peaceful means.

The issue of delinkage between Abu Musa and Greater and Lesser Tunb as the basis for the settlement of the problem was introduced initially by Tehran. The UAE was adamant in its refusal to accept such a proposal on two grounds: first, the fact that the UAE is a federal state and the federal authority is constrained constitutionally on the issue of territorial integrity of the member emirates; and second, the issue of sovereignty over Abu Musa island was not resolved through the MOU whereas the case of the two Tunbs, which are occupied territory, is totally different. By not accepting the delinkage approach to settle the question, the UAE intends to enhance its negotiating position with the Iranians and regain its sovereignty over the three disputed islands.

The possibility of peaceful settlement of the islands question is strengthened by the winds of change sweeping Iran, culminating in the electoral success of the reformists on both the executive and legislative levels, the American-Iranian indirect dialogue, and interregional developments. The election of Mr. Khatami as president of Iran in 1997 brought new hope for settlement of the islands question. A new Iranian regional policy centered on Khatami's call to settle all the remaining contentious issues. During his early years in office, Khatami succeeded in opening a new chapter in Iran-GCC relations, culminating in his state visits to Saudi Arabia and Qatar in May 1999. Despite the setback Khatami encountered on the domestic front, Iran-GCC relations have entered a new phase of cooperation. The second term of Khatami's presidency could culminate in closer regional security cooperation and economic integration.[86]

Iranian foreign minister Kharrazi's visit to the UAE in May 1998 reflected the new Iranian attitude toward the issue of Abu Musa and led to cautious optimism over settling the islands question.[87] However, Iran refused to receive an arbitration committee formed by the GCC in 1999 which was subsequently dissolved. The visit of Shaikh Hamdan bin Zayed Al-Nahyan, the minister of state for foreign affairs, to Tehran in July 2001, and the reciprocal visit to Abu Dhabi by a special envoy of President Khatami, may be regarded as a positive development in the search for mutual cooperation.[88]

Momentum toward peaceful resolution of the conflict over the islands is likely to increase if the reformists in Iran are able to consolidate their hold on power. On the other hand, the Saudi-Iranian rapprochement has caused a conflict of interest between the UAE and Saudi Arabia. The UAE viewed the new move in a zero sum game perspective that was intended to weaken its position on the islands. On the one hand, the Saudis hold the view that such a development would eventually help in finding an acceptable peaceful formula to settle the islands question. The UAE, on the other hand, believes that the normalization of relations between Saudi Arabia and Iran could end up in new arrangements and possibly secret deals at the expense of the disputed islands. The Emiratis argue that the Iranians could interpret recent developments as meaning that they are no longer required to settle the islands issue as a precondition for such normalization.[89]

A new American approach toward Iran and the possibility of détente in the relations of the two countries increases the probability of reaching a peaceful settlement of the crisis.[90] Iran-U.S. rapprochement may gain momentum under the Bush administration. An American-Iranian opening would inevitably remove one of the main obstacles hindering settlement of the islands question and possible regional integration. The Iranians would no longer see the American-GCC special relationship and the American presence in the Gulf as directed against them. Analysts argue, however, that the United States is not particularly interested in achieving stable GCC-Iran relations and the settlement of the islands question does not occupy the U.S. agenda as one of the conditions for future U.S.-Iran rapprochement.[91]

NOTES

1. It lies at the entrance of the Arabian Gulf, west of the Strait of Hormuz and about 45 miles from Sharjah. Abu Musa has a square shape (4.4 miles in length and 4.4 miles in width) with an area of 18.5 square miles and a population of about 1,500 people, all of them Arabs.

2. These two islands lie in the mouth of the Strait of Hormuz. Greater Tunb lies about 15 miles from Qeshm island and is about 7.5 miles long and 4.4 miles wide, constituting an area of 33 square miles. Its 700 Arab inhabitants belong to the Tamim and Huraiz tribes. Lesser Tunb is 1.3 miles long and 0.6 miles wide and assumes the shape of a triangle. It is about 8 miles west of Greater Tunb and is virtually uninhabited.

3. As part of this development, Iran, in January 2001, exempted GCC citizens visiting Iran from visa requirements.

4. AFP (Tehran), January 2, 2001 (online). The GCC states decided to terminate the committee that was set up in 1999 to mediate between the UAE and Iran in protest against Iran's refusal to cooperate on the issue.

5. *Mukhtara Iraniya,* No. 6 (Cairo: Center for Political & Strategic Studies, Jan. 2000), p. 5.

6. Pirouz Mojtahed-Zadeh, "The Issue of the UAE claims to Tunbs and Abu Musa vis-à-vis Arab-Iranian Relationships in the Persian Gulf," *The Iranian Journal of International Affairs*, Vol. VIII, No. 3 (Fall 1996), pp. 601–26.

7. *Dirasa hawla al-khilaf bayn dawlat al-Imarat al-'Arabiya al-muttahida wa Jumhuriyat Iran al-Islamiya 'ala siyadat al-juzur al-thalath Tunb al-Kurba, Tunb al-sughra wa Abu Musa* [Strategic Study Related to the Sovereignty Dispute between the UAE and the Islamic Republic of Iran over the Three Islands: Greater Tunb, Lesser Tunb and Abu Musa] (Washington: Washington Center for International Studies, 1998), confidential report.

8. Abdul Wahab Abdul, *Al-juzur al-'Arabiya al-thalath fi al-khalij al-'Arabi wa mada al-mashru'iya al-taghyirat al-iqlimiya al-natija 'an istikhdam al-quwwa* [The Three Arab Gulf Islands and the Legitimacy of the Regional Changes Due to the Use of Force] (Ras al-Khaimah: Documentation and Studies Center, series no. 9 (1993) pp. 109–18).

9. Mohammed Morsy Abdulla, *Dawlat al-Imarat al-'Arabiya al-muttahida wa jiranuha* [The UAE and its Neighbors], (Kuwait: Dar Al Qalam, 1981), pp. 323–24.

10. *Dirasa hawla al-khilaf . . .* op. cit.

11. Mohammed al-Rikyn, *Al-bu'd al-ta'rikhi wa al-qanuni li al-khilaf bayn dawlat al-Imarat al-'Arabiya al-muttahida wa Iran hawla al-juzur al-thalath* [The Historical and Legal Dimensions in the UAE-Iran Dispute over the Three Islands], (Al-Ain: UAE University, Research Series no. 3, 1996), p. 7.

12. *Dirasa hawla al-khilaf,* op. cit.

13. Walid al-Adhami, *Al-Niza 'bayn dawlat al-Imarat al-'Arabiya al-muttahida wa Iran hawla juzur Abu Musa wa Tunb al-kubra wa al-sughra fi al-watha'iq al-Baritaniya* [The UAE-Iran Dispute over Abu Musa and the Greater and Lesser Tunbs in the British Documents 1764–1971] (London: Dar al Hikmah, 1993), p. 31.

14. Mohammed al-Mahmoud, "The Merit of Iran's Claim to Abu Musa and Tunbs," San Diego, California: United States International University, 1983, M.A. Thesis, unpublished, p. 49.

15. Al-Adhami, op. cit., p. 78.

16. Mohammed al Roken, op. cit., p. 8.

17. Rosemary Said Zahlan, *The Origins of the United Arab Emirates* (London: Macmillan Press Ltd., 1978), pp. 126–27.

18. London: Foreign Office, (FO 371/74968 40612 E5158).

19. Abdul Wahab Abdul, op. cit., pp. 96–97.

20. Geographical maps in international law are either official or private. Official maps are those attached to international agreements or treaties and carry no value by themselves.

21. Mohammed al Roken, op. cit., p. 18.

22. Abdul Wahab Abdul, op. cit., pp. 42–48.

23. Hassan Hamdan al Alkim, *The Foreign Policy of the United Arab Emirates* (London: Saqi Books, 1989), p. 140.

24. Ibid., p. 142. There are other versions of what happened.

25. Mohammed al-Mahmoud, op. cit., p. 50.

26. Anthony H. Cordesman, *The Gulf and the Search for Strategic Stability* (Boulder: Westview Press, 1984), p. 417.

27. *The Guardian,* September 28, 1971.

28. *The Sunday Telegraph,* September 27, 1992.

29. Al Alkim, *Foreign Policy of the UAE,* op. cit, p.141.

30. Zahlan, *Origins of the United Arab Emirates,* p. 128.

31. Al-Alkim, *Foreign Policy of the UAE,* pp. 141–42.

32. Anthony Cordesman, *The Gulf and the Search for Strategic Stability* (Boulder: Westview Press, 1984), p. 417.

33. *Al-Nahar al-'Arabi wa al-Duwali,* no. 151, March 30, 1980, cited in Al-Alkim, *Foreign Policy,* p. 160.

34. *The Times,* November 18, 1971.
35. *Arab Record and Report* (ARR) 1971, p. 599.
36. *Al-Khalij,* January 22, 23 and 25, 2000.
37. M. S. Agwani, *Politics in the Gulf* (New Delhi: Vikas, 1978), p. 61.
38. Al-Alkim, *Foreign Policy of the UAE,* pp. 137–68.
39. *Arab Report and Memo,* no.10, June 6, 1979, p. 2.
40. Kuwait News Agency (KUNA), April 1, 1979.
41. Al-Alkim, *Foreign Policy of the UAE,* p. 159.
42. *Arab Report and Memo,* no. 10, June 20, 1979, p. 31.
43. Al-Alkim, *Foreign Policy of the UAE,* pp. 159–60.
44. *The Times,* September 2, 1992.
45. *Al-Quds al-Arabi,* September 2, 1992.
46. Hassan H. Al-Alkim, "The United Arab Emirates and Sub-regional Powers," in Joseph A. Kechichian, ed., *A Century in Thirty Years: Shaikh Zayed and the United Arab Emirates* (Washington, D.C.: Middle East Policy Council, 2000), p. 183.
47. *Al-Khalij,* March 11, 2000. See also *Jane's Defense Weekly,* March 8, 2000, pp. 28–29.
48. A memorandum published by the UAE Foreign Ministry, op. cit.
49. Shimlan el-Issa, "The Dispute Between the United Arab Emirates and Iran over Three Islands," in *Arab-Iranian Relations,* ed. Khair el-Din Haseeb (Beirut: Centre for Arab Unity Studies, 1998), 244.
50. *Al-Khalij,* November 12, 1996. This has not happened.
51. A memorandum published by the UAE Foreign Ministry, op. cit.
52. Sultan bin Zayed bin Sultan Al Nahyan, "Gulf Security: The View from Abu Dhabi," in Kechichian, *A Century in Thirty Years,* p. 275.
53. David Long, "Saudi Arabia and its Neighbors: Preoccupied Paternalism," in *Crosscurrents in the Gulf,* Richard Sindelar and J. E. Peterson, eds. (New York: Routledge, 1988), p. 190.
54. Anwar Gargash, "Iran, the GCC States, and the UAE: Prospects and Challenges in the Coming Decade," in Jamal S. al-Suwaidi, ed., *Iran and the Gulf: A Search for Stability* (Abu Dhabi: The Emirates Centre for Strategic Studies and Research, 1996), p. 136.
55. Nadav Safran, *Saudi Arabia: The Ceaseless Quest for Security* (Cambridge: The Belknap Press of Harvard University Press, 1985), p. 265.
56. Tim Niblock, "Iraqi Policies towards the Arab States of the Gulf," in *Iraq: The Contemporary State,* ed. Tim Niblock (London: Croom Helm, 1983), p. 127.
57. Mordechai Abir, *Saudi Arabia in the Oil Era* (London: Croom Helm, 1988), p. 219.
58. *al-Ittihad,* January 17, 1991.
59. Al-Alkim, *The Foreign Policy of the UAE,* 1990, p. 24.
60. Sophia Beernaerts, Economic, Political and Legal Aspects of Cooperation Between the European Economic Community and the Countries Party to the Charter of the Cooperation Council for the Arab States of the Gulf (Dissertation presented to the Institute of European Studies, Universite Libre de Bruxelles, 1989), English version, the UAE Foreign Ministry Archive, p. 18.
61. Anthony Cordesman, op. cit., 1984, p. 419.
62. *MEED,* November 29, 1986, pp. 4–5.
63. Abdul Ridha Assiri, *Kuwait's Foreign Policy: City-State in World Politics* (Boulder: Westview Press, 1990), p. 102.
64. Tim Niblock, "Iraq's Policies towards the Arab States of the Gulf," in *Iraq: The Contemporary State,* ed. Tim Niblock (London: Croom Helm, 1983), p. 127.
65. Shahram Chubin, "Iran and Regional Security," *Survival,* vol. 34, no. 3 (Autumn 1992), p. 68.
66. Ibid., p. 69.
67. Safran, *Saudi Arabia,* p. 234.

68. Jamal S. Al-Suwaidi, "Gulf Security and the Iranian Challenge," *Security Dialogue,* vol. 27/3 (1996), p. 277.
69. Shahram Chubin, op. cit., p. 65.
70. Gargash, "Iran, the GCC States, and the UAE," p. 138.
71. Chubin, p. 66.
72. Al-Alkim in Kechichian, ed., pp. 184–86.
73. Anthony Cordesman, "Iranian Military Capabilities and 'Dual Containment,'" in *The Persian Gulf at the Millennium: Essays in Politics, Economy, Security and Religion,* ed. Gary G. Sick and Lawrence G. Potter (New York: St. Martin's Press, 1997), p. 190.
74. *Jane's,* p. 28.
75. *The New York Times,* October 13, 2000, A30.
76. In 1999 Iran announced the production of different types of missiles, including surface-to-air and surface-to-surface models. For more details, see Medhat Ahmed Hamad, "Iran 1999–2000," in *Al-taqrir al-Istratiji al-khaliji* [The Strategic Gulf Report] (Sharjah: Dar Al-Khalij for Press and Publication, 2000), p. 172.
77. Jamal S. Al-Suwaidi, op. cit., p. 283.
78. *Al-Ittihad,* November 11, 1996.
79. *Al-Khalij,* March 11, 2000.
80. *Jane's,* p. 28.
81. *Washington Post,* January 15, 1991.
82. Al-Arab, December 10, 1992.
83. For more details, see Hassan Al-Alkim, *The GCC States in an Unstable World,* op. cit., pp. 145–48.
84. Information obtained from an informed source at the UAE Foreign Ministry who prefers to remain anonymous.
85. Hassan Hamdan al Alkim, *The GCC States in an Unstable World* (London: Saqi Books, 1994), p. 114.
86. Environment, water, free trade zone, common market, energy, and oil investment are possible sectors for economic integration.
87. *Al-Khalij,* May 26, 1998.
88. *Gulf News,* July 25, 2001 and IRNA (Abu Dhabi), August 6, 2001 (online).
89. Mohammad Al Said Idrys, "Majlis al-ta'awun al-khaliji 1999–2000" [The Gulf Cooperation Council], *Al-taqrir al-Istratiji al-khaliji* (Sharjah: Dar Al-Khalij for Press & Publication, 2000), p. 124.
90. See Madeleine Albright's speech to the American-Iranian Council in *Al-Khalij,* March 21, 2000.
91. Ali Ahmed Al-Gafli, "'Alaqat al-khalijiya al-Amirikiya" [The Gulf-U.S. Relations], in *Al-taqrir al-Istratiji al-khaliji* [The Strategic Gulf Report] (Sharjah: Dar Al-Khalij for Press and Publication, 2000), p. 214.

CHAPTER 7

ANYTHING BUT BLACK AND WHITE
A Commentary on the Lower Gulf Islands Dispute

RICHARD SCHOFIELD

INTRODUCTION

The prime importance of the Lower Gulf islands dispute has often lain in what it symbolizes, rather than in its detail, and never more so than since its resurrection in 1992. Largely as a consequence, the detail is little known, under-appreciated, and frequently misrepresented. It is ironic, therefore, that a close inspection of the specifics of the dispute and the evidence for its evolution ultimately leaves nearly as many questions unanswered as it does answered. In this commentary, a brief characterization of the recent dynamics of the dispute will be followed by a selective examination of some of its key historical and contemporary episodes. These will serve to underline that a distinct lack of clarity has usually distinguished the finer print of the dispute over Abu Musa and the Tunbs, that even those parties claiming the features over the last century and a quarter have paid little attention to its details, and that exaggeration and misrepresentation have—especially in recent times—been a feature of pronouncements on the issue.

A SYMBOLIC AND CYCLICAL DISPUTE

For most of the 1990s, the Lower Gulf islands dispute served, as much as any territorial dispute may, as the focus of Arab-Iranian rivalry across Gulf waters. Facilitated by Iraq's regional and international isolation, the dispute seems to have temporarily displaced the Shatt al-Arab's traditional symbolic role in this respect. The propensity for boundary and territorial disputes to reflect wider tensions between states has been noted for as long as social scientists have been writing about international boundaries. Certainly, Arab-Iranian rivalry has often found expression in territorial disputes, and within a regional territorial framework that is fast moving toward completion the Shatt al-Arab and Lower Gulf islands disputes remain alive, albeit to varying degrees.

A decade after its resurrection, the ultimate willingness of Iran and the United Arab Emirates (UAE) to contemplate settling the Lower Gulf islands dispute on any terms other than their own might now reasonably be questioned. Admittedly, since 1993, the

UAE has consistently recommended reference of the Abu Musa and Tunbs dispute to the International Court of Justice for settlement, a proposal that has consistently received solid backing from the Gulf Cooperation Council (GCC) and several Western states. Initially this standpoint appeared at variance with GCC policy toward its own, in-house territorial disputes, where a clear preference for settlement by bilateral negotiations over third-party intervention was expressed at the summit in Manama, Bahrain, in December 1994. The nervous and uncertain silence with which the GCC has viewed the ICJ's treatment of Bahrain-Qatar disputes has contrasted with its obvious enthusiasm to see the Lower Gulf islands dispute referred for judicial settlement in The Hague.

Why should this have been so? Primarily, there was and remains a genuine belief in the UAE and the GCC that if the Abu Musa dispute was judged on its historical merits, the UAE's territorial claims would have a strong chance of prevailing. At the same time, the UAE must have realized that the prospects of Iran ever allowing reference of the Lower Gulf islands dispute as a whole to the World Court were slim. For Iran's professed willingness during this last decade to talk about the status of Abu Musa has contrasted with its steadfast insistence that Iranian sovereignty over the Tunb islands was non-negotiable.[1] It is, as it always has been, the basic reality of who controls what in this dispute that has dictated the strategies of the dispossessed party and the degree to which the occupying power is prepared to compromise its own stance. The contemporary reality is that Iran has held all the aces in the three decades since Britain left the Gulf as protecting power in 1971, inasmuch as it has occupied the Tunb islands since that time and consented—in the run-up to Britain's withdrawal—to a suggestion from Sharjah that the administration of Abu Musa island should be shared.

Since its formation as a federation in 1971, the UAE has sought to regain the control that Ras al-Khaimah had exercised over the Tunbs (under British guarantees of protection) for the previous century. Moreover, since Iranian heavy-handedness resurrected the Abu Musa dispute with the incidents of 1992, the UAE federal government has seemingly sought to gain more beneficial terms for Sharjah on the island than those defined by the 1971 Memorandum of Understanding.[2] This was an agreement that had been concluded voluntarily, if reluctantly, by Sharjah on the basis that it was the best deal then attainable. The UAE argues that the Iranian actions of 1992 terminally damaged the validity of the 1971 MOU, even if Iran has repeatedly stated in the period since that it remains bound by the instrument's provisions. Whatever the merits of that argument, the contemporary geopolitical context of the dispute is of a politically youthful state attempting—albeit peacefully—to wrest back control of the features from its considerably more powerful northern neighbor. The federal government in Abu Dhabi must also be seen to be treating its component emirates equally, and therefore any resolution of the Lower Gulf islands dispute must deal with both Abu Musa and the Tunbs on the same footing at the same time.

It is this context that makes a reference of the dispute to the ICJ for judicial settlement unlikely, at best, for the foreseeable future. Not only does it take two to tango before a dispute can be settled at the World Court (i.e., the consent of both parties is needed for discussion to proceed), but fairly obviously, in so doing, each party must be in agreement about the scope of the dispute itself. For the UAE, it involves all three of the Lower Gulf islands. Seemingly for Iran, if any legitimate dispute exists at all, it concerns the island of Abu Musa only.

Though a wholly reasonable move in itself, the UAE's call for a reference of the Lower Gulf islands dispute for judicial settlement at The Hague should be seen as part of a deliberate strategy to internationalize it. The most obvious tactic for achieving such internationalization in the early 1990s was to allow the islands dispute to be symbolized in terms of regional rather than national rivalries. So, as already mentioned, the islands question inherited the Shatt al-Arab's traditional mantle as the principal territorial dispute in the region upon which Arab-Iranian rivalries could be focused. Indeed, pronouncements from both sides of the Gulf—but especially its western littoral—would soon directly employ much of the symbolic rhetoric previously directed at the Shatt. Certainly, the furor in the Arab media during 1992 was wholly disproportionate to anything that might have happened on the island itself.

Largely by "Arabizing" the issue, the UAE government would succeed in internationalizing the Lower Gulf islands dispute. It had been the GCC summit in Abu Dhabi in December 1992 that would set the ball rolling in terms of both internationalizing the dispute and adopting it as a regional symbol. Here the GCC's Supreme Council would affirm "its complete solidarity and absolute support for the UAE's position and all the peaceful measures and means it deems appropriate to regain its sovereignty over the three islands in accordance with international legitimacy and the principle of collective security." The mention of "three islands" strongly suggested, of course, that the UAE wanted more than the modification of the 1971 MOU that was offered. Tehran's defiant riposte, to be repeated on many occasions in response to successive restatements of the above position, was colorful and dismissive but also underlined its comparative advantage in the dispute at the interstate level: "Iran is surely stronger than the likes of you . . . to reach these islands one has to cross a sea of blood . . . we consider this claim as totally invalid."[3]

The war of words soon became stalemated but continued throughout the decade. It had been set in motion despite the fact that life at the local level on Abu Musa had soon returned to something approaching normal. Not long after the incidents of April and August 1992, the ferry was running to the island as normal from Sharjah, while the oil-sharing arrangements for output from the nearby offshore Mubarak field had never even been interrupted in the first place.

The UAE's successful internationalization of the dispute gathered pace after Sultan Fahim bin Sultan al-Qasimi's accession to the post of secretary-general of the GCC in 1993. The proposal was now made that the island disputes be submitted to the ICJ. Then, during the early summer of 1994, King Fahd of Saudi Arabia appeared to take a personal interest in promoting proposals for peaceably returning the islands to Emirati sovereignty. Iran took notice, repeating its warning of December 1992. The United States now took the surprising—albeit involuntary—step of departing from its traditional position of neutrality in the territorial disputes of the region. On March 12, 1995, in Jeddah, former secretary of state Warren Christopher added his name to a joint communiqué issued by the foreign ministers of states signatory to the March 1991 Damascus Declaration. This read as follows: "[T]he ministers expressed their deep appreciation of the UAE's efforts to peacefully resolve the issue of the Iranian occupation of the three islands—the Greater Tunb, the Lesser Tunb and Abu Musa, which belong to the UAE."[4] This would soon prove much less significant than it might have been. It transpired that a weary Christopher had somewhat carelessly added his name to a number of documents after a short, exhausting tour of the region. Once the mistake had been recognized, the U.S. government withdrew its support for the above statement.

The episode, however, illustrates the extent to which the UAE had successfully internationalized the islands dispute by the mid–1990s. Yet, doing so and materially improving the

UAE's prospects of regaining territorial control were clearly not one and the same. Though the dispute had soon assumed the characteristics of a stalemated war of words, there were real concerns by spring 1995 that the waters of the Lower Gulf were becoming too militarized, the consequence of the large number of exercises being undertaken by the navies of Iran and the United States. Many of these exercises were taking place close to Abu Musa itself. Both formally and informally, currents of opinion within the UAE began to question the likely endgame of Abu Dhabi's strategy of internationalizing the dispute as an Arab-Iranian issue. For example, Crown Prince Muhammad of Dubai would comment during February 1995 that recent tensions over the islands had been "fabricated."[5] Perhaps there was a general fear that a naval incident might occur between Iran and the United States in the vicinity of the islands over which the federal government could exercise no control. There were other complications, too. Sharjah's interest in the continuance of the 1971 MOU that regulated Abu Musa's status did not necessarily square with the obligation felt by the federal UAE government to deal with all three of the Lower Gulf islands on a more or less identical basis. Hence, Sharjah's barely disguised disappointment at the manner in which the ill-fated bilateral Iran-UAE negotiations were conducted in the autumn of 1992. It is therefore a reality that there are three parties to the dispute over Abu Musa: Iran, the emirate of Sharjah, and the federal government in Abu Dhabi.

It was the response of Iran to the UAE's successful internationalization of the Lower Gulf islands question that is of most relevance to this discussion and the prospects for the dispute's ultimate resolution. For the UAE's very success would engender a defensive posture in Iran and the adoption of the islands question as a national issue, one that was inextricably linked to regime legitimacy. At the risk of generalizing, it might be commented that the 1980–88 Iran-Iraq War was the first conflict of modern times in which the Iranian state did not lose territory. To the minds of many Iranians, Abu Musa and the Tunbs were wrongfully taken by Britain in the nineteenth century and rightfully returned to Iran on Britain's departure from Gulf waters in 1971. The extension of such logic dictates that a regionally isolated and defensive Iran cannot entertain requests from a small state like the UAE that Iranian territory be handed over. The defensive posture engendered in Iran by the mid–1990s was reflected in its announcement in 1996 that plans were afoot to build a university on its half of Abu Musa. Should such an action ever be undertaken, it would be typical of the type of symbolic measures that states often resort to when trying to underline their control of a disputed feature.[6]

The Lower Gulf islands constitute one of a small but significant group of boundary and territorial questions that have seemingly escaped all of the progress made toward finalizing the regional territorial framework in the last decade. What has been the nature of this progress? Within an Arabian context, not only has the glass of settled land boundary delimitations moved from half to nine-tenths full but the states of the region have processed their recent boundary settlements in the manner expected by the international legal community. Boundary treaty texts, old and new, have generally been lodged at the Secretariat of the United Nations in New York. This has been a recent phenomenon, beginning essentially with the conclusion of the Gulf War in 1991. It has convinced many commentators that the territorial arrangements introduced by Arabian boundary agreements are designed to be permanent. This will have reassured Saudi Arabia's historically mindful neighbors, who will recall that Iraq was not the only territorially acquisitive state in the region during the twentieth century. Lastly, the GCC, largely by accident and always reactively, has evolved a set of basic principles that aim for the entrenchment of the current territorial framework. Increasingly, it would seem to be left to regional organizations to regulate territorial issues, especially in those areas of the world where there is no continental commitment to existing boundaries.[7] Saudi Arabia, too, can take some satisfaction from all of this material progress achieved over the last decade or so. For it can now claim to have to have replaced all of the old territorial settlements and understandings reached with the British during the 1920s and 1930s with modern bilateral boundary treaties agreed with neighboring independent states.

Moreover, progress toward finalizing the political map on land and sea in the region continued to gather pace in 2001. In June 2000, Saudi Arabia and Yemen finally (yet rather suddenly) agreed upon the course of what until then had been Arabia's last indeterminate land boundary.[8] Then, in July, the same, decisive momentum that Crown Prince Abdullah of Saudi Arabia had brought to bear in boundary negotiations with Yemen seemingly also broke the long stalemate in the kingdom's negotiations with Kuwait over a lateral maritime boundary delimitation in the Persian Gulf. The two sides signed such an agreement on July 2, 2000. The final resolution of Kuwaiti-Saudi maritime disputes also opened the door to the onset during September 2000 of formal negotiations between Iran and Kuwait over an opposite maritime boundary delimitation in northern Gulf waters.

Last but not least, the ICJ delivered its verdict on the Bahrain-Qatar island and maritime disputes on March 16, 2001. Here, Bahrain emerged largely as the winner since the sovereignty of the Hawar island group—unquestionably the chief bone of contention in the case—was confirmed as lying with the island state. Effectively, the ICJ has therefore recognized the status quo as far as ownership of the Hawar group is concerned in ratifying Britain's earlier ruling of July 1939.[9] Qatari sovereignty over the locality of Zubarah on its northwestern shoreline was confirmed, though this part of the ruling was every bit as predictable as the court's treatment of the Hawar group. Although including Zubarah in the range of questions to be decided had originally appeared a boon for Bahrain, it is probably more realistic to surmise that by doing so, the ICJ was ensuring that Qatar would at least go home with something when judgment was made. So much for reaffirmation of the status quo in the ICJ judgment. What about the court's treatment of the disputed shoals and its announcement of a maritime boundary delimitation between the two states? In dealing with these issues, the court arguably had a little more flexibility. Until the judgment, both the Dibal and Jaradeh shoals had been occupied by Bahrain and had previously been recognized as belonging to the island state (albeit within a seabed area provisionally characterized as Qatari) after a British ruling of 1947. The court has now ruled that the Dibal shoal belongs to Qatar but that Jaradeh belongs to Bahrain as an island.[10] Such a distinction is important, for Jaradeh's newly recognized island status has projected the maritime boundary between the states further eastward than would otherwise have been the case. Bahrain probably has more reason to be satisfied with ICJ's maritime delimitation than Qatar has.

In recent years the dynamics of this dispute had altered completely. Back in 1995, Bahrain was openly challenging the ICJ's decision that it possessed jurisdiction to try the dispute, and one of its ministers was reported as commenting that the disputed features would be handed to Qatar "over our dead bodies." Undoubtedly, much of Bahrain's discomfort stemmed from the fact that in any future ICJ decision, it had everything to lose and Qatar everything to gain, since the features in question had been occupied by Bahrain and had previously been recognized by Britain to belong to the island state. Yet, in the last two or three years of the case, Bahrain had showed a much greater appetite for the fray. It can only have been encouraged by Qatar's request that the ICJ disregard as evidence 82 suspect maps and documents included as annexes to the Doha government's memorial and countermemorial. Their authenticity had previously been challenged by Bahrain and, when asked to account for their provenance by an ICJ court order, Qatar basically had had to back down on the whole issue. In so doing, Qatar had withdrawn much of its historic (and apparently new) evidence for ownership of the Hawar group. In the end, as already mentioned, the court would agree with Britain's earlier treatment of 1939.

So much for the progress we have just discussed. What of the lack of it? It must be said that the remaining territorial issues involve non-GCC member states. While one could presume that the Shatt al-Arab boundary (as well as the remainder of the Iran-Iraq land boundary further north) continues to be regulated by the package of agreements signed in 1975, this is contentious and many observers would reckon that the dispute is dormant rather than finally settled. Similarly, while the Iraq-Kuwait boundary is settled in international law as a result of the United Nations Iraq-Kuwait Boundary Demarcation Commission's deliberations between 1991 and 1993 and Iraq's unequivocal acceptance of its award in November 1994, it would be reckless to predict that the last has been heard of Iraqi claims on Kuwaiti territory, given the vexed history of this territorial limit. For, as the fate of the 1975 Iran-Iraq agreements demonstrated, a boundary resolved in international law is not necessarily a regional problem removed. To this list of "usual suspects" may be added the Lower Gulf islands dispute. For these disputes (including the Iraq-Kuwait boundary before 1990) are the ones that have ultimately proved resistant to all manner of proposals for their settlement over the last century or so. If one looks at the detailed record of their evolution, it will be seen that each of these disputes possesses a distinct cyclical nature, typically moving from long periods of dormancy to shorter, intense periods of activity. Exactly what awakens a territorial dispute from a state of dormancy is difficult to establish with any precision, but as far as these "usual suspects" are concerned, it relates clearly to the coincidence and interplay of a number of factors, with perception of regional power dynamics within the Gulf region probably more instrumental than anything else.[11]

One point that can be made quite validly about the Lower Gulf islands is that changes—intrinsic or merely perceived—in the power dynamics of the region have marked decisive stages in the history of the dispute. And to a large extent, might has proven right. Back in 1887, the Persian Qajar government asserted its authority much more directly along the coastal tract to the west of the Strait of Hormuz, resulting in the banishment of the Qawasim from their northern outposts of Lingeh and Sirri island and a retreat back to their principal power bases of Ras al-Khaimah and Sharjah along the southern Gulf littoral. Only a decade and a half later, in 1903, the British India government would advise the Qawasim to place flags on Abu Musa and the Tunbs. These were removed by Belgian-run Persian customs officers, who hoisted the Persian flag. Britain then used the threat of force to get Persia to back down with the result that in 1904 the Qasimi flag was rehoisted on Abu Musa and Greater Tunb.

Iran would move on the islands in November 1971, when Britain departed the Gulf as protecting power. Prior accommodation had been reached with Sharjah (reluctantly if voluntarily on the part of its ruler) for the shared administration of Abu Musa, though the Tunb islands were taken forcibly from Ras al-Khaimah. As already established, the period since 1992 has witnessed the revival and internationalization of the Abu Musa/Tunbs dispute. Iran's clumsy reactivation was almost certainly attributable to its frustration at being excluded from post–Gulf War plans for regional security.

Meanwhile, the conduct of the resurrected Lower Gulf islands dispute continued throughout the 1990s to be dictated by perceived windows of opportunity. For almost a decade, as has already been established, the dispute has symbolized Arab-Iranian rivalries across Gulf waters. In the medium term, presuming Iraq's eventual reintegration within the Arab fold, it seems likely—if history is anything to go by—that the Shatt al-Arab will resume its traditional symbolic role as a barometer of Arab-Iranian relations and the recent concentration on the Lower Gulf islands will subside. However, the nature of the islands dispute is already changing as a consequence of yet another tangible (if admittedly tentative) shift in the power dynamics of the region—the emerging Iranian-Saudi entente of the last two or three years. It is within this bigger regional picture that the UAE has charged the Riyadh government with failing to fully support its claim to the islands. Notwithstanding the creation during 1999 of a special GCC subcommittee (which includes Qatar, Oman, and Saudi Arabia) charged with the task of promoting a peaceful settlement of the dispute, there has been a feeling among some Emirati officials that the window of opportunity has narrowed and a private recognition that after eight years in the spotlight, the islands question is not the regional issue it once was.

So having internationalized the islands question as an Arab-Iranian issue, perhaps the only route left to the UAE federal government is to change strategy and reclaim the dispute as a national question. At least this could force a greater concentration on the specifics and details of the dispute. For the lesser the symbolic value of the dispute, the easier it may be to tackle directly. There is sometimes a value or convenience in keeping island or territorial disputes alive—or at least short of final settlement—to symbolize competing national or regional rivalries. One only has to look at the way in which the status of the Senkaku/Diaoyutai and Tok-Do disputes symbolizes national rivalries between Japan and China and Taiwan and Korea respectively to see that this is not a phenomenon restricted to the Persian Gulf region. Also, while island disputes have a proven utility in symbolizing rivalries, there is also arguably an element of safety in treating them as such. For surely the potential for a dispute over contiguous land territory (i.e., over an international land boundary) developing into actual conflict is much greater than is the case with a disputed island. This holds, of course, only if one accepts that there is no chance that the UAE will try and recover its control of the islands by resort to force.

Perhaps the more that Iran and the UAE address the specifics of the Abu Musa dispute in the future, the more they will appreciate that the imaginative if flawed accommodation of 1971 was by no means as bad a solution of a disputed island as it is sometimes portrayed. For effectively managing this dispute may be a more realistic and durable option than trying to reach final agreement on sovereignty.

THE SPECIFICS

The British Attitude: Irritation and Impatience

While historically the potential of Iraq's boundary disputes at the head of the Gulf to threaten regional stability had long been recognized by the British government, other territorial disputes in the region were often regarded as tedious irritations. Occasionally the Lower Gulf islands would fall into this category.

Having been involved in efforts at various levels to resolve the Lower Gulf islands dispute while serving as a diplomat along the western and southern Gulf littoral, Sir Glen

Balfour-Paul later commented that the dispute had, by the turn of the 1970s, assumed a scale in Anglo-Iranian relations "grossly disproportionate" to the size and importance of the islands.[12]

Likewise, former British Resident William Luce, having been brought back at around the same time specifically to broker a settlement of outstanding issues with Iran in the face of Britain's impending departure from the Gulf, was heard to mutter in a moment of obvious exasperation, "[T]he Persians took Sirri while we weren't looking in 1887. I sometimes wish they had taken the Tunbs and Abu Musa as well."[13]

Also worth mentioning here is a candid, recently declassified FCO memorandum penned by FCO official Donal McCarthy. This reviewed the status of the various unresolved boundary questions that Britain would likely bequeath to the region on its departure in December 1971. Again, irritation was the predominant characteristic of the following, more general comment:

> [T]he mentality of these rulers is such that they are prepared to dispute a barren sand dune till judgment day, while tribal views on e.g., access to wells are pressed with an urgency which does not comprehend Western ideas on rigid frontiers.

In a sense, of course, this last quote was a bit rich. Having introduced a Western-style consciousness of territoriality to Arabia (or at least its rulers), it really ought not to have been a cause for complaint when the ownership of specific localities became the subject of fierce contention, albeit usually for reasons best explained by personal or dynastic rather than national rivalries.[14]

A Distinct Lack of Clarity

1. The allegiances of the coastal communities.   Political and territorial control of the Lower Gulf region before Britain's arrival on the scene—and for a good while thereafter—was marked by its fluidity and impermanence. As such, evidence for ownership of the islands located there before the mid-nineteenth century barely exists. Historically, there was a considerable degree of contact and interchange among the coastal communities of the Gulf, and Arab populations on both sides traditionally moved back and forth across this body of water. Since the economies of the coastal tribes were geared to exploitation of the resources of the Gulf waters themselves, it follows that the inhabitants of the Lower Gulf littoral enjoyed appreciably more contact with their counterparts on the opposite shore than they did respectively with central authority in Persia or the resource-poor Arabian interior.

2. The official record of the origins of dispute.   Iranians are often frustrated by the tendency of non-Iranian historical accounts of the dispute to begin with the nineteenth-century record maintained in the files of Britain's Persian Gulf Residency, based until Indian independence in the Iranian port of Bushehr. These files, recently rehoused at the British Library's Oriental and India Office Collection (OIOC) at St. Pancras in London, are patchy and disorganized but seemingly represent the only primary record of the origins of the dispute that has been publicly unearthed to date. The problem Iran has faced when arguing that the Qawasim, protected by Britain, had displaced its own administration of the Lower Gulf islands during the nineteenth century is that it has not yet come forward with any records of its own that display or document any earlier connection with Abu Musa or the Tunbs. Indeed, contemporary Iranian accounts of the dispute tend instead to make rather selective use of those minority sections of the British archives that support the Persian claim to the islands.[15] Certainly where Abu Musa is concerned, the OIOC record makes depressing reading for the substantiation of Iranian claims.

3. "Clear geography, unclear politics." The geography of the nineteenth century dispute over the Lower Gulf islands is much clearer than its politics. All of the everyday contacts with the island of Abu Musa appeared to be from the southern Gulf littoral. The weight of documentation in the British archives suggests that Abu Musa was administered directly from Sharjah during the nineteenth century. From 1863 onward, pearlers and fishermen visiting the island paid dues annually to the ruler of Sharjah, whose claims to the feature Britain actively defended from 1870. The issue during 1888 of the first informal Persian claim to the island of Abu Musa (which was in truth more of an indirect mention but acknowledged internally by government departments in British India) had only been induced by the British Admiralty's carelessness. The first edition of its *Persian Gulf Pilot* (1864) erroneously stated that the Qawasim at Lingeh maintained contact with Abu Musa, in addition to Sirri and Greater Tunb. This was patently not the case, as evidenced by the issue of a request by the Persian authorities at Lingeh during the late 1880s that the ruler of Sharjah return a fugitive who had taken refuge on the island.

The political situation with respect to the Tunbs was considerably less clear though virtually all of the contacts maintained with the islands were from the northern coast. Up until 1873, the Bushehr Residency had held that the Tunbs probably belonged to Persia, because of the close connection of these islands with the port of Lingeh. By the mid–1880s, however, Britain was increasingly of the opinion that the Qawasim ultimately held rights over the Tunbs. Though the Qawasim would effectively control Lingeh until 1887, their main bases of power were located along the southern Gulf littoral. Britain's opinion as to ownership of the Tunbs changed after it received original documentation suggesting that the Qawasim in Lingeh were subordinate politically to their counterparts in Ras al-Khaimah. Following the expulsion of the Qawasim from southern Persia in 1887, Britain developed the following, rather bizarre explanation of the way in which the northern wing of the Qasimi federation had administered Sirri and, by extension, Greater Tunb before this point. They had governed Lingeh in their capacity as Persian officials but had maintained contact with Sirri and Greater Tunb only as members of the Qawasim federation and as subordinates to their southern counterparts in Ras al-Khaimah. This was all a little contrived, to say the least.

4. The lowering of the Qasimi flag on Greater Tunb in 1934. The British authorities in the Gulf were hugely embarrassed when the ruler of Ras al-Khaimah withdrew the Qasimi flag from Greater Tunb in December 1934. There are two rival explanations of why such an action was taken that illustrate neatly the frequently inconclusive nature of archival sources as evidence for territorial claims. One stated that the flag had been lowered as the result of an exchange of correspondence entered into directly between the ruler of Ras al-Khaimah and the Persian government. Before Britain eventually persuaded the Ras al-Khaimah shaikh to rehoist his flag on the island in the late spring of 1935, its diplomats in Tehran had more or less resigned themselves to aiming for a compromise whereby Persian claims to the Tunbs would have been admitted in return for Tehran's recognition of Sharqawi claims to Abu Musa. The other explanation for Ras al-Khaimah's action went as follows: the shaikh had taken this action to draw attention to the fact that no rent was received from Britain for its use of the lighthouse on Greater

Tunb. It will come as no surprise that funds were made available once the Qasimi flag was back in place.

5. Linkage, packages, and the Lower Gulf islands. As is clear from a reading of subsection 3 above, the nineteenth-century histories of Abu Musa and the Tunbs were not one and the same. Yet there has always been a tendency to link the status of the Lower Gulf islands. This may be because for most of the twentieth century, the power that held one island also controlled the others. It also had much to do with further Government of India sloppiness. An evidently influential memorandum of 1928 held that what affected one island during the nineteenth century generally affected the other.[16] Successive, derivative British memoranda perpetuated this misplaced notion of historical linkage.

All manner of schemes for territorial tradeoffs would be discussed, formally and informally, between the British and Persian governments at the time of the General Treaty negotiations during the 1920s and 1930s. On several occasions the Persian government offered formally to drop its claim to Bahrain if Britain would recognize its claims to the Lower Gulf islands. On other occasions, Britain toyed with the idea of trying to persuade the Qasimi rulers to lease the features to Persia. The Persian minister of court, Abd al-Hussein Taimurtash, informally suggested in 1930 that the Tehran government might relinquish its claim to Abu Musa in return for Ras al-Khaimah dropping its claims to and administration of the Tunbs.[17] Britain tried to refloat these ideas for territorial tradeoffs during the mid–1950s but, again, to no avail.

The speculation surrounding linkage and possible island tradeoffs naturally resurfaced once Britain, in January 1968, had declared its intention to vacate the Gulf as protecting power. It is often suggested that Britain's eventual tolerance of Iran's moves on the islands in 1971 was the price paid for the Tehran government's relinquishment of its historic claim to the sovereignty of Bahrain. A close inspection of the British and American archives confirms that there was no such explicit deal before the shah of Iran announced in January 1969 that the inhabitants of Bahrain were free to determine their own political destiny. Yet a suggestion for an arrangement along these lines was broached directly to the shah in the spring of 1968 by the United States government or, to be more precise, its ambassador in Tehran, Armin Meyer. Since Meyer's overriding concern was the facilitation of an Iranian-Saudi agreement on a continental shelf boundary in central Gulf waters,[18] the following scheme was proposed: in return for the relinquishment of the Iranian historical claim to Bahrain, arrangements would be made through British auspices for the cession of Abu Musa and the Tunbs to Iran, while a joint economic zone for the exploitation of hydrocarbon reserves might be set up in the central Gulf between Saudi Arabia and Iran.[19] Once the October 1968 Iranian-Saudi maritime boundary agreement had been concluded and seabed areas either side of it opened up for hydrocarbons development, American suggestions for territorial tradeoffs disappeared.

Britain had talked in terms of "packages" rather than linkage as such. There would be frequent suggestions for broader "packages" in the Foreign Office record for 1968, packages that would see the roughly simultaneous settlement of outstanding Anglo-Persian questions and disputes before Britain would leave the Gulf as protecting power at the end of 1971. One of these suggestions was broached directly by Denis Wright, the British Ambassador in Tehran, to the Iranian government in August 1968. There was, however, no explicit deal within the arrangement whereby in return for abandoning the claim to Bahrain, Iranian claims to Abu Musa and the Tunbs would be admitted. By the end of 1968, the British government seems to have concluded that since the individual components of any possible package were being addressed by bilateral negotiations anyway, no overall package could be guaranteed in any case. Furthermore, it appeared that one was no longer needed. For the British Gulf authorities were by now genuinely of the opinion that the shah was keen to dispose of the Bahrain claim on its own merits, without the need for any compensating inducements. As a Foreign and Commonwealth Office [FCO] minute of the late autumn of 1968 would testify:

5. I told the Shah that HMG fully understood his anxieties and the importance of satisfying public . . . opinion: we felt however (and I know that he did not accept this point of view, which I had already voiced) that it would be possible for the Shah to abandon his claim in the context of an over-all settlement of the median line and the disputed islands, of our withdrawal from the Gulf in 1971, and an overall agreement with King Faisal over the future of the Gulf. The Shah made it clear that the inclusion of Bahrain in a package solution was not acceptable. If he were to abandon the claim in this way, it would be a one-man decision by himself which could be reversed by his successors. If the Bahrain issue was to be settled permanently it must bear the stamp of legality and recognised procedures for settling territorial disputes and not be the decision of one man. In going so far as he was prepared to go he was taking considerable risks and doubted whether any other person (in the future I think he meant) would be in a strong enough position to do so.[20]

Let us now look at these developments in a little more detail. The general package settlement of outstanding Gulf problems suggested by Denis Wright to the shah of Iran in May and August 1968 consisted of the following:

. . . he [His Majesty] might drop his claim [to Bahrain] in the context of an over-all settlement of median line and disputed islands, the creation of the UAE, the British withdrawal from the Gulf and an agreement between Iran and Saudi Arabia.[21]

Later, during February 1969, the same Donal McCarthy mentioned previously would pen a minute in which the following comment was made:

[W]hen we discussed a possible "package" settlement in the Gulf with the Shah last May we made it clear that since three different rulers were involved (Bahrain, Sharjah *qua* Abu Musa, and Ras al-Khaimah *qua* the Tunbs) a simple trading of an Arab solution over Bahrain for the Iranian acquisition of the other islands was not one we could negotiate. We also proceeded [sic] on the assumption that the vital question was Bahrain; and while we could not give away the other islands we let the Shah understand that the Tunbs, being on the Iranian side of any median line, might well go to him in the end. Since then the Shah, while making it clear that he maintained his claim to both Abu Musa and the Tunbs, has not pressed it hard with us.[22]

How, precisely, did this overall package envisaged by Britain affect the islands of Abu Musa and the Tunbs? In a sense it did not, at least not directly. There was the clear reality, though, that a median line maritime boundary agreed for the Lower Gulf between Iran and the future UAE would leave the Tunbs to its north and Abu Musa to the south. Iran may have been led to believe, as is partially supported by the above quote, that Britain expected the Tunbs to go to it in the future, even if Britain would continue to insist that their ultimate fate could be decided only through direct negotiations with the ruler of Ras al-Khaimah. Such negotiations would take place in the latter months of

1968. By way of contrast, in its communications with the rulers of the southern Gulf littoral, Britain could argue—technically correctly, of course—that agreeing to a Lower Gulf median line in no way predetermined the sovereignty of Abu Musa and the Tunbs:

> Pol. Agent Dubai can give confirmation he proposes, but point out that median line even if settled does not in itself affect sovereignty of islands.

> . . . that in our view he [Shaikh Saqr of Ras al-Khaimah] is in his rights in standing by his sovereignty over the Tunbs and that if Iranians want use of islands they must use the carrot and not the stick.[23]

After meetings in late October 1968, Britain would apparently be left in no doubt about the attitude of the Iranian government toward Wright's "package":

> 2. Mr. Afshar told me that the Shah only that morning had impressed on him that he was to let me know that there could be no bargaining over the Iranian position on the various islands, which was well known to us. I said that I was sorry to hear this as it seemed to me that the only way of reaching a settlement was through a package deal such as I had outlined to the Shah in early August. I could see no settlement or possibility of compromise if the Iranians insisted on Abu Musa as well as Sirri and the Tunbs. Mr. Afshar took this but made no attempt to argue the Iranian case on the islands.[24]

All this is on the record, yet it is probably fair to say that Iran, once it had begun to rescind its claim to Bahrain (beginning with the Shah's New Delhi statement of January 4, 1969), hoped that Britain might play ball by allowing the Tehran government to make good its claims to the Lower Gulf islands. Afshar certainly indicated that this was the view of the Shah: "In turn, having demonstrated his goodwill over Bahrain, the Shah believed the British government was obliged to recognize his claims to Abu Musa and the islands of Tunbs."[25]

This, as we have seen, had never really been in the cards and there would certainly be no express linkage or tradeoff. The same Mr. Afshar would comment as much long into his retirement in London during January 1991: "[T]here was no tradeoff deal with the British during our negotiations on the separate issues of Bahrain and the three islands of the Strait of Hormuz."[26]

6. The November 23, 1971 Iran-Sharjah Memorandum of Understanding [MOU] regarding Abu Musa. This essentially pragmatic MOU was most notable, of course, for the manner in which it accommodated the full sovereign claims of both Iran and Sharjah to the island. The question of sovereignty was completely fudged in the agreement, which provided instead solely for the island's divided administration. The preamble to the agreement read bizarrely as follows: "Neither Iran nor Sharjah will give up its claims to Abu Musa nor recognize the other state's claims." A distinct and deliberate lack of clarity, yet again!

Carelessness and a Lack of Concern for the Details
1. The British War Office map of 1886. Iran has always lain great stress on a British War Office map series in which all of the Lower Gulf islands were shown clearly in Persian colors. The series was presented to the shah of Iran by Sir Henry Drummond Wolff, British minister in Tehran, on the instructions of Foreign Secretary Lord Salisbury dur-

ing the summer of 1888. Britain's overriding concern in presenting the maps had been Persia's eastern frontier with British India, and all other details were evidently considered of marginal importance as far as the Foreign Office was concerned. Yet Britain had flagged the map series as authoritative. Wolff had been instructed to "present this map to His Majesty's Government with an expression of their hope that it might be useful and interesting to His Majesty as His Majesty has on several occasions asked to be supplied with geographic information."[27]

This was, of course, highly embarrassing for the British authorities, who were attempting to buttress Qasimi claims in the Lower Gulf following their banishment from Lingeh and Sirri a year earlier. It was no wonder that the map series question had caused the shah "so much satisfaction."[28] Yet the cartographic sloppiness would continue, underlining that in the wider realm of things, the ownership of this or that little island in Lower Gulf waters at this juncture of history was simply not a major British foreign policy concern. Incredibly, maps continuing to show the disputed islands in Persian colors would appear on the inside cover of Lord Curzon's classic two volume 1892 work, *Persia and the Persian Question*. For no one would be more determined in the next decade and a half to maintain the Persian Gulf as a British lake and to deny the unwelcome claims of any power— regional or European—that might conceivably threaten this state of affairs.

2. The events of 1992. Many observers were initially confused by what exactly had occasioned the resurrection of the dispute over Abu Musa during the spring and late summer of 1992. An often hysterical Arab media has variously accused Iran of having invaded the island of Abu Musa or else of having taken over the southern, Sharjah-controlled part of the island. Both claims were clearly erroneous. Yet Iran's actions in 1992 and thereafter have obviously altered the status quo on the island. Whether they have contravened the express clauses of the 1971 MOU must be open to considerably more doubt. Only by demonstrating that the territorial reality introduced by the MOU has been deliberately altered to its own permanent advantage by Iran could one claim that more than the spirit of the agreement has been broken. Despite frequent claims to the contrary, there is very little evidence—other than the extension of a landing strip in recent years[29]—that Iran has brought large areas of the southern, Sharjah-administered part of Abu Musa under its aegis.

Distortions and Exaggerations

1. Articles of faith and Iranian nationalism. As alluded to earlier, Iranians are often frustrated by the tendency for non-Iranian accounts of the origins of the islands dispute or of modern histories of the Persian Gulf more generally to be based so squarely on the British archival record. In Iran's view, this inevitably presents a distorted picture in which its own earlier-established supremacy over the waters and islands of the Gulf is ignored. Whether or not history affords Iran the right to claim such a hegemonic position has to be balanced against the fact that most influential Persians, from the nineteenth century onward, believe that it has: "Despite all the vicissitudes of its stormy existence in the past, contemporary Iran seems to perceive its role in the Persian Gulf as almost uninterrupted and as always active. Facts would not seem to support this perception, but the important point is that this belief influences Iran's behavior today."[30] Such a point was reinforced rather eloquently in a recent work by Fuller (1991). Where Iran's role in the Persian Gulf is concerned, "The national memory is far more important than any reality or legal brief could be."[31]

Until the last quarter of the nineteenth century, when reasonably specific and detailed territorial claims would be entered to Bahrain and the Tunbs on an individual basis, Persian claims to the islands of the Persian Gulf would be framed in a generalized, collective fashion. In February 1845, for instance, the Persian prime minister, Haji Mirza Aghassi, would claim all the waters and islands of the Gulf as Persian, seemingly on the basis that ownership followed from the name of the body of water.[32] Britain would get frustrated by the obvious vagueness of such a claim, with Lord Elphinstone of British India commenting as follows in the early 1820s: "[It is based] solely upon the argument that all the islands in the Gulf had once been Persian and that they still were, regardless of what had happened over the centuries."[33]

It is the widespread persistence of such articles of faith within Iranian society that partially explains the context for Iran's resurrection of the contemporary phase of the dispute in 1992. It is a matter of debate as to whether Iran's action of denying access to the southern, Sharjah-administered part of the island to non-UAE nationals was a local administrative blunder, a knee-jerk reaction to its exclusion from collective security arrangements for the Gulf or a calculated move designed to enhance its strategic position in the Lower Gulf. However, at a time when American policy was being formulated to isolate Iran (as well as Iraq) internationally, no Iranian was likely to disapprove of actions that might underline to the Arab western littoral states that Iran remained a force to be reckoned with.

2. Iran's seizure of the Tunbs in 1971. There remains some confusion about the degree to which the island of Greater Tunb was manned by Ras al-Khaimah nationals in the immediate period before its forcible capture by Iran on November 30, 1971. One source claims, perhaps rather fancifully, that 120 Qasimi inhabitants of Greater Tunb were expelled from the island to the Ras al-Khaimah mainland.[34] Other reports testify that the Tunbs were uninhabited in the run-up to Iran's move but that three officials from Ras al-Khaimah were stationed on Greater Tunb at the very last moment as a futile gesture of defiance. Of these, one was apparently killed.[35]

3. Iran-UAE bilateral negotiations over the Lower Gulf islands, 1992 and 1995. To date there have been two rounds of bilateral negotiations between the Abu Dhabi and Tehran governments since the resurrection of the dispute in 1992. Both were short-lived and failed conspicuously. The first round of negotiations between delegations of the Iranian and UAE governments took place in Abu Dhabi but soon broke down, ostensibly when the UAE demanded at the outset that Iran immediately end its military occupation of the Tunb islands.[36] Yet, there were unconfirmed reports circulating at the time that the Iranian delegation had surprised their UAE counterparts by immediately agreeing to abide fully by the 1971 MOU over Abu Musa. According to this alternative version, talks then broke down when the UAE delegation tied such an agreement to demands that the future of the Tunbs should be decided by either third party arbitration or judicial settlement.[37]

The second round of bilateral negotiations took place in Qatar during November 1995 and broke down every bit as quickly as had been the case three years earlier. However, breakdown on this occasion had seemed inevitable, given the consistently stated position of each party over the previous months and years. The UAE government had published the agenda it would defend in advance of the negotiations themselves. Again, the first item on its published agenda was a demand that Iran terminate its military occupation of the Tunb islands. The talks collapsed amid mutual recriminations, some of which were directed at the conduct of the Qatar government, as host to the talks.

CONCLUDING REMARKS

If there were important strides taken during the 1990s toward finalizing the political map of the Arabian peninsula, the first eighteen months of the new millennium has witnessed a further intensification of efforts to resolve surviving regional territorial questions. A transformation in political will more than anything else facilitated the conclusion of Saudi Arabia's respective recent boundary settlements with Yemen and Kuwait in June and July of 2000. The manner in which the ICJ's March 2001 judgment on Bahrain-Qatar disputes has been received in Manama and Doha gives some grounds for optimism. It would not be surprising if the two sides announced the institution of some kind of joint development zone to cover seabed areas on both sides of their new maritime boundary at some point in the near future. For where ownership of the seabed and its resources is concerned, pragmatism usually reigns. And in this instance, Bahrain may have won the legal arguments, but Qatar possesses the financial muscle. A similarly pragmatic outcome might be expected from the ongoing Iranian/Kuwaiti maritime boundary negotiations. For it is difficult to invest maritime jurisdictional questions with the same symbolic value that has characterized disputes over land, even where (as is the case between Iran and Kuwait) there are important questions of access to resources at issue and the potential for regional (i.e., Arab-Persian) rivalry exists.

For the reasons outlined in this chapter, it seems unlikely that any resolution of the Lower Gulf islands dispute will be added to this list of progress in the near future. That is not to argue that it is necessarily bound to be a festering source of tension between Iran and the United Arab Emirates. This seems to be one dispute that is more susceptible to effective management than final resolution in international law. In itself, the 1971 Iran-Sharjah MOU was a reflection of this reality. Its original rationale might beneficially be further developed. At the same time, there is every likelihood that this symbolic and cyclical dispute will continue to be activated during periods of heightened Arab-Iranian tensions. For as long as this happens, the detail of the dispute will continue to be secondary to what it represents. Given that the detail is so lacking in clarity, maybe this is not all bad.

NOTES

1. This reality reminds us that the respective histories of Abu Musa and the Tunbs have never been one and the same. It is largely because historically the power that has held Abu Musa has generally also controlled the Tunbs that this linkage is continually made.
2. For background, see Richard Schofield, "Border Disputes in the Gulf: Past, Present and Future," in Gary G. Sick and Lawrence G. Potter, eds., *The Persian Gulf at the Millennium: Essays in Politics, Economy, Security and Religion* (New York: St. Martin's Press, 1997), pp. 142–56.
3. See Richard Schofield, "Boundaries, Territorial Disputes and the GCC States," in David E. Long and Christian Koch, eds., *Gulf Security in the Twenty-First Century* (Abu Dhabi: Emirates Center for Strategic Studies and Research, 1997), pp. 133–68.
4. See Schofield, "Border Disputes in the Gulf: Past, Present and Future," p. 152.
5. Ibid., p. 153.
6. Ibid., p. 155.

7. While there is nothing in place for the Arab world as a whole, the independent states of Latin America (with their institutionalized acceptance of the legal principle of *uti possidetis juris*) and Africa (with the OAU "sacrosanctity" declaration of 1964) have committed themselves to the boundaries of the colonial territories they replaced.

8. It should be stated, however, that Oman and the UAE still have to conclude an overall land boundary settlement that will ratify all of the earlier agreements on separate stretches of the boundary that have been agreed in a piecemeal fashion since the late 1950s. With only minor boundary problems remaining to be ironed out between Oman and the emirates of Sharjah and Ras al-Khaimah, it is expected that such a settlement will be concluded in 2001.

9. "Affaire de la delimitation maritime et des questions territoriales entre Qatar et Bahrein (Qatar c. Bahrein)," Arrêté, 16 Mars 2001/"Case concerning maritime delimitation and territorial questions between Qatar and Bahrain (Qatar v. Bahrain)," Judgment, March 16, 2001, International Court of Justice, The Hague.

10. Ibid.

11. These issues are central to this author's current research of boundary and territorial disputes in the Persian Gulf region.

12. Glen Balfour-Paul, *The end of empire in the Middle East: Britain's relinquishment of power in her last three Arab dependencies* (Cambridge: Cambridge University Press, 1991), p. 127.

13. Confidential source.

14. Richard Schofield, "Down to the Usual Suspects: Border and Territorial Disputes in the Arabian Peninsula and Persian Gulf at the Millennium," paper presented at a conference entitled *Iran, Iraq and the Gulf Arab States*, UCLA Center for Near Eastern Studies, Los Angeles, May 3–4, 2000.

15. This tendency is illustrated perfectly by the four chapters in Hooshang Amirahmadi's edited book, *Small islands, big politics: the Tunbs and Abu Musa in the Gulf* (Basingstoke, U.K.: Macmillan Press, 1996). This presents an unashamedly direct if useful, articulation of the Iranian claim to the islands.

16. India Office (1928) Memorandum entitled "Status of the islands of Tamb, Little Tamb, Abu Musa and Sirri" by J. G.Laithwaite in OIOC file: L/P&S/18/B397.

17. Although its should be pointed out that the Persian foreign ministry showed no inclination whatsoever toward such a scheme.

18. This would ultimately be achieved with their October 24, 1968 maritime boundary agreement.

19. Telegram no. 186, dated March 15, 1968 from the U.S. ambassador in Tehran to Dean Rusk, U.S. State Department, in National Security files, "Iran cables," vol.2, nos. 66–69, box 136, Iran Country File, Lyndon B. Johnson Library, University of Texas, Austin, Texas.

20. Account of meeting during late October 1968 between Wright and the shah of Iran in minute entitled "Persian Gulf/Union of Arab Emirates," October 28, 1968 in PRO file: *FCO 8/938/1.*

21. Telegram dated October 29, 1968 from Sir Denis Wright in Tehran to the Foreign and Commonwealth Office [FCO] in PRO file: *FCO 8/938/1.*

22. Memorandum entitled "Bahrain and Iran" by D. J. McCarthy, FCO dated February 25, 1969 in PRO file: *FCO 8/942.*

23. Telegram dated October 30, 1968 from Stuart Crawford at the Bahrain Residency to the FCO in PRO file: *FCO 8/960/1.*

24. Wright's account of his meeting with Minister of Court Asadollah Alam and Amir Khosrow Afshar, deputy foreign minister, enclosed in dispatch dated October 24, 1968 from M. C. S. Weston in Tehran to A. J. Beamish, Eastern Department, FCO in PRO file: *FCO 8/938/1.*

25. Quoted in Asadollah Alam, *The Shah and I: The Confidential Diary of Iran's Royal Court* (New York: St. Martin's Press, 1992), p. 119.

26. Interview with Pirouz Mojtahed-Zadeh in Pirouz Mojtahed-Zadeh (1995), *The islands of Tunb and Abu Musa,* Occasional Paper no.15, Centre for Near and Middle Eastern Studies, SOAS, p. 55.

27. Dispatch dated July 27, 1888 from H. Drummond Wolff in the PRO file: *FO 406/93.*

28. Dispatch dated August 17, 1888 from the Persian minister of foreign affairs to Drummond Wolff in the PRO file: *FO 406/93.*

29. Against which written formal protests have been delivered to the United Nations by the UAE federal government.

30. Rouhollah Ramazani, *The Persian Gulf: Iran's Role* (Charlottesville, Virginia: University of Virginia Press, 1972), p. 26.

31. Graham E. Fuller, *The "Center of the Universe": The Geopolitics of Iran* (Boulder, Colorado: Westview/RAND, 1991), p. 58.

32. As J. G. Laithwaite of the India Office would comment in his memorandum of July 1934, "It may be remarked that the Persian claim [to Bahrain of February 1845] was largely based on a general claim that the Persian Gulf from the Shatt-el-Arab to Muscat and all the islands in it belonged to Persia; that the employment in English of the term 'Persian Gulf' was itself evidence of this . . ." J. G. Laithwaite, "Historical memorandum on Bahrain," India Office, July 14, 1934 in OIOC [Oriental and India Office Collection, British Library] file: R/15/1/358].

33. Paraphrased in J. B. Kelly, *Britain and the Persian Gulf, 1795–1880* (Oxford: Oxford University Press, 1968), p. 185.

34. Husain M. al-Baharna, *The Arabian Gulf states: their legal and political status and their internal problems,* 3rd ed. (Beirut: Librairie du Liban, 1978), p. 339.

35. Confidential Sharjah-based sources.

36. Press release, Embassy of the United Arab Emirates, London, October 1992.

37. Confidential Sharjah-based sources.

CHAPTER 8

THE NEW GENERATION IN SAUDI ARABIA
Cultural Change, Political Identity, and Regime Security

MAI YAMANI

INTRODUCTION

The degree of change that Saudi Arabia has witnessed since the 1930s has been phenomenal. This chapter investigates the major cultural, political, and economic transformations that have led to the growth of new concepts of identity in the kingdom. These changes have implications for the political consciousness of the population and over the medium to long term may even pose a threat to regime security.[1]

Saudi Arabian as well as wider Gulf security issues often are studied at the state level and above. Considerations of political security in Saudi Arabia need to take serious account of domestic factors, using the tools of sociology and anthropology instead of international relations. The connection between culture and politics in the Saudi context cannot be underestimated, especially within the context of the increasing politicization of the country's new generation.

Since the 1950s, existing economic, political, and religious behavioral standards have come under siege within the Saudi kingdom. This process has resulted in old standards of behavior either being discarded or modified, inevitably resulting in the reinvention of new levels and forms of identity. The symbolism of Islam combined with the unique heritage of Saudi Arabia continue to be central to the Saudi identity and therefore to Saudis' sense of stability. However, a more complex and dynamic process of sweeping cultural change has left the new generation feeling unsettled, to say the least.

Identity, whether conceptualized as "given" (natural) or "constructed" (social), endows groups and individuals with a place, a function, a purpose, and, in the modern world, with the capacity for action.[2] Thus identity is indivisible from modern politics. The basis of an individual's identity within a given society is determined from numerous sources. Each input gains or loses importance depending on the social circumstances of the individual. Since the founding of the state, Saudi identity has been determined by various overlapping and competing sources, including religion, tribal belonging, family, and the nation. The direction of this evolving sense of identity has been linked to the processes of economic development and government policy. The ruling elite has sought to control the process in ways that support its own political agenda and strengthen its position at the heart of the state.

In times of economic growth, the Saudi population, optimistic about the future and supported by a financially strong state, has received ideas from the outside world with a degree of confidence that facilitates its coherent assimilation. However, in times of economic and political uncertainty (the current Saudi context), the population as a whole tends to seek cultural reassurance in notions of "tradition." The people become preoccupied with the mosque and public displays of piety or the region or tribe from which their grandparents came. This retreat into certainty is an attempt to interact with a rapidly changing and uncertain world from a secure and recognizable base. Although it may be true that identities cannot necessarily be defined in a straightforward fashion, under conditions of "complex modernity" it becomes even more difficult to attempt any systematic delineation. People identify themselves on various levels and in various ways depending on a given social situation or context. The main objective of this study is to analyze the manner in which these identities (familial, tribal, regional, religious, and national) and the existing interaction among them have evolved over the last three generations. It will examine the form this interaction has taken as well as the gap that has developed between the identity of the new generation and their parents. The new generation has absorbed information and experiences that could lead them to question the basis of Saudi society and their sense of belonging.

ECONOMIC DEVELOPMENT, CULTURAL CHANGE, AND THE GROWTH OF SAUDI ARABIAN IDENTITIES

The extent to which society has been transformed and the cultural references of ordinary Saudi Arabians radically changed is best portrayed by taking an "ideal type," in this case the life experiences of a typical Saudi family during the oil era. Thus, the effects of modernization can best be judged by looking at a family whose grandparents would have been born in the 1930s, parents in the 1950s, and the new generation, the central focus of this article, would have been born in the 1970s and 1980s. Such a family provides a story of three generations that can explain evolving cultural identity and political consciousness against the backdrop of changing economic circumstances. Over a period of 60 years the horizons of each successive generation have expanded, from the purely local, to those bounded by the state, to the present generation that is challenged by the processes of globalization.

The grandparents of this typical family would have been born in a decade of great historic significance for the kingdom, namely that of political unification in 1932. At the time, the majority of the kingdom was a vast desert with oases of largely nomadic rural communities. Identity was based on a sense of regional belonging, i.e., to the Hijaz, Najd, Asir, or Ahsa, as well as on familial or tribal identity. As far as macropolitical allegiances were concerned, the transition from loyalties based on a tribal or regional identity to a national one promoted by the central government did not impact on the daily existence of the vast majority of the population. National homogeneity was certainly the objective of the newly established government under the al-Saud family, but this goal was unrealized in the 1930s and 1940s.

The practical (as opposed to religious) horizons of the grandparents' imagination did not extend beyond the boundaries of their home town or village[3] The grandfather's only means of transport was on foot or later by truck, and extended journeys usually were undertaken only once in a lifetime and then to Mecca. This reflected the economic circumstances of the time, characterized by a country with almost negligible resources. Villages outside main trading centers and ports were connected tenuously to the areas surrounding them rather than to the world economy. As far as education was concerned, the grandfather's education did not go beyond religious instruction at a *kuttab,* with studies based on the Quran, although he was also knowledgeable about tribal and local affairs. In modern terminology, one would describe him as semiliterate.

The typical grandfather had one wife, unlike a minority of men who were better off tribally and/or economically and had more than one wife. His grandmother's major occupation in life was to produce and rear the offspring. Like other women of her generation, she raised an average of seven children, excluding those who unfortunately became part of the high infant mortality rate. These grandparents came into adulthood when oil revenues were beginning to make their effects felt, but they still remembered pre-oil times.

The parents, those of the second generation, were born in the 1950s. They reached adulthood after the institutional structures of the state had emerged. National homogeneity became the norm with the unification of dress (all Saudi men adopted the national *thoub* and headdress and all Saudi women the black *abbaya* in public), a national education curriculum, and the beginnings of mass communication with the first national newspapers and radio. With these innovations it became possible to speak of the emergence of a Saudi Arabian identity. Travel throughout the kingdom was commonplace. Saudis began to come into regular contact with, and to depend on, state institutions. They began to read about their fellow citizens in national newspapers and to hear the pronouncements of a national government on the radio. There was also a homogenizing of religious practice under the dominant Hanbali school of jurisprudence as prescribed by the established religious elite. The father's macroallegiances became synonymous with the Saudi state and beyond that with the wider causes of Arab nationalism.

If the father went on to higher education, he probably did so at a university in the United States, where he was supported by government grants. When he returned to the kingdom, he worked in the government sector, where he was guaranteed a job. During the 1970s, the wages paid by state employment allowed him to provide his wife, children, and other dependents in the extended family with a standard of living far in excess of anything that the average member of his parent's generation could have imagined.

His wife, although educated at one of the new schools for women, nonetheless maintained the traditional role of a woman of her generation in terms of rearing children. However, she had to her advantage modern medicine and health care and could make use of foreign nannies. This led to a reduction in levels of infant mortality and a baby boom that greatly increased the size of the population.

The result of that population increase is the third generation and the main focus of this article. The sons and daughters, the members of the new generation, were born during the peak of the oil boom of the 1970s (1973–1979). They do not remember anything prior to oil. All notions of "tradition," of a bedouin past, indeed of a life lived primarily in the desert have been handed down to them through the stories and recollections of the two previous generations.

During their upbringing the members of this new generation took for granted mass education, regular travel abroad, television and radio, and more recently, satellite broadcasts. They are left to grapple with a very uncertain set of beliefs about "modernity."

They know much more than their parents' generation because of their exposure and education, but this knowledge creates problems. Change has been so swift that they still do not have the cultural terms of reference to put this new society and their role within it into perspective. The unanswered questions that trouble the new generation are many: whether they will be given the chance to usefully apply the new skills and concepts learned in a greatly expanded and generously funded education system; whether they even will have the guaranteed employment and the same living standards of their parents; and crucially who they are and what is the basis and location of their identity.

Following this amazing cultural transformation, these young people lack the certainties of their grandparents, the villagers whose position and role in life appeared stable and predictable. They also lack the economic security of their parents who grew up in a time when oil delivered plenty. The conflicting choices and uncertain future that face the new generation are seen as threatening. Although there are still numerous advantages (housing, food, and other material benefits), rapid urbanization has created a sense of dislocation. The move, in the space of two generations, from a self-supporting village, weakly connected to the outside world, to the cities of a modern state at the heart of a region undergoing the effects of globalization has assaulted the identity of these young people with the sense of a vague and apparently superficial way of life.

The uncertainty that modernity brings can be challenged and placed in perspective by confronting its effects and questioning its outcomes. These young people, however, have not been given the personal autonomy to question a profoundly disorienting experience because of basic beliefs, traditions, and religious and political practices that constrain and censor their thoughts and actions. One can identify two broad categories of problems with which they are grappling. First and most noticeable are the economic transformations and second are the cultural values and norms that are increasingly coming under scrutiny as being anachronistic.

THE CENTRALITY OF THE NEW GENERATION

The centrality of 15– to 30–year-olds to the future of Saudi Arabia needs to be stressed. Their numbers alone make them the crucial political constituency of the next five years. The *Saudi Gazette* estimated that more than 50 percent of the population was below the age of fifteen,[4] while the National Commercial Bank gave a figure of 43.5 percent.[5] The Gulf Cooperation Council (GCC) Economic Databook estimated that the number of Saudis and expatriates under 15 represented 33.6 percent of the whole population—which translates into 40.9 percent of the purely Saudi population. Despite the discrepancies in the estimates, even the most conservative figures demonstrate the very high proportion of Saudis who are still under, but rapidly approaching working age. About 50.9 percent of Saudis are below the age of 20 and only 17.2 percent are above the age of 40. Of all those in Saudi Arabia aged 30 to 39, only 47.5 percent are Saudi nationals.

In 1974 the official census estimated the population of the kingdom at 6,218,381 Saudis. The United Nations estimated that the population of Saudi Arabia in 1975 was 7,251,000, rising to 8,9600,00 by 1980. The 1992 census, however, put the Saudi population at 12.3 million. The almost doubling of official Saudi population figures in eighteen years cautions one to treat all official figures with skepticism. Government figures for 1998 estimate the population to be approximately 18 million, including foreign workers and their families who form 29 percent of the total population. This tendency for official statistics to overestimate the population has serious implications for any demographic analysis, especially estimates of the extent and effects of unemployment.

Even if these population estimates are considered to be reasonably accurate, the kingdom, like other countries in the GCC, is facing major problems in terms of absorbing its youth into the labor force and containing expectations for wider political participation. At a time when private investment is leveling off, oil revenues are unstable, and massive public spending exceeds revenues, Saudis are bewildered as to how they can manage an expanding population, a decreasing mortality rate, and an increasing demand for female employment.[6] Currently, around 3.5 million Saudis (approximately 27 percent of the population) are in schools, colleges, and universities.[7] By the year 2000, an estimated 660,000 Saudi nationals were expected to join the labor market.[8]

The government's concern is driven by the combination of a decline in the Saudi standard of living combined with a projected annual population growth rate of 3.3 percent between 1992 and 2000. This means that an average of 125,000 Saudis will enter an already constricting job market each year (a projected 700,000 in the years between 1995 and 2000).[9] There are differences between the figures given by the NCB Economist and those of the World Bank; hence, these figures are approximate. Examples from across the developing world, specifically from North Africa, show that the specter of political instability haunts regimes that fail to provide for the economic needs and social expectations of a youthful and expanding population.

THE PLACE OF THE NEW GENERATION IN A CONSTRICTING SAUDI ECONOMY

Economic conditions in Saudi Arabia started to decline in the mid–1980s when oil prices dropped dramatically. This process accelerated after the 1990–1991 Gulf War, with the kingdom having to find extra resources to pay for the costs incurred. Compared to the early 1980s, when Saudi foreign assets were at their highest, the kingdom's overseas investments had been greatly reduced by the early 1990s. This resulted in the unprecedented step of the government raising a loan from overseas banks in an attempt to avert a fiscal crisis. By early 1998, the economic situation was even more problematic, with the price of Saudi crude as low as $11 per barrel. The low price of oil necessitated a government policy of cutbacks and a reduced social security program. Even with the recent steep rise in the world price of oil since 2000, there is still a sense of economic vulnerability in the kingdom and a belief that the danger of oil price fluctuation has not been overcome.

The fall in oil revenues during the 1980s resulted in the reduction of state-sponsored development projects across the Gulf area. According to the International Monetary Fund (IMF), living standards in Saudi Arabia slipped from one of the world's highest in 1981 to the level of a middle income nation by 1993.[10] This has meant that governments could no longer afford high levels of expenditures on social services such as welfare, health, and education. Yet, welfare and development have been the central tenets of the ruling ideology and so far have cushioned the indigenous populations from the sort of social and political problems endemic in other states of the Middle East and North Africa. The IMF has forecast increasing levels of indebtedness, and it has advised that there be further readjustment of development policies to reflect more accurately the market values of international finance.[11] Beginning in January 1995, Saudi Arabia has been obliged to raise the cost of gasoline, water, electricity, and telephone service. The recent surge in the oil price has yet to filter through to the state budget, with government spending declining by 3.6 percent in 1998 and a predicted fall in GDP of 7 percent in 1999.[12] Overall the current healthy price of oil will result in the postponing of the radical restructuring and hard socioeconomic decisions that the Saudi state and society so desperately need to make.

There is an assumption among some Western analysts that by accentuating Islamic values in education, especially gender segregation, the Saudi Arabian government has not prepared its population for the necessary structural adjustments that the economy and society will have to undergo in the coming decades to prepare for the demands of the global economy and the goal of joining the World Trade Organization (WTO). One can find this analysis in both World Bank reports as well as in the journals and newspapers that rely on these reports. However, this type of analysis offers little insight into how the economic and social restructuring of GCC states may progress in the future. Saudi Arabia is the foremost example of a GCC state that has undergone a major societal transformation in a relatively short period of time. It is certainly not a coincidence that Saudi Arabia also has witnessed demands for political and social reform.

The al-Saud have successfully maintained a high degree of organic solidarity as a patronymic group while becoming a national elite. The ruling family controls the important government positions and has strengthened its base of support by forming alliances with the religious establishment, the al-Shaykh, and the regional elites. The al-Saud princes number 6,000, and with their al-Shaykh supporters they number altogether as many as 12,000 men who are related by marriage to all the other local lineages, such as the al-Sudayris. This extended ruling class numbers around 20,000 people. Together with other non-royal partners, the total number of the kingdom's elite is as high as 100,000. Thus, the influence of such a substantial ruling class must not be underestimated.

The rule of the al-Saud family is portrayed in terms of stability and piety, values that attempt to substitute for the absence of representative institutions. The system of monarchic rule is a form of patronage, depending on the immense oil wealth controlled by al-Saud. The system has been described in Western terms as one of "no taxation no representation." The government does not collect taxes based on income. Instead, taxes follow the pattern of religious obligation, *zakat,* an obligatory alms tax of 2.5 percent of surplus wealth per annum. The issue of an income tax is a controversial one, because *zakat* is considered the only legitimate form of tax according to Islamic law.

The royal family has followed a traditional pattern of rule: the distribution of patronage, both in the form of influence over public sector jobs and by the provision of welfare schemes for the remainder of the population, has remained the material basis of its rule. The welfare programs included the provision of free health care and education, and subsidies for medicine, bread, electric power, and gasoline. The state also offered interest-free loans and gifts of land. There has also been the novel phenomena of young men relying on the state's gift of $5,000 for the marriage dower, a program to encourage marriages between Saudi nationals. The state thus has attempted to adapt the "traditional" social and moral practices of paternalism to the new conditions of a modern state, a phenomenon often described as the patrimonial state. This has been a remarkable adaptation of tradition to the modern state; yet, when considering the attitudes of the younger generation in society, one needs to ask whether the moral concepts that attend patronage and charity have been transmitted to the young Saudis, or whether such values have been compromised by recent financial constraints. In the present situation, the legitimacy of the patrimony of the ruling family has become questioned, since a large section of the population finds itself excluded from the immediate benefits of state patronage. Although the IMF has urged the expansion of the private sector, in the short term, although certain market sectors are growing, the economy remains dominated by the oil sector and largely unreformed.

The immediate problem posed by fiscal austerity is how to accommodate the growing number of young Saudis reaching the job market. The rapid population growth that accompanied the modernization of Saudi society created a unique problem for the integration of this generation into society. The public sector already is over-manned, and the potential of the private sector to employ Saudi nationals has been impeded by a variety of cultural and economic factors. With young people representing such a large percentage of the population, the state's inability to provide them with employment in the long term will prove a major source of social tension that could result in the destabilization of the current regime.

THE PERCEPTIONS OF THE NEW GENERATION

During 1998 I interviewed members of the new generation (15– to 30–year-old Saudi Arabians). I have been attempting to gauge the effects of increased economic insecurity and exposure to the globalization of culture. I have tried to interview as broad a sample of Saudi youth as possible. They can be categorized loosely into six overlapping groups. First, young people who belong to the royal family, both those close to the throne and those at the periphery. Second, young people whose families are powerful politically and whose relatives are high-ranking state functionaries. The third category is those young people of recent rural or bedouin origin. The fourth group includes young people related to key trading and business families. In category five are those who can loosely be described as belonging to the intelligentsia or "educated class"; this would include people who have spent extended time in higher education and those whose parents are or who themselves are working in educationally related employment. The largest category are those lower-class Saudi Arabians who make up the vast majority of the population; their welfare and work depend directly and solely on state employment, and they rarely travel abroad in comparison to the Saudi elite. In interviewing I used open-ended questions, favoring a qualitative as opposed to a quantitative approach.

In this paper, the focus is the attitudes of those in category five, the educated class. These people are perhaps the most influenced by modernization. Therefore they offer the best example of its likely results, the changing identity of Saudis, and future political developments. I focus first on cultural influences and the identity of the new generation, then on education, employment, and gender. These themes allow us to examine the concerns of the new generation, the change in their attitudes, and their response to the policies of the Saudi state.

GLOBALIZATION OF CULTURE AND
THE IDENTITY OF THE NEW GENERATION

The social experiences of an individual determine his or her perception and identity. Given the much broader exposure of the new generation to what rapidly is becoming a globalized culture, its attitudes tend to differ significantly from those of its parents. Their mothers' and fathers' sense of social and political identity had a greater stability, partly due to the state's ability to control their access to the wider world. By the late 1990s, identity no longer could be taken for granted because the new generation had access to seemingly endless sources of information and entertainment that have expanded greatly the borders of its imagination. This global classroom and playground stand in sharp contrast to local social and political structures that constrain permissible behavior.

This radical expansion in cultural exposure can be detected in nearly all the young people interviewed irrespective of the social categories to which they belong. For example, Said is 27 and comes from a rural village. His parents were illiterate, and his sources of cultural exposure were extremely limited, with the radio providing their main window to the outside world until 1977, when television arrived. New forms of media were not welcomed by his mother, who used her "strength and dominance in the family" to oppose the latest intrusion, a satellite dish. After several years, the family convinced her, and Said has had access to satellite TV since 1993. Thus in the space of sixteen years Said has witnessed the widening and ultimate transformation of his cultural sphere.

With a greater variety of entertainment programs available on satellite television channels, the state-run media has lost its dominance over young people. The drab appearance and limited scope of programs featured on TV means it increasingly has been rejected. It also has drawn attention to the issue of censorship. Muhammad, 30 years old from Jeddah, was critical of local censorship, claiming that Saudi television is commonly referred to as force-feeding (*ghasab*) Channel 1 and force-feeding Channel 2. However, the increasing influence of television generally and satellite TV specifically has not been celebrated by all Saudi youth. The ambivalence of its reception is reflected in Said. Although he clearly enjoyed watching television and fought with his mother for many years to get a satellite dish, he claims that television contributed to creating a new generation of consumers and "the U.S. is behind the whole thing because they want us [Saudi Arabia] to remain dependent upon them." He also thinks that satellite television will cause deep-rooted change, "especially American songs will have an influence on the culture and we must fight to keep our tradition of the country." Maysa, 27, agrees that Western television has had a negative effect on society: "this is the day of confrontation (*yaum al-tahaddi)"* with Saudi Arabia being divided between two extremes, the conservatives and the eccentrics *(munharifin)* and TV being the main cause.

The majority of those interviewed saw satellite television as a positive innovation. Both Malak (educated class) and Maha, 17 (new middle class) saw it as a crucial link to the wider world. According to Maha, "technology is very important, especially satellite television; it makes you aware of the outside world, likewise mobile phones. These things are a blessing." Salman, a 25–year-old (a youth whose families are powerful politically) agreed: "Satellite is a big source of relief for Saudi society, offering a window on the outside world. They enjoy what they otherwise would not have."

This ambivalence of outlook, embracing technology and the information it brings while seeking security in a reinvention of tradition, permeates the identity of the new generation. This perception of "tradition" allows the youth to interact with a changing and possibly threatening world from a position of certainty. Princess Nauf from the ruling family, for example, travels regularly in Europe, reads widely, and frequently uses satellite TV and the Internet. However, she also writes poetry, because "it expresses my traditional Arabic heritage which is both Salafi Islam and pure desert Najdi culture. . . . I value Islam and especially Salafi." She also values the purity of desert architecture and language. She thinks Saudis should maintain the extended family phenomenon as well as traditional gender segregation because of the general conservative Islamic trends that still exist in society.

Balance between the perception of a secure and reassuring tradition and an innovative and positive modernity is difficult to sustain. Maha sums up modernity as "people's perception of you: what you wear, your home, appearance are the symbols of modernity for most people." Maha finds those attitudes to constitute a form of pressure, and she thinks that modernity clashes with the traditional in Saudi Arabia. Malak also sees modernity as having a negative effect: "Young people have the wrong attitude, a selfish attitude to modernism." If modernity cannot be wholly rejected, however, Malak believes it should be adopted selectively: "We should avoid the negative sides. Change should be for the good. Change is often not necessary." Alaa', 24 (from the new middle class) summed up the duality in perception by saying modernity "is to respect the past and to build the future on it."

This perception of using tradition as a stable base to interact with a rapidly changing world depends on the strength and stability of Saudi state-society relations. The sharp decrease in government largesse has given rise to doubts both about what the future might hold and also about how the state is run. For example, Abdullah, 26, the son of a prominent businessman, sums up this sense of uneasiness by saying:

> In the past everything was easier. There were more opportunities . . . The oil benefited my generation superficially. We got toys out of it while the older generation benefited most . . . During the 1970s, 30 to 40 percent of the older generation had the chance to go abroad, find the right job; their life was secure, highly admired, and they were compensated. The smallest thing they did was considered impressive. Today the upper class have the same chances while the middle-lower class have more competition facing them. Before, if a man went to a "Mickey Mouse" university, people would be impressed and think it was a big deal. In the 1960s there was no kingdom of Saudi Arabia as there is today and thus the standards were different. No matter what he learned, a man felt that he achieved a lot. He came from heaven [meaning America].

EDUCATION

In the context of a society that has undergone rapid modernization over the past generation, family and education represent radically different influences for future developments. Among the older generation the unquestioning upholding of "traditional" attitudes persists, and parents often try to transmit traditional social values. For instance, Said, the young man from a rural village, said that he had studied business administration and marketing at King Abd al-Aziz University in Jeddah because he admired his father's "business sense." However, he noted that his father was illiterate, having been educated only in the "school of life" (harij madrasat al-hayat) and having begun his career as a simple worker, shepherd, and carrier.

Said's only desire is to follow in his father's footsteps and work in the family business. Yet, his education has influenced his attitudes. For instance, he says that he resisted his parents when they wanted him to marry his cousin because he is aware that there are medical complications associated with the practice of endogamy. Nonetheless, in accordance with traditional practices, he would prefer that his future wife did not work. On the issue of work, he said that his generation was remarkable for its overdependence on the luxuries and conveniences of modern life. He blames the government for this situation because its development programs "spoiled" the people so that they cannot work in the sun. Said's views represent the dramatic transformation of society as a result of education, travel, and media during the past thirty years.

One may ask whether traditional norms of respect for authority will be maintained under the impact of this transformation. Education has been used by the state to help shape the attitudes of youth. The new business and professional classes, for example, were educated abroad until the opening of the first Saudi university, King Saud University, in 1957. Because education tends to transmit values emanating from outside the cultural tradition, the state allowed the *ulama* to organize the religious curriculum of schools to ensure that Islamic tradition would be emphasized. In fact, the first schools for girls were organized by the *ulama* beginning in 1959, and religion was a central part of their curriculum. Prior to the opening of the first women's college, women were not permitted to attend classes at the (all-male) universities, although they could study for degrees at home as external students. Currently, in primary and secondary schools for both boys and girls, the teaching of Islamic tradition takes up as much as two-thirds of the curriculum and normally involves the memorization of the Quran.

In the 1970s and 1980s, the government expanded the number and size of universities so that male Saudis could fill positions in the state industries and bureaucracy. Free education, housing, food, and books were provided by the government; until recently, a job also was guaranteed. The government encouraged the conservative tendency by giving the *ulama* supervisory control over educational policy, even in the secular universities, resulting in a strong Islamic influence in university curriculum. Not only did education tend to turn out people with conservative attitudes, but the teaching of foreign cultures and beliefs was restricted and foreigners were excluded from the state schools.[13]

The education system in Saudi Arabia, although greatly expanded, represents the conservatism of a state legitimated by Islamic culture. Therefore, education has had a restricted impact on the development of new cultural or social attitudes. Thus, Said retains many characteristics of his rural background even while he aspires to an education for career reasons. In spite of his traveling abroad to attend a British school to acquire proficiency in English for "international business dealings," Said cannot converse in English and actively cultivates his Arab and Islamic identity. In contrast, Khalid, a member of the educated class from Riyadh who has a university degree from the United States, said that because of the present influence of the media, particularly satellite TV, if he were a schoolboy today he would despise what is taught in school because of the conservatism and limitation of the curriculum. Khalid is more supportive of and enthusiastic about cultural change and adaptation.

The Saudi educational system emphasizes the transmission of cultural norms. For example, in 1990, 25 percent of university students were enrolled in Islamic universities and taught solely in Arabic.[14] The result is a duality or conflict in cultural orientation often represented by proficiency in English. The dilemma is conveyed by the the observation of a professor in the Saudi university system: "English and Arabic are forces with powerful symbolic value in Saudi Arabia; they stand for modern/traditional; secular/sacred; alien/comfortable."[15] It also is represented by a conflict between modern and conservative teaching methods. Malak, a *muhajjaba* (a women who abides by Islamic dress codes at all times) of 17, living in Jeddah and from the educated class, stressed the traditional method of teaching by noting that in schools teachers do not care if students understand as long as they memorize.

Although critical of the schools, Malak says she loves the respect *(ihtiram)* of tradition and regrets that there is less and less respect in society, blaming this decline on the values of modernity that stress only material comforts. Yet, for Malak tradition is not the extremism of the religious authorities who impose religious values on others and restrict educational aspirations: "In order to be part of the global community, we need to become more international while keeping something for ourselves."

Muhammad, from Jeddah, reflects the more international attitudes of the new generation. Educated in computer science at the University of Jeddah and in America, he says that his aspiration is not to make money but to be the "best man" in his field. He believes that in the future life will be more difficult and that it is necessary to adapt to science and technology because these are the only means to develop the economy. Muhammad says that his education in the United States has made him more aggressive, an attribute that is necessary for survival in the new conditions of the future.

The views of two sisters from the new middle class, Haifa and Hind, 17 and 19 years of age respectively, provide an idea of the doubts and fears of other young people when confronting the future. Although Haifa has traveled to the United States and United Kingdom and wants to study medicine she would prefer to marry a "rich man" who would provide her with a house and servants. Hind is studying medicine but could not contemplate traveling abroad to further her career. The sisters were not from a wealthy background and were critical of the fashionable tastes of more affluent families. Hind said she did not want a lot of servants. Another pair of sisters, Jumanah and Arwa, have studied at King Abd al-Aziz University and the House of Tenderness School respectively, and they claim that the choice of subjects to study is limited. They regret that the authorities restrict their choices and remark in addition that their families are overprotective and do not permit them to travel abroad for further education.

The younger generation is definitely conscious of the world beyond the borders of Saudi Arabia and believes that this is an arena where life possibilities would be enhanced. This is a normal perception even among those young girls who have been sheltered at home from outside influences. Although there is both implicit and explicit frustration with the quality of education, as well as with the existing censorship, the youth continue to cling to the family and the conventions of Saudi society as part of its social identity. This ambiguity undoubtedly will influence future opinions about both political and cultural issues.

EMPLOYMENT

The state is the largest employer, employing a total of 88 percent of the work force in the public sector.[16] A study of Saudi society in the 1970s, made by the IMF, showed that most Saudis with an education desired a government job, because such employment was seen as providing more secure income for raising a family. Therefore, access to government influence, usually through family connections, is the usual method of career advancement, resulting in a high degree of personal dependence of the individual upon the state. The ruling family dominates this sector through employment contracts and control of positions in the bureaucracy and state utilities. The current policy of Saudiization, however, involves a more active effort to include Saudis in the private sector. The sixth five-year plan (1995–2000) stated its aim was to "replace non-Saudis with appropriately qualified and willing-to-work Saudi manpower in all occupations" and to develop "Saudi manpower through meticulous evaluation of educational curricula and training programs."[17]

However, employers in the private sector must operate in a global market and, as a result, prefer not to invest in the costly job training programs supported by the government for nationals. Many employers claim that Saudi nationals are not adaptable to employment and business because of cultural attitudes that encourage regional and family preferences. Hence, Najdis prefer to reside in the Najd, and Hijazis in the Hijaz, whereas expatriate communities are mobile and adaptable. Thus, the younger generation is forced into a job market where secure government jobs have become scarce and where employers have a preference for foreign workers.

The new generation believes they see uncaring employers supported by devious foreigners intent upon protecting themselves by creating barriers to entry. Young Saudis believe they know a double standard when they see one. Given the general use of English as a discriminator in achieving employment and possessed of a generally limited capability in terms of job search and self-marketing, Saudi youth often find the employment search a degrading and frustrating experience.[18] In fact, inherited extended family values influence these attitudes. Because most businesses in Saudi Arabia are family-owned, there is an unwillingness to allow any Saudi national outside the family access to business information. Most businesses, therefore, prefer to employ foreign workers. Even those Saudis who have attended trade or vocational schools tend to set up businesses that seek government contracts and then hire foreign companies and/or workers with the expertise to carry through the project. As a result the huge migrant class employed by the government in the state sector of the economy is replicated in the private sector, and the migrant class makes up 41 percent of Saudi Arabia's total population. The total number of expatriates in the 1990 labor force was 2,878,000, or 60 percent of the total. These percentages are not expected to change before the year 2005. The situation became a cause of some social tension during the 1990s, particularly in the cities where 83 percent of the total Saudi population live.[19] This is particularly true of the younger generation of Saudis who must compete with foreigners when seeking employment. In a total labor force of 4,382,500, Saudis make up only 12 percent of the service sector and 7 percent of the private sector. In industry, a mere 4 percent of Saudis take up positions in the more desirable banking sector, where they compromise 65 to 70 percent of the work force, as well as in the privately owned petrochemical industries. More than 50 percent of the migrant workers are unskilled.[20]

For instance, Khalid, 29 (the educated class), who wants to start a clothes design factory, said he would employ Egyptian, Indian, and Filipino workers because of their expertise. "The Saudis do not want to work." What is contradictory is that although he is critical of Saudi attitudes toward work, at the same time he liked the custom of *ihtiram* (respect) in his country, saying that the younger generation should not "exceed their boundaries." This indicates the ambivalent attitudes of young Saudis toward the sort of social changes that attend economic restructuring. Other young men with exposure to American cultural values were also upset about the habits of both Saudi employees and employers. Muhammad, from Jeddah, contrasted the aggressiveness and efficiency of American business culture with the "IBM" (*inshallah, bukra,* and *maleish,* "God willing." "tomorrow," and "it will be all right") attitudes of Saudis toward work. He said that finding a job in Saudi Arabia is very frustrating because of the employers' attitude of *maleish* and *haram aleikum* towards employers. *Haram aleikum* is the attitude of protectiveness toward those to whom employers feel either a personal obligation as friends or as family connections or else a moral obligation, such as *abu a'iyal,* a man with children to support. This attitude has an impact upon business efficiency. In addition, Muhammad says that businesses employ Filipinos only because it is cheaper, even though the Filipinos do not perform better than the Saudis. In the same conversation he said that even basic necessities require *wasita,* or connections, in Saudi Arabia. In his view his expectations are limited because of the excessive dependency of people on the government; he believes that government controls should be relaxed and the private sector developed.

Previously it was shown that Said recognizes the need to develop skills to make international contacts for his business, but otherwise he shows a strong attachment to the ancestral home where his father has re-created a farm reminiscent of the pastoral days. He wants to work in the family business with his brothers. When in Britain he spent most of his time in Saudi upper-class circles, because he was eager to make connections with important patrons. In spite of his travels and education in business administration, Said is insular in his attitudes. He condemns the luxuries of consumer society and sees them as the work of the Americans who want to keep the Saudis dependent. He blames the government for this dependency. Said's views suggest the continuing popularity of conservative values in the populace, rejecting developments that are seen as eroding Arab and Islamic virtues.

Faiz, a member of an important business family and a student of 16 who has studied in Jeddah and America, says that technology is important in Saudi Arabia—air travel, media, telephone, Internet—and that big business families are very aware of international events because the Saudi economy is involved in a world economy. He sees progress in the application of technology: "We need progress to develop industry and become independent of America." Faiz believes tradition is important. "Religion is tradition," he says, but in Saudi Arabia it is applied incorrectly and has impeded progress. He maintains that strict social rules should be abolished because "everything was permitted by Islam. Likewise, laws should be applied consistently; although the satellite dish was illegal, the king had the biggest satellite dish of all." His argument was directed not against the West but against contradictions that are created by the authorities in these times of change. Faiz also referred to the government's decision to forbid women the right to drive in the name of Islam, contending that people should be allowed more opportunities.

GENDER

Cultural values are determined by the most important social organization in these societies, the family, one that remains patriarchal. Ideally, boys and girls never meet after kindergarten, courtship is forbidden, and marriages are arranged. Young women stay at home and learn "domestic virtues," while boys go to school for a career-oriented education. Men are expected to provide for women and children as their dependents, with women bearing the enormous responsibility of rearing an average of five children. The husband is required by *iltizam,* obligation, to supervise all household expenses. The wife makes only one-third of food purchases, while the husband makes all purchases of durable commodities, including the satellite dish. Therefore, although 95 percent of households own a television set and 60 to 70 percent own a stereo or video, the patriarchal character of society is maintained.[21] Women are not allowed to drive a car, a custom that became law in 1990 after a demonstration of 47 women in Riyadh. The codification of this law has made sexual inequality official.

The gender distinctions are evident in the consumer sector, with special branches of banks set up for women. Likewise, most banks offer different bank cards for men, women, and the young (those under 25 years of age). These distinctions are taken for granted by the youth. The separation of genders is indicated by shops for women as seen in all the big malls with signs clearly saying: "For women only. Men are not allowed."

In the major trading and commercial enterprises, women have their own niche through which they actively engage in the private sector. It is estimated that women hold 25 percent of the property in Riyadh and 50 percent in Jeddah, as a result of the rights afforded women under Islamic law, such as autonomous control over inherited wealth and dowries.[22] Certainly, a question that must be asked is whether the expansion of educational institutions and the development of new industries and services have enabled a new generation of women to become more integrated in male-dominated public and professional life.

To date the exclusion of women from the work force has meant that although 55 percent of all university graduates in Saudi Arabia are women, they make up only 5 percent of the work force. Those who have found work do so behind the veil (*hijab*). Likewise, women feminists who have made demands for rights do so in Islamic terms. Beginning in the universities, this movement was nurtured by lecturers who were influenced by Egyptian ideas on women's Muslim rights. The movement spread rapidly through gatherings led by charismatic leaders. In their meetings, numbering as many as 300, these women remained veiled to represent their solidarity and their commitment to Islam. This distinguishes the new Islamic feminist from the traditional attitude that required women to veil only when in public; it also distinguishes the Islamic feminists from liberal protesters who have less support within an Islamic society. The worldly aims of the young feminists are not yet clearly defined. They do not demand the right to vote or to work with men. However, they seem to be in the forefront of all public professions that are open to women, such as women's branches of banks and the universities. Therefore, although this group clearly represents the educated new generation, the Islamic motive provides them with a moral power to challenge patriarchal norms that stand in the way of their professional achievements. The aggressive attitude provides a significant distinction between the new women and those of the same generation who have accepted the traditional role of women in the family. Thus, the appearance of Islamic attire belies a new and even modern attitude of women in relation to education, employment, and private life.

Among some of the young women interviewed there was great frustration that their aspirations, nurtured by education and foreign travel, could not be fulfilled within Saudi Arabia. Two of the female interviewees from the families dependent on state employment railed against the sexism inherent in the present Saudi system. For example, 15–year-old Nasrin's ambition is to become the first Saudi woman pilot, "But it is almost impossible. If we cannot drive, how can we fly?" Therefore she says she has little choice but to "study mathematics until I die."

Ashwaq is also 15 years old and wants to become an archaeologist after completing higher education. However, she fears she will be forced to become a teacher or a secretary because although archaeology is her passion she will not be able to travel as a woman and to go on digs. She will, under the present circumstances, have to compromise and get an acceptable job such as a teacher.

Role expectations are also articulated ambivalently by young women. Amina (a member of the educated class), who is 18, wants to study law, despite the fact that there are no women lawyers in Saudi Arabia. "By the time I graduate I hope there will be opportunities to practice law. I hope things will move, Otherwise I will start it." She wants to earn her own money, not to take from her husband. She says that her education in Britain taught her to depend on herself, but she also values the virtues of self-control and respect in Saudi society. She intends to be a wife and mother first because, she said, the family is something lasting. Interestingly, she says she expects her husband to fulfil the customary obligation, *iltizam,* of maintaining the household: "My money will not go towards maintaining the house." Finally, she expects she will get her job through connections: "Contacts will get you there." Apparently, Amina is unaware of the contradiction between being an innovator and challenging patriarchal dominance yet relying on contacts that necessarily would issue from the establishment. Yet this girl, like Malak, contrasted her interest in a career with the traditional female role of simply finding a husband and starting a family.

Likewise, Maryam (intelligentsia or educated class), who is older at 27, said that she wanted to do something useful and therefore works with disabled children. Although an exceptional person in her devotion to her professional career before marriage and family, nonetheless she chose her career only in consultation with her family, who encouraged her to follow a course in keeping with social conventions in which women are carers and nurturers. Moreover, Maryam chose the career to please an influential patron in her family. She is marrying only now, and intends to live a modest lifestyle according to her needs.

Similar aspirations were expressed by Hind, eight years younger, who wanted to study medicine and has chosen the career of pediatrician. She hopes to meet her husband while working. She was critical of the DJ (disc jockey) parties specially organized by mothers, social parties for the young where there is dancing and sometimes even the mixing of the sexes, so that the sons and daughters of well-to-do families can meet and form engagements. Hind said that at these parties it is necessary to have the latest in Western fashions. Therefore, her parents would have to spend beyond their means to meet social status requirements in dress and gifts to keep up appearances. However, Hind wanted to work to provide a better quality of life, not just for appearances (*mazahir*) or material benefits. She said that her husband would have to adapt to this aspiration; they would have to *natafaham,* find understanding.

The young *muhajjaba* mentioned earlier, Malak, did not see herself as a career woman. She said that most of her teenage friends were already conforming to customary practice, but this was only for material or practical reasons. For her marriage and motherhood are a form of worship, *ibada.* This is probably not a reflection of traditional or customary beliefs, but her spiritual or religious idealism.

Alaa (educated class) has just divorced her husband at the age of 18 because her husband refused to let her work. She was able to divorce because her family had included permission to continue her studies as one of the conditions in the marriage contract. Increasingly women are asking for the *ismaa,* the right to ask for divorce, as part of the contract. In Alaa's case when her husband resisted her choice of a more public social role, she sought her father's permission to divorce. "I am ambitious. I cannot just sit at home." When I asked Alaa, Amani, Jumanah, and Arwa if they thought women should drive, they said that they would love to drive, but that such a goal was unrealistic because of the attitudes of men. This suggests some of the unique conditions imposed by gender segregation, such as the courting rituals carried out in cars or at DJ parties.

Women are still subject to the aggressive attentions of men in public places. In my own experience as an ethnographer I observed the customary approach of *ghazal,* by which a man establishes a dominant and aggressive role through sexualizing the conversation and deploying set phrases and gestures. Men would protect their wives from exposure to the opposite sex. For instance, Said aspired to marry a beautiful and educated woman who would not want to work although he said—at least to me—that he was open to the idea if she wanted to work. Generally, in the educated class men claimed to be open to the idea of women working; however, at this stage of economic development, additional income from a working wife is not a pressing issue. The male preference is to be the traditional provider. Muhammad said that he wanted to marry an educated woman who was "next to me rather than behind me." He expected that he would meet her not through an arranged marriage, but at a mixed party. "Someone will arrange a meeting for me. It is like a blind date." He is not in a hurry to marry because he does not want "to choose a bride and then choose another one afterwards." Faiz said that he would marry at 25 and have four children, but he would not object if his wife wanted to work; he said his mother would choose his bride for him.

CONCLUSION

The views of the new generation show that the patriarchal extended family still dominates the thinking of both genders. Kinship remains the organizing principle for social and economic life. There is still a strong sense of the need to conform. Yet, most youth, if not all, put educational and career ambitions as a first concern, with women committed to the idea of having both a career and a family. It should be noted that education was seen as a way to improve the quality of life, both materially or spiritually. Some traditional roles and norms have persisted, while former modes of life have disappeared. Patriarchal autonomy has been maintained through the ownership and control of property, although this is beginning to be challenged. Women are not necessarily discarding altogether their customary roles as mothers and wives, although they do seem to seek more power outside the home as a natural result of education, exposure, and an awareness of economic rights. The sense of certainty based on familial and traditional norms is being slowly transformed, giving rise to ambivalence, contradictions, and ambiguity. Satellite channels like al-Jazira have contributed to the development of new role models. However, there is understandable confusion in the adaptation of traditional role models to the new conditions, evident in the desire to have traditional status advantages in private and public life while seeking new career options.

Most of the young people interviewed agreed that their own individual development and that of the larger society have been impeded by government controls on resources and restrictions in education and media. Yet the educated class remains ambivalent about transformation that would threaten the stable world of family, patrons, and customary practices. The Saudi government has worked hard to maintain its control over a state structure that has increased rapidly over the last sixty years. The patron-client ties that it has maintained within a diverse administration have been key to its power. However, there is increasing scrutiny of how resources are used at a time when there is increasing demand for greater transparency. This means that as the new generation reaches the job market, the state's ability to constrict its autonomy is in question. The process of education and the cultural exposure of the new generation are giving rise to a new political identity. As yet, however, it is incoherent and partly formed. But if it is to develop in harmony with the rest of Saudi society and in partnership with the state, it needs to be given more space, both socially and politically, in which to evolve. The path that the new generation's collective identity takes in the future is as yet unpredictable, but the outcome of its uncertain journey is crucial to Saudi Arabia's long-term stability in a turbulent Middle East.

NOTES

1. By regime, I mean the political ruling family and the established religious elite.
2. For greater detail, see Kathryn Dean, "Politics and the End of Identity," in K. Dean, (ed.) *Politics and the Ends of Identity* (Ashgate, 1977), pp. 4–43.
3. For a theoretical explanation of this argument in the European context, see Benedict Anderson, *Imagined Communities: Reflections on the Origins and Spread of Nationalism* (London: Verso, 1991), pp. 9–45.
4. *The Saudi Gazette,* September 1, 1995
5. NCB Economist. "Gulf Population and Labour Force Structure." Economic and Financial Publication Issued by the Economics Department of the National Commercial Bank. Issue no. 4, vol. 5 (June-July 1995), p. 2. More recent figures broadly support these estimates. For example, the *1999 Population Reference Bureau,* World Population Data Sheet estimates that 42 percent of the population are under 15 and just 3 percent is over 65 percent, p. 6.
6. *NCB Economist.* "Gulf Population and Labour Force Structure." Economic and Financial Publication Issued by the Economics Department of the National Commercial Bank. Issue no. 4, Vol. 5 (June-July 1995), p. 3.
7. Ibid., p. 5.
8. Ibid., p. 3.
9. The World Bank, World Tables.
10. *The Financial Times,* December 22, 1993.
11. See, for example, Catherine Caufield, *Masters of Illusion: The World Bank and the Poverty of Nations* (London: Macmillan, 1997).
12. *The NCB Economist* January/February, 1999, p. 3.
13. Cyril and Christine Simmons, "Personal and Moral Adolescent Values in England and Saudi Arabia," *Journal of Moral Education,* vol. 23, no. 1, 1994.
14. F. Gregory Gause III, "The Middle East: A Crucial Moment," *The Washington Quarterly,* Winter 1997, vol. 20, no. 1, pp. 145–65.
15. Mordechai Abir, *Saudi Arabia in the Oil Era: Regime and Elites: Conflict and Collaboration* (London: Croom Helm, 1988), p. 170.
16. *Saudi Development and Training Company Ltd.,* July 6, 1996.
17. "Saudi Arabia, Special Report," *Middle East Economic Digest (MEED),* vol. 39, no. 10, March 10, 1995, p. 40.
18. *Saudi Development and Training Co.*
19. See World Population Data Sheet, ibid, p. 6.
20. Institute of International Finance, Washington, D.C., August 11, 1994 and World Bank, *World Tables,* 1994; also *MEED Special Report, Saudi Arabia, MEED,* vol. 40, no. 14, April 5, 1996, p. 56, and Saudi Arabia, *MEED,* vol. 39, no. 10, March 10, 1995, p. 40.
21. *The Saudi British Bank, The HSBC Group: Business Profile Series,* Saudi Arabia, sixth edition, Third Quarter, 1994, p. 15.
22. The Middle East Executive Reports, vol. 5, no. 5, 1982, p. 22.

CHAPTER 9

THE COMING GENERATION IN IRAN
Challenges and Opportunities

MOHAMMAD HADI SEMATI

INTRODUCTION

Great social revolutions, though rare in history, leave important marks on social and political structures as well as people's mindsets. The Islamic revolution in Iran is one of those cases in which a clear transformation took place in most aspects of life and its structural impacts cannot be overlooked. The collapse of the shah's regime in 1979 and the establishment of the Islamic Republic in Iran set a revolutionary cycle in motion. Protest movements normally have life cycles of their own, and different cycles tend to exhibit both continuity and change.[1] Continuity arises from underlying ideals and revolutionary activism, which is reflected in committed cadres and supporters of the movement; change takes place because of new members or supporters who embark on redefining original goals and who come up with new objectives for the movement. The Iranian revolution is still in the process of unfolding, which makes it quite difficult to study. Despite the remarkable resiliency of the revolution to stand against all odds, external and internal, with little evident change in course and nature, I argue that one can actually detect a considerable degree of innovation in adjusting to new circumstances or cycles.

Scholars have mostly tried to explain the causes of the revolution while policymakers have had a hard time coping with its impact. Few studies have dealt with the outcome of the revolution, and no successful attempt, to the best of my knowledge, has been made in predicting its future direction. Prediction is always a risky endeavor in the social sciences and even more hazardous when dealing with the Iranian case. The purpose of this paper is to underline and discuss change and continuity in the Islamic revolution of Iran. I will analyze the changing trajectory of the revolution in light of new developments since the election of President Mohammad Khatami in 1997. I argue that despite retaining some major ideals, the revolution is entering a new cycle characterized by the formation of new collective identities and aspirations and a break with the past. More specifically, I will attempt to explain the internal dynamics of the new cycle and general characteristics of the generation that functions as the agent of the present cycle.[2]

A NEW SOCIAL MOVEMENT

The landslide election of President Mohammad Khatami in May 1997 caught the world by surprise. It was a shock also to longtime observers of politics inside Iran and was a turning point in Iran's contemporary history. A fairly democratic and competitive electoral process brought to power a marginal candidate whose chances looked slim just a week before the election. What happened? What were the social forces behind this astonishing victory? The May election was indeed fueled by a new social movement in many respects similar to other new social movements across the world. This movement is a new cycle in the history of the Iranian revolution, which has its own dynamics and new constituencies and leaders. The election was for change and supporters of the movement opted for modest goals within the framework of the constitution. What made this cycle a new one and different from the previous phases of the revolutionary process?

First, it is a movement that advocates specific and concrete issues. The central theme of Khatami's campaign was civil society and the rule of law. It was the primacy of these issues that set this movement apart from previous movements which had aimed at cataclysmic and full-fledged social reorganization. Contrary to other cycles of protest, this time Khatami used a single overarching issue, namely political development, to galvanize popular sentiment. It was a master framework with which different social groups could identify, at least partly, and act accordingly. In other words, a sense of ambiguity in the movement's aspirations made it possible for various forces to place their hopes in it. The framework was broad and participatory enough that actors of the new generation could contextualize it for collective action.

Second, in sharp contrast to old-time revolutionary struggle, reformism and gradualism became the general tactical guidelines of political life. The art of bargaining and compromise is increasingly manifest in the day-to-day give and take of politics. Shifting alliances and coalition formation among the elite are signs of a tacit understanding of the significance of consensus formation for policy advocacy. In the words of one observer, "It is time to be revolutionary in goals but not means." This indicates the widespread feeling that one could still be committed to the ideals of the revolution by pursuing reformist strategy. The subsiding of revolutionary slogans and the routinization of everyday politics, though, should not be exaggerated. A conflicting trend could emerge, and to some extent has already revealed itself, which could lead to further polarization of factional politics and society at large. Revolutionary mobilization from above could be used again to stem the tide of reform.

Third is the centrality of dialogue in settling disputes among competing factions. Nowadays the catchphrases of every intellectual circle and many papers and periodicals are *dialogue* and *discourse*. This should not come as a surprise from a movement whose essential platform is civil society. Dialogue, although not totally absent in Iranian history, is becoming harder to neglect as the principal mode of communication. The other side of the coin is tolerance, which is the common theme in many of Khatami's speeches. The revolutionary absolutism of the previous cycle is crumbling and becoming increasingly harder to sustain. Tolerance is not foreign to Islamic culture, but reconfiguring it for the modern age and in a turbulent world full of uncertainties is not an easy and painless process. Nonetheless, despite resistance from traditional quarters and in spite of genuine fear and concern on the part of many who are trying to cope with rapid changes in the world, tolerance is becoming an issue played out in public discourse. Interestingly enough, the debate is extended to areas rarely heard before, including religion itself. The ideas of "religious pluralism" and "true paths" are examples of the growing awareness of and concern for the built-in contradictions in an Islamic state.

The fourth difference between old and new movements is the conception of the "enemy," or fundamentally how we define ourselves relative to others. "Sameness" and "otherness" is not as sharply and antagonistically delineated as before. This is virtually a new phenomenon in post-revolutionary Iranian society. There is a tendency among movement participants not to look at their opponents as evil personified and themselves as the absolute truth and the symbol of virtue. Khatami is preaching about tolerance and diversity and genuinely building a generation of devotees whose trademark will be pluralism and tolerance. Accepting a plurality of ideas and even opposing discourses underlies the civil society movement. In other words, the time of black-and-white, right-and-wrong, and good-and-evil politics is over. A note of caution is in order at this point. One should not forget that many actively involved in the reform movement might have joined it out of political expediency or that still others will change and resume the old practices as time passes. Here I am referring to a general tendency that may be reversed.

Last but not least is the movement's constituency and social base. It was quite clear by the election results that supporters of Khatami came from diverse backgrounds. The traditional social cleavages of class, rural/urban, young/old, and many other similar dichotomies were not at work in this cycle. Khatami's support cut across major social cleavages, which put him in a unique position with a strong popular mandate. However, two of the social groups without whose support such a result would not have been achieved deserve special attention, and they are the youth and women. It is precisely from these groups that Khatami and the civil society movement draw their strength. The latter group played a pivotal role in Khatami's triumph, but its impact is very limited for it lacks the institutional and legal power on the one hand and a sense of collective identity on the other. The new political momentum has accelerated the germination of a new political consciousness among women. This last feature has serious implications for the trajectory of the revolution in the future. The social composition of the electorate and massive outpouring of sympathy for Khatami were signs of changing political fields. The agents of change will be the new generation born after or right before the revolution (1978–79). It is thus essential to scrutinize in more detail the nature of this evolving army of voters who will play an indisputable role in political mobilization for years to come. We will do so after a cautionary note on the specificity of the new social movement in Iran.

The emerging discourse and practice of civil society promulgated by the new generation of reformers should be understood in the specific context of the Iranian experience with social and political change. The features of the new movement outlined above reveal a sharp contrast with new social movements in the Western world. The conflict in the Iranian case is primarily within the polity rather than civil society, and major protagonists seem to be speaking for a constituency that is not necessarily in the conflict, at least directly. Therefore, one must not mistake the "civil movement" in Iran for the feature of a highly developed industrial and affluent society. It is indeed a political contestation fought at the top and it finds resonance in civil society. The resistance to reform by some among the elite and the insistence of others to change the political equation in favor of a more transparent and open polity shape the nature and form of conflict. While discord and bargaining take place at the top, growing pressure is mounting from below, and one could make a good case that the evolving discourse of rights and republicanism will spill over to the civil society. The segmented polity along with multiple separation of powers built into the constitution of the Islamic Republic of Iran help further to institutionalize conflict among contenders.

THE POLITICS OF DEMOGRAPHY

UNESCO has estimated that in the year 2000 the world population of the age group of 15 to 24 reached 1.28 billion, with Iran among the top contributors to this global trend. Relative to total population growth, the share of age group 15 to 24 has been the largest. Over the last four decades, the total population has increased 3.6 times while the youth category (15 to 24) soared 4.8 times. Proportionately the youth population has increased from 15.6 to 20.9 percent. If one adds the percentage of age group 11 to 14 years, the proportion reaches nearly 32.8 percent. Table 9.1 shows the general demographic change from 1956 to 1998 and the relative share of youngsters between the ages of 15 and 24.

Table 9.1 Demographic Change in Iran, 1956–1998 (in thousands)

	1956	*1966*	*1976*	*1986*	*1991*	*1998**
Total population	18,755	25,079	33,708	49,445	55,473	67,331
Age group (12–24)	2,918	3,811	6,393	9,386	10,856	14,050
% of total	15.6	15.2	19	19	19.6	20.9

Note: *Predicted estimate of 1998 is based on data used in the Second Development Plan (1994–1998), "Macro Models for Predicting Demographic Change," Budget and Plan Organization.
Source: Census data of various years published by statistical center of Iran.

The trend shown in table 9.1 is continuing, and there seems to be no reversal or slow-down in the near future. A closer look at the projected population growth over the next decade makes clear that the issue will be critical for the general socioeconomic development. It is evident in table 9.2 that the percentage of the youth (15 to 24) in the total population will be nearly 24 percent in 2006. This is even more alarming if one takes into account the undesirable rate of economic growth projected in the next few years.

Table 9.2 Projected Population in 2006 by Age and Sex

Age Group	Male and Female	Male	Female
10–14	6,263,817	3,217,303	3,046,514
15–19	8,419,651	4,291,657	4,127,994
20–24	8,990,293	4,572,840	4,417,453
Total population	71,726,368	36,384,276	35,342,096

Source: Compiled from "The Study of Labor Market Condition and Its Predicted Changes in the Decade of 1996–2006." Plan and Budget Organization, Office of Macroeconomics, February 1997.

Demographic change in and of itself may not be a prelude to social change.[3] It could be a precursor to change if combined with other structural changes. One such change is how the population dynamics is played out in the context of the trend toward urbanization. Tables 9.3 and 9.4 illustrate the changing urban population between 1956 and 1998, and the increasing number of youth over these years.

Table 9.3 Change of Urban Population, 1956–1998 (in thousands)

	1956	1966	1976	1986	1991	1998
Total urban population	5,935	9,795	15,855	26,845	31,837	38,678
% of total population	31.7	39.1	47	54.3	57.4	57.4

Source: Ibid.

Table 9.4 Urban Population Change for Age Group 15–24, 1956–1998 (in thousands)

	1956	1966	1976	1986	1991	1998*
Number	1,079	1,725	3,446	5,265	6,058	7,896

Note: *Estimated based on census date of 1991.
Source: Ibid.

These figures indicate that the urban population has increased 4.5 times while the youth component has gone up 7.3 times. This becomes alarming when gauged by employment opportunities. Table 9.5 shows the unemployment picture among urban youth aged 15 to 24 between 1956 and 1998, and table 9.6 compares the general unemployment of age group 15 to 24 and other categories. The number of unemployed youth in urban areas has increased 1,350 percent in four decades, and the prospect for improvement is very low at best.

Thus, based on the preceding tables, there should be little doubt that Iranian society will get younger and younger over the next decade. Could this demographic change produce pressures undermining stability? One cannot downplay the prominence of demographic transition for sociopolitical processes. What could these shifts mean? How is this general population dynamic going to influence the future of Iran? In the following pages

Table 9.5 Change of Urban Population for Unemployed Youth (in thousands)

	1956	1966	1976	1986	1991	1998*
Number	169	374	915	1,414	1,653	2,268

Note: *1998 figure is estimated based on 1991 statistics.
Source: Ibid.

Table 9.6 Number of Employed and Unemployed for Age Group 15 to 24 and Other Age
Groups

	Male and Female			Male		
	Employed	Unemployed	% of Unemployed	Employed	Unemployed	% of Unemployed
15–24	3,164	883	21.8	2,765	625	18.4
Other ages	9,933	757	7.1	9,100	617	6.3

Source: Ibid.

I will try to deal with these issues and suggest some insights into the possible challenges
facing Iran in the future.

POLITICAL ECONOMY OF THE YOUTH

A quantitative change of population and shift in the composition of the youth could certainly put pressure on government institutions and available resources. But this is just
one side of the story. Even more troublesome is the changing structure of the youth population. While the number of young people is increasing, contrary to previous generations, the demand for employment among them is also increasing. Traditionally many
people in the 15 to 24–year-old category were dependent on their parents, thereby reducing strain on the labor market. Economic imperatives and changing value structures
will increasingly encourage the younger population to search for employment, and if
economic growth and job creation do not match that upward trend, we could run into
severe social dislocations.

At the same time, educational chances for all age categories are improving hence
making the labor force more skilled and conscious of its destiny. This is particularly important as far as women are concerned. Since women were traditionally less active as a
part of the labor force and less educated, development policies were not much concerned about their role. Women are now being educated in larger numbers and will definitely be a crucial and active force in the youth population. Taking into account the
increasing organizational strength of women's activism, I expect to see a more unified
youth population regardless of gender, particularly when facing common problems. In
other words, a youth population more educated, and certainly less dependent on traditional household structure, could create potential crises if other sociopolitical ingredi-
ents are present and their demands are not met.

Concentration of the youth population in urban centers is one of the most serious
implications of migration from rural to urban areas. Despite a decreasing rate of migration from rural areas, there is still a strong willingness to choose the attractive city life.
The city can provide numerous opportunities and a vast array of resources for an ambitious young man that would hardly be available in the villages and small towns. Moreover, the huge historical gap between rural and urban areas does not exist anymore.
Educational infrastructures, both at secondary and college levels, are rapidly reaching
even rural areas. Nonetheless, the city life has given and will give the youth a far better
chance to move up the ladder of social mobility. As more youth move to the city, the
collective identity based on similar experiences and lifestyles could become a frame for

action. Therefore, urbanization, along with the major demographic shift that is taking place in Iran, are among macroprocesses to watch.

What are the cultural underpinnings of this new generation of youth? How does it perceive itself? Is there a sharp distinction between this group and its predecessor as far as value structures are concerned? At one level, the coming generation of youth in Iran, as in any other transitional society, faces serious identity questions. For one thing, the free flow of information keeps it informed about the world. Iran has always been fairly open when it comes to information exchanges, notwithstanding certain restrictions maintained by the government. Information technology, such as the Internet, is gradually but surely infiltrating all walks of life, and in the next five to ten years people will be more in touch with their peers outside their home country than any other period in history.

This brings us to the issue of value changes in the age of the global communication revolution. It is getting harder to resist powerful images and symbols produced by alien cultures. Although a great number of young people will resist changes forced upon them, a considerable portion of this generation will share, at least partly, the world-view of its counterpart outside Iran. In other words, one can see the "relativization of reference groups" when looking at the youngsters' values, norms, and behavior. Relativization, though, does not mean total submission to the pressure exerted from outside.[4] On the contrary, there is a greater sense of reflexivity among the youth in the encounter with postmodern conditions. However, there is no denial of reciprocity in shaping new identities or reconstructing old ones. In a recent study, over 50 percent of the youngsters of Tehran who were surveyed believed that their parents do not understand them. According to the same study, over 80 percent believed that society had forgotten them. Both of these sentiments underscore the changing position of traditional reference groups and a feeling of frustration over societal responses to the problems of youth. Here is why the election of President Khatami assumes a greater significance: Khatami has become a symbol of hope and optimism for a generation whose connection to the past and reliance on the future are both somewhat weak.

An energized youth population will create both opportunities and challenges for the government. As stated earlier, major demographic changes could have a serious impact on political institutions, particularly in the age of information explosion. It seems that a motivated and politically conscious generation can create crises if institutional structures responsible for the distribution of values (goods and power) fail to accommodate some of its demands. Groups as social categories simply have common characteristics and may pursue even common interests. When they become conscious of their interests and form a collective identity, they could make claims on the state. Indications like the reactivation of campus politics and more vocal youth representation throughout the country, given emerging "transnational power networks," are signs of evolving solidarity structures.[5] Demands for political participation and economic prosperity are frequently heard from this new generation, and the government is trying hard to be responsive, while no one is suggesting that the changing composition of the population will facilitate social change. It is therefore necessary to take a look at possible transformations in other social groups or agents.

ELITE TRANSFORMATION

Aside from changes stemming from generation shift, certain mutations and reorientations are apparent at the elite level. I take a broad conception of elite to include individuals in and outside the polity. There are two mechanisms of new recruitment and conversion that are responsible for changing elite composition. As young and newly educated professionals are recruited, they bring with them new blood and somewhat new ideas. New members are gradually incorporated into state apparatuses leading to potential realignments. Notwithstanding their power considerations, new recruits tend to be familiar with global trends and time-space imperatives.

Secondly, a conversion process seems to be at work as well. Having gone through tumultuous periods ever since the victory of the revolution, a growing number of elite perceive the world differently or more objectively. Pragmatism is the result of maturity and experience. Some may quarrel with this conception of conversion but empirical records in the history of social movements and revolutions are testimony to the argument advanced in this paper. Part of the conversion is the result of election impact and other events of the same nature. Even hard-core revolutionaries eventually change course or at least become sensitive to career and family pressures. Conversion, however painful it may be to committed activists, is a fact in the life span of revolutionary movements and cannot be ignored.

An interesting consequence of the mechanisms I have just discussed is worth mentioning. We will witness a greater degree of fluidity in political identification, which in turn will make alliance shifts less difficult for the elite. In other words, mid-level managers and professionals will more frequently get involved in changing partisan affiliation. This is not to ignore the parallel and more macro societal trend toward stronger partisan identification, one that pushes a vast number of politicized masses to choose sides in the political spectrum. People are becoming more conscious of their political orientation and feel freer to align themselves with a specific faction. These two contradictory trends will eventually be resolved in favor of a more sharply divided and less blurred political landscape. We have already seen the beginning of this trend.

Continuous economic crises will eventually compel the elite to take coalition building and consensus formation more seriously. As they are confronted by the realities of modern power politics, the need for strategy, resources, and above all allies will be demonstrated. This could be the introductory step toward a politics of which compromise is an important element. The experience through which Iran is going may not be exactly similar to that of some other countries but the underlying logic seems to be the same. "In countries such as Algeria, Jordan, Tunisia, and Morocco, by the late 1980s the acute financial crisis of the state put the politics of consensus and coalition building on the political agenda, albeit in limited and manipulated forms."[6] Coherent state policy in times of acute crisis dictates a tacit political agreement on the basis of which different factions can accommodate each other. The parameters of consensus building and factional politics are changing in the context of an evolving discourse of compromise. Compromise and bargaining are alien concepts to Iranian political culture, and any development in this regard should be welcomed. Khatami's election and the civil society movement that followed it have been instrumental in reinforcing compromise as a value not to be despised. Consequently we are witnessing a process through which the elite feels obliged to operate by the rules of the game set by President Khatami.

After Khatami came to power, the public benefited immensely from the publication of numerous periodicals that represented diverse political and philosophical persuasions. The titles and areas included politics, philosophy, religion, art, and communication. New magazines and newspapers mushroomed at the national as well as local level, and the prolific marketplace of ideas created a vibrant intellectual atmosphere that has been almost unknown in recent Iranian history. The intellectual discourse was an enriching experience from which fundamental questions pertaining to the future of Iranian society were being raised. Although many publications were subsequently closed, the soul-searching climate that emanated from the exchanges between these publications is a vital step toward authenticity. The quest for authenticity is providing a sense of self-confidence among the elite and intellectuals. This is an arena where civil society is being further consolidated and intellectuals are playing the leading role.

The present debates signify a discernible shift in the outlook of the intellectual community compared to previous generations of intellectuals.[7] First, the new generation is departing from a simplistic categorization of human experience and is showing great competence in coping with diversity and plurality of ideas. Openness to new ideas from other cultures and other philosophical traditions and a desire to be synthetic in formulating ideas is fairly new among Iranian intellectuals.

Secondly, the new intellectual community is well versed in Western social theory and cutting-edge research in the social sciences and humanities. This capability has given it a chance to be involved in a constructive dialogue with the Western world. Last but not least, the present generation seems to be reflecting upon the past while looking to the future. In other words, from religious to secular intellectuals, an inclination to be attentive to the forces of tradition is undoubtedly present. A generational shift in the intellectual community has proven to be crucial to any social and political change in Iran; once again, such a shift is in sight, and people have high hopes from it.

CONCLUSION

What seems to be taking place in Iran is indicative of fundamental structural changes that will have profound social and political impacts both internally and externally. Although identifiable changes beneath the surface can be observed, all are in a dynamic, fluid, and quite possibly reversible phase. Our political-generations approach suggests that a tangible shift is occurring for the first time in post-revolutionary society and that it is not restricted to demographic dynamics. It goes beyond mere population shift and will influence the power elite and intellectuals, thereby molding state-society relations. Development imperatives will make the state retreat even further from economic activities, which will pave the way for the politically conscious new generation to articulate its demands and challenge the state. The rapidly expanding middle class will find itself more and more allied with Khatami and his reform policy.[8] Certainly the demands of this growing educated class and the society at large will strain the resource capability of the government and increase the likelihood of clashes between these conflicting forces. Nonetheless, the trend seems to be unavoidable, and the avalanche of new demands can be halted briefly but not forever.

Fortunately, the Islamic Republic of Iran has demonstrated a remarkable maturity in dealing with these intense pressures. Two distinct but related processes are at work. At the top, the elite is involved in institutional building and bargaining, and at the bottom people are exerting pressure and constantly making new claims. The interplay of these two trends and the consolidation of a stronger republicanism are promising signs of a brighter future.

NOTES

1. Davis S. Mayer, "Protest Cycles and Political Process," *Political Research Quarterly,* vol. 46 (1993).

2. Karl Mannheim, "The Problem of Generations," in *Essays on the Sociology of Knowledge,* ed. P. Kecskemeti (London: Routledge and Kegan Paul, [1928] 1952), pp. 276–332.

3. See the monumental work of Jack A. Goldstone, *Revolution and Rebellion in the Early Modern World* (Berkeley: University of California Press, 1991).

4. Roland Robertson, *Globalization: Social Theory and Global Culture* (London: Routledge, 1992), pp.25–31.

5. Peter Waterman, "A New Worldview: Globalization, Civil Society, and Solidarity," in Sandra Braman and Annabelle Sreberny-Mohammadi, eds., *Globalization, Communication and Transnational Civil Society* (Cresskill, NJ: Hampton Press, 1996), pp. 37–61.

6. Manochehr Dorraj, "State Petroleum and Democratization in the Middle East and North Africa," in Manochehr Dorraj, ed., *The Changing Political Economy of the Third World* (Boulder: Lynne Reinner Publishers, 1995).

7. A brief but succinct analysis of the state of the intellectual field in Iran can be found in Ahmad Naraghi, "On Religious Intellectualism," *Rahe Nov* (New Path), vol. 1, no. 9 (1998).

8. The middle class is increasingly looking for a political voice, and apparently Khatami is going to be the spokesman of the emerging middle class. For a discussion of the new class structure, see Hossein Bashirieh, "Presidential Election of 1997 from a Class Struggle Perspective," *Rahe Nov* (New Path), vol. 1, no. 8 (1998).

CHAPTER 10

MUTUAL REALITIES, PERCEPTIONS, AND IMPEDIMENTS BETWEEN THE GCC STATES AND IRAN

ABDULLAH K. ALSHAYJI

INTRODUCTION

A rabs and Iranians live in the same region and share the same history, geography, religion, and fate, yet sectarian differences, culture, politics, and ethnicity separate them and contribute in no small measure to creating a wall of mistrust and contention stretching back over a thousand years. These factors do not help in bridging the gap for the two distinct races to assimilate, integrate and cohabit peacefully. It is true that Iran in recent years, mainly following the election of President Khatami in 1997, has followed a moderately pragmatic trend in its foreign policy, in a region that is undergoing major transition. Iran has broken out of its isolation and achieved rapprochement with European countries, and the prospect of better relations with the United States lies ahead.

Nevertheless, Iran continues to be misunderstood and demonized as a threat to its Arab neighbors and as a rogue state or nation of concern to the Americans. Is it powerful and resurgent, or weak and defiant? For generations, whether it was under the shah or the clerical ayatollahs, a host of differences, perceptions, and misperceptions have kept the two sides at arms' length. Iran follows the minority Shi'i sect of Islam, although perhaps half of its population is either not ethnically Persian or Persian speaking, which compounds its nationalist dilemma. Iran's neighbors in the littoral states, on the other hand, are by and large Arab and Sunni Muslims.

Iran of late has been patching up its long feud with the Saudis and the Kuwaitis and even going as far as promoting serious rapprochement with the Egyptians and entertaining a quasi axis with American regional allies, such as Egypt and Turkey. This Iranian change of course toward pragmatism and détente has been well received and embraced by the Gulf Cooperation Council (GCC) countries, which include Bahrain, Qatar, Oman, Saudi Arabia, Kuwait, and the UAE. Historically, the relationship between the two sides has been fraught with animosity, rivalry, and distrust.

The fragility and volatility of the Gulf region are well recognized. This area has witnessed two devastating wars in the last two decades and now relies on an external security regime provided by the United States. This regime excludes the two major powers in the region, Iran (the most populous state) and Iraq (the second most populous). Such a system is subject to instability and lacks the needed balance of power that provides stability from within. The outside presence is not a lasting formula and substitute for a long-term, indigenous, home-grown security system that would include Iraq and Iran, the two "rogue" states. Before such a scenario can come to fruition, however, Iraq has to be completely transformed into a state that can live with its neighbors and Iran has to refrain from mischief and sustain its reformist trend. It has to be a system of full incorporation and inclusion rather than exclusion. The emphasis has to be on economic reform and political openings, rather than on militarization and brinkmanship politics. The Gulf also must be declared a region free of all weapons of mass destruction. These would be the first genuine confidence-building measures that would reduce tension and change the security and the political landscape of the Gulf.

The Gulf region is a vital area of international significance not only because of its huge oil reserves, but also because it contains the birthplace of Islam. Regional powers have fought for influence and hegemony there, including Iran under both the shah and the Islamic Republic, and Iraq under Saddam Hussein. The struggle for dominance by the strongest and largest regional states over the peripheral smaller ones is a continuing factor, as is the military might and de facto permanent presence of the United States.

Oil, the competition for regional hegemony, and international efforts to assure security by manipulating the major powers in the region have all contributed to the instability that has been a hallmark of Gulf politics. These factors plus the Iranian revolution generated intense suspicion on the Arabian side of the Gulf toward Iran, its politics, its real intentions, and hidden agenda. Coupled with the absence of accountability and democratic practices in the larger Gulf countries, these conditions have produced a region that is fragile, easily manipulated, and prone to instability.

As a major regional power, Iran plays a pivotal role in the politics of the Middle East and beyond—from countering Russian influence in the southern Caucasus to standing up to Israel, allying itself with China, or even continuing its inherited role from the shah's regime as the guardian of the Gulf. From a GCC perspective, Iran continues to assume the mantle of a tireless crusader fulfilling the ideological principles of the Islamic revolution. Iran mixes ideology with realpolitik and sometimes appears to be using bullying and menacing tactics to intimidate and cajole others to toe the line. At the same time, Iran is experiencing domestic upheaval, polarization, and internal battles among the reformist-pragmatist camp, led by President Khatami, who is ranged against a clique of hardline clerics and revolutionaries bent on derailing the reformist march. Their opposition handicaps the president's conduct in foreign and domestic policies.

With this background, this paper will highlight the perceptions and the misperceptions that characterize the GCC-Iran relationship. It will discuss the macro and geopolitical factors of the relationship as well as the bilateral realities that contribute to the negative images and perceptions that the Iranians have about the Arabs and vice versa, in all their historical, sectarian, cultural, and power dimensions. This paper argues that there is not a unified GCC relationship with Iran, but rather there are two distinct views among the GCC states. The chapter will assess the current rapprochement underway between Iran and most of the GCC states, especially Saudi Arabia, and the ongoing flirtation between the Americans and the Iranians and its wider impact on the perceptions and geopolitics of the region. It will examine whether the pragmatic approach espoused by Iran is a lasting trend or is necessitated by other factors, and will highlight the impediments facing a GCC policy of inclusion vis-à-vis Iran. Moreover, the paper will discuss the geopolitical impact on the future relationship. This includes the United States' negative role in attempting to exploit and capitalize on the atmosphere of rivalry and distrust that prevails in the region for its own interest. The United States indeed represents one of the major hurdles for a full-blown rapprochement to become a reality. The study concludes with some suggestions and recommendations for both sides in order to reduce the distrust and implement some confidence-building measures to encourage coexistence and cooperation in the new millennium.

THE COMPLEXITY OF THE RELATIONSHIP: MACRO FACTORS

Although the Arabs on the western shore of the Gulf share with their Iranian neighbors religious and cultural affinity and a dependence upon the same commodities (oil and gas), we see that these very elements are not unifying factors, but rather divisive ones. The problematic Arab/Persian–Sunni/Shi'i divide and competition are the major cause for much under-the-surface tension and mistrust, factors that will be referred to as the macro factors. These factors contribute to mutual misperceptions over issues such as nationalism, religion, ideology, ethnicity, and oil. I will first discuss historical and cultural competition and issues, including mutual ignorance between Arabs and Iranians, as evidenced by the present lack of think tanks, strategic centers, and linguistic institutions to narrow the gap between the two sides. The focus will then shift to security issues such as the geopolitical competition, conflicting Iranian foreign and security policies, and the alteration of accommodation and confrontation that at times leads Iran to take a proprietary view toward the smaller Arab states in the Gulf. This hegemonic attitude, and inconsistent policies contributes a great deal to maintaining the Arabs' genuine impression of Iran as a power that should be watched, and one that has not changed much under the Islamic revolution or even after President Khatami assumed the presidency.

HISTORY AND NATIONALISM: ARAB VS. 'AJAM

I agree that the relationship between Iran and her neighbors in the Gulf is different from Iran's relations with the other Arab countries, as noted by Bijan Khajehpour-Khoei in his chapter "Mutual Perceptions in the Persian Gulf Region: An Iranian Perspective."[1] This is due mainly to geographical proximity and human migrations, as well as an economic relationship, whether it is in the oil sector or the re-export trade with Dubai. Additionally, there is the presence of a huge Iranian expatriate work force in all of the GCC states. All these elements contribute to create misperceptions.

Since the days of the Arab conquest of Persia in the seventh century, the relationship between the two culturally distinct peoples has witnessed much rivalry. While acknowledging the distinct Persian contribution to Islamic culture and civilization, the fact is that some Persians looked down on the bedouin Arabs at that early stage. Some Iranians lamented that the "backward" Arabs who conquered Persia and spread Islam degraded the glorious pre-Islamic Persian civilization. This attitude persisted, and the shah's patronizing policies failed to foster any warmth or reconciliation either with the small littoral states of the Gulf or the wider Arab world.

From an Arab perspective, the Persian mentality is influenced by strong nationalistic sentiment wrapped in chauvinistic Aryan feelings which the shah manipulated and fostered in the Iranian psyche. One of the first orders of business of Reza Shah when he assumed power in the 1920s was to "cleanse" the Persian language of Arabic words. This anti-Arab trend in the Pahlavi dynasty continued for 60 years.[2]

RELIGION: SUNNI MAJORITY VS. SHIʻI MINORITY

One would think that religion would play a unifying role between Arabs and Iranians, but on the contrary it has been a divisive force. One cannot fathom the impact of Islam on Iran as a religion and as a way of life and politics if one does not understand Shiʻism and its feeling of grievance and victimization and persecution since the death of Imam Hussein, the grandson of the prophet Mohammad, in the seventh century at the hands of Sunnis.

As acknowledged by an Iranian scholar,

Iran, a Shiʻi state (though overall the Shiʻis only account for some 15 percent of Islamic adherents), is a peculiarity in Islam, and this gives Iran's actions a special flavor. Iran's claims to represent Islam are not so readily entertained by other Sunni Muslim states. Indeed some, like the Wahhabi Saudis, consider Shiism at best as a heterodox sect. The result is that when it comes to universal Islamic issues such as Palestine, Iran has to try harder. The Shiʻi factor may also account for Iran's cultivation of a sense of victimization, or martyr complex. Its leaders have found it congenial to point to Iran's isolation, claiming that it is meritorious and desirable.[3]

One cannot understand Iran without first comprehending "Al'tashiyooh" Shiʻism as a minority sect and political movement, according to Abdullah Al-Naffisi, the former chairman of the political science department at Kuwait University. Al-Naffisi argues that one has to understand Shiʻism (which is the official Iranian religion, according to the Iranian constitution) both as an Islamic sect and as a political movement. Without that, one cannot fully appreciate and comprehend the grievances and ideological behavior that have been the driving force behind it over the last thousand years.[4] Article 152 of the Iranian constitution states that Iran's foreign policy is based on the "defense of the rights of all Muslims,"[5] i.e., that Iran attempts to rectify the past injustice and to appoint itself as the crusader and the champion of the *mostazafin*, the meek and the downtrodden.

One cannot underestimate the divisive impact of the religious divergence between Iran and its mainly Sunni Arab neighbors in the Gulf, especially since the Islamic revolution presented Iran as the champion of Islamic causes. Moreover, the revolution also adopted an anti-monarchical rhetoric of deposing the Gulf monarchies and "cleansing" the region. The Islamic revolution is thus a major ideological competitor to Saudi Arabia, the country that boasts the two holiest shrines in Islam, Mecca and Medina. (The low point of this rivalry occurred in 1987, when more than 400 Iranian pilgrims were killed during the Hajj after conducting political demonstrations. In Sunni Islam, the Hajj is a spiritual journey to cleanse one's soul and not to get involved in any political demonstrations, which the Iranians regularly conduct. The subsequent reaction to that massacre was the ransacking of the Saudi embassy in Tehran and the cutting off of relations between Iran and Saudi Arabia for years.)

The election of President Khatami and his pragmatic, reformist approach toward the littoral states in the Gulf, which culminated in his historic visit to Saudi Arabia in May 1999, led to a rapid rapprochement between the two powerful regional actors. In addition, for three years beginning in December 1997, Iran served as chairman of the Organization of the Islamic Conference, an alliance of 55 Muslim states. This helped to tone down the rhetoric and project a gentler image of Iran. Officials of the Gulf monarchies, who were once suspicious of Iranian revolutionary mischief, flocked to Iran to attend the 1997 summit. (What gave that occasion great impact was that it came on the heels of an almost-unanimous boycott of the U.S.-sponsored MENA summit in Qatar a few weeks before.) This atmosphere of détente between the two rival camps of Islam represented by the Saudis and the Iranians was in direct contrast to the derogatory statements made by the Iranians accusing the Saudis and the other monarchies in the Gulf of representing "Islam al-rasmi" (official Islam or Americanized Islam) vs. the true real Islam which is represented by the Iranians. Thus, the Iranians are no longer—or so the Arabs hope—representing themselves as the only true Muslims and creating an acrimonious atmosphere of bickering and mistrust.

CULTURAL DIFFERENCES AND MUTUAL IGNORANCE

Winston Churchill once described Russia as "a riddle wrapped in a mystery inside an enigma." For many Arabs in the GCC states and the wider Arab world, this applies to Iran. For them, Iran resembles an intricate, sophisticated Persian rug, with its complex designs and elaborate colors. The Persian carpet by itself speaks volumes about the Persian personality—its endurance, its patience, its glorious past, and its complexity. No wonder it is hard to understand the Persians.

One of the main reasons for the misunderstanding between Arabs and Iranians is the lack of ongoing communications, travel, debates, exchanges of scholars, and learning of languages. A sense of mistrust was stoked on the one hand by the shah's demonizing and belittling of Arabs and on the other by a devastating war launched by an Arab country, Iraq, against Iran in the early years of the revolution.

Serious academic publications in the Arab world about Iran are few and far between. A scholar who wants to conduct research on Iran will spend half his time looking for books and data. There are some exceptions, however. A symposium entitled "Arab-Iran Relations: Present Trends and Future Prospects," which was held in Doha, Qatar, in 1995 produced a major volume.[6] The Iranians, for their part, hold an annual conference sponsored by the Iranian foreign ministry at the Institute for Political and International Studies, which held its eleventh meeting in January 2001. The writer has attended several of these conferences and can attest to their importance as a mechanism in breaking down the wall of mistrust and ignorance.

What contributes more to negative mutual perceptions between Arabs and Iranians are the impediments represented by the lack of mastering each other's language, despite the fact that Arabic is a major influence on Persian. The language of communication when Arabs and Iranians meet and discuss issues is mainly English. In addition, the main source for each side to learn more about the other has been for a long time the Western media.

Another factor that prevents the Arabs from fully embracing their Iranian neighbors is the power struggle taking place there, and the perception that the Khatami administration is under siege by hardline clerics. It remains to be seen if Khatami will be the

Mikhail Gorbachev of Iran and open up the political system. But he has already begun to lead the nation down a path that seems inevitable.

The negative image the Western media has fostered of Iran since the revolution has left a lasting impression, and contributes to the stereotypes of Iranians in Arab minds. Dr. Abdullah Al-Naffisi has warned how that media shapes and influences the Arabs' perceptions of Iran and probably Iranians' perceptions of the Arabs, at least within the intellectual community that has access to the Western media.[7] The Iranian perception of the Arabs is a stereotype of bedouins, the backward conquerors, and now pawns in the hand of the "Great Satan" who conspires against the Islamic Republic of Iran and appeases Israel. Moreover, the Iranians' perception of the Arabs is that they despise and do not appreciate Persian civilization. All of this contributes greatly to distort one's picture of the other.[8]

THE GULF: ARABIAN OR PERSIAN OR AMERICAN?

One of the most contentious issues from an Arab perspective is the Iranians' insistence on naming the body of water that divides them the "Persian Gulf." From an Arab perspective, this demonstrates the arrogance and hidden agenda for dominance that the Iranians harbor toward them. The Arabs are quick to point out that eight countries border the "Arabian Gulf" and only one—Iran—is not Arab. The Arabs note also the Iranians' bellicose posture and occupation of the three United Arab Emirates islands and their recent drilling in the Dorra (Kuwaiti-Saudi) oil field as indicative of their real intentions in the region.

From an Arab perspective, the label "Persian" was coined by the British in the eighteenth century to serve their own interests, since they did not want the alternative names Arabian or Ottoman to be associated with the Gulf at that time. Although Arabs have called the body of water separating them from the Iranians the "Arabian Gulf" since President Nasser of Egypt fanned pan-Arabist sentiments in the 1950s, the "name game" of calling the Gulf Arabian, Persian, or American illustrates the ongoing serious competition and competing perceptions of who "owns" the Gulf. In early January 2000 President Khatami was quoted in the Arab press in his visit to Bandar Abbas as saying, "the Gulf is Persian and it will be Persian forever."[9] Such a statement was angrily received in the GCC states and the rest of the Arab world, especially coming from a leader regarded as pragmatic and moderate. It sparked numerous editorials describing the statement as a step backward in the confidence-building process that President Khatami wants to embark on.[10] The truth that both Arabs and Iranians would agree to is that this important Gulf is turning into an American lake. There does not seem to be an easy solution to this dilemma of the politically correct name of the Gulf from the perspective of either the Iranians or the Arabs.

In an anecdotal contribution to the Gulf/2000 electronic forum, M. R. Izady related that only a few weeks after the fall of the shah, a Palestinian representative arrived in Iran as the guest of the provisional revolutionary government. Among other places, he went to Ahwaz, Khuzistan, where he treated the eager Arabic-speaking populace to a long speech in Arabic. In the midst of his fiery anti-imperialist rhetoric, he had advertently or inadvertently referred to the need for liberating the rest of the "Arabian" Gulf from the imperialists. What happened in Ahwaz after such a pronouncement is unclear. Ayatollah Khomeini's response upon hearing the report is the point to note. Those who had brought the news were hoping for a final pronouncement on this pedagogical point of contention between the Iranians and their Arab neighbors—something along the lines of "Islamic Gulf." Khomeini's response was even better: "Those who control it and milk it, should also name it. For the time being, it should be called the American Gulf."[11]

The Arabs will always refer to the body of water between them and Iran as the Arabian Gulf and the Iranians will forever call it the Persian Gulf. Their leaders, whether they are moderates or hardliners, will fan the flame of nationalism and play to the domestic audience. Such is the case in the dispute with the UAE over the islands, which keeps poisoning the mutual relationship over what seems to be a trivial issue but is blown out of proportion by nationalistic camps on both sides of the divide. As Khomeini rightly stated, this body of water is becoming in the eyes of Arabs and Iranians the American Gulf.

THE COMPLEXITY OF THE RELATIONSHIP: SECURITY ISSUES

IRAN'S FOREIGN AND SECURITY POLICIES TOWARD THE GCC

It is clear that Iran's paramount interest is to secure and maintain stability along its lengthy borders, from the Caucasus and the republics of the former Soviet Union in the north to Turkey and Iraq in the west and Afghanistan and Pakistan in the east. The countries that represent the least threat to Iranian national interests—and the only area where Iran can flex its military might—are the GCC states as a whole.

Even before the internal bickering began between the competing camps of moderates and hardliners, Iran's foreign and domestic policies were at best contradictory and confusing for the outside world. Many Arab officials and laymen wonder whether there is any difference between Iran's security policy toward the Gulf during the shah's rule and under the Islamic Republic. Indeed, not much has changed in terms of the aim of hegemony and the occupation of the UAE islands. For example, in an inflammatory statement Iranian foreign minister Kamal Kharrazi announced in Beirut, in reference to the occupied UAE islands, that "those islands belong to Iran."[12] According to an Iranian scholar, "Iran has traditionally claimed for itself a large voice and a leading role in Persian Gulf affairs, whether under the shah or the Islamic republic, by virtue of its size, population, and long coastline on the Gulf. . . . Thus, Iran is extremely sensitive to exclusion, or any perception of an attempt at exclusion, from arrangements regarding Persian Gulf security."[13]

Iranian leaders speak in many and often conflicting voices on both domestic and foreign policies, whether in their dealings with the GCC countries or others. As Shaul Bakhash rightly observes: "Since 1992, a degree of incoherence has characterized Iranian foreign (and domestic) policy, in the sense that Iran appears to be pursuing conflicting and incompatible ends. . . . At the same time, the government has engaged in rhetoric and a pattern of behavior that has caused concern in Europe and the United States and among Arab states of the Middle East, exacerbating relations with individual states and undermining long-term economic objectives."[14] For example, President Rafsanjani warned GCC leaders in December 1992 that they would have to swim through "a sea of blood" to recapture the United Arab Emirates' occupied islands.[15] The same bellicose sentiment from Iran toward the GCC was repeated by Abbas Mohtajj, then the deputy commander of the Iranian Navy. He stated that "Iran has fought Iraq for eight years over a dispute of one hundred meters in the Shatt Al-Arab waterway, and Iran is willing to fight eighty years to hold on to Abu Musa and let everyone be aware of that."[16] A few days following this stern warning, a diplomatic overture came from Hussein Sheikholislam, the assistant to the Iranian foreign minister, who indicated Iran's willingness to sign a non-aggression security pact with its GCC neighbors.[17] One should juxtapose these remarks with Iran's meddling in the GCC's internal affairs by allegedly fomenting disturbances in Bahrain in June 1996. Iran was quick to deny accusations of providing aid to a conspiracy to topple the government, but not before a unanimous condemnation was heard from all the GCC states, as well as some Arab and Western countries.[18]

Iran has moderated its foreign and security policies since President Khatami assumed power in 1997. It has toned down its revolutionary zeal and the ideological drive that colored its foreign policy, especially with the GCC states. Iran today follows a policy of accommodation and pragmatism, away from confrontation and brinkmanship with both the Gulf States and to a certain extent with the U.S. and the European Union. Over two decades after the revolution, economic interests now prevail over ideology and Iran has started to show some maturity and responsibility in its dealings with the international community. The GCC states welcome the continuation of this trend, which could help solve the issues—especially that of the UAE's islands—that still cause much distress and poison the relationship.

HEGEMONIC IRAN: THE VIEW FROM THE GCC

Iran is convinced it should be the superpower of the Gulf region because it is the largest and most populous littoral state, because of its strategic position between the Gulf and the Caucasus and its huge military might. Just as a comparison, the whole GCC native population is not larger than the population of the Iranian capital, Tehran. The total military manpower of the GCC states (half of it comprised by the Saudis) is less than one third of the Iranian military personnel including the Revolutionary Guards. After the defeat of Saddam Hussein in the second Gulf war, Iran not only achieved parity in terms of balance of power, but also eliminated, at least temporarily, the archenemy that for a decade was the major threat to its national security. Another major threat to Iran's national security disappeared with the collapse of communism in the former Soviet Union, so the stage was set for Iran to be the undisputed leader of the Gulf region. This is, in fact, the only region in which Iran could exercise such a role.

Iran's dilemma is understandable. It suffers from what could be labeled the "Rodney Dangerfield" complex of getting no respect, due mainly to its exclusion from the security arrangements in the Gulf by both the GCC and the United States. Iran perceives its role not as one of dominance, but as one of leadership. The GCC states see the Iranian role as overbearing, dominant, and eager for opportunities to capitalize on the GCC's inherent weakness. Iranians would argue that the Arabs on the other shore of the Gulf are too sensitive, because leadership means to lead while dominance means to control, and Iran, due to the factors explained earlier, is more than qualified for the leadership role in the Gulf region. At the same time, if in the future this leadership role becomes a dominant role, that will be due more to the Arabs' weakness than to the Iranians' intentions. It is not easy to convince Arabs of the GCC states or, for that matter, in the wider Arab world that the real Iranian objectives in the Gulf region in the past, present, and the future have not been based on dominance and hegemony.[19] Hegemonic tendencies are one of the basic principles and fixtures in international politics for regional superpowers in any area, and Iran is no exception to that rule.

The inconsistency in Iranian foreign policy has been criticized more by some Iranian scholars than their Arab counterparts. In order to give this essay more neutrality and objectivity, I will quote Iranian scholars rather than their Arab counterparts. Shaul Bakhash, for example, argues that

> Iran's foreign-policy posture—even on the questions of Islam and Palestine—is not consistent. The revival of an activist, interventionist, confrontational style in foreign policy is selective, and it applies to some areas or countries and to some issues, and not to others. . . . The Iranian government has sought to exploit opportunities for expanded trade, but, like the shah's regime, it has accorded priority to order and stability along its borders. . . . It saves its Islamic radicalism for countries and places distant from Iran—Lebanon, the West Bank, Sudan. In Europe (and now also in the Persian Gulf), pragmatism and economic interests prevail over ideology. . . . Iran's foreign policy, whether in its ideological or in its pragmatic variety, is not of one piece. . . . The ability to pursue radical and pragmatic foreign policies simultaneously has been a source of both strength and weakness for the regime.[20]

The GCC states are aware of the predicament the current status quo poses to Iran. Iran is contained and checked by the huge American armada in the region, and American officials do not miss a beat in their warnings to the GCC that Iran is the real long-term threat to the region with its weapons of mass destruction and ballistic missiles, in addition to its arms-producing and developing capabilities.[21] The GCC states are aware that the Iranians feel excluded from any arrangements related to Gulf security. The Iranians also still feel bitter about the unconditional monetary and logistical support these small Gulf states, especially the Kuwaitis and the Saudis, provided to the invading Iraqi forces.

The Iranians, however, seem to forget two things. First, they made threats against Arab Gulf states, such as when Imam Khomeini stated that one day he might forgive Saddam Hussein for the war with Iran, but he would never forgive the Saudis for their role of aiding and supporting the Iraqis.[22] Moreover, many Kuwaitis still remember vividly the threats Khomeini used to make and the bombing of Kuwait's oil refineries in Al-Shuaibah and Al-Ahmadi. In addition, there were the sabotage operations committed by some Kuwaitis of Iranian extraction and the direct threats made against the shaikhdom of Kuwait after Iran had finished with Iraq. The Kuwaitis, indeed, bore the brunt of Iranian wrath more than any other GCC state. Its oil tankers were attacked 178 times by the Iranian air force in reprisals for the Kuwaiti aid to Iraq.

Second, the Iranians seem to forget that they turned down all the Iraqis' pleas for a ceasefire after the third year of the war, especially after they liberated all their occupied land including Khorramshahr, in Khuzestan province (or as the Arabs refer to it, "Al-Mohammarah" in "Arabistan" province). The Iranians were consumed by vengeance and a ceaseless drive to depose Saddam Hussein in an ideological crusade that unnecessarily prolonged the war and the suffering. That war threatened the stability and the well-being of the respective GCC states that had no choice but to support Iraq for lack of other options, especially after Iranian threats to export the revolution.

IRAN–GCC RELATIONS: PHASES AND POINTS OF CONTENTION

R. K. Ramazani, a prominent Iranian professor living in the United States, has chronicled Iranian–GCC relations in the first decade of the Islamic revolution from 1979 to the election of President Rafsanjani in 1989. He points out that there were four major factors that contributed to poison the relationship.

> First, Ayatollah Ruhollah Khomeini's Islamic ideology . . . led Iran to take on both super-powers. The United States, the "Great Satan," was the major object of vilification. The Soviet Union was the "Lesser Satan," and, hence, America's friends in the Gulf were to be redeemed by revolutionary Iran, where a "Government of God" had been established. Security in the Persian Gulf could be achieved only if the Arab peoples of the region rebelled against the ruling monarchs and created governments similar to, but not identical with, Iran's; cut their subservient ties with the United States; and acknowledged Iran's primacy in the Gulf, *primus inter pares.*
>
> Second, Iran's domestic politics contributed to hostile relations with the Gulf Arab states in two ways. The crusade to export revolution satisfied not only Iran's ideological quest, but also helped the Khomeinist factions to project domestic problems abroad in order to monopolize power at home. Freelance revolutionaries threatened the Arab sense of security in the earliest phase of the revolution when, for example, Ayatollah Ruhani called for the annexation of Bahrain . . . [23]
>
> A third factor was the Iraqi invasion of Iran in 1980. . . . Saudi Arabia and Kuwait bankrolled Iraq's war efforts, intensifying Iranian antagonism toward them. And Mubarak's Egypt aided the Iraqi war effort by providing needed manpower, increasing Iranian hostility toward Cairo.
>
> A fourth and final factor was the policies of the superpowers. The United States tilted increasingly toward Iraq with intelligence and other kinds of help, and destroyed most of the Iranian navy and offshore oil fields during the tanker war. The Soviet Union supplied arms to its old ally Iraq, especially because at the time Iran appeared to Moscow, as it did to Washington, to be the greater of the two evil in the region.[24]

Add to this account other anti-GCC policies, such as the views of the first Iranian president Abolhassan Bani Sadr. Bakhash asserts that he "believed the conservative Arab states of the Persian Gulf deserved to be swept away by popular revolutions. . . ." In addition, Iranian officials were implicated in the sabotage of Kuwaiti oil installations in 1987.[25] Such calculated and menacing behavior coming from a hegemonic power, Iran, was deeply engraved in the memory and the psyche of the GCC states' leaders and people.

This cold war atmosphere gave way to a pragmatic new détente under the Rafsanjani presidency (1989–97). Arab-Iranian relations improved following the end of the Iran-Iraq War and the death of Imam Khomeini, and the Iranian position opposing the Iraqi occupation of Kuwait helped Iran's standing among the GCC states and in the Arab world. The collapse of the Soviet Union also freed Iran from a kind of a siege mentality. Ramazani labels this period as one that witnessed the shift in Iran's foreign policy orientation from ideological confrontation to "pragmatic peace." The thaw was completed with President Khatami's landslide victory in May 1997. Khatami moderated Iran's foreign policy and called for a dialogue among civilizations.[26]

Although rapprochement with the GCC states started under President Rafsanjani, it blossomed under Khatami with his pragmatic, conciliatory approach. The eighth summit of the Organization of the Islamic Conference (OIC), held in Tehran in December 1997, attracted a number of Arab leaders who broke all taboos and helped moderate the tensions and alleviate hostility between Iran and much of the Arab world, especially the GCC states. This ushered in not only the ascendance of Iran as the chairman of the largest gathering of Islamic states, but also a new chapter of Iranian relations with old foes and a change of the old image of the "ugly Iranian" or the bullying Iranian, to the gentler and friendlier Iran, the new Iran.

The GCC leaders, policymakers, and intellectuals demand the same thing from Iran as the Americans—that is deeds and not words. Or as President Ronald Reagan characterized his policy toward the Russians, "Trust, but verify." Iranians are overly sensitive and too quick to label any move or policy as a conspiracy against them, while they fail to appreciate and fully comprehend how they are perceived and how official Iranian remarks and rhetoric are being read and interpreted across the Gulf.

The Contentious Issues: The GCC Perspective

The GCC also has a list of complaints and grievances that it regards as the stumbling blocks that Iran must address to create an atmosphere of confidence, so reconciliation and accommodation that has been unfolding for the last few years will continue as a lasting trend rather than an aberration. For the rapprochement to be built on solid and lasting ground, Iran has to allay the GCC's fears about the intentions and objectives of its current and future policies in the Gulf. The pragmatic approach in Iranian foreign policy needs to prevail over ideological rhetoric and hegemonic tendencies, and Iran should refrain from any bellicose and threatening remarks. Iran should end the confusing and mixed messages that it has been sending for years to its Arab neighbors about security, cooperation, the islands, armaments, and military maneuvers. These keep the GCC states suspicious and wondering whether any Iranian overture is a genuine one, and they keep the relationship at a level of low expectations. Iran also needs to resolve its domestic power struggle between the moderates and the hardliners, which has a spillover effect into the foreign policy arena. This not only makes Iranian foreign policy confusing and hard to read, but also makes it appear contradictory, counterproductive, and menacing, damaging Iranian national interests and compromising its economic well-being.

In the view of the GCC, both camps seem to have convergent views regarding Iran's relations with the GCC states and the Arab world at large (which is not the case regarding the rapprochement with the United States). Nevertheless, the hardliners tend to be more dogmatic in their views, policies, and conditions when it comes to dealing with the GCC states, while the liberals tend to be more chauvinistic and attempt to capitalize on their relationship with the GCC to be used as a tool for domestic consumption.[27]

The dispute over the islands is the litmus test. Both hardliners and moderates refuse to negotiate and reconcile the dispute with the UAE, and they belittle it by referring to it as a bilateral "misunderstanding." Those who blow the issue out of proportion are playing into the hands of those who want to isolate Iran from its Arab surroundings.[28] The Iranians maintain that the other Arabs in the GCC, or those who signed the Damascus Declaration, or the Arab League, should not concern themselves with this bilateral dispute. In July 1999 a tripartite committee made up of Oman, Qatar, and Saudi Arabia was formed to seek a solution to the row after the UAE threatened to pull out of the GCC, mainly because of the rapid Saudi rapprochement with Iran.

At their summit meeting in Oman in 1999, the GCC leaders agreed to work for strong ties with Iran and urged Iran to join in seeking a peaceful end to its territorial dispute with the UAE. They "stressed their keenness to forge strong relations of mutual trust and good neighborly ties." They urged Iran to "respond positively" to the efforts of the Tripartite Committee, and expressed hope that Iran would respond positively to the noble objective for which the committee was formed.[29] The final communiqué issued following the seventy-fifth meeting of the foreign ministers of the GCC states held in Jeddah, Saudi Arabia, stressed that "The GCC is concerned that relations with Tehran should be based on good neighborliness, mutual respect, non-interference in each others' internal affairs and resort to peaceful means to solve disputes."[30]

At the twenty-first GCC summit in Bahrain in December 2000, the final communiqué of the leaders rejected the continuing Iranian occupation of Abu Musa and Greater and Lesser Tunb and condemned Iranian military exercises on the three occupied UAE islands and in adjacent waters. It called on Iran to halt these exercises, which it said threatened peace and stability in the Arabian Gulf and did nothing to promote trust. It rejected Iranian claims to Abu Musa and expressed its support for all steps taken by the UAE to restore its sovereignty over the three islands through peaceful means, and called on Iran to accept referral of the conflict to the international court of justice.[31]

The committee was later dissolved since the Iranians refused not only to cooperate with it, but even to meet with it to discuss the islands dispute. The islands issue is still unresolved, and it is a ticking bomb with huge negative consequences. The GCC leaders have been cautious and conciliatory in their posture with Iran over the islands, as seen in the 1999 summit.

The islands issue continues to be a festering wound that poisons the Iranian-Arab relationship. The ayatollahs are unwilling to compromise so no one could accuse them of relinquishing a piece of territory captured under the shah. They do not want to be perceived in the eyes of Iranians as less patriotic than the shah. Such logic contradicts Islamic principles that espouse tolerance and forgiveness and preach against occupations, incursions, and taking others' property by force and call for reconciling disputes through deliberations and peaceful means. This untenable Iranian position forced the UAE foreign minister, Rashid Abdallah Al-Nuaymi, to denounce Iran and to compare the Islamic Republic's unreasonable position over the islands with the shah's.[32] This dilemma has consequences not only for Gulf security, but also exacerbates the rift within the GCC states and the opportunity it provides for American exploitation, which will be discussed in the geopolitical section below.

IRAN'S DOMESTIC POWER STRUGGLE

Iran's competing and conflicting foreign policy is held hostage to the ongoing power struggle among the multilayered Iranian decision-making apparatus. The forces of moderation and reform led by President Khatami initially were able to score three consecutive victories, first in 1997 with the landslide election of Khatami, followed in 1999 by a major victory for reformists in the municipal elections, and finally the major upset by reformers in the 2000 elections for the Sixth Majlis (Parliament), where conservatives were reduced to a minority. However, the hardliners retaliated—by intimidation tactics, by arresting moderates, by jailing reformists, and by muzzling the press. Despite the reelection of Khatami in 2001, the hardliners still control the judiciary, the armed forces, and Iran's Islamic Revolutionary Guards (IRGC).

The *New York Times* assesses the situation thus:

> With most of their newspapers silenced and many of their activists jailed by conservative courts, Iran's reformers have scaled back their once-defiant agenda for change and are concentrating on regaining a public voice through their control of the new Parliament. . . .

There is a sense of reduced expectations. It is a mood far different from the euphoria that followed their sweeping victory in the first round of parliamentary elections in February (2000). . . . But their ambitions were visibly trimmed by a conservative backlash—the press crackdown, the detention of pro-democracy activists, the voiding of more than a dozen races won by pro-Khatami candidates, and a three-month delay in certifying the election results for many others.[33]

IRAN AND THE GCC: THE DILEMMA OF DEMOCRACY

In the early years of the revolution, Iran frightened the Arabs in the GCC states by threatening to export the revolution. Nowadays, with all the shortcomings and pitfalls of its democratic experience, Iran is setting an example of merging Islam with democracy. Clearly, Iran has a long way to go down the democratic road, but it has come a long way since its early revolutionary days when it was bent on exporting a commodity no one wanted to buy. Iran's democracy and reforms worry the Arabs now, as did militant Islam before. Clearly, Iran aspires to be not only a democratic model and an example of political reform in the Middle East, but, following the victory by Hezballah in South Lebanon in the summer of 2000 with the Islamic Republic's support and assistance, even an inspiring flame of resistance.

The Iranian democratic trend, as the *Washington Post* puts it, is "prompting democratic activists and commentators in the generally less pluralistic Arab world to look east and wonder: What about us?" The transfer of authority (in the Arab world) is typically prompted by assassination or natural death instead of the ballot box. As Kamal Abu Jaber, the former Jordanian foreign minister who heads Jordan Institute of Diplomacy stated, "People realize that what is taking place in Iran is a new face that the revolution is wearing, a new ideology."[34]

Fawaz Sherif, a former Jordanian ambassador to France and the United States, told the *Post*, "If I'm a Saudi Shaikh I would not be sure how to explain why we don't have parliamentary elections when Iran, a country that also claims to be guided by Islamic principles, is in the midst of an increasingly freewheeling political debate." The article goes on to state, "The implications are not lost on Iranian officials. They note that while their country remains under U.S. trade restrictions, regional American allies less tolerant of pluralism escape public criticism and benefit from military protection and economic aid." Mohammad Abtahi, President Khatami's chief of staff, remarks: "The will of the people makes governments legitimate. This is basic. You can compare us with the regional countries—the countries nobody talks against. Women cannot fly without someone, or driving is not allowed, or they don't have the right to vote."[35]

Iran admittedly represents a different political landscape than its Arab counterparts, where monarchies, window-dressing democracy, and authoritarian leaders are the norm. Iran's democratic trend is a beacon of reforming the system from within. The jury is still out as to whether the Iranian experiment to make Islam and democracy compatible can be duplicated in the Arab world. Naturally, Iran poses both a real predicament and an embarrassment to the Arab totalitarian regimes. As Bijan Khajehpour-Khoei concludes in his chapter in this volume, "the degree of democratization in Iran compared to other Islamic nations in the region will have the potential of generating new, possibly negative perceptions on the Iranian side."[36]

The real danger for the GCC states is what happens if Iran becomes unstable due to its severe economic crisis. Neither the Iranian revolution nor President Khatami has been able to deliver Iran from its economic stagnation and improve the well-being of the Iranian people. Over twenty years after the revolution, the Iranians are worse off, and the revolution has failed to achieve its twin goals of providing social justice and economic reform. The reasons for this ongoing economic crisis, according to the government, are the devastating war with Iraq and the embargo and sanctions by the Americans. What kind of ramifications and consequences would that create for its wealthy little neighboring states, which are witnessing an upsurge in Iranian couriers as smugglers of drugs across their borders? The real dilemma is Iran becoming engaged in a low-intensity adventure to deflect attention from the economic plight at home, unlikely though that seems.

From the GCC's perspective, Iran remains a threat to the stability of the region, whether it is a powerful and resurgent Iran or a weak one beleaguered with economic woes and domestic upheaval. In both cases, Iran represents a potential flashpoint. The silver lining in this economic cloud is the ability of the Iranian leadership to comprehend fully the severity of its economic situation and the need to stay on the course of moderation and pragmatism, so Iran will be able to attract loans, investments, joint ventures, credit, and high technology to improve its foundering economy and to upgrade its oil industry.

GEOPOLITICS:
IRAN, IRAQ, AND THE UNITED STATES

THE IRAN-US RELATIONSHIP AND
ITS IMPACT ON THE IRAN-GCC RELATIONSHIP

Iran's relations with the other two major players, the United States and Iraq, negatively affect the scope, depth, and achievement of rapprochement between Iran and the GCC, in the perception of the latter. In the aftermath of the Iranian revolution, when the United States was declared the "Great Satan," the Iranian revolutionary ayatollahs believed that the greatest threat to the revolution and to their survival was the Americans and not their Russian neighbors. Shahram Chubin argues that

> from the perspective of the Islamic republic, the threat posed to it by the United States through the local states is not something that can be ignored. At the least, the U.S. military presence is a potential threat . . . [that] acts to inhibit Iran's diplomacy in the region, which is what it is designed to do. It certainly makes the Arab Persian Gulf states more resistant to Iran's overtures. This type of containment adds to Tehran's frustration. It may be an additional reason for looking at nuclear weapons. In the meantime Iran's interests would be best served by good relations with the Arab states.[37]

Iran has insisted that the U.S. military presence is the source of instability in the Gulf region. It has steadfastly rejected the presence of Western troops and called for signing security pacts with the individual GCC states. By and large, notwithstanding the Iran-Saudi pact signed in April 2001, such overtures have not been heeded by the individual GCC states for the reasons outlined in this study, and due to the contradictory and mixed signals emanating from Tehran.

Moreover, Iran perceives the GCC states as playing a conspiratorial and negative role as a pawn in the grand game of conspiracy against the Islamic Republic. From an Iranian point of view, such a feeling does not help in creating confidence-building measures for normal relations with the smaller Gulf states. These states continue to legitimize and sustain the United States presence in the region. Iran feels that it is not only excluded from playing any role in security arrangements in its own front yard, but to add insult to injury, it has even, at least for the time being, been lumped together with Iraq in the same category as a rogue state or "state of concern."

What troubles the GCC states is that the depth of their relationship with Iran is tied to the results of the "pistachio diplomacy" that is unfolding between the United States and the Islamic Republic. How far can this develop? The relationship between the GCC states and Iran cannot go too far as long as United States–Iranian relations continue to be hostage to domestic divisions and lost opportunities caused by hardliners in both Tehran and Washington.

THE IRAN-IRAQ RELATIONSHIP AND ITS IMPACT ON THE IRAN-GCC RELATIONSHIP

For a long time, Iraq has been Iran's nemesis and it continues to represent the real threat and danger to Iran's national interest. Iraq launched a devastating war that lasted for eight years, although it sought an exit strategy in the third year after it started losing. Iraq has not signed a peace treaty with Iran, and both countries host the main factions of each others' opposition. Over a decade after the end of the Iran-Iraq War, both countries are still exchanging and releasing prisoners of war. Nor have they settled other outstanding issues. Iran's condemnation of the Iraqi occupation of Kuwait gained it a lot of praise from the GCC states, mainly the Kuwaitis and the Saudis. It did not go unnoticed in the Gulf states, though, that this was a calculated and prudent undertaking, which bore dividends in the future. But the same states were also well aware that a complete defeat of Iraq would lead to the automatic dominance of Iran.

The Americans and the GCC states stopped short of toppling the Iraqi regime in order to maintain a semi-balance of power and to prevent Iran from turning into the Goliath of the Gulf. The collapse and defeat of Iraq in the second Gulf war reduced but did not remove a major threat to Iran's national security and a major competitor for dominance of the Gulf region. Since the end of the Gulf war, the UN has contained Iraq and placed it under the severest sanctions regime in modern history. Iraq has been absent from the Gulf scene, sanctioned, ostracized, and isolated, with its economy in a shambles. This has meant the resurgence of Iran. The Iran-Iraq War put to rest the idea that Iraqi Shi'is would support the Iranian Shi'is in a war against their own country. Thus, nationalism in Iraq prevailed over ethnic affiliation. Iran is fully aware that the Americans are exploiting the Iraqi threat to stay indefinitely in the region. Iran fears that Iraq will emerge from its current situation to threaten its national security and compete with it for dominance of the Gulf.

It is ironic that the Iraqis perceive the Iranian-Saudi rapprochement as a ploy and conspiracy against them. Iraqi officials and press are critical of this thaw in relations between the other two largest states in the region. Although Iran and Saudi Arabia have no territorial claims against each other, both vie for supremacy and hegemony in the Gulf. They are both courted by the states in the GCC, each for its own national security purposes and to balance the power in a fragile region.

Thus, there is not a unified view in the GCC toward either Iran or Iraq. The GCC countries seek to hedge their bets with both countries and to have one counterbalance the other. The much-debated fear of an alliance between the two common enemies, Iran and Iraq, never materialized. In the Middle East, diehard grudges and animosities still run deeper than strategic alliances.

THE TWO VIEWS OF THE GCC STATES TOWARD IRAN: THE NORTH-SOUTH DIVIDE

In Gulf politics, the GCC states represent the smallest and most vulnerable player, while the United States, an outsider, is the most powerful one, with Iran and Iraq completing the picture. The jockeying for power and alliances and counteralliances foments instability and promotes dissension. Seeking a perceived or realistic balance of power is what adds to the intrigue and complicates the Gulf scene even further. The United States remains the surest protector for all the GCC states. Among the local players, the northern Gulf states (Saudi Arabia and Kuwait) depend on Iran to counter Iraq, whereas Iraq is favored by the southern Gulf States (mainly the United Arab Emirates and Bahrain), and Qatar and Oman could go either way as swing states toward Iraq or Iran.[38]

The southern Gulf states have a perception of Iran as the dominant hegemonic power that is bent on dominating the region if circumstances are favorable. They cite Iranian intransigence and unreasonable posturing over the occupied islands, its offensive armaments, its ballistic capabilities, and the provocative military maneuvers that Iran conducts routinely in disputed territorial UAE waters.

For example, the Iranian Revolutionary Guard air and naval forces conducted exercises in October 1999 in the Persian Gulf and Sea of Oman, where for the first time all three of Iran's new submarines were deployed together. Another, called "Unity 77," incorporated a mock attack on targets from the Strait of Hormuz and the Sea of Oman using submarines, frigates, and helicopters with anti-submarine weapons. "While these maneuvers were officially supposed to mark the anniversary of the start of the 1980–1988 Iran-Iraq war and demonstrate Iran's readiness to defend the region, it is clear that submarine exercises and mock raids on shore facilities are far from defensive operations. Such exercises might be aimed at showing the GCC states that a joint Iran-GCC naval capability could replace the United States as a regional defense," according to Stratfor Reports.[39]

Iran has repeatedly called for the GCC to help rid the Gulf region of foreign militaries—namely that of the United States. This is not the view expressed by some GCC scholars, especially from the UAE. Dr. Jamal Al-Suwaidi, the director of the Emirates Center for Strategic Studies and Research, stated that

> the huge conventional and nonconventional Iranian military buildup ignites an arms race in the region which threatens its countries, and prolongs the presence of foreign forces which runs contrary to the intentions and wishes of Iran. Furthermore, the attempt by Iran to force its own perception based on its own historical justification vis-à-vis the USA, on the rest of the GCC states is dangerous because it is an interference in the domestic affairs of these (GCC) states. . . . The show of force which Iran conducts in the Gulf goes to show that the future theater of operations is the Strait of Hormuz and the Arabian Sea. The objective of these exercises is an offensive one and that contradicts the Iranian contention of being defensive exercises, especially, the role of the Revolutionary Guards, and its dogma of exporting revolution and fomenting troubles and instability in the region.[40]

The collective air and naval forces of the GCC states, although larger and more advanced than their Iranian counterpart, are largely ineffective and dominated by the Saudis. The GCC tries to remedy its weakness by conducting its own exercises. However, the GCC states suffer from deficiencies in their joint command and control systems, and past exercises have been mired in communications and logistical problems that are not an issue in Iran's navy.

Enter Iraq as a counterbalance for Iran, which splinters the GCC into factions. The southern Gulf states have been pushed into an alliance of convenience with the Iraqis. This is due to Iran's occupation of the UAE islands, its fomenting of instability in Bahrain, its long-term potential threat to Qatar's rich northern gas fields, and its provocative exercises and meddling in the domestic affairs of the GCC states, such as drilling in the disputed Dorra oil field in Kuwaiti-Saudi territorial waters. Furthermore, the Iranian mixed signals and bellicose rhetoric push the GCC states to embrace the Americans, to sign military pacts and purchase American-made weapons (the UAE's purchase of 80 F–16 jet fighters in 2000 is a case in point), and to fend off Iranian bullying and threats. This creates two views in the GCC states vis-à-vis Iran. Such polarization complicates the picture and increases the negative perception of Iran, not to mention its negative consequences on intra-GCC solidarity and cooperation.

THE U.S. FACTOR IN IRAN-GCC RELATIONS

The continued stagnation of relations between the United States and Iran, the trading of accusations, and the attempt by the United States to promote the Iranians as the major threat to the region do not help in creating the environment needed by the regional countries to embrace Iran. All attempts to moderate the U.S. stance toward Iran have fallen on deaf ears. Martin Indyk, the former U.S. State Department assistant secretary for Near Eastern Affairs, stated on October 14, 1999, "It is time for the United States of America and the Islamic Republic of Iran to engage each other as two great nations face to face, and on the basis of equality and mutual respect."[41] This was a clear departure from the failed dual containment policy that he himself helped formulate in 1993. The United States, Iran, and GCC all could benefit from such a rapprochement between Tehran and Washington. The United States, for example, could help mediate over the disputed islands. This would enhance stability and secure U.S. oil interests in the Gulf, as well as help to reassure the GCC states and strengthen the confidence-building environment between the suspicious Arabs and Iran.

There is a sinking feeling among some GCC intellectuals that the Gulf countries are under siege from all sides. Even their own solidarity amounts to nothing more than a fragile facade. Some believe that the United States is fueling some of the discord that currently exists within the GCC states, which gives credence to the conspiracy theory that is circulating all over the Gulf of the "real" American intentions.[42]

"The fundamental guiding principle of U.S. policy in the Persian Gulf is to prevent any one country other than the United States from being the regional hegemon or from controlling the export of Gulf oil," according to Stratfor Intelligence.[43] American officials, on the other hand, do not miss a beat in reminding the GCC leadership and peoples about the real danger Iran poses to the entire region. A case in point was former secretary of defense William Cohen's visit to Kuwait in April 2000. As the *Washington Post* reported, "visiting Kuwait, Cohen watched U.S. marines lob grenades and fire 'bunker buster' assault weapons, telling them later that he hoped film of the exercise

234 / ABDULLAH K. ALSHAYJI

would be broadcast so Iran might 'see how good you really are.'" Each country must be very careful in dealing with Iran, Cohen said, to "make sure they can satisfy themselves that Iran wants a peaceful, stable relationship with them."[44]

The demonizing of Iran through such American posturing and scare tactics, which foments tension and insecurity, will thwart the ongoing rapprochement, is counterproductive and ill-serves the fragile and volatile relationship between Iran and the GCC. It exaggerates fears, adds to unwarranted tension and keeps the two suspicious parties at arms' length indefinitely.

CONCLUSION

The above macro and geopolitical factors, whether they are real or imagined, fabricated, fomented by others or exaggerated by sectarian, ideological, and political factors, collaborate in keeping both Iran and the GCC states suspicious of each other. They must be studied and understood by both parties if they are to cohabit and advance their rapprochement from a tentative process into a lasting experience in which all will gain dividends.

Iran has to demonstrate to the GCC that its drive toward reform and fence-mending is real and genuine. As an Iranian scholar commented, "the Iranian resolve to forge relations with her southern neighbors has developed out of the positive experience of her relations with the northern neighbors. . . . A continuation of hostile policies toward the southern neighbors goes along with the potential of new confrontation in the north and would have been fatal for Iran's regional policy. Hence the Iranian government saw it expedient to improve relations with the southern neighbors to better confront challenges in the Caspian region."[45]

This view is echoed by some Arab scholars, who see that economic integration would help in insuring much-needed stability in the region. Thus, as Saleh Al-Mani, a Saudi political science professor, remarks, "Iranian moderation is due mainly and more than anything else to economic pressure and needs and not to a genuine tilt toward pragmatism and deep belief in moderation per se."[46]

Iran's domestic scene is not encouraging. Iran continues to experience internal upheavals between its two feuding factions and continues to be captive to its domestic politics. This makes for a volatile situation and results in a foreign policy of mixed and conflicting signals. While Iran has moderated its posturing and begun down the road of pragmatism, it needs to prove that its fence-mending is not an aberration. A good start is to assuage the UAE and send a clear and major confidence-building signal by agreeing to discuss, or better yet, to make concessions over the island dispute with the UAE. This step will cause a cosmic change across the Gulf and will dispel the notion that the Iranian rapprochement is no more than a ploy.

Some of the factors discussed in this chapter, especially the macro ones, are hard to overcome as they have been with both the Arabs and Iranians for over a thousand years and will not disappear. But both the Arabs and the Iranians could collaborate in removing the other manufactured, perceived, and geopolitical factors, and especially the cultural ones. As the Kuwaiti scholar Mohammad Al-Rumaihi declared recently, "the cultural environment in both its Arabic and Persian dimensions is poisoned by some fascist slogans, and cultural understanding between Arabs and Persians is the first step toward eradicating the mutual accusations and recriminations between Sunnis and Shi'is, and toning down the nationalistic fervor which the Iran-Iraq war deepened." He calls for tearing down this unseen cultural impediment that blocks the rapprochement between Arabs and Iranians.[47] In the same symposium, Fahmi Howeidi, the well-known moderate Egyptian Islamist thinker who is a specialist on Iran, blamed the lack of understanding between Arabs and Iranians on political systems, officials, and intellectuals: "Politics have separated us and poetry has brought us closer." He asked for "the reinvigoration of translation, and for the correction and reforms of school texts and for more outreach programs between the Arabs and the Iranians."[48]

Iran has to give up what Chubin describes as "a proprietary attitude toward the Persian Gulf; this is an outgrowth of geopolitics as much as ideology. But it is also a reminder that Tehran is sensitive about the U.S. presence, the Arab military buildup, and loose and provocative talk about the security of the region being exclusively an Arab affair."[49] Iran cannot keep playing contradictory games and think it can get away with them. Its policy toward Iraq needs to be very clear. How does it explain its sudden zeal in implementing UN Security Council resolutions by one day interdicting and capturing tankers smuggling Iraqi oil, while a few days later allowing, as it has for years, smuggled Iraqi oil to sail unrestrained through its water in a lucrative trade? Such behavior by Iran has to change if it is to be taken as seriously embracing reform.

If demographic growth and the demands of political participation pose the real future threat to the Gulf, and if we subscribe to the notion that the wave of the future is regional alliances and economic integration, then the first step is a genuine GCC-U.S. endeavor to take Iran to task and help it break out of its siege mentality. Under President George W. Bush, the United States should begin a real and constructive engagement not beholden to narrow partisan and domestic lobbyists' whims. Early developments in the new administration lent hope that a cautious thaw in relations was at hand.

The GCC for its part has extended numerous gestures toward Iran. This is especially true of the Saudis, who have appointed the first Shi'i ambassador to Tehran and have increased the Iranian quota of pilgrims annually from 60,000 to 85,000. After Saudi Arabia and Kuwait demarcated their maritime boundaries and settled their disputes over the continental shelf, it is now up to the Iranians to show some flexibility and pragmatism to its closest friends in the region. (After all, it was Iranian mischief—drilling in the disputed Dorra gas field—that forced the rapid conclusion to the border demarcation between Kuwait and Saudi Arabia.)

If and when Iran shows some reasonableness, the GCC states should engage Iran economically, through joint ventures and by providing employment to skilled Iranian expatriates. We would like to see what has become known as "the code of conduct" embodied in the Tehran Vision statement as the real code of conduct in Iran-GCC relations. This affirms "the principles of respect for sovereignty, territorial integrity, and national independence of states, rejection of the use, and the threat, of force or interference in internal affairs, inviolability of internationally recognized borders and resolution of disputes through dialogue and negotiations, and cooperation for combating terrorism."[50] We in the GCC states are hoping that the remarks by President Khatami at the eighth Islamic summit held in Tehran, in which he remarked that "Iran poses no threat to any Islamic country," do not remain only as a promise, and that Iran will be judged by deeds and actions and not words and slogans.

The Iranians have a nice saying: "The one who moves forward is not the one who moves fast." We know the Iranians are patient and hard bargainers, and they usually do not move fast, but to reap the benefits and to capitalize on the dividends, they have to change their course and move fast and forward at the same time; otherwise, they might arrive too late. As a consequence, all parties in the neighborhood will stand to lose. Such a scenario would not necessarily transform the Gulf into a tranquil lake, but it is a good start. Maybe later on, the Arabs and Iranians can agree on an appropriate name for the body of water that separates them.

NOTES

1. Bijan Khajehpour-Khoei in this volume, p. 239.
2. Riad N. El-Rayess, *Masahif wa suyuf: Iran min al-shahanshahiya ila al-khatamiya* [Qurans and Swords: Iran from the Shah to Khatami] (Beirut: El-Rayess Books, 2000), p. 244.
3. Shahram Chubin, "Iran's National Security: Threats and Interests," in Geoffrey Kemp and Janice Gross Stein, eds., *Powder Keg in the Middle East: The Struggle for Gulf Security* (Lanham, Maryland: Rowman & Littlefield, 1995), p. 112.
4. Abdullah Al-Naffisi, *Iran wa'l Khalij: Diyaliktik al-damj wa'l nabdh* [Iran and the Gulf: The Dialectic of Inclusion and Exclusion] (Kuwait: Dar Qortas Publishing, 1999), pp. 5–9.
5. Ibid. See also *Constitution of the Islamic Republic of Iran,* trans. Hamid Algar (Berkeley: Mizan Press, 1980), p. 82.
6. *Arab-Iranian Relations,* ed. Khair el-Din Haseeb (Beirut: Centre for Arab Unity Studies, 1998).
7. Al-Nafissi, op. cit., p. 12.
8. Al-Nafissi, op. cit., p. 12.
9. Abdulaziz Al-Kuwari [Qatari columnist], article in *Al-Khalij* [UAE], January 29, 2000.
10. Ibid.
11. M. R. Izady, comment in Gulf/2000 electronic forum, May 18, 1999.
12. *An-Nahar* (Beirut), March 3, 2000.
13. Shaul Bakhash, "Alternative Futures for Iran: Implications for Regional Security," in Kemp and Stein, *Powder Keg in the Middle East,* p. 94.
14. Bakhash, "Alternative Futures," p. 91.
15. *An-Nahar* (Beirut), January 28, 1992, p. 1.
16. *Iran Hava'i* (Tehran), December 13, 1995, p. 1.
17. *Keyhan Arabi* (Tehran), December 16, 1995, p. 1.
18. Abul-Jalil Marhoon, *Amn al-khalij ba'd al-harb al-barida* [Gulf Security After the Cold War] (Beirut: Dar Al-nahar Publishing, 1997), pp. 237–38.
19. Riad N. El-Rayess, op. cit., pp. 63–69.
20. Bakhash, "Alternative Futures," pp. 102–103.
21. Anthony Zinni remarks on the Iranian threats, Kuwaiti dailies, February 2, 2000.
22. Riad El-Rayees, op. cit., p. 65.
23. R. K. Ramazani, "The Emerging Arab-Iranian Rapprochement: Towards an Integrated U.S. Policy in the Middle East?," *Middle East Policy,* vol. 6, no. 1 (June 1998), p. 46.
24. Ramazani, "The Emerging Arab-Iranian Rapprochement," pp. 45–46.
25. Bakhash, "Alternative Futures," pp. 88–89.
26. Ramazani, op. cit., p. 46.
27. Riad N. El-Rayees, op. cit., p. 84.
28. Kuna Bulletin, Kuwait, May 9, 1999.
29. Reuters online, April 29, 2000.
30. Gulfwire online (Weekly e-newsletter), No. 48, June 9, 2000.
31. See the twenty-first Gulf summit final communiqué.
32. *Al-Sharq al-awsat* (London), March 12, 2000, and Stratfor Report, March 7, 2000.
33. *New York Times* online July 5, 2000.

34. "Democracy in Iran Prompts Arab Introspection," by Howard Schneider, *Washington Post Foreign Service,* March 10, 2000, p. A15.
35. Ibid.
36. Khajehpour-Khoei, p. 243.
37. Chubin, "Iran's National Security," pp. 128–29.
38. See Ghanim Alnajjar, "The GCC and Iraq," in *Middle East Policy,* vol. 7, no. 4 (October 2000), pp. 92–99.
39. Stratfor Special Report online, October 5, 1999.
40. Jamal Al-Suwaidi, ed., "Ma'zaq al-siyasa al-Iraniya fi al-khalij wa mutaliba al-taghyir," [The Dilemma of Iranian Policy in the Gulf and the need for Change], paper delivered at a symposium in Kuwait on GCC-Iran Future Relations. Kuwait University, May 15, 1999.
41. *Iran Times,* October 22, 1999.
42. Abdullah Alshayji, "Gulf Views of U.S. Policy in the Region," *Middle East Policy,* vol. 5, no. 3 (September 1997), pp. 1–13.
43. Stratfor Special Report online, December 3, 1999.
44. *Washington Post,* April 10, 2000, p. A14.
45. In Khajehpour-Khoei chapter in this volume, p. 247.
46. In Jamal Al-Suwaidi, ed., *Iran wa'l khalij: al-ba'th 'an istriqrar* [Iran and the Gulf: Searching for Stability] (Abu Dhabi: The Emirates Center for Strategic Studies and Research, 1997).
47. *Al-watan* [Kuwait], July 5, 2000, p. 22. This was at an Arabic symposium organized in Tehran to recognize the achievement of Sa'di, the great Iranian poet from Shiraz who wrote his poems in Persian and Arabic in the twelfth century. The symposium was arranged under the auspices of Al-Babtain Foundation, a Kuwaiti non-profit literary foundation.
48. *Al-watan* (Kuwait) July 5, 2000, p. 22.
49. Chubin, "Iran's National Security," p. 127.
50. R. K. Ramazani, op. cit., p. 55.

CHAPTER 11

MUTUAL PERCEPTIONS IN THE PERSIAN GULF REGION
An Iranian Perspective

BIJAN KHAJEHPOUR-KHOEI

In contemporary times, the Persian Gulf has been the scene of tension and international confrontation, including two massive wars in the last two decades of the twentieth century. Though a number of analysts argue that it is the existence of oil and the consequent international interest in the Persian Gulf that have contributed to the tensions and conflicts there, one cannot dismiss the significance of a number of historical processes that have shaped the region's present realities. Viewed simply in terms of its contribution to the development of civilizations and religions, the Persian Gulf region has been of international significance throughout history.

Scholars and observers of the region have extensively discussed the events of the past, and a historical perspective is clearly necessary to understand present circumstances. This paper will concentrate, however, on the present and the future, with the aim of identifying and discussing the main factors influencing Iran's relations with her neighbors in the Persian Gulf region. Before examining this set of factors as perceived in Iran and the region, it is important to underline two points.

First, the relations between Iran and her neighbors in the Persian Gulf are not equal to Iran's relations and perceptions of the Arab world. Though all Persian Gulf states are Arab except for Iran, the nature of mutual relations and perceptions in the region is influenced by a number of additional factors, such as physical proximity and economic interaction.

Second, it is important to note that some of the elements discussed below influence popular perceptions and others governmental perceptions on the Iranian side. Eventually, these two sides will interact, so it is crucial to identify each element individually and examine what processes might change perceptions and improve the level of understanding. In addition, a number of tendencies will be identified that play a role in the medium to long-term process of regional integration.

FACTORS INFLUENCING
MUTUAL PERCEPTIONS

The discussion of regional political realities by Middle Eastern researchers is often hampered by an emotional response to the fact that Islamic civilization has lagged behind Western civilization, leading to a tendency to blame "foreign forces" for a number of current problems. Clearly, foreign powers have played a significant role in shaping the realities of the twentieth-century Middle East. However, the aim of this paper is to identify the indigenous factors that have been derived from the political, geopolitical, religious, and cultural evolution of this important region. Furthermore, it is important to be able to conduct an academic approach to discussing the indigenous factors that influence mutual perceptions, free of emotions and desires. Though such a task is difficult for a Middle Eastern researcher, the following will attempt to identify the key factors influencing Iran's perceptions of her Arab neighbors in the Persian Gulf.

FACTOR 1: NATIONALISM

Nationalism can be considered one of the products of the movement in search of national identity in the twentieth century. The creation of modern governments required the establishment of modern nations, which was not an easy process, especially in the tribal societies of the Middle East. This process has played a significant role in shaping contemporary realities in a number of countries in the region.

In the case of Iran and relations with her neighbors, the growth of nationalism has had an effect on regional and political developments. At the same time, the historical legacies and elements that influence the degree of nationalism in Iran, as well as their impact on Iranian perceptions toward Arab neighbors, are older than the twentieth century. These elements can be summed up as follows:

First, the division between "Arab" and "'Ajam,"[1] which has roots in the Iranian belief that the Arab-Islamic invasion of Iran in the seventh century put a tragic end to Iran's "glorious" pre-Islamic civilization. This feeling has been intensified through nationalistic sentiments, which have been kept alive for generations through Persian literature and have been confirmed through hostility throughout history.[2] The general "anti-Arab" sentiment is a factor that has to be taken into account when analyzing Iran's perceptions toward her Arab neighbors.

One other important element affecting nationalistic sentiments in Iran has been the fact that Iran, as the only non-Arab nation of the Persian Gulf region, has been considered a "peripheral minority" in the Arab world. This element intensified in the 1950s when the Egyptian leader Gamal Abdel Nasser increased anti-Persian rhetoric in the Arab world by using the term "Arabian Gulf."[3]

More recently, anti-Arab sentiments were confirmed in Iran through the Iraqi invasion. Sadly, from an Iranian perspective, the fact that almost all Arab countries in the region supported Iraqi atrocities against Iran does not help the cause. Putting this historical legacy into present perspective, one is faced with the unfortunate reality that the average Iranian has a negative prejudice about his Arab neighbors, due not only to deeply ingrained hostility throughout the past millennium, but also to more recent events.

At the same time, there are enough indications to believe that the average Iranian is capable of correcting that incorrect perception. The best proof for such a capability was displayed in 1990, when a large number of Kuwaiti citizens sought refuge in Iran following the Iraqi invasion of Kuwait.[4] The reception of the Kuwaitis by their Iranian neighbors was unique, especially since they mainly arrived in the province of Khuzistan, where most of the Iraqi atrocities in the 1980–88 Iran-Iraq War took place. Though some observers explained the warmth in human relations by the fact that Khuzistan has an indigenous Arab community, in the author's view, the main reason was that the crisis generated unprecedented human contact between the peoples of the two countries, in fact a contact that corrected images and perceptions on both sides.

Considering the future impact of nationalistic sentiments on Iran's perceptions of its Arab neighbors, one needs to address the issue from different angles:

First, the above example indicates that an increase in human contacts and people-to-people encounters, which could be achieved through the promotion of tourism and religious pilgrimage, will improve images and perceptions on both sides.

Second, there is a need for an educational campaign in Iran, such as the revision of school textbooks, to correct historical misperceptions.[5] The UNICEF campaign entitled "Peace Education," which has been implemented successfully in other countries, might be an appropriate tool to influence the perceptions by Iranians of their Arab neighbors. Iran's young population[6] clearly presents an opportunity in this regard.

Finally, Iranian government officials have to be careful in how they utilize the positive aspects of nationalistic sentiments in Iran (especially in regards to national unity and integration). There is increasing need for transparency and communication with the people in projects that might be misunderstood. For example, the campaign to confirm the legitimacy of the name "Persian Gulf" has the potential of increasing anti-Arab emotions among Iranians.

FACTOR 2: RELIGION

As much as nationalism and the Arab-Persian division might have contributed to the deterioration of relations in the past, one might suppose that the predominant religion among the region's countries would have the opposite effect. However, the fact that Iran chose to follow the Shi'i branch of Islam while most of her Arab neighbors are predominantly Sunni has also had a dividing effect on the region's countries. Undoubtedly, the ideological division between Sunni and Shi'i is less a concern of the ordinary citizen on both sides. However, the very same division and difference have implications for governance in Iran as opposed to governance in Arab countries, thus leading to tensions between the two sides. While the issues of governance will be tackled under the heading "political issues" below, religion as a factor has influenced mutual perceptions, especially from an Iranian perspective.

Both prior to and especially since the 1979 Islamic revolution, Iran has claimed to be one of the leaders of the Islamic world. In this sense, Iran stands in direct competition with Saudi Arabia, which, as the birthplace of Islam and the location of Islam's holiest shrines, considers itself the natural leader of the Islamic world. This competition has led to tension between the two sides, especially in the 1980s, when Iran was at the height of her revolutionary fever and a number of incidents intensified the tension. The climax was the massacre in 1987 of more than 400 Iranian pilgrims in the holy city of Mecca during a political rally initiated by Iranian organizers.

Tensions subsided in the 1990s, symbolized above all by the fact that the summit of the Organization of the Islamic Conference (OIC) was held in Tehran in December 1997.[7] The successful staging of this important meeting granted Iran a leading role in the Islamic world, this time in cooperation rather than in confrontation with Saudi Arabia. Based on this new chapter in relations, which was made possible through a rapprochement process over the several preceding years,[8] the Iranian government seemed to move away from its past perceptions and developed a new atmosphere of cooperation with its Arab neighbors in religious matters. The climax of the continuously improving relations was the signing of a security accord between Iran and Saudi Arabia in April 2001.[9]

Furthermore, one major source of tension in regard to religion has been the question (mainly posed on the Iranian side) of who represents the true path of Islam. In the past, Iranian leaders have referred to the Iranian concept of "pure Mohammedan Islam" while denouncing the practice of Islam in the Arab countries as "Americanized Islam." Although this rhetoric was clearly politicized, the key issue of Islamic practice subsequently appeared to be losing some of its weight on the Iranian side, both in government and among the public. In other words, as the focus in Iranian politics begins to shift more toward national interests and away from strictly Islamic interests, the notion of "religious" practices and interpretations could lose some of its previous emphasis, eventually easing potential tensions between the two sides. Still, differences in religious interpretation will remain a source of friction and misperception between the two sides, especially on the politicized level of religious interpretation discussed below.

FACTOR 3: POLITICAL ISLAM

Islam and Islamic nations claim to be developing a new set of values for human development. What we consider the "Islamic bloc" or "Islamic civilization" strives to challenge the values set forward by Western civilization. That Islamic values and rules can be put into modern and constructive practice is today witnessed through the rapid growth of Islamic banking and the role it plays in international finance. At the same time, the growth of political concepts derived from Islamic rulings and teachings leads to friction between the different interpretations of Islam. This fact is currently reflected in the interpretation of Islam by the Taliban militia in Afghanistan, which Iran denounces but Saudi Arabia partially accepts. This factor has the potential to become the most destructive element in the relations and perceptions of the two sides. There is already a degree of unhappiness among Iranians about the image of Islam presented by the southern Persian Gulf countries (as there must be on the other side). The reason for this fact is not the division between Shi'i and Sunni, but rather the drive of "Islamic civilization" to generate an internationally respected image. In his opening speech at the 1997 OIC summit in Tehran, President Khatami emphasized this very issue, i.e., the objective of the Islamic world to create a modern civilizational bloc that would be "even better than our past." At the same time, Khatami recognized that this progress would be possible only if "we have the fairness and capability of utilizing the positive scientific, technical and social achievements of Western civilization." He concluded that "with awareness, effort, and solidarity we are capable of changing our destiny."[10]

Khatami's remarks reflect the very heart of the matter: on one side the desire to revive Islamic civilization as a constructive international element, on the other the need to merge a number of ideas and developments with Western civilization, and finally the challenge to unite the Islamic world behind this theme. To achieve this goal, President Khatami has put forward the concept of "dialogue among civilizations"—a proposal that has achieved a positive international resonance. In fact, the year 2001 was recognized by the United Nations as the Year of Dialogue Among Civilizations in which a number of events and exchanges took place.

While governments will be at the heart of potential disagreements and frictions over political Islam, the peoples of the region will also develop perceptions and misperceptions about each other as a result of Islamic interpretations in their countries. The potential for such misperceptions from an Iranian perspective is very high as throughout history the Iranians have tended to consider themselves distinguished Muslims who have contributed greatly to Islamic civilization.[11] On the other side, citizens of Arab states in the southern Persian Gulf region perceive the religiosity of Iranians as hypocrisy. The divide in political progress between the two sides—in other words, the degree of democratization in Iran compared to other Islamic nations in the region—will have the potential of generating new, possibly negative perceptions on the Iranian side.

Consequently, many of the future political tensions between Iran and her Arab neighbors will arise from the fact that the region's societies are caught in the transition from traditionalism to modernity, or in the merger of Islamic values with Western concepts. As a result, the role of religion in governance and society, which is of significance in all Persian Gulf states, will undergo changes and reforms, and the solutions presented in the different countries are certain to cause friction. However, if increased political and cultural exchanges take place among the countries, a number of new moves and formulations can be aimed at increasing mutual understanding between nations and governments. In fact, the recent exchanges between Iran and her Arab neighbors, especially Saudi Arabia, seem to have led to some relaxation in this regard. Another important element will be increased contact between intellectuals and scholars on both sides who could lay the theoretical ground for Islamic and political interpretations.

FACTOR 4: REGIONAL ISSUES

In addition to the three elements discussed above, perceptions and relations between Iran and her Arab neighbors are influenced by a number of regional issues. Clearly, Iran, Iraq, and Saudi Arabia have all had the ambition of being the key player in a number of regional matters, which has led to strains in their relations. As far as governmental and public perceptions are concerned, some regional issues have united Iranians with their Arab neighbors and some have divided them. These include:

The Palestinian Cause

For decades, the Palestinian issue has been uppermost in the minds of Islamic countries, including the Persian Gulf states. It should be noted that the Organization of the Islamic Conference, which is the main political organization uniting the Islamic countries, was established in reaction to the Israeli threat and with the objective of solving the Palestinian issue. In that sense, the Palestinian cause, which is very important for the Iranian people, has had a uniting effect on the Persian Gulf nations. Despite all other areas of tension, the Palestinian issue and the Israeli threat to Muslim countries in the region has given them a sense of unity. Though some analysts argue that this unity is only situational and that the division between the Persian Gulf nations is too deep to achieve unity, it is evident that the cohesion that has resulted from having a common enemy will create opportunities for both sides to increase contacts and exchanges, which, as discussed above, will be constructive. The proof for this assertion can be witnessed in the

244 / BIJAN KHAJEHPOUR-KHOEI

current Israeli-Palestinian crisis. In fact, the ongoing Palestinian crisis has helped the process of rapprochement between a number of regional players.

Regional Hegemony and Persian Gulf Security

Since the 1971 withdrawal of British forces from the Persian Gulf, Iran, Iraq, and Saudi Arabia have all had ambitions to play a hegemonic role in the region. Iran's hegemonic behavior, mainly prior to the Islamic revolution, Iraq's hegemonic behavior in the 1980s, and Saudi Arabia's behavior, especially in border disputes with the smaller countries in the Persian Gulf, have all contributed to the creation of an atmosphere of mistrust among these nations. From an Iranian perspective, the issue is even more complicated, as Iran was the victim of an Iraqi invasion supported by other Arab countries in the region. Unfortunately, this element of mistrust has been intensified through lack of political and intellectual exchange throughout most of the 1980s and 1990s. Recent initiatives in generating intellectual and political contacts have certainly had a positive impact; however, one should not underestimate the degree of mistrust, which can only be healed over time, and through further effort on both sides.

One of the issues connected to regional hegemony is the desire of all Persian Gulf states to provide a secure environment for the production and transport of oil and gas as well as to carry out other economic activity. As far as Iran is concerned, the government believes that the littoral states can themselves provide for security in the Persian Gulf; however, historical legacies, current tensions, and the atmosphere of mistrust have so far prevented the development of a regional security scheme that would include Iran, and her Arab neighbors. As mentioned earlier, the signing of a security accord between Iran and Saudi Arabia in April 2001 can be considered the starting point of a process that could lead to a more relaxed security relationship between the regional states. The big question remains relations with Iraq. It is clear that Iraq under Saddam Hussein still has the ambition of emerging as the region's hegemon, although new regional and international realities have reduced the possibility of such a scenario. The Iran-Saudi accord has also put pressure on Iraq's position. Nevertheless, future perceptions, and policies will continue to possess a dual nature. On the one hand, in regional security issues we will continue to see a rather tense relationship between Iraq and the rest of the Persian Gulf players, and on the other, relations on the commercial and diplomatic level are improving. This duality increases the complexity of relations between Iran and her Persian Gulf neighbors.

Military Equations

Due to the issues of hegemony, and security, the larger states in the Persian Gulf have also invested in military capabilities. One of the indicators of the degree of regional cooperation and understanding is how the different states understand and interpret current investment in military capability by the other side. As far as perceptions in Iran are concerned, the huge investments in military equipment by the southern Persian Gulf states add to the element of mistrust. Though the existence of Iraq's Saddam Hussein as a threat to all Persian Gulf states is fully understood in Iran, there are two arguments in regards to the military expenditure: first, some interpret the expenditure as partly oriented against Iran; secondly, it is understood as a weakness on the side of Arab countries who, in the opinion of Iranians, are fully dependent on the West, especially the United States. Both of these interpretations lead to prejudice, and negative perceptions on the Iranian side.

There is no doubt that Iran's Arab neighbors have similarly negative perceptions about Iranian military expenditure, and activity. Hence, what seems to be very necessary is communication between the two sides of the Persian Gulf, and transparency about the objectives of military investment and activity on the part of both. The more defensive the nature of military equipment, and war games staged, the more one can hope that this issue will be resolved in the future. Recent exchanges between the Iranian, Omani, and Saudi defense ministries and emerging high-level contacts in this field are among the positive signposts pointing to a reduction of misunderstandings in mutual relations.

Border Disputes

Another element that has hampered relations and perceptions in the Persian Gulf is the existing border disputes. From an Iranian perspective, two major border disputes have caused tension in the past.

First is the dispute with Iraq over the Shatt al-Arab river. According to Richard Schofield, the 1975 Algiers Accord that settled this dispute was "one of the most sophisticated river boundary treaties ever signed in international law."[12] However, in 1980 prior to the Iraqi invasion of Iran, Saddam Hussein declared the accord annulled, thus reviving the old dispute. Though Saddam Hussein, in a strategic move, accepted the Algiers Accord in 1990 to attract Iranian support for his atrocities against Kuwait, there is little doubt that the dispute is not fully settled. As a result, Iran and Iranians are still concerned that any revival of the border dispute could lead to catastrophic consequences.

Secondly and more acutely, Iran is faced in the Persian Gulf with a dispute with the United Arab Emirates over the islands of Abu Musa and Lesser and Greater Tunb. This dispute is discussed in much greater detail elsewhere in this volume; however, it is important to realize that the existence of the dispute and the fact that the majority of Arab states, and certainly the Gulf Cooperation Council (GCC) countries, are backing the UAE's position have affected Iranian perceptions. In recent years, there has been a degree of commitment to dialogue to solve this issue. Most significantly, Iranian foreign minister Kamal Kharrazi visited the UAE on May 22, 1998, and the two sides "agreed to resort to peaceful means to resolve their territorial dispute."[13] However, there has been little progress since that visit. Clearly, the ability of the two countries to enter into a constructive dialogue would be very fruitful for their relations, and undoubtedly a peaceful and lasting settlement in this matter would have a very positive influence on future perceptions between Iranians and Arabs.

The Iraq Issue

Another key regional issue is the position of Iraq. Currently, Iraq is perceived as a potential threat to the Persian Gulf states. At the same time, the elimination of Iraq's military potential is crucial to Iran's security. Consequently, an alliance against Iraq's threat could potentially work in favor of Iran's rapprochement with the southern Persian Gulf states.

At the same time, the Iraqi threat is one of the justifications for the presence of Western, especially U.S., forces in the region, which Iran criticizes. Consequently, as long as Persian Gulf Arab states insist on the presence of foreign forces there, tension between Iran and these states will remain and Iran will be critical of their commitment to regional cooperation.

The Iranian government feels that its responsible behavior during the Iraqi invasion of Kuwait and recent increased contacts should pave the way for security agreements between Iran and her southern neighbors. A failure from the Arab side to move in this direction would greatly disturb Iran's perceptions of the Arab states. That said, it should be noted that Iran and Saudi Arabia have made some progress in paving the way for military contacts and confidence building measures.

Attitudes toward Smaller States

Finally, some Iranian perceptions of her Arab neighbors are derived from the fact that Iran has the largest population,[14] and the second largest area (after Saudi Arabia) in the region. The combination of these two facts with the reality that Iran controls almost the entire northern Gulf coast have created a "big brother" attitude on the Iranian side. The relationship of protector (Iran) and protected (Arab neighbors) was clearly also implanted in the region by the U.S. policy of the 1970s that declared Iran under the shah the regional "gendarme." The result is that Iranians tend to perceive their Arab neighbors as states that need Iranian protection and support, thus belittling them. Increased political and cultural exchanges would potentially reduce the negative impact of such a perception, but the reality is that Iran will remain one of the key military players in this tense region.[15]

FACTOR 5: GEOPOLITICS

Two geopolitical processes are influencing Iran's perceptions of and relations with her Arab neighbors in the Persian Gulf. Though geopolitical realities are very fluid, especially in the aftermath of the collapse of the Soviet Union, some tendencies can be identified, as will be explained below.

Persian Gulf Geopolitics

Since the 1979 Islamic revolution, one of the key issues in the Persian Gulf region has been the threat posed by Iran to Persian Gulf states. While initial revolutionary rhetoric suggested an Iranian desire to replace the region's monarchies with revolutionary Islamic governments, a number of developments have reversed that process, and today Iran is less concerned with exporting its revolutionary ideas than with its own national security and domestic politics. Therefore, while current Iranian policy has reversed this direction, the existence of threat perceptions in the past has produced a number of negative perceptions in Iran.

First, the creation of a political front between the GCC countries supported by the United States on one side and Iran and Iraq on the other side has automatically put Iran and her southern neighbors in a conflict situation. Even if today all regional countries are working toward overcoming that image and establishing a new relationship, the antagonism produced by earlier threat perceptions has its own residue and a negative impact on current perceptions. Iran and Iranians are not at ease with the fact that the front lines that have been drawn in the region put Iran and Iraq on the same side, i.e., the side threatening the region's security. Though this division was a product of the now dormant "dual containment policy,"[16] Iran still feels that it is not perceived as a partner in the Persian Gulf. One interesting phenomenon in this regard is the fact that from a GCC perspective, while the northern GCC states (Kuwait and Saudi Arabia) consider Iraq the main threat, the southern states, especially the UAE, are more focused on the potential threat from Iran.

Secondly, the almost unconditional cooperation between GCC countries and the United States has generated an impression on the Iranian side that these states are more concerned with U.S. interests in the region than with their own and broader regional interests. Indeed, the situation is a reverse of the conditions prior to the Islamic revolution, when the shah of Iran seemed to be the protector of U.S. interests in the region working against the interests of the littoral states. The existence of such a belief can only be destructive for the development of mutual perceptions. In the case of Iran, the strategic links between the GCC and the United States have had a negative impact on perceptions.

Caspian Sea Geopolitics

There is no doubt that the events of the past decade in the region bordering Iran's northern territories, i.e., Central Asia and Trans-Caucasia, have changed Iran's geopolitics to a significant extent. The creation of independent states in the north and the prospect for the Caspian basin to become a major energy source for the international community have brought about a number of new challenges for Iran. In the light of this development, there are different interpretations of Iran's regional policy.

Some researchers believe that Iran's new experience of relations with its northern neighbors, which were based on cooperation and partnership from the very start, opened the Iranian government's eyes toward the potential of regional cooperation as an alternative to confrontation. Consequently, the Iranian resolve to forge relations with her southern neighbors has developed out of the positive experience of her relations with the northern neighbors.

On the other hand, a number of observers believe that Iran had to reorient its policies to cope with the new situation. A continuation of hostile policies toward the southern neighbors along with the potential of new confrontation in the north would have been fatal for Iran's regional policy. Hence the Iranian government saw it expedient to improve relations with the southern neighbors to better confront challenges in the Caspian region.

Whatever the reasoning behind Iran's new chapter in foreign relations, it is clear that geopolitics, especially the fact that Iran is now the connecting element between the Persian Gulf and the Caspian basin, will play a role in shaping common interests among the Persian Gulf states, thus affecting mutual perceptions. As far as Iran is concerned, economic growth as a result of regional cooperation and exchange with her northern neighbors has certainly encouraged a number of forces, especially the country's business community, to favor better relations with the southern neighbors.

FACTOR 6: OIL AND GAS DEVELOPMENT

Oil and gas reserves provide the most significant engine for economic growth and wealth in the Persian Gulf countries. In regard to oil and gas, from an Iranian perspective the Arab countries in the southern Persian Gulf could be considered either competitors or partners. While in the past an atmosphere of competition was felt in many situations, it seems that Iran now would like to see the Arab Gulf countries as partners in oil and gas activity.

This attitude is manifesting itself more and more, as the formerly powerful oil cartel, the Organization of Oil Exporting Countries (OPEC), is regaining its international edge as a direct consequence of active cooperation between Saudi Arabia and Iran.[17] Currently, there are indications that a new era of cooperation might be developed among Islamic countries, especially the oil producing countries in the Persian Gulf. Such a process would clearly help the cause of rapprochement between Iran and her neighbors. Furthermore, it is expected that oil-rich Saudi Arabia and the United Arab Emirates will invest in Iran's oil and gas industry, increasing the interdependency of these nations in the crucial energy sector. One of the interesting chapters of the new relationship is the emerging cooperation between Iran's National Petrochemical Company and the Saudi conglomerate SABIC (Saudi Arabian Basic Industries Corporation).

In addition, the existence of shared oil and gas reserves in the Persian Gulf, which are slowly being developed, offers another justification for increased cooperation. Iran has joint hydrocarbon resources with Kuwait, Saudi Arabia, Qatar, the United Arab Emirates, and Oman. Cooperation based on mutual respect and a peaceful demarcation of boundaries in joint fields would clearly enhance the atmosphere of trust between Iran and her southern neighbors.[18] Furthermore, through joint investments in the energy sector, the two sides will learn to appreciate each other's business and technical capabilities—itself an important element in improving mutual perceptions.

FUTURE TENDENCIES

Having discussed current realities in regard to mutual perceptions in the Persian Gulf from an Iranian perspective, the following will attempt to identify the potential future trends that will influence relations and perceptions among the Persian Gulf states.

IMPORTANCE OF CIVIL SOCIETY

As discussed above, in the past the majority of issues were influenced by the relationship between governments and also by political priorities. Notwithstanding, the countries of the Persian Gulf are also influenced by a number of global developments, including the growth of civil society that has been witnessed over the past decade. Undoubtedly, the growing influence of civil society institutions, such as business and intellectual circles and non-governmental cultural and educational institutions, in a country's relationship with others will in turn play its role in shaping and correcting perceptions among the Persian Gulf nations. The future trend in this regard has already started with limited contacts between civil society institutions, especially universities, and in intellectual circles between Iran and her Arab neighbors. The enhancement of such activities and encounters will not only improve perceptions on both sides, but it will also ease the tension between governments over a number of issues such as Islamic interpretations.

ECONOMIC INTERACTION

The key realization that currently seems to exist on both sides is that needed economic growth can be achieved only in an atmosphere of trust and cooperation. There is little doubt that increased trade and investment activity between Iran and the other Persian Gulf states will have favorable results in improving perceptions and correcting erroneous beliefs on both sides. Economic interaction and integration have already led to fruitful cooperation in other parts of the world, so even though relations among the Persian Gulf nations are affected by their historical legacies, this region will not be an exception to the rule.

One important element that will increase the pressure on Persian Gulf countries to ease tensions and seek the advantages of economic integration is the current demographic structures in these countries. Most of the Persian Gulf states have a very young population that demands extraordinary economic growth patterns, which in turn strongly requires regional cooperation and stability. In other words, the need for job creation in all Persian Gulf states will increase the element of commercialization in political relations. The consequence will be a greater effort to reduce tensions and increase the region's stability in order to attract the needed investments.

What is needed at this stage is an augmented level of confidence-building measures (CBMs) between the two sides. Interestingly, foreign policy thinkers in Iran are increasingly discussing the introduction of CBMs between Iran and her southern neighbors.[19]

IRAN'S MAIN CONCERN

As mentioned earlier, over the course of the past two decades a number of Islamic and revolutionary agendas have overshadowed Iran's relations with her Arab neighbors. While that attitude does not exist anymore, it is important to realize that the key concern of Iran's national security revolves around the issue of the country's national integrity. There is no doubt that both state and society on the Iranian side would perceive any threat to Iran's integrity as a danger to the country's future development. Therefore, Persian Gulf states have to appreciate that any statements that would favor a disintegrated Iran, especially in regard to the country's Arab minority in the south, would be perceived as hostile and could lead to the return of old negative perceptions.

UNITED ISLAMIC CIVILIZATION?

The desire of a number of Islamic governments and scholars to create an Islamic political bloc has manifested itself in a number of currents in the Islamic world; clearly President Khatami,[20] who headed the OIC from 1997 to 2000, has promoted this idea. In the medium term, the promotion of an Islamic bloc has the potential of becoming an official goal of the major Islamic countries. To some extent, such a desire was also an engine for the creation of the D–8 Group of Islamic countries.[21] If one believes that Islamic countries will strive toward the creation of an Islamic bloc, the question would be how this effort would impact on Iran's relations with her Arab neighbors. In other words, would the creation of an Islamic bloc, which would probably give Iran a dominant role, improve Iran's relations with her Arab neighbors, or would it lead to new threat and hegemony perceptions in the region?

According to Mohammad Ali Azarshab, lecturer at Tehran University, Iranians and Arabs will play the key role in unifying the Islamic world and reviving Islamic civilization.[22] One could reasonably conclude that an Islamic civilizational bloc would be possible only if Iran and the Arab world increasingly cooperate and manage to develop a mutual understanding for each other's concerns. The small steps that have been taken so far, especially the relationship between Iran and Saudi Arabia, have proven to be constructive in this regard.

CONCLUSION

The above outline aims at identifying the key factors influencing Iran's perspectives and perceptions of her neighbors in the Persian Gulf region. Clearly, the factors mentioned are interrelated and interdependent in many cases. Today, as Iran and her Arab neighbors are working toward a genuine rapprochement, it would be a grave mistake to sweep the existing perceptions and misperceptions under the carpet and believe that the goodwill of a number of governments will solve all issues. In the author's view, each element that influences mutual perceptions should be studied and dealt with in an unprejudiced way.

An examination of individual factors on the one hand, and new currents and developments that influence mutual perceptions on the other, underlines the fact that the Persian Gulf is in a period of transition. Increased self-confidence among the littoral states in political affairs, the growth of civil society as a balancing element, the importance of economic interaction and integration, and finally the demographic profiles are all elements that require new patterns of regional thinking and regional integration. In this light, one challenge is to deal with the past and the other is to deal with the future. Undoubtedly, governments and intellectuals on both sides have to work toward promoting a higher level of relations and improving the existing negative perceptions. At the same time, they should not underestimate the role that can be played by the civil societies and business communities on both sides of the Persian Gulf.

Even if some historical legacies and disputes impede a rapid process of integration, common historical roots as well as common economic and regional interests will help the Persian Gulf nations overcome the old perceptions and define a new set of perceptions that are based on current realities rather than old hostilities. It can also be predicted that the new generations emerging in these countries will be more inclined to develop new patterns of relationships based on more realistic perceptions. Undoubtedly, the emerging elites of these countries have developed a more modern view of the world and will tend to take a more pragmatic approach to issues and challenges, including the review of old perceptions, contributing to better mutual understanding.

NOTES

1. 'Ajam is the term, often used in a pejorative sense, given in medieval Arabic literature to the non-Arabs of the Islamic empire, particularly the Persians. It later became an ethnic and geographic designation to separate Arabs from Persians (see *Encyclopedia Iranica*, I, 700–01).
2. Joya Blondel Saad, *The Image of Arabs in Modern Persian Literature* (Lanham, Maryland: University Press of America, 1996).
3. According to an Iranian scholar, Mahmoud Shamsolvaezin, on many occasions in the past Arab leaders and scholars referred to Iran, Turkey, and Pakistan as the "peripheral minorities" of the Islamic world. Interestingly, these three are the most populous Muslim countries of the region. For more detailed analysis of this issue, see "Iran and the Arab World: Interview with Mahmoud Shams," *Iran Focus*, vol. 9, no. 7, July/August 1996, p. 12.
4. It is estimated that some 300,000 Kuwaiti citizens sought refuge in Iran in 1990.
5. See the interesting article by Talal Atrissi, "The Iranian Image in Arab School Books," in *Discourse: An Iranian Quarterly*, vol. 1, no. 1 (Summer 1999), pp. 103–56. This article finds a very negative image of Iranians in Iraqi school books, for example, whereas Saudi books present a more positive image.
6. Currently, some 67 percent of the Iranian population are below 30 years old, 51 percent below 20 years.
7. The decision to hold the OIC summit in Tehran, which automatically gave the presidency of the OIC to Iran for three years, had been taken with Saudi Arabia's blessing. This fact had eased the tension on the Iranian side in regard to Iran's leading role in the Islamic community.
8. In a gesture of historical reconciliation and in order to demonstrate Iran's commitment to improving ties with Saudi Arabia, Iran's former president and powerful political figure,

Hashemi Rafsanjani, visited Saudi Arabia in February 1998. That visit was the initial step in a very successful series of political exchanges that have paved the way for a more normal relationship between Tehran and Riyadh.

9. This security accord covers areas such as the "fight against organized crime, terrorism, narcotic drug trafficking and illegal immigration as well as surveillance of borders and territorial waters" (*Iran News,* April 17, 2001, p. 15).

10. Opening speech by President Khatami to the OIC summit on December 9, 1997 in Tehran. Source: *Iran* (newspaper), December 10, 1997, p. 10.

11. For an excellent overview, see *The Persian presence in the Islamic world,* ed. Richard G. Hovannisian and Georges Sabagh (Cambridge: Cambridge University Press, 1998).

12. For further detail, see Richard N. Schofield, "Border Disputes: Past, Present and Future," in *The Persian Gulf at the Millennium,* Gary G. Sick and Lawrence G. Potter, eds. (New York: St. Martin's Press, 1997).

13. *Iran Focus,* vol. 11, no. 6, June 1998, p. 16.

14. Iran's population in 2001 was estimated at 67 million (including about 2 million refugees). That is more than the combined population of all other Persian Gulf states.

15. In a major speech about Iran on March 17, 2000, U.S. secretary of state Madeleine Albright recognized Iran's importance in the Gulf and expressed hope that Iran would fulfill its promise to act as an "anchor of stability" in the region.

16. Official term used by U.S. Department of State officials describing their policy toward Iran and Iraq in the second half of the 1990s.

17. OPEC's largest and second largest producers.

18. This fact was underlined in the incident involving the Dorra gas field that is shared between Iran and Kuwait. Interestingly, Iran, Kuwait, and Saudi Arabia managed to come to an agreement on demarcation of borders and exploitation of resources of the Dorra field. For more details, see Menas Associates' *Iran Energy Focus,* vol. 2, no. 10, June 1, 2000.

19. For example, see Tahere Ebrahimifar, "Confidence-Building Measures as Instruments of Regional Security in the Persian Gulf," in *The Journal of Foreign Policy* [Tehran], vol. 14 (Fall 2000) and Bijan Asadi, "Iran and the Persian Gulf: Détente, Dialogue Among Civilizations and New Arrangements," *The Journal of Foreign Policy,* vol. 14 (Winter 2001).

20. President Khatami has been outspoken in this matter. He talks not only of an Islamic civilization, but also of the need for a dialogue among civilizations, especially a dialogue between the West and the Islamic countries.

21. This group was established in 1997 upon the initiative of former Turkish prime minister Necmeddin Erbakan. D–8 includes Iran, Turkey, Pakistan, Nigeria, Egypt, Bangladesh, Indonesia, and Malaysia. It notably does not include Saudi Arabia, as the founding members wanted to include the most populous Islamic nations. The key premise is economic cooperation, and sooner or later other Islamic countries will be included.

22. Mohammad Ali Azarshab, "The Status of Iranians and Arabs in the Islamic World," *Middle East Studies Quarterly,* vol. 4, no. 4, Winter 1997, p. 61.

CHAPTER 12

IRAQ AND THE GULF SINCE 1991

The Search for Deliverance

RAAD ALKADIRI

INTRODUCTION

Iraq's formal attendance at the October 2000 Arab heads of state summit in Cairo marked a significant reversal of fortune for the Baghdad government. Struggling to escape the stranglehold of over a decade of stifling sanctions, President Saddam Hussein's regime suddenly found itself a welcome player once again at the highest levels of Arab politics. As Egyptian president Hosni Mubarak remarked of what was perhaps Baghdad's greatest single foreign policy achievement in ten years of grappling with the sanctions issue, Iraq was close to being fully integrated back into the Arab fold.[1] The fact that the Iraq issue dominated discussion at the subsequent summit in Amman in March 2001 underlined Mubarak's assessment. Although efforts to find an acceptable compromise formula that would accelerate Baghdad's rehabilitation failed, it was nevertheless clear that it could no longer be completely isolated on the Arab scene as it had just a few years earlier. Moreover, Iraq's diplomatic success had been achieved at least partially on its own terms.

Iraq's reemergence on the regional stage was due to a number of reasons. Sanctions had clearly weakened it militarily and economically, and as a result the country was viewed as less threatening by many of its neighbors in spite of its occasionally bellicose rhetoric. Popular antipathy to the embargo in the Arab world and beyond, and dismay over its humanitarian impact, also contributed to sanctions fatigue. But perhaps the most important factor underlying Iraq's partial rehabilitation was the crumbling of the Israeli-Palestinian peace process in an explosion of violence, and with it the unraveling of the very basis of eight years of U.S. Middle East policy under the Clinton administration.

Put on the defensive by a more assertive Israel and dismayed by Washington's unwillingness to play a more effective role in ending the violence in the West Bank and Gaza, both the regional Arab states and Iran were forced to make strategic reassessments. Under these new circumstances, Iraq was suddenly viewed as less of a threat and more as a potential partner in the new regional system of alliances that was emerging. Consequently, constructive engagement of Saddam Hussein's regime came to replace containment. This new, softer approach was also a signal by Arab states of their frustration with the United States' inability to rein in Israel, as well as a means of assuaging popular Arab demands for action by their governments in response to the Israeli challenge.

While Iraq's diplomatic gains represented progress toward its ultimate goal of having UN sanctions lifted, Baghdad still had some way to go. It was still denied access to its all-important oil export revenue, it remained under military embargo, and foreign investment in the country was heavily constrained. Furthermore, not all Arab states shared the same enthusiasm for Iraq's rehabilitation. Saudi Arabia and Kuwait in particular were conspicuous in their opposition to re-engaging the Iraqi regime, even as they were pulled along by the tide of events. Long the most ardent Arab supporters of sanctions on Iraq, neither state welcomed Baghdad's participation at the Arab summit—although under the circumstances they were powerless to resist the initiative—and Saddam Hussein's political gains did nothing to weaken their support for U.S.-led efforts to enforce the international embargo as well as the much-contested no-fly zone over southern Iraq.

Saudi and Kuwaiti refusal to moderate their policies in line with other Arab states earned them stinging rebukes from Baghdad. Iraq accused both Gulf states of being the willing pawns of the United States and Israel and called for the overthrow of their governments,[2] prompting some observers to conclude that the Iraqi regime remained an unreformed threat to its neighbors. But in reality, Iraq's rhetoric betrayed its vulnerability rather than its strength. The attacks on Saudi Arabia and Kuwait were not a sign of Iraq's renewed territorial ambition, but rather Baghdad's tacit acknowledgement that these two states, particularly Saudi Arabia, were regional linchpins for keeping Iraq contained and consequently posed a significant obstacle to its full rehabilitation. Indeed, the Iraqi regime had recognized ever since the end of the second Gulf war that restoring good relations with the Gulf states would be crucial if it was to succeed in attaining its primary foreign policy objective: political and economic rehabilitation without military denudement. As a result, the region in general, and Saudi Arabia in particular, had been a particular preoccupation of Iraqi foreign policy efforts over the decade of the 1990s.

GULF RELATIONS PRIOR TO THE GULF WAR

Iraq's focus on the Gulf was not unique to the post–Gulf War era; the region had long been of strategic importance to Baghdad. Economic imperatives relating to the export of oil, combined with geopolitical ambition, encouraged successive Iraqi governments in the post-monarchy era to extend their influence southward, a process that was given additional impetus by the United Kingdom's withdrawal from the Gulf in 1971. At the same time, Iraq's leaders had cast a wary eye eastward toward the country's large, regionally ambitious, and—until 1979, at least—militarily more powerful neighbor, Iran, Baghdad's principal rival for Gulf hegemony.

In the last two decades of the century, the Gulf became even more central to Iraq's broader strategic calculations, and as a result, the region emerged as a principal focus of the Iraqi regime's attention. The defining events of Iraqi history over those twenty years, namely the eight-year war with Iran, the 1991 Gulf war, and the economic embargo that followed, were all played out in this arena. Not surprisingly, therefore, the nature of Baghdad's relationship with the states of the Gulf was an important determinant of the regime's ability to achieve its immediate and longer-term foreign policy objectives. This remained as true in 2001 as it did during the war with Iran, despite the obvious antipathetic shift in sentiment toward the Iraqi regime that had taken place in most Gulf capitals. Indeed, one of the features of Iraq's regional relations since 1980 was that Baghdad, despite its hegemonic posturing, was forced to depend in one way or another on the Arab Gulf states in order to achieve some of its most important political goals. After the invasion of Kuwait in 1990, the Iraqi regime also looked intermittently to Iran for assistance.

Ironically, Iraq's dependence on its fellow Arab Gulf governments in the 1980s and 1990s—a relationship that ran contrary to the relative balance of military power between the two sides—was primarily the product of the regime's attempts to secure and assert its power in the region. Baghdad's desire to assume the role of Gulf superpower and to gain formal recognition of its elevated status were important driving factors behind the war with Iran and the invasion of Kuwait, arguably the two most fateful decisions in the previous half-century of modern Iraqi history. Both acts also incorporated a clear territorial component: Iraq's southern boundaries afford the country a minimal coastline and very limited access to the Gulf. Revising these borders in Iraq's favor, and thereby providing the state with a secure maritime outlet, was deemed a matter of strategic importance by a regime that perceived the existing geographic status quo as an economic and political vulnerability deliberately imposed by the country's former colonial masters when they drew up the state's frontiers at the beginning of the twentieth century.

However, Baghdad's resorting to force against both Iran and Kuwait ultimately led to outcomes that were contrary to the regime's strategic and territorial objectives. Regime survival, not expanded borders, ultimately became the principal gauge of the success of the war with Iran; and having been expelled from Kuwait, a much weakened and politically isolated Iraq was actually forced to cede coastal territory to the emirate, thereby narrowing its access to the Gulf yet further. More broadly, the two conflicts altered regional dynamics and in the process created a somewhat artificial situation whereby the traditional determinants of relative power were rendered moot.

Thus, despite its superior conventional military strength and geographical size, Iraq found itself on the defensive and in a position of practical weakness vis-à-vis its fellow Gulf states for much of the two decades after 1980. During the war with Iran, this was manifest in Baghdad's desperate need for financial support from the Arab Gulf, especially Kuwait and Saudi Arabia, to augment the huge cost of its war effort, while maintaining the partisan political support of these states was crucial to ensuring this flow of funds. Solidifying the relationship was helped by the Gulf Cooperation Council's (GCC) fear of Iran's perceived revolutionary zeal and the threat that this potentially posed to the existing regional order, a danger that the Iraqi regime played upon explicitly in drumming up Arab support for its cause.

IRAQI FOREIGN POLICY AFTER 1991

This reliance on the GCC states—and to a much lesser extent on Iran—as a means of achieving key foreign policy objectives became even more pronounced after the Gulf war, as Baghdad looked to these countries to deliver it from its political and economic isolation. However, while it was able to generate some favorable sentiment, particularly in the southern Gulf, by appealing both to common security concerns in the face of a perceived Iranian threat and to humanitarian misgivings as the social and economic conditions inside Iraq worsened, latent opposition to rehabilitating President Saddam Hussein's regime persisted, expressed most forcefully by Kuwait and Saudi Arabia. Iraq's efforts to use improved relations with Iran as a vehicle for overcoming its isolation appeared no more successful. Political reconciliation was limited by an ongoing legacy of mutual mistrust and conflict, and Tehran's own diplomatic efforts to improve its standing in the Gulf made it resistant to Iraq's appeals for closer ties.

Iraq's overriding objective after the end of the Gulf War was simple: deliverance from its postwar political and economic isolation, and the recovery of its regional status without divesting itself completely of its non-conventional weapons arsenal or at least the capacity to reconstitute this capability in the future. Thus, Baghdad focused its efforts on garnering political support for the lifting of UN sanctions by appealing both to states' economic and political self-interest as well as to their humanitarian heartstrings. In the meantime, it performed an elaborate dance with the UN disarmament bodies established to dismantle its non-conventional weapons arsenal, mixing cooperation with concealment and confrontation, leading to eventual expulsion of the inspectors in 1998 and refusal to countenance their return.

Baghdad's actions were based on the regime's stubborn refusal to submit to the role of the vanquished and to accept the full consequences of the invasion of Kuwait and its aftermath. Justifying its intractability in the face of international pressure for compliance with UN Security Council resolutions, the Iraqi government insisted that the country was resisting an aggressive U.S.-led conspiracy designed to bring Iraq to its knees, a claim that gained popular credence as the humanitarian devastation wrought by sanctions grew (and that helped not just to deflect domestic criticism for the hardship suffered by the Iraqi population away from the regime but actually enhanced support for it). At the same time, it was evident that the Iraqi government clung doggedly to the hope that the terms of the Gulf War ceasefire and the provisos for the regime's rehabilitation were negotiable. As such, the regime repeatedly sought to engage its adversaries, including the United States, in a dialogue aimed at establishing a modus vivendi that would facilitate Iraq's political reintegration and an end to the economic blockade, while meeting some—but by no means all—of the international community's concerns.[3]

The most important reasons for Iraq's obstinacy in the face of international pressure for its disarmament, however, went beyond pride and hope. Principally, Baghdad was driven by its overriding fixation with security and, more specifically, with regime survival—long the common denominator of its decision-making. Put simply, even the most favorable interpretation of UN Security Council conditions for lifting the international embargo on Iraq was perceived by the regime as incommensurate with its political and national security interests. Viewed from Baghdad's perspective, the complete elimination of its weapons of mass destruction (WMD) mandated by the UN Security Council would have left the country (and the regime) painfully exposed by robbing it of its capacity to deter hostile regional powers, many if not all of which had non-conventional weapon capabilities of their own. Under these conditions, life in the "tough neighborhood" that is the Middle East would not be simply difficult for Saddam Hussein's government—it could be fatal. At the very least, disarmament would severely undermine Iraq's hopes of resuming a regional role if and when sanctions were removed (although at least one analyst maintained that its conventional army remained a match for its principal regional rival, Iran).[4]

Baghdad's resistance to disarmament efforts increased over time as the regime came to realize that, whatever its level of cooperation with UN weapons inspectors, Washington would never countenance lifting sanctions while Saddam Hussein remained in power. Interestingly, it took until 1997 and the failure of the regime's efforts to parlay cooperation with weapons inspectors into tangible movement toward easing sanctions to irrevocably convince senior Iraqi officials that nothing could be done to make the United States budge. This was despite the fact that the Clinton administration's adamant refusal to make concessions was in line with the policy pursued by the U.S. government since the end of the Gulf war. Washington always clung to a broad interpretation of what was demanded of Iraq under the terms of postwar Security Council resolutions, insisting that, in addition to disarmament, Baghdad must return Kuwaiti prisoners of war (POWs), respect the human rights of domestic minorities, and prove that it was not a threat to peace and security in the Gulf. Moreover, it was abundantly clear from 1991 onwards that no U.S. administration perceived the Iraqi regime as capable of meeting those standards. Thus, while regime change was only formally introduced as a U.S. policy goal in late 1998, there was little doubt after the end of the Gulf war that the containment of Iraq through sanctions was designed to achieve more than just disarmament.

The perversity of Washington's approach, from the perspective of the Iraqi government at least, was that it is all stick and no carrot. The only incentive for Baghdad to comply with its Security Council obligations was to avoid punishment; otherwise the best that it could hope for from the council was a continuation of the status quo with some amendments at the margins, as in the case of the oil-for-food program, which the Iraqis finally accepted in 1996. The passage of Security Council Resolution 1284 in December 1999 did little to alter this underlying contradiction: the text was purposefully ambiguous on the key issues of what Iraq must do to satisfy the Security Council and what it could expect thereafter, reflecting the divisions among the permanent council members over how much the containment of Iraq should ever be eased while Saddam survived. As such, it continued to give Washington considerable latitude over the demands that could be made of the Iraqi regime before an easing of the embargo was discussed, and not surprisingly, the United States consistently rejected calls for a formal interpretation of the text.

Washington's rigidity after the Gulf war contributed to a highly volatile situation, which at times produced Iraqi acts of desperation (such as its mobilization on the Kuwaiti border in 1994) and which ultimately culminated in late 1998 with Baghdad's refusal to cooperate with UN weapons inspectors in the absence of a guaranteed and tangible quid pro quo on sanctions. It also created clear incentives for the Iraqis to wear down the international community's resolve to maintain sanctions rather than cooperate with disarmament efforts.

In testing international resolve to maintain the embargo, Baghdad pursued two separate but interrelated foreign policy avenues. First, it appealed to the political, economic, and commercial self-interest of states, emphasizing its regional importance and the wealth of economic opportunities that it offered, not least in the oil and gas sector. Second, it attempted to create anti-sanctions sentiment by highlighting the devastating humanitarian costs of the embargo, a blockade that it maintained was unjust given Iraq's avowed compliance with Security Council resolutions.

THE GULF STATES IN IRAQI FOREIGN POLICY

Much of Baghdad's diplomatic effort in support of its foreign policy was focused on the permanent members of the Security Council, especially China, France, and Russia. Nevertheless, the Iraqi regime also appreciated early on that support from the Arab Gulf states would provide an important boost to its rehabilitation efforts. Thus, the lines of dependency running from Baghdad to the Gulf, so evident throughout the 1980s, were accentuated in the 1990s. In appealing to the GCC for support, Iraq used both of its aforementioned foreign policy tacks. Appeals to self-interest were largely political in nature, and nuanced according to their intended target. They included threats, both immediate and future, in an apparent bid to coerce the Gulf states to acquiesce to Baghdad's rehabilitation. This was particularly evident in the aftermath of the Gulf War, but periodic bursts of bellicose rhetoric continued to be heard during times of tension and frustration, particularly against Kuwait and Saudi Arabia (although other GCC states were not immune).[5] Clearly, this did little to diminish fears that the regime was an enduring threat to peace and the security of at least some GCC states, and it provided useful ammunition for those states that sought to focus on the need to remain ever vigilant and contain Iraq while President Saddam Hussein remained in power.

Iraq's repeated resort to the use of threats was also ironic, given the regime's predilection for emphasizing the importance of its rehabilitation in order to counter *other* potential external dangers faced by the GCC states. Beginning in late 1992 with Tehran's moves to assume unilateral control of Abu Musa, Iraqi officials and the media regularly raised the specter of Iranian expansion, asserting that Iraq was the only capable defender of Arab interests in the Gulf region. In the words of one writer in the Iraqi newspaper *Babil*, "confronting the enemies of the Arab nation is impossible if Iraq is absent from the confrontation arena."[6]

In asserting their genuine concern for the GCC states and the Arab world more generally, Iraqi officials repeatedly pointed to the country's sacrifices to protect the "eastern flank" during the eight-year war with Iran. For example, speaking in 1997 on the ninth anniversary of the end of the war, Saddam Hussein lauded Iraq's performance, remarking that he "did not imagine there would be ones who could drive evil away from the Arabs and from their eastern flank with more efficiency."[7] Iraq's rhetoric was similarly strident, and in many ways more effective, with the onset of Israeli-Palestinian violence in September 2000. Adopting an extremely hard line against Israel, Baghdad asserted that it was the only true defender of Arab rights, a claim that resonated in the Arab "street."

The need for Iraqi-GCC reconciliation, and hence for Iraq's rehabilitation, was expressed in similarly broad Arab nationalist terms. Emphasizing the need to restore Arab unity, Iraqi leaders alluded to various "costs" that the post–Gulf War fragmentation of the Arab world imposed on the GCC states. By relying on a U.S. security umbrella, Baghdad noted that the Arab Gulf states were required to spend billions of dollars to finance Washington's local operations and in the process conceded a large measure of their sovereignty. More importantly, these states had, in Saddam Hussein's view, promoted "imperialist internationalism" and consequently "pave[d] the way for imperialism, led by the United States and its ally Zionism, to impose hegemony under the pretext of providing protection."[8] Iran was also held responsible for attracting a foreign presence to the Gulf.[9]

Underlying the Iraqi regime's thesis was the assertion that the dangers posed by this foreign encroachment and exploitation of the GCC states, as well as other threats to the Arab world (including a resurgent Israel), could be confronted only through dialogue among the Arab states, including Iraq. This in turn would eventually restore solidarity and cooperation among them—a prescient assumption in hindsight, although neither the manner of Iraq's gradual transformation from pariah to partner, nor the underlying forces that drove this shift, matched Iraqi thinking at the time.

As Iraqi leaders saw it, ending "differences of opinion" between Iraq and the Arab Gulf states should be the first step toward wider Arab cooperation,[10] thereby allowing Iraq to reassume the role of Gulf protector and provider (and, more importantly, to free itself from the shackles of sanctions and present the rest of the Arab World with a fait accompli). Only in this way, Baghdad argued, could the long-term security of the Gulf be guaranteed. As a first step toward this end, Iraqi officials repeatedly emphasized their willingness to conduct dialogue not just with the Arab Gulf states, but with any or all of their Arab brethren as well.[11]

RELATIONS WITH THE SOUTHERN GCC STATES

There is little to suggest that Iraq's appeals for solidarity directly influenced policy in any of the GCC governments. However, independent of Baghdad's efforts, support grew for ending Iraq's isolation, largely among the southern Gulf states—ironically the very countries that adopted a more ambivalent position toward Iraq during its war with Iran. A number of factors explained this policy shift. In part it reflected the narrow strategic interests of the individual states, whether in terms of seeking a measure of independence from Saudi dominance of the GCC or a desire to counteract Iranian power in the Gulf (some Gulf governments clearly agreed with Iraq's contention that it was an important element in maintaining the balance of power in the region). The failure of sanctions to unseat Saddam Hussein's regime and growing unease about the embargo's humanitarian toll on the Iraqi people also influenced the policies of these Gulf states.[12]

Adding to all of these considerations were concerns over U.S. policy toward the Middle East in general and Iraq in particular. All GCC states welcomed Washington's commitment to Gulf security. At the same time, however, repeated standoffs with Iraq, not to mention periodic large-scale military attacks against it, proved unpopular domestically in many Gulf states and therefore a potential source of instability and a focus for internal discontent. The Clinton administration's seemingly ad hoc and often ambiguous policy toward the Iraq issue also proved unsettling, leading these Gulf governments to conclude that Washington lacked a clear and workable long-term plan for dealing with Saddam Hussein and his regime, not to mention the internal political chaos that could follow the present Iraqi government's demise.

In the early 1990s, the GCC states most clearly identified with a "sympathetic" policy toward Iraq were Oman and Qatar. Muscat was the only Arab Gulf capital not to sever relations with Iraq following the invasion of Kuwait, while Doha restored diplomatic relations in 1992. By early 1995, both governments were openly calling for an easing of Iraq's isolation, although both consistently paid lip service to Iraq's need to implement UN resolutions. Qatari statements were particularly outspoken: in February 1995, Foreign Minister Shaikh Hamad bin Jasim Al Thani termed the humanitarian situation inside Iraq "a disgrace for Arabs." Qatari officials subsequently maintained this stance, arguing further that Iraq's rapid return to the fold would be in the best interests of Arab states.[13] In February 1999, for example, bin Jasim—who twelve months earlier had become the first GCC foreign minister to visit Iraq since the Gulf war—proposed the convening of a UN conference to settle the ongoing Iraqi crisis and pave the way for a lifting of the economic embargo on the country. Thereafter, senior Qatari officials persisted with efforts to bring about Iraq's rehabilitation through a reconciliation with its most ardent foes in the Gulf.[14]

However, the GCC's most vocal supporter of Iraqi rehabilitation from the mid–1990s onward was the United Arab Emirates (UAE), despite the country's initial reluctance to restore full diplomatic relations with Baghdad.[15] Signs of a shift from its initially cautious post–Gulf war policy (it dispatched a token force of troops to Kuwait during the October 1994 crisis) were evident in statements by Defense Minister Shaikh Mohammed bin Rashid Al Makhtoum in early 1995. He asserted that the Arabs "should stand by Iraq and its people" and called on the Kuwaitis to restore gradually its links with Baghdad. These statements proved to be a prelude to an impassioned plea for Arab rapprochement and the lifting of sanctions on Iraq by UAE president Shaikh Zayed bin Sultan, who insisted in a speech in October that year that the Arabs should work to ease the economic stranglehold irrespective of the West's policy.[16] After that, UAE leaders, including Shaikh Zayed, consistently reiterated this line, a policy founded in part at least on the federation's concerns over Iran's military ascendancy in the Gulf and the ongoing dispute with Tehran over sovereignty of Abu Musa and the two Tunb islands.[17] Senior UAE officials also took an outspoken stand against the use of force against Iraq. At the height of the Iraqi-UN standoff in early 1998, for example, Shaikh Zayed called possible U.S.-led military action against Iraq "loathsome" and argued that Iraq posed no threat to its neighbors in the Gulf.[18] He took an equally strong position against the Anglo-American air strikes in December that year, attacks that a UAE foreign ministry spokesman described as "unacceptable."

In spite of this political rhetoric, however, humanitarian assistance represented the most practical expression of UAE policy. The various emirates were the source of considerable medical and food aid, particularly after 1997. In early 1998, Shaikh Zayed's wife, Shaikha Fatima bint Mubarak, ordered a comprehensive plan to be drawn up for the dispatch of humanitarian aid to Iraq.[19] Bilateral trade also developed at a steady rate. A UN-sanctioned trade route opened in May 1997, and regular exchanges of trade, industry, and financial delegations took place. Iraqi traders were quoted as saying that they found duty-free Dubai easier to deal with than neighboring countries (presumably a reference to Jordan). Meanwhile, senior Iraqi officials insisted that the UAE, along with Jordan and later Syria, would remain Iraq's principal—and expanded—market once sanctions are lifted, replacing Kuwait (which acted as Iraq's major intermediary depot prior to the Gulf war).[20]

However, on a political level, neither the UAE nor its fellow southern Gulf states were able to influence significantly collective GCC or Arab policy toward Iraq. With brief exceptions, Baghdad clearly appreciated the support it received from these three states within the Gulf organization, publicly lauding their leaders for their good sense and true Arabism.[21] Moreover, intermittent consultations at ministerial level and above took place: Qatari Emir Shaikh Hamad bin Khalifa Al Thani met Iraqi vice president Taha Yasin Ramadan on the margins of the Islamic summit in Tehran in December 1997, and in January 2000 he visited Baghdad to discuss the implementation of the newly passed UN Security Council resolution 1284; Saddam Hussein's half-brother Barzan al-Tikriti reportedly held secret meetings with Shaikh Zayed both in the summer of 1996 and in the autumn of the following year.[22] Iraqi officials also met with their counterparts from the UAE and Qatar during the Arab summit in Cairo in October 2000. Nevertheless, the support of these states on the whole proved little more than a valuable propaganda tool for the Iraqi regime. Reports of secret initiatives aimed at Arab reconciliation and encouraging dialogue between Baghdad and Washington—efforts associated in particular with Shaikh Zayed—came to naught.[23] Moreover, Iraq's efforts to use these states as a conduit for reversing the GCC's public backing of sanctions were fruitless.

Indeed, despite clear differences of opinion among its member states, GCC unity on Iraq was maintained at the organizational level. This was clearly evident in the outcome of successive GCC summit meetings. In December 1997, for example, a proposal by Shaikh Zayed to send a Gulf delegation to Baghdad with a set of demands as a prelude to Iraq-GCC reconciliation was rejected. Instead, the summit's final statement repeated the organization's existing tough line on Iraq, calling on Baghdad to implement all post-war Security Council resolutions, including those calling for the release of Kuwaiti POWs and for Iraq to refrain from acts of aggression or provocation against its neighbors. The GCC leaders also insisted that Iraq must apologize publicly for its invasion and occupation of Kuwait.[24]

A similar dichotomy between the views of individual states and council decisions continued to be evident into 2001. Meeting in Jeddah in late 2000, the GCC foreign ministers did formally agree to consider a Qatari initiative to bring about a rapprochement with Baghdad, but their underlying message remained unchanged.[25] The outcome of these meetings clearly demonstrated the relative political weakness of the GCC's southern states compared to their northern allies Kuwait and Saudi Arabia. More importantly, the willingness of these states to subsume their individual policy preferences in favor of consensus indicated the extent to which intra-organization unity and consensus remained priorities for its member-states, irrespective of their independent political and security objectives.

CONTINUED CONFRONTATION WITH KUWAIT

The combination of these two factors—weakness and desire for consensus—ensured that Kuwaiti and Saudi policy preferences on Iraq remained paramount within the GCC. Indeed, both states enjoyed an effective veto over reconciliation efforts. Of the two, Kuwait was the most vociferous in refusing to countenance a rapprochement with Baghdad. The psychological wounds inflicted by the Iraqi invasion were very slow to heal; indeed, there was no ambiguity in the emirate's adamant refusal to deal with Saddam Hussein's regime, regardless of the opinion of its fellow GCC partners.[26] This resulted in a reactive and somewhat vengeful policy. Unwilling to let bygones be bygones, Kuwaiti leaders responded with alarm to the various southern Gulf initiatives toward Iraq. They attempted to nip these efforts in the bud, not least by refusing to participate in any such reconciliation efforts, as was the case with a Qatari initiative in November 2000. Instead, the emirate consistently demanded that Iraq admit its culpability for the 1990 invasion and respect and implement all Security Council resolutions. In the latter regard, Kuwait's approach was somewhat similar to that of Washington. The difference, however, was that for the Kuwaitis, these resolutions were not merely a convenient diplomatic cover for rejecting the Iraqi regime's rehabilitation but rather raised issues of direct concern to the emirate, particularly the return of POWs and worries over future Iraqi behavior. Thus, there was no letup in Kuwait's demands for the return of over 600 POWs who it claimed were still being held by Baghdad, and it was clear that the emirate had no faith in Iraq's protestations of peaceful intent.

Iraq's approach to Kuwait after 1991 did little to calm the emirate's fears. Baghdad's policy had a tactical bent: its undulations acted as a barometer of the regime's own sense of its foreign policy fortunes. Thus, in the immediate aftermath of the war and in line with Iraq's general obstructionism, Iraqi officials and media persisted in their occupation-era rhetoric, refusing to recognize the emirate's independence or the restored al-Sabah regime. This was accompanied by a large number of relatively small cross-border incursions, not all of which were politically motivated.

It took until 1993, and the more general softening of Iraqi foreign policy, for the first public hints of moderation by Iraq. In spite of its evident anger over the UN boundary commission's demarcation of the joint border with Kuwait, Baghdad publicly expressed a willingness to cooperate with Arab League efforts to resolve the POW issue. Midway through the following year this had evolved into clear signals from Saddam Hussein and other Iraqi officials that Baghdad was more eager to overcome its differences with Kuwait through "unconditional" dialogue.[27] However, it took until late 1994 for a definitive change in Iraqi policy, when Russian mediation to resolve diplomatically the October border crisis led the following month to Iraq's formal recognition of Kuwaiti sovereignty and the newly demarcated border. Nevertheless, the Iraqi action, born largely of the regime's frustration with the continuing embargo, illustrated clearly that Kuwait's security was seen as something of a pawn for Baghdad's broader policy ambitions.[28]

After the recognition decision, Baghdad's public attitude toward Kuwait fluctuated between conciliation and threats. Iraqi officials repeatedly expressed their desire to put the past behind them and restore ties with Kuwait as part of a broader Arab reconciliation.[29] Moreover, there was a very significant decline in cross-border incidents along the Kuwaiti border. Nevertheless, Iraq leaders left their southern neighbor in no doubt about their absolute refusal to acquiesce to Kuwait's broad demands for the sake of better ties. Baghdad continued to insist that Kuwait was the master of its own fate in 1990. In mid–1998, Taha Yasin Ramadan was quoted as rejecting calls for an Iraqi apology for its aggression, arguing instead that the Arabs should apologize to Iraq for imposing the economic blockade upon it.[30] Deputy Prime Minister Tariq Aziz adopted a similar tack in a series of four hard-hitting articles entitled "Who Should Apologize to Whom" that were published in the daily *al-Thawrah* in January 1999.[31] Meanwhile, regular criticisms of the al-Sabah regime and intermittent attacks on the legitimacy of the Kuwaiti regime continued—particularly during times of heightened Iraqi frustration with the continued imposition of sanctions or when Baghdad felt vulnerable.

Kuwait's rejection of Baghdad's reconciliation offers and the emirate's close ties to the United States were assailed in the Iraqi media. The tone of these attacks was illustrated in the immediate aftermath of the standoff with the UN in early 1998, when Sami Mahdi, chief editor of *al-Thawrah,* called the emirate's policy "reckless" and charged that it served only "the enemies of the Arab nation; that is, the Americans and the Zionists."[32] In an apparent bid to turn the tables on the Kuwaitis, he also insisted that it was the emirate that threatened Iraqi national security in violation of UN conventions through its close military relationship with the United States.[33]

Kuwait was the focus of similar vitriolic rhetoric in the aftermath of the December 1998 bombings and the airstrikes that followed in the northern and southern no-fly zones. Baghdad launched a series of vicious verbal attacks on the emirate, accusing its leaders of carrying out an "aggressive hateful war" in alliance with the United States, and demanding an immediate end to the policy.[34] After a brief let-up in late 1999 and early 2000, this rhetorical campaign was revived, in an effort that Iraq claimed was designed to expose Kuwaiti and Saudi ongoing cooperation with U.S. efforts to undermine the regime.

With regard to the issue of Kuwait's POW allegations, Iraq was dismissive, insisting that it returned all prisoners in 1991. Officials conceded that an indeterminate number of Kuwaitis missing in action may remain; but Kuwait's insistence on dwelling on the issue and using it as a means of obstructing Iraq's rehabilitation was a source of anger for the Iraqis, who noted that missing persons are a legacy of all wars. For political reasons alone, any captive Kuwaitis still held by Iraq were unlikely to be released except as part of a broader deal with Kuwait that met key Iraqi demands, notably its rehabilitation; one report in late 1997 suggested that Barzan al-Tikriti had proposed that Iraq would hand over the remaining POWs to the UAE as part of a reconciliation scheme led by Shaikh Zayed. Nevertheless, Baghdad maintained that it was cooperating with the International Committee of the Red Cross efforts to resolve the matter, although it ceased attending formal meetings on the POW issue after Operation Desert Fox in 1998.[35]

Faced with Kuwait's dogged focus on the POW issue and other examples of what it regarded as arrogant Kuwaiti obstinacy designed to block reconciliation efforts, Baghdad was not averse to resorting to threats, both actual and rhetorical. Iraq's scope for practical military action in the south was severely constrained by the allied air-exclusion zone, the U.S. presence in Kuwait, and the imposition of limits on the movement of Iraqi troops in the aftermath of the 1994 border crisis. Intermittent rumors of Iraqi moves toward the Kuwaiti border after 1994—often raised by the Kuwaitis themselves—proved groundless. Nevertheless, this did not stop the media and officials in Baghdad from reminding Kuwait about its vulnerability, pointing out that its weakness had already been the cause of the al-Sabah's temporary downfall at Iraq's hands once before. Kuwait, they cautioned, should therefore be wary of repeating its past mistakes with regards to Iraq.[36]

Iraqi statements also underscored the limits of their patience with the status quo: "brothers living in one tent and sharing one common destiny should not be starving to death while others are full to the point of death," insisted Saddam Hussein during a speech in September 1997.[37] Such a policy, Baghdad warned, was creating an enduring legacy of Iraqi hatred toward Kuwait, the possible implications of which, while left unstated, were nevertheless clear. The possible dangers for Kuwait were underscored when, following Operation Desert Fox, the issue of the common border was raised publicly once again, with calls in the Iraqi National Assembly for the government to revoke its 1994 recognition of the new boundary demarcation. In August 2000, the assembly met again to discuss the Kuwait issue, this time in the context of Iraq's allegations of Kuwaiti "aggression" against it, and questions about Kuwaiti sovereignty were raised occasionally by Iraqi officials thereafter.

APPEALS AND THREATS TO SAUDI ARABIA

While Baghdad generally adopted a far more measured public stance toward Saudi Arabia compared to Kuwait, Riyadh's rejection of Iraq's reconciliation efforts and its support for U.S. policy in the Gulf also made Riyadh the focus of stinging Iraqi rhetoric and insults, particularly after Operation Desert Fox in December 1998. This represented something of a turnaround; in the years leading up to the Anglo-American campaign, media attacks against the kingdom had become rarer. Instead, the Iraqi regime chose to emphasize its lasting desire to restore full relations with Saudi Arabia and to highlight what it perceived as indications of shifts in Saudi policy in favor of Iraq.

The difference in Baghdad's approach to its two southern neighbors reflected their relative political weight. Iraq's disposition toward Kuwait appeared to be based on a belief that in the long run, Kuwaiti sensibilities could safely be ignored without any lasting detriment to Iraqi national interests. It was clear, however, that the same did not apply to Saudi Arabia. Indeed, some senior Iraqi officials had long believed that Riyadh held the key to Iraq's fate—a feeling that was allegedly shared by Saddam Hussein.[38]

This perception was hardly surprising, given Saudi Arabia's regional and international position. Despite occasional acts of independent defiance by other members, the kingdom remained the leader of the GCC by virtue of its political and economic weight. As such, its views were crucial in determining policy within the council, and it was therefore the only state capable of overriding the Kuwaiti veto on the issue of Iraqi rehabilitation. This political weight also extended to the Arab world more broadly, something that was plain to see in the diplomatic tumult that followed the December 1998 Anglo-American bombings. In a shift away from the traditional conservative reticence that generally characterized its foreign policy, Riyadh took a forceful stand, delaying efforts to convene an Arab heads of state summit to discuss Iraq and the attacks and ensuring that the eventual gathering was downgraded to foreign ministerial level. In doing so, the Saudi leadership effectively blocked Iraq's initial hopes that the Arab states were on the verge of providing it with a rapid means of escaping its economic and political isolation, something that earned Riyadh the wrath of the Iraqi regime.[39]

An additional factor adding to Saudi Arabia's importance in Baghdad's eyes was its close relationship with the United States. Clearly there was a military dimension to Iraq's thinking: not only was the kingdom the only Gulf state large enough to act as a base for a major ground assault against Iraq (as it did during the Gulf war), but it also played host to a significant contingent of U.S. military forces, including aircraft used in the patrol of the southern no-fly zone. There is little doubt that the Iraqi regime would have viewed convincing the Saudis to rid themselves of these forces as a significant victory: in the immediate term, it would have complicated the prosecution of U.S. operations against Iraq; more broadly, it would also have undermined what the Iraqis saw as the direct existential threat in their midst. However, while this military dimension was clearly a significant issue for Iraq, it was the political aspect of the U.S.-Saudi relationship that was perhaps most important as far as Saddam Hussein's regime was concerned. The desire to improve relations with Saudi Arabia went beyond simply wanting to undermine U.S. policy toward Iraq and the Gulf region more generally (although this would clearly have been greeted with glee in Baghdad); the Iraqi regime also probably entertained hopes that Riyadh could act as a conduit to improved relations with Washington given the close ties between the two. Over the years, Iraqi officials made no secret of their desire to reestablish better relations with the United States, something that they realized would help their beleaguered position immensely. They also recognized that, even if Washington had entertained the notion of softening its stance toward Saddam Hussein's regime, a significant thaw in the U.S.-Iraqi relationship would be unlikely in the face of Saudi opposition

Given these factors, it was not surprising that Baghdad took active steps to establish direct channels to the Saudi leadership in a bid to restore bilateral relations. These efforts began in the immediate aftermath of the Gulf war—at a time when anti-Saudi rhetoric was at its loudest—when Barzan al-Tikriti and Shaikh Abd al-Aziz al-Tawaijari, deputy commander of the Saudi National Guard and a close associate of Crown Prince Abdullah bin Abd al-Aziz, met in Geneva. However, Iraq's proposals for a rapid rapprochement, which reportedly included the immediate restoration of diplomatic ties, the resumption of Iraqi oil exports via Saudi Arabia and Saudi mediation with Washington on Iraq's behalf, were rejected outright by Riyadh.[40] Nevertheless, this link was maintained as the principal channel between the two states for a considerable period of time. In addition, Baghdad used other indirect communication routes with the Saudi leadership, taking advantage of established personal relationships and cross-border tribal links.

Not surprisingly given its policy, Baghdad was quick to seize upon any developments that might be interpreted as a turnaround in the Saudi position (as well as any indication of Kuwait's growing isolation within the GCC). Prior to December 1998, there were hints of a subtle change in the kingdom's policy toward Iraq, signs of which were evident in statements by Saudi officials, including Foreign Minister Prince Saud al-Faisal and Crown Prince Abdullah. Speaking prior to the December 1997 GCC summit, the latter remarked cryptically on the need for "going beyond preoccupation with the ruins of the past," which Baghdad, among others, took as a reference to the Iraq question.[41] Overall, however, the Iraqi leadership's efforts, including proposals for direct open dialogue and the opening of interest sections in the two states, resulted in no explicit shift in Saudi policy.[42] Riyadh consistently adopted a line very similar to that of Kuwait, insisting that Iraq must comply fully with Security Council resolutions and that responsibility for the country's plight lay solely with the Iraqi regime. In the aftermath of Operation Desert Fox, Saudi criticism of the regime became more direct, including calls in the media for Saddam Hussein's overthrow and his indictment for war crimes.[43]

In fact, while the regional status quo remained unchanged, Riyadh never looked likely to take significant strides toward a rapprochement with Iraq in the absence of indications that some political change was taking place in Baghdad itself.[44] A number of factors underlay the Saudi position. Fear of Iraq's military potential and a reluctance to see the country restored to its former strength (particularly under Saddam Hussein), were consistent concerns after 1990, and they may explain in part Riyadh's moves later in the decade to improve relations with Iran. The kingdom also faced pressure from the United States to keep up its tough stance, thereby supporting Washington's containment policy that explicitly targeted Saddam Hussein's regime. Convincing Riyadh to maintain its tougher approach may not have been too difficult in the short term; there were clear signs that it had grown increasingly frustrated with the repeated standoffs seen after late 1997 and their regional fallout (particularly in terms of Arab popular opinion).

However, the kingdom never showed any great enthusiasm for participating directly in efforts to bring about regime change in Iraq, and as Baghdad's regional position improved, questions emerged about how much Riyadh was willing to cooperate with efforts to unseat Saddam Hussein and his government. As far back as the mid-1990s, the Saudi leadership had begun to show a growing reluctance to support the use of force against Iraq. It failed to endorse US attacks that followed the Iraqi military incursion into Irbil in August/September 1996, and reportedly refused Washington's request to launch these strikes from Saudi bases.[45] The Saudis rebuffed similar US requests during the repeated Iraqi-UN crises of 1998 that led up to Desert Fox.

Meanwhile, the kingdom also demonstrated a certain ambivalence toward the U.S.-backed Iraqi opposition in exile. Much was made of Riyadh's contacts with and funding for opposition groups in the period immediately following the Gulf War. However, its actual contribution to removing Saddam Hussein was far more limited. Reports suggested, for example, that Saudi support did not extend to a willingness to participate directly in the overthrow of the Iraqi regime,[46] something it insisted was up to the Iraqis themselves. As the external Iraqi opposition regained its political prominence in 2001 under the patronage of the Bush Administration and the U.S. Congress, questions reemerged about Saudi Arabia's willingness to back plans for overthrowing the Iraqi regime, which included proposals for opposition training and operational bases to be established in neighboring countries. But initially at least, Saudi Arabia maintained a low profile on the issue.

Indeed, in the absence of some watertight guarantee of the Iraqi opposition's success, Riyadh seemed likely to persist with its low-profile approach to regime change in Iraq. The kingdom's concerns regarding the stability of Iraq and its future territorial integrity remained paramount. Such worries were understandable. Saudi Arabia recognized that its overt participation in moves to unseat the Iraqi regime could backfire dangerously in the event that such efforts failed. Moreover, any disintegration of the existing political order in Iraq threatened a spillover of domestic violence into neighboring countries (which themselves wanted to influence events in Iraq), not to mention possibly shifting the regional balance of power in favor of Iran, which despite its closer ties with Riyadh, nevertheless remained the kingdom's principal rival for regional power.

A DANGEROUS OPPORTUNITY—IRAQ'S IRAN POLICY

Relations with Iran posed a major tactical dilemma for the Iraqi leadership in the decade after the Gulf war. On the one hand, the Islamic republic was the source of opportunities that could have potentially facilitated the success of Iraq's foreign policy. Moreover, Tehran's own regional problems and its removal from the immediate political arena of the Gulf war and its aftermath gave Baghdad slightly more scope for initiative than was the case with its GCC policy. On the other hand, Iran remained a threat. These two aspects, both of which involved complexities in their own right, created a series of opposing forces on Iraqi decision-making that in turn influenced its view regarding relations with Iran.

Iran has acted as a source of opportunities in a number of ways. First, the specter of the Islamic republic's regional ambitions and its perceived military strength provided Iraq with a useful vehicle to emphasize its own value as a source of strategic balance. This was used not merely in relation to the GCC states; Baghdad also played on Western fears of Iranian expansionism. In August 1996, for example, it used claims of Iranian encroachment into northern Iraq to justify in part its active military support for the Kurdish Democratic Party (KDP), a ploy that forestalled briefly a U.S. response to the central government's armed incursion. Secondly, Iraqi leaders appeared to hope that signs of improving relations between Baghdad and Tehran would prompt a regional and international rethink of strategy in Iraq's favor. At the same time, however, Baghdad clearly viewed Iran as a potential ally due to their common sanctions experience. Iraqi officials called for closer bilateral ties as a means of relieving the isolation imposed on both states by the United States.

In spite of this rhetoric, practical cooperation was limited. The clearest example was Iranian involvement in illegal Iraqi oil exports, a significant source of income for the cash-strapped regime in Baghdad—some estimates suggest that exports reached up to 100,000 barrels per day after 1996.[47] Progress on the political front was more cautious.

Saddam Hussein exchanged letters with President Ali Akbar Hashemi Rafsanjani before the latter stood down in 1997, and a series of high-level meetings took place, including a visit by Vice President Taha Yasin Ramadan to Tehran in December 1997 for the Organization of the Islamic Conference summit, where he held talks with Iranian president Mohammed Khatami. In the aftermath of the Ramadan-Khatami meeting, Iraqi foreign minister Mohammed Said al-Sahhaf spoke optimistically about the possibility of normalization with Iran.[48] Indeed, gestures designed to improve ties between the two states became more frequent after Khatami's assumption of the presidency in August 1997. The Revolutionary Command Council—Iraq's highest decision-making body—passed a decree the same month allowing Iranian pilgrims to visit Shi'i holy sites in the country. In doing so, Baghdad acquiesced implicitly to a longstanding Iranian condition for better relations. The decision was eventually implemented in May 1998, but not before Iraq made a further concession by agreeing to Tehran's demands for the establishment of a joint committee to determine procedures for the pilgrimages.

Meanwhile, there was also progress toward resolving the POW issue, a central Iraqi prerequisite for reconciliation (Baghdad accused Iran of holding over 18,000 Iraqis captive since the 1988 ceasefire, almost 9,000 of whom are registered with the International Committee of the Red Cross). A series of prisoner swaps in early 1998 culminated with the handing over of 800 Iraqi POWs in April as part of an Iranian pledge to release almost 6,000 Iraqi captives. The deal, arranged during a meeting in New York in September 1997 between al-Sahhaf and his Iranian counterpart Kamal Kharrazi, included the return to Iran of Hussein Reza Yashkuri, a pilot who had been held since being shot down on September 18, 1980, in a bid to bolster Iraq's claim that Iran initiated the eight-year war.[49] Prisoner swaps took place intermittently thereafter, and joint searches by officers from the two states were carried out to uncover the remains of soldiers in the areas along the southern border.

These initial steps were followed by further signs of a significant thaw in bilateral relations, although the road was bumpy. After a period of violent tension in early and mid–2000, high-level dialogue was restored after Iraqi vice president Ramadan met Iranian president Khatami during the OPEC summit in Caracas in September 2000. One month later, Kharrazi became the most senior international official since the Gulf war to fly to Baghdad, where he met Saddam Hussein and other senior Iraqi leaders. This was followed by a meeting between Khatami and Izzat Ibrahim, the vice chairman of the Iraqi Revolutionary Command Council, during the Organization of the Islamic Conference summit in Doha, after which the Iranian president spoke of his country's willingness to open a new chapter in relations between the two countries. Speaking a few days earlier, Iraqi foreign minister Mohammed Said al-Sahaf announced that Baghdad and Tehran were working to normalize relations via a set of committees that had been established to resolve outstanding issues.[50]

In spite of the softer rhetoric, however, a rapid improvement in relations did not appear likely. While strategic changes in the region enhanced the value of bilateral relations, the legacy of history, particularly war, between the two states created an enduring set of deep-seated and antipathetic differences that would prove very difficult to overcome. Each side, for example, continued to support armed organizations dedicated to the removal of the neighboring regime, something that led to heightened bilateral tension and that both capitals identified as a key issue in future negotiations (early in 2000, Iranian forces were reported to have pursued attacking Mujahedin-i Khalq rebels across the border into Iraq, and in April 2001 Iran launched more than fifty missiles at Mujahedin camps in Iraq after a series of cross-border attacks). The gulf separating the two sides was reflected in the conditions they set for a restoration of relations. In Iraq's case, these included not only the repatriation of POWs but also the return of Iraqi aircraft (including 115 military and 33 civilian planes) that were flown to Iran during the Gulf war. Of greater significance were Iraqi calls on Iran to prove conclusively its commitment to better relations, accusing it of pursuing a two-faced policy and of failing to match words with deeds. Tehran was similarly critical of Baghdad's purported desire for reconciliation.[51]

Underlying the Iraqi stance was the fact that despite Iran's utility, Baghdad still perceived the Islamic republic as an untrustworthy, threatening rival, and one that it was yet again being forced to court at a time of weakness rather than strength. Iraqi officials repeatedly accused Tehran of interference in Iraq's domestic affairs. This included providing logistical and military backing for the March 1991 Shi'i uprising, after which Baghdad claimed to have captured a number of Iranian agents. Allegations of Iranian backing for Shi'i rebels in the south persisted, apparently with due cause. Meanwhile, Tehran attempted to exploit the political vacuum created by the ongoing violent factionalism in northern Iraq. In addition to providing material support to Patriotic Union of Kurdistan forces, Iranian troops and the Badr Brigade of the Tehran-backed Shi'i opposition group, the Supreme Council for the Islamic Revolution in Iraq, intervened intermittently in fighting in northern Iraq, most notably in 1996. Iranian forces also mounted raids against Kurdish Democratic Party of Iran targets in the region. These areas were politically sensitive to Baghdad as sources of continued armed opposition to the central government that could conceivably threaten the territorial integrity of the state. This was particularly the case in the north, where the regime had been prohibited from re-establishing control. Iran's involvement there and its intermittent efforts to promote itself as the principal mediator in the Kurdish dispute threatened to weaken further Baghdad's tenuous hold over the area. While the Iraqi regime's position in the south was stronger, it was nevertheless fragile, and Iranian interference was seen to exacerbate this weakness and threaten the integrity of the state, particularly given the confessional dimension of the domestic struggle.

The Khatami administration's regional policy aimed at improving ties with the GCC posed further dangers for Iraq. Better relations between Tehran and the Gulf states weakened Baghdad's case for being a regional defender against Iranian aspirations, at least in the short term, and thereby undermined the urgency of the need for Iraq's strategic rehabilitation. Of particular importance in this regard was the developing relationship between Iran and Saudi Arabia. A formal alliance between the two threatened to create a strategic environment broadly similar to the one that existed in the area during the early and mid–1970s and that would leave Iraq surrounded by potentially hostile, militarily powerful states, a situation that would certainly heighten Baghdad's feelings of isolation and vulnerability.

PROSPECTS FOR THE FUTURE

The dynamics of Iraq's relationship with the GCC states and Iran after the Gulf War were influenced by two key factors: the country's political and economic isolation following its invasion of Kuwait and Saddam Hussein's survival in power. As suggested, this postwar environment left Baghdad bereft of much of its military and political power, and therefore of its capacity to act independently in pursuit of its primary foreign policy goals. This is not to suggest, as some analysts have, that Iraq lacked the will to pursue a regional policy, but rather that circumstances left it somewhat at the mercy of smaller states' whims, whose very lack of stature made them inappropriate vehicles for promoting Iraqi aims. Meanwhile, Iraq lost ground to its two main regional rivals, Iran and Saudi Arabia, and the emerging alliance between the two states from the mid-1990s onward only exacerbated Baghdad's insecurity.

The new strategic dynamic that emerged in the Middle East in the wake of renewed Israeli-Palestinian violence in late 2000 clearly improved Iraq's position somewhat, leading a number of Arab states—and to a lesser extent, Iran—to shift toward more constructive engagement with Baghdad. But this reorientation looked likely to remain cautious while Saddam Hussein survived in power. This, in turn, suggested that Iraq's post–1991 strategic view of the Gulf states as a simultaneous source of opportunity and danger was likely to remain largely unaltered. Moreover, the regional instability engendered by these conditions over the previous decade also looked set to continue. While there had been no major overt acts of Iraqi hostility in the direction of the Gulf states since 1994, the regime's propensity to lash out verbally at neighboring states during times of crisis and frustration, and occasional cross-border incidents along its boundaries with Kuwait and Saudi Arabia, added to the sense of insecurity felt by Iraq's Gulf neighbors. Meanwhile, continued Iraqi refusal to cooperate with UN weapon inspectors after 1998 further raised tension, and meant that the prospect of U.S.-led military action was a persistent one.

In the longer term, the question that remained was whether Iraq's eventual rehabilitation or the demise of Saddam Hussein would alter the strategic equation in the Gulf. There was little indication that the existing regime in Baghdad had forsaken its desire to resume a regional role in the Gulf eventually and to reestablish itself as a local superpower, a position it apparently believed was rightfully its own. Clearly, there would be limits on how far Baghdad could extend its influence beyond enhanced trade links while sanctions, particularly prohibitions on Iraqi access to its oil revenue, remained in place.[52] However, once the embargo was removed, Iraq seemed poised to resume its "big brother" mantle, as it termed it. Iran and Saudi Arabia appeared certain to respond to such moves with alarm, and tension between the three states would be heightened as they jostled for relative supremacy, whether individually or in an alliance of two against the third.

Iraq's aspirations were also likely to clash with territorial realities in the post-sanctions era. Baghdad's acceptance of both joint control over the Shatt al-Arab boundary with Iran and, more particularly, of the redrawn border with Kuwait represented concessions in the face of extreme circumstances (the prelude to the Gulf war in the former case and as a means of extricating itself from the 1994 border crisis in the latter case). These two decisions robbed Iraq of much of its already limited access to the Gulf, thereby undermining its ability to play an effective regional role in the future. The 1992 demarcation of the Iraqi-Kuwaiti border by a special UN boundary commission was particularly galling and detrimental to the regime's wider interests. The commission stripped Iraq of a significant part of its de facto southern coastline, including the southern part of the port of Umm Qasr and the main navigation lanes of the Khawr Abdullah—the country's only effective alternative to the Shatt al-Arab as a Gulf outlet.[53]

Historical precedent suggested that these border problems, which essentially remained unresolved, would resurface as a source of friction in the future. For the existing regime, the borders were an enduring symbolic testament to its weakness. This reason alone seemed likely to provide Baghdad with sufficient political motivation to try to induce a territorial change in the future, especially given the fact that the border with Kuwait left Iraq even more strategically vulnerable than it was prior to August 1990, thereby making Iraqi control over the Kuwaiti islands of Warba and Bubiyan of greater importance as a means of insuring unimpeded access to the Gulf. Comments by senior Iraqi officials challenging the legitimacy of the UN-demarcated border was a possible portent of things to come.[54] Tension along the Shatt al-Arab probably will depend on Baghdad's view of the balance of power between Iraq and Iran and broader strategic considerations. Ultimately, however, history suggested that in the absence of effective regional security guarantees for both states, the existing boundary would be the cause of future crises.

There was no guarantee that a change in political order in Iraq would relieve the latent territorial tensions in the long term. Both border disputes predated Saddam Hussein's regime, and it was noticeable that some of the Iraqi opposition joined Baghdad in condemning the UN demarcation of the border with Kuwait in 1992. Given that extending Iraq's regional influence seemed likely to remain an article of faith for any future government, irrespective of its hue, the borders issue will likely continue as a source of tension. This seemed likely to apply even if Saddam Hussein's regime was removed by force. Iraqi history demonstrates that the overthrow of incumbent regimes—traditionally with military involvement—often led initially at least to periods of unstable government during which extreme Iraqi nationalist tendencies were exhibited. If such circumstances repeated themselves in the future, it seems conceivable that the question of Kuwaiti sovereignty and Iraq's alleged claims to the emirate could resurface yet again. Ultimately, it appeared that much would depend on how enduring the legacies of both the Iran-Iraq War and the Gulf War turned out to be.

An optimistic assessment in late 2001 suggested that the disastrous outcome of these two conflicts would act as a sufficient deterrent against the future use of force by either the existing or any future Iraqi regime to revise the territorial boundaries or to promote Iraq's regional role. History and experience, however, suggested this was unlikely to be the case.

NOTES

1. "Iraq Coming Back Into the Fold," *Washington Post,* November 22, 2000.
2. See, for example Baghdad's attack on Riyadh in the aftermath of the Cairo summit, "Iraqi Leadership Condemns Arab Summits, Iraq TV, October 22," *Iraq News* (online), October 23, 2000.
3. For an example of an Iraqi initiative, see "Saddam Said Ready for Peace with Israel," *Jerusalem Post,* October 8, 1999; "Saddam Message to U.S. Undelivered," Associated Press, October 12, 1999.
4. Kenneth Katzman, "Searching for Stable Peace in the Persian Gulf," *Strategic Studies Institute Monographs* (online), February 2, 1998, p. 17.
5. Threatening Iraqi rhetoric was particularly intense in the aftermath of Operation Desert Fox in December 1998, when Saddam Hussein publicly called on the people of the Gulf to overthrow their leaders. Similar attacks against the Kuwaiti and Saudi governments were heard repeatedly from July 2000 onward, as Iraq attempted to "shame" the two governments into supporting the lifting of sanctions and ending their support for the no-fly zones.
6. *Babil,* November 30, 1996, in FBIS-NES–96–239. See also *Middle East Contemporary Survey* (henceforth *MECS*), 1992, pp. 159–69; *al-Thawrah,* November 28, 1996, in FBIS-NES–96–239; *al-Jumhuriyah,* November 8, 1997, in FBIS-NES–97–315.
7. *Iraq Television Network,* August 8, 1997, in FBIS-NES–97–220.
8. *Republic of Iraq Radio Network,* September 23, 1997, in FBIS-NES–97–266.
9. *al-Thawrah,* December 23, 1996, in FBIS-NES-97–003.
10. *INA,* December 20, 1997, in FBIS-NES 97–354.

11. See interview with Iraqi representative to the UN headquarters in Geneva, Barzan al-Tikriti, *al-Wasat,* December 9–15, 1996, p. 21; Iraqi vice president Taha Yasin Ramadan, quoted in *al-Dustur,* November 28, 1997, p. 20; interview with Iraqi foreign minister Mohammed Said al-Sahhaf, *al-Quds al-Arabi,* March 31, 1997, p. 6; interview with Iraqi interior minister Mohammed Zimam Abd al-Razzaq, *al-Bayan* (Internet edition), January 4, 1998, in FBIS-NES–98–04; Ramadan quoted in "Iraq Prepares to Hold Dialogue with All Arab States," *ArabicNews.com,* August 2, 1999; Ramadan quoted by *Agence France Presse,* February 19, 2000.

12. Huda al-Husseini, "Gulf Agreement to Delay the Iran Plan for Change in Iraq," *al-Sharq al-Awsat,* January 2, 1997, p. 12.

13. *Agence France Presse,* February 12, 1995, in FBIS-NES–95–029; *Petra-JNA,* July 8, 1996, FBIS-NES–96–132; interview with Shaikh Hamad bin Jasim Al Thani, *al-Watan al-Arabi,* March 27, 1998, pp. 24–25.

14. See statements by Shaikh Hamad bin Jasim Al Thani, *Agence France Presse,* May 13, 2000. Qatar also spearheaded a failed Arab League initiative on the sidelines of the Organization of the Islamic Conference summit in November 2000, designed to break the deadlock between Iraq and Kuwait. See Reuters, November 12, 2000.

15. The UAE eventually restored diplomatic relations with Baghdad in April 2000, and in July 2000 Iraq reopened its embassy in Abu Dhabi.

16. Interview with Dubai Crown Prince Shaikh Mohammed bin Rashid Al Makhtoum, *al-Sharq al-Awsat,* April 17, 1995, p. 5; Najm Jarrah, "Shaikh Zaid's Appeal," *Middle East International,* November 3, 1995, p. 9.

17. See Shaikh Zayed quoted by Reuters, November 26, 1997; "UAE Deputy Premier Calls for Finding an Arab Solution to the Iraqi Problem," *ArabicNews.com,* February 1, 1999; Shaikh Zayed quoted by *Reuters,* November 30, 2000. On the link to the islands dispute, see UAE foreign minister Rashid Abdullah Al-Nuaimi quoted in Reuters, November 23, 1996.

18. *ArabicNews.com,* February 24, 1998.

19. *Khaleej Times,* February 24, 1998.

20. See interview with Iraqi trade minister Mohammed Mahdi Salih, *al-Wasat,* May 26–June 1, 1997.

21. See, for example, Iraqi presidential adviser Hamid Yousef Hammadi quoted in *al-Bayan,* February 19, 1998, p. 1; Iraqi justice minister Shabib al-Maliki quoted by the *Iraq Television Network,* March 30, 1998, in FBIS-NES–98–090. The most recent example of Iraqi castigation of its GCC sympathizers was in September 2000, when the Baghdad press lambasted the emirates for publicly calling on the Iraqi regime to implement UN Security Council resolutions. See *Reuters,* September 18, 2000.

22. *al-Quds al-Arabi,* April 5–6, 1997, p. 1; *Agence France Presse,* January 6, 2000; Nail Mukhaiber, "What Went On between the Iraqi President's Brother and the Emirates President in Rabat?," *The Iraq File,* No. 71, November 1997, pp. 64–65.

23. On reports of these efforts, see *al-Bilad,* December 11, 1996, p. 4; *al-Riyah* (Internet version), in FBIS-NES–08–097.

24. *al-Wasat,* December 29, 1997, pp. 12–13; *KSC Television,* December 22, 1997, in FBIS-NES–97–356.

25. See, for example, *al-Quds al-Arabi,* January 2–3, 1999, p. 1; *Agence France Presse,* September 3, 2000.

26. See, for example, *MECS,* 1993, p. 404; Kuwaiti defense minister Shaikh Salim al-Sabah quoted in *al-Sharq al-Awsat,* November 14, 1996, pp. 1 and 4; interview with Kuwaiti foreign minister Shaikh Sabah al-Ahmed al-Sabah, *al-Sharq al-Awsat,* December 1, 1997, p. 4; interview with Kuwaiti information minister Yusuf Mohammed al-Sumayt, *al-Bayan,* May 25, 1998, in FBIS-NES–98–145; "Kuwait Blasts Iraqi Policy—Top Priority Security," *Kuwait Times,* November 29, 2000.

27. *MECS* 1994, p. 353.
28. Saad al-Bazzaz, a former regime insider, speculated that Iraq's decision to instigate the crisis was designed as a convenient way for the regime to recognize Kuwait and the new boundary without appearing to be making concessions to the international community, *Ashes of Wars: Post–Gulf War Secrets* (Philadelphia: Al Warrak, 1995), pp. 278–79.
29. See, for example, Iraqi deputy prime minister Tariq Aziz quoted in *al-Sharq al-Awsat,* November 11, 1996, p. 1; interview with Barzan al-Tikriti, *al-Wasat,* December 9–15, 1996, p. 21; interview with Iraqi National Assembly Speaker Saadoun Hammadi, *al-Ahram al-Masa'i,* April 10 1998, p. 5; Tariq Aziz interview with *al-Ittihad* newspaper, quoted in *Agence France Presse,* September 25, 1998; letter from President Saddam Hussein to Arab League Chief Esmat Abdel-Meguid quoted in "Iraq says it is ready for talks with Arab states," *Reuters,* February 21, 1999; statements by Iraqi vice president Taha Yasin Ramadam, quoted in "Iraq Prepares to Hold Dialogue with All Arab States," *ArabicNews.com,* August 2, 1999.
30. INA, June 3, 1998, in FBIS-NES–98–154. See also statements by Iraqi deputy prime minister Tariq Aziz on *Larry King Live, CNN,* March 2, 1998, in FBIS-NES–98–062.
31. In the articles, Aziz provided a detailed account of the Iraqi version of events leading up to the Gulf war, as well as a critique of Kuwaiti policy toward Iraq since 1991. For the full text, see *al-Thawrah,* January 10, 11, 13, and 14, 1999.
32. *al-Thawrah,* March 9, 1998, in FBIS-NES–98–072.
33. *al-Thawrah,* March 2, 1998, in FBIS-NES–98–063.
34. See statements by Iraqi foreign minister Mohammed Said al-Sahhaf in "Iraq Labels Saudi Arabia, Kuwait as Backers of U.S.," *Reuters,* January 15, 1999; *Iraq Television Network,* February 14, 1999, in *Iraq News,* February 15, 1999; Iraqi vice president Taha Yasin Ramadan interviewed by *Iraq Satellite Channel Television,* February 15, 1999; *al-Iraq,* February 18, 1999, pp. 1 and 6.
35. See interview with Iraqi foreign minister Mohammed Said al-Sahhaf, *al-Quds al-Arabi,* March 31, 1997, p. 6; *al-Thawrah,* May 11, 1998, in FBIS-NES–98–137.
36. *al-Thawrah,* March 9, 1998, in FBIS-NES–98–072.
37. *Republic of Iraq Radio Network,* September 23, 1997, in FBIS-NES–97–266.
38. Bazzaz, *Ashes of Wars,* pp. 266–67.
39. See, for example, Iraqi deputy prime minister Tariq Aziz quoted by *Republic of Iraq Radio Network,* in *Iraq News,* January 13, 1999.
40. Bazzaz, *Ashes of Wars,* pp. 246–48.
41. Crown Prince Abdullah quoted in *al-Wasat,* December 29, 1997, p. 13. For the Iraqi response, see Amatzia Baram, *Building Towards Crisis: Saddam Husayn's Strategy for Survival* (Washington, DC: The Washington Institute for Near Eastern Policy, 1998), p. 144.
42. Mohammed Said al-Sahaf quoted by *INA,* May 18, 1998, in FBIS-NES–98–138.
43. See, for example, *Saudi Press Agency,* January 10, 1999, in *Iraq News,* January 13, 1999; "Saudi Press Urges Iraq Uprising," *Agence France Presse,* January 16, 1999; "An Insane Tyrant," *al-Jazirah,* January 7, 1999.
44. This aspect was reportedly a partial motivation behind the reform proposals allegedly submitted to Saddam Hussein by his half-brother Barzan Ibrahim al-Tikriti in early 1997.
45. Baram, *Building Towards Crisis,* p. 143.
46. Bazzaz, *Ashes of Wars,* pp. 260–61.
47. Robin Wright, "Iran Cracks Down on Iraq's Illegal Shipments of Oil," *Los Angeles Times,* March 16, 1998, p. 1.
48. Interview with Mohammed Said al-Sahhaf, *Radio Monte Carlo,* December 12, 1997, in FBIS-NES–97–346.
49. Dilip Hiro, "Politics—Iraq: Iraq Making Unlikely Friends with Iran and Syria," *World News* (online), April 7, 1998.

50. Sahhaf quoted by *Reuters,* November 10, 2000; "Iran and Iraq in Top Level Contacts," BBC Online, November 14, 2000.

51. See, for example, speech by Saddam Hussein, *Iraq Television Network,* August 8, 1997, in FBIS-NES–97–220; interview with Mohammed Said al-Sahhaf, *al-Bayan,* October 11, 1996, in FBIS-NES–96–200; interview with the director of the Iraqi Ba'ath Party Foreign Relations Bureau, Saad Qasim Hammudi, *al-Hadath,* December 30, 1996, p. 8.

52. On the issue of Iraq's efforts to enhance its trade links with its regional neighbors, see Raad Alkadiri, "The Iraqi Klondike: Oil and Regional Trade," *Middle East Report* 220 (Fall 2001), pp. 30–35.

53. On this issue, see Richard N. Schofield, "Border Disputes: Past, Present and Future," in Gary G. Sick and Lawrence G. Potter (eds.), *The Persian Gulf at the Millennium: Essays in Politics, Economy, Security and Religion* (New York: St. Martin's Press, 1997), pp. 139–41.

54. See, for example, Iraqi vice president Taha Yasin Ramadan quoted in "Iraq Poses New Threat over Demarcation of Border: Kuwait," *Agence France Presse,* June 7, 1998; article by Iraqi deputy prime minister Tariq Aziz in *al-Thawrah,* January 14, 1999.

CONTRIBUTORS

LAWRENCE G. POTTER has been Deputy Director of Gulf/2000 since 1994 and Adjunct Assistant Professor of International Affairs at Columbia University since 1996. A graduate of Tufts College, he received an M.A. in Middle Eastern Studies from the School of Oriental and African Studies, University of London, and a Ph.D. in History (1992) from Columbia University. He taught in Iran for four years before the revolution. From 1984 to 1992 he was Senior Editor at the Foreign Policy Association, a national, nonpartisan organization devoted to world affairs education for the general public, and currently serves on the FPA's Editorial Advisory Committee. He specializes in Iranian history and U.S. policy toward the Middle East. He co-edited (with Gary Sick) *The Persian Gulf at the Millennium: Essays in Politics, Economy, Security, and Religion* (St. Martin's Press, 1997) and published "The Persian Gulf in Transition" in the Foreign Policy Association's *Headline Series* (January 1998). His most recent article is "Dealing with Iraq: Which Way Forward?" (January 2001) in the FPA's *Great Decisions* briefing book.

GARY SICK is the Executive Director of Gulf/2000 and Director of the Middle East Institute at Columbia University. Dr. Sick served on the U.S. National Security Council staff under Presidents Ford, Carter and Reagan, where he was the principal White House aide for Persian Gulf affairs from 1976 to 1981. He is the author of two books on U.S.-Iranian relations and many other articles and publications on Middle East issues. He co-edited (with Lawrence Potter) *The Persian Gulf at the Millennium: Essays in Politics, Economy, Security, and Religion* (1997). Dr. Sick is a captain (ret.) in the U.S. Navy, with service in the Persian Gulf, North Africa, and the Mediterranean. He was the Deputy Director for International Affairs at the Ford Foundation from 1982 to 1987. Dr. Sick holds a Ph.D. in political science from Columbia University, where he is Senior Research Scholar and Adjunct Professor of International Affairs. He is a member of the board of Human Rights Watch in New York and co-chairman of the advisory committee of Human Rights Watch/Middle East.

HASSAN HAMDAN AL-ALKIM is the adviser for studies and research to the Crown Prince of Ras al-Khaimah in the United Arab Emirates. He was a member of the Department of Political Science at UAE University from 1986 to 2000, becoming Professor of International Relations in 1997 and Chairman of the Department. He received his B.A. in political science from Seattle University in 1981 and his M.A. and Ph.D. (in 1986) from the University of Exeter. Prof. Al-Alkim has written widely on issues related to the Gulf subregion, the politics of the Arab world, and international relations. He has published more than 25 articles and is the author of *The GCC States in an Unstable World* (1994), *The Foreign Policy of the United Arab Emirates* (1989), and *The Islamic Political System* (1991, in Arabic), and the editor of *The Contemporary Islamic Issues* (Cairo, 1998).

RAAD ALKADIRI is a Senior Country Risk Analyst in the Markets and Countries group of the Petroleum Finance Company, where his primary focus is on political-economic developments in the oil-producing states of the Middle East and Africa. Prior to joining PFC, he was Middle East Analyst and Deputy Managing Editor for the UK-based consultancy Oxford Analytica, where he focused in particular on the northern Gulf states. From 1990 to 1991, Alkadiri was a Teaching Fellow of Politics at the University of St. Andrews. He received his D.Phil. from St. Antony's College, Oxford University, in International Relations in 1995. A fluent Arabic speaker, he has lived and traveled extensively in the Middle East and has authored a number of articles on Iraq and regional affairs.

ABDULLAH ALSHAYEJI is the Director of the Kuwait Information and Media Office in Beirut, Lebanon. He is on leave from Kuwait University, where he is an Associate Professor of Political Science. He is former Political Adviser to the Speaker of the Kuwaiti National Assembly *(Majlis al-umma)*, and to the Foreign Relations Committee in the Parliament. His areas of specialty include Kuwait and GCC politics, the Middle East and Gulf, U.S. Foreign Policy, and Political Development and Democratization. Dr. Alshayeji received his Ph.D. in 1989 from the Department of Government at the University of Texas in Austin. His publications include numerous articles on Kuwaiti political development and parliamentary experience, Gulf security, U.S. policy in the Gulf, and GCC-Iran relations.

M. R. IZADY has been teaching simultaneously at the Department of History, Fordham University, New York, and at the Joint Special Operations University, United States Air Force, Florida, since 1997. He received his Ph.D. from the Department of Middle Eastern Languages and Cultures at Columbia University in 1992, with a dissertation on the evolution of Kurdish sociocultural identity. He obtained his B.A. from Kansas University (1976) and M.A. from Syracuse University in 1979. From 1991–1995 he was a full-time lecturer in Persian and Kurdish at Harvard University. Dr. Izady is the author of *The Kurds: A Concise Handbook* (second edition, 2000), and a forthcoming multivolume annotated translation of *The Sharafnama*, a key work on medieval Kurdish history. He has written numerous articles on Kurdish and other socioethnic topics and edited *The International Journal of Kurdish Studies* from 1992–1998.

IBRAHIM A. KARAWAN is Director of the Middle East Center and Professor of International and Middle East politics at the University of Utah in Salt Lake City. Between 1995 and 1997 he was Senior Fellow for the Middle East at the International Institute for Strategic Studies (IISS) in London and a Research Fellow at the World Economic Forum in Davos, Switzerland. His work has focused on the political role of the Arab military establishments, the Islamic resurgence, inter-Arab relations, nuclear weapons and Middle East conflicts, and Egyptian foreign and defense policies. His recent publications include *The Islamist Impasse* (New York: Oxford University Press, 1997); "Implications for the Arab World," in *Al-Aqsa Intifada* (Washington: Georgetown University, 2000); "Political Parties Between State Power and Islamist Opposition" in

Between the State and Islam, eds. I. W. Zartman and C. Butterworth (Cambridge: Cambridge University Press, 2001); and "Identity and Foreign Policy: The Case of Egypt," in *Identity and Foreign Policy Making in the Middle East,* eds. S. Telhami and M. Barnett (Ithaca, NY: Cornell University Press, 2001).

BIJAN KHAJEHPOUR-KHOEI is founder and Managing Director of Atieh Bahar Consulting, a strategic consulting firm in Tehran. He is also co-founder and member of the Board of Trustees of Jomhur Research Institute in Tehran. Further, he is an editorial member of *Goftogu* (Dialogue), a Persian-language quarterly review. Mr. Khajehpour-Khoei holds a Diploma in Economic Studies from Reutlingen University (Germany) and a B.A. (Hons.) degree in European Business Administration from Middlesex University (London). He also serves as a consultant on Iranian politics and economy for foreign companies and organizations.

SAIDEH LOTFIAN is an Associate Professor in the Faculty of Law and Political Science at the University of Tehran. She is also the Deputy Director of the Center for Middle East Strategic Studies and the Director of the Middle East Program at the Center for Strategic Research in Tehran. Formerly, she was an Assistant Professor, Department of Political Science, Boston University (1987–91); Visiting Assistant Professor, Department of Political Science, at Texas Christian University (1986–87) and the University of Iowa (1985–86). Professor Lotfian earned a Ph.D. in political science from Michigan State University (1986) and a B.A. in accounting from the University of Tehran. In 1995, she was a Guest Researcher at the Stockholm International Peace Research Institute. She writes regularly on topics related to Iran's foreign and security policies, non-proliferation, the political economy of defense, and ethnic minority rights. Her most recent book is *The Role of the Military in the 1979 Revolution* (in Persian, forthcoming).

J. E. PETERSON is a historian and author on the Arabian Peninsula and Gulf. He spent the 2000–2001 academic year at the International Institute for Strategic Studies in London. Prior to this he served in the Office of the Deputy Prime Minister for Security and Defence in the Sultanate of Oman, where he wrote a history of the Sultan's Armed Forces. He received his Ph.D. from the Johns Hopkins University and has held various teaching and research positions in the United States. His books include *Oman in the Twentieth Century* (1978), *Yemen: The Search for a Modern State* (1982), *The Politics of Middle Eastern Oil* (ed., 1983), *Defending Arabia* (1986), *Cross-currents in the Gulf* (co-ed., 1986), *The Arab Gulf States: Steps Towards Political Participation* (1988), and a *Historical Dictionary of Saudi Arabia* (1993). He published "Succession in the States of the Gulf Cooperation Council" in *The Washington Quarterly* (Autumn 2001) and his *Adelphi Paper* on "Saudi Arabia and Gulf Security" is forthcoming.

JALIL ROSHANDEL is currently a Visiting Professor at the University of California at Los Angeles. He was a Visiting Scholar at the Center for International Security and Cooperation at Stanford University in 2000–2001. Prior to that, he served as Visiting Associate Professor at Middle East Technical University in Ankara (1999–2000) and earlier held a fellowship at the Copenhagen Peace Research Institute. From 1992 to 1998, he was a Senior Research Fellow at the Institute for Political and International Studies in Tehran. He also has taught contemporary strategy and foreign policy at the University of Tehran, where from 1989–1993 he was Vice-Dean in Charge of Academic Affairs. He holds a

Ph.D. from the University of Social Science, Toulouse, France (1989). Dr. Roshandel's research has included the implications of nuclear proliferation and confidence-building measures. He has numerous publications in Persian, including *Current Military and Strategic Issues* (1995; reprint 2001), *National Security and International Systems* (1995), and *Politics and Government in Armenia* (1994; reprint 1998). Dr. Roshandel has worked with the Stockholm International Peace Research Institute and has contributed to its publications. Recent publications in English include "Towards Cooperative Security in the Persian Gulf" in *Oil and Water,* ed. Bjorn Moller (I. B. Tauris, 2001) and "Iran's Foreign Policy and Security Policies," in *Security Dialogue* (March 2000).

RICHARD SCHOFIELD is a Lecturer in Boundary Studies in the Department of Geography at King's College, London (KCL). He was associated with the Geography Department at the School of Oriental and African Studies, University of London, for the previous decade until its merger with that of KCL in August 2001. He is also the Academic Director of the Masters program in International Boundary Studies, which he founded in 1997. Mr. Schofield is the author *of The Evolution of the Shatt al-Arab Boundary Dispute* (Menas Press, 1996*), Kuwait and Iraq: Historical Claims and Territorial Disputes* (Royal Institute of International Affairs, 1991; second ed., 1993), and *Unfinished Business: Iran, the UAE, Abu Musa, and the Tumbs* (forthcoming). He is the editor of *Arabian Boundary Disputes* (Archive Editions, 1992), and *Territorial Foundations of the Gulf States* (UCL Press/St. Martin's Press, 1994), and was founder and editor of the journal *Geopolitics and International Boundaries* (Frank Cass, 1996 -). He is currently preparing an atlas of Arabian boundary disputes and is working on a political geography of land boundaries and territory with J. R. V. Prescott.

MOHAMMAD HADI SEMATI is Assistant Professor of Political Science and Associate Dean for Research in the Faculty of Law and Political Science at the University of Tehran. He holds a Ph.D. in Political Science from the University of Tennessee in Knoxville (1993). Dr. Semati's research interests include international relations theory, comparative politics, culture and international relations, Middle East politics, and Iranian national security. He has published on the subjects of Iran's foreign policy, civil society and democratization in Iran, globalization and Iran, and resource mobilization in the Islamic revolution.

MAI YAMANI is a research fellow at the Royal Institute of International Affairs at Chatham House. She is also Research Associate at the Centre of Islamic and Middle Eastern Law at the School of Oriental and African Studies, University of London. Dr. Yamani received a B.A. in anthropology from Bryn Mawr College and both an M.A. and a Ph.D. from Oxford University. She has taught at King Abdul Aziz University in Jeddah and has been a Research Fellow at Oxford's Centre for Cross Cultural Research on Women and an adviser to the Center for Contemporary Arab Studies at Georgetown University. Among her publications are *Feminism and Islam: Legal and Literary Perspectives* (edited) (Ithaca Press, 1996), *Changed Identities: The Challenge of the New Generation in Saudi Arabia* (London: Royal Institute for International Affairs, 2000), and *The Rule of Law in the Middle East and the Islamic World* (co-edited with Eugene Cotran) (I. B. Tauris, 2000).

INDEX

Italicized numbers refer to tables, figures, and maps.